To Jill

With

GW01464774

Dorothy Campbell

*Memories of an Eas...*

# FAR-EASTERN TRAVELS & TRIALS
## Memories of an Expat. Wife

An autobiography covering the writer's early years in England, including a disastrous marriage, which ended in the author being left alone in Calcutta with a nine-month-old baby and no income, and her eventful life which followed.

Fate stepped in and she had a very happy and fulfilling life with a wonderful partner, with time spent in Calcutta, Bombay, Karachi, Malaysia, Hong Kong, Singapore, Turks & Caicos Islands and the Philippines.

Friendships made overseas were long lasting — having been forged in shared uprisings, riots, wars, typhoons and earthquakes, creating a life-long camaraderie.

This life style gave rise to many situations which are the basis of this book.

# FAR-EASTERN TRAVELS & TRIALS

*(Memories of an Expat. Wife)*

# DOROTHY CAMPBELL

***Goodwin Books***

30 York Court, The Albany, Albany Park Road,
Kingston-upon-Thames, Surrey, KT2 5ST, U.K.

First published in Great Britain 1997 by
*Goodwin Books*
30 York Court, The Albany, Albany Park Road,
Kingston-upon-Thames, Surrey, KT2 5ST, U.K.


British Library Cataloguing-in-Publication Data.
A catalogue record for this book is available
from the British Library.


ISBN: 0-9531118-0-6

Printed by *Manuscript ReSearch Printing*
P.O. Box 33, Bicester, Oxon, OX6 7PP, U.K.
Tel: 01869 323447/322552    Fax: 01869 324096

# CONTENTS

**Chapter**                                             **Page**

## APPRECIATION

I would like to express my appreciation to all the friends who encouraged me to get this published when I really felt it should be confined to the wastepaper basket. So rather than throw the manuscript away — I decided to try to publish it myself, and for this I have to thank Val Miller of Manuscript ReSearch for all her help and encouragement.

My thanks, of course, go to my husband, who tolerated all the hours I have spent poring over the computer. Also Tony Henderson, Pat and Leslie de Swart, Donald Smith, David and Anne Archibald, who helped with all my computer problems. I also want to thank Maureen Abel for her assistance.

Finally, I apologise in advance for any inaccuracies arising from references to individuals mentioned in this book. Conducting long range research and relying on memory whilst living overseas has its drawbacks.

Dorothy Campbell, 1997.

# PREAMBLE

I was inspired to write this "Diary" after I had tried to console a distressed teenager, I should add with no apparent success, and was told that I really knew nothing about life and the trials and tribulations that the youth of today face! I was told I had no idea what it was like to be hard up, and that in "my day" we had none of the problems that the young face today; unemployment, drugs, drink, and safe sex, — altogether the inference was that my life had been a "doddle"!

I was quite speechless at this tirade, but felt this erroneous impression should be corrected and therefore decided to write a few lines to correct this misapprehension. I guess I got carried away!

Whilst I had to agree on one or two points — for instance they may have been right on the drug scene — but they certainly did not invent sex, safe or not, and most certainly I had known what it was like to be short of cash. Times certainly have changed — and this generation gap is truly a GAP in every sense of the word.

When I was brought up, Grass was for cutting; Pot was a cooking utensil; a Gay person was the life and soul of the party; Aids were helpers in the Headmaster's office; Joints became stiff with age — they certainly weren't smoked; Screws were bought by weight, and a Bang occurred when cars collided. We Sucked sweets; didn't shoot people or heroin, Coke was a cold drink, Closets were for clothes not for coming out of: "filth" meant dirty; we were well before the sex change — we made do with what we had: and were the last generation that was so dumb as to think you needed a husband to have a baby — how quaint could one be! No wonder we are confused and there is such a generation gap today.

A few years have passed since I started this — but recently Jeanne Mason, an old friend from our days in Kuala Lumpur, encouraged me to continue.

I had met Jeanne and her husband whilst we were living in Kuala Lumpur, her husband was attached to The Australian Embassy. Over the years we had corresponded from the various countries we had been living in and she had kept all my letters as she said she had found them "so interesting". She was moving from her large home to a Unit where there was not the same storage space and she didn't want to throw the letters away, so returned them to me and said she thought I should incorporate them in a book!

Before throwing them out, I started to read one or two of the letters and, to my amazement, I too found them "interesting" so thought maybe I should add extracts to the 60 pages I had already written! Perhaps it might be of interest to others, and help people to see there is a light at the end of the tunnel, be it sometimes faint.

So this is where I started my reply to the accusations that I really had never met any real problems in my life. At the time it made me feel better having written it — and perhaps my grandchildren might be interested in some of the family history. But now I have added to the initial "preamble" and, according to my friends, other people may be interested. Time will tell — but I have enjoyed all the reminiscing!

My birth was not a particularly joyous occasion; my brothers were 14½ and 16 when I was born, and my parents far from enthusiastic about the thought of returning to sleepless nights, changing nappies and four hourly feeds.

Mother was well into her 40's, which in those days was quite old to have children, consequently she had a difficult and tiring confinement, and her general state of health was poor. My brothers in later life repeatedly told me how they had virtually brought me up in the early months, as besides my Mother not being in the best of health, my Father really was not interested in this additional mouth he had to feed and educate, or the sleepless nights.

I subsequently learnt that if I had been a boy, I was to have been adopted by the local vicar and his wife who had been unable to have children of their own.  For the first time in my life — Fate stepped in and decreed otherwise — I was a girl and they decided to keep me!

The state of the country after the first World War was depressing in the extreme.  Financially the country was in the doldrums — the political climate confusing, there was massive unemployment — many of the men who had returned from the war were seriously ill suffering from the effects of gas poisoning, malnutrition, dysentery and illness from which they never really recovered.  Food continued to be scarce and expensive for many years to come.

I arrived in the early 20's amidst all this doom and gloom.

I make mention of this background as I feel I have had such an interesting and full life but in no way was I born with a silver spoon in my mouth.   Perhaps this might give encouragement to many young people today who wonder what future there is and what life has to offer — but we never know what is around the corner, and I profoundly believe that life is what you make it.

I was born in Durham  though my family at that time were living in Northallerton.   My mother came to Durham for the confinement as she had a friend who was a mid-wife — and this meant that my birth would be less expensive.

We left Northallerton when I was two and moved to Yeadon, a small Yorkshire village which had been a centre for wool manufacture, but had been used for ammunitions during the War. Now most of the Mills were closing and depression had hit this small village.   As a result my father was able to purchase a very pleasant bungalow for the princely sum of £700!  It was surrounded by fields and farms — and appeared an ideal place to bring up this addition to the family.

My Mother's family had originated in Ireland but came to Liverpool when she was a child — this is where she met my father — though little else is known of her background.   She had a brother

Tom and the family name was Leigh.

My father came from a wealthy Liverpool family which owned the chain of Restaurants in Liverpool called "Kirklands," named I believe after my Great Grandfather and subsequently known as "Slaters". The family lived in a superb Edwardian house with nine bedrooms and on the top floor three large bedrooms for the Staff. It was on the water front between Birkenhead and New Brighton. They had three or four maids who always wore little starched caps and aprons and my Grandparents travelled around Birkenhead in a carriage and pair. Obviously for those days they were considered to be well off.

I only remember visiting my Grandparents in their home on two occasions and I was quite awed by their affluence, though my cousins seemed to take the life style for granted.

The second and last visit to my Grandparents, which I remember, was for their Golden Wedding when all the family gathered together. An Aunt and Uncle flew in from Australia and brought all their nieces delightful little opal bracelets. I was naturally thrilled to pieces and very upset when a few years later mine was stolen.

My Uncle apparently was quite shocked at the obvious serious rift between his parents and his brother — my father — and was obviously upset at this state of affairs.

Uncle Eric and his wife Winnie were there. Uncle Eric was a dentist in Birkenhead and I had only seen them once before, they had no children of their own, were great fun and we had wonderful games of hide and seek all over this huge home, with all the Grandchildren participating. This truly was a side of life I had no idea existed, and without doubt the most memorable time of my young life.

After the age of 10 the Grandchildren were allowed to stay up for evening dinner but were expected to change and dress suitably for the occasion! This obviously caused my mother some concern; she had assumed that I would be included in the Nursery Supper and would be in bed during the grown-ups Dinner, so when my

14

Grandparents suggested that I stay up for Dinner with the older cousins, I had no suitable clothes for the occasion. My Grandmother, who reminded me of Queen Victoria and seemed equally unapproachable, had anticipated this situation and gave me a gift of two of the most lovely dresses and the situation was saved. To be waited on at the table by several maids with heavily starched caps and similar little frilled aprons and *not* have to clear the table and wash up, was indeed an experience.

My various cousins looked upon me with avid curiosity, as they were apparently quite accustomed to this life style and could not understand my shyness and bewilderment.

My father had been in the family business, but there had been a serious confrontation in the family, and my father had left home and become a representative for a Dairy Products Company. He was provided with a car and seemed to travel 4 days out of 7. This meant he was away from home a great deal and often had to spend three to four nights away. His main area of operations seemed to be around Scarborough and the North East, so instead of paying Hotel bills he felt it would be cheaper to rent a small flat in that area and managed to convince the Company of this!

I never did discover the cause of the conflict with my father's family, but it would appear my father was the "black sheep". All enquiries as to why this had happened met with a stony silence, but it was very obvious that my father had been the financial loser. When my Grandparents died a few years later, he received a gold chain, a set of Crown Derby, a Gold Tie Pin and a very nice Silver Dressing Table set for my mother. These were given by his brothers and sisters as I assume they felt guilty or sad that he had been completely omitted from any inheritance.

From an early age I was very conscious that I was the product of old parents. When other children were taken on picnics, rambles in the country, and holidays, my father wanted to rest to recover from his hectic week and all the travelling he had done. Consequently I spent a lot of time on my own.

On the few occasions I was allowed to accompany my father on his local trips, I was never allowed to speak in the car as it "distracted the driver"!   When I wanted to answer the call of nature, this was equally frowned on, as we always seemed to be in a frantic hurry to get to the next village!   When I saw fields of bluebells and poppies and wanted to pick some to take home to Mother, we again were in a hurry and could not stop. So these spasmodic trips which I initially looked forward to with great excitement became tantalising insights into "what might have been".

On about three occasions when my Mother insisted that we had a holiday, arrangements were made for us to go and stay in the Scarborough flat.   It always seemed to rain during these visits, and I have visions of my Mother standing on the beach holding an umbrella over me whilst I made sand castles!   When we became too wet we wandered onto the Pier where there was a small band playing and people were singing and everyone seemed to be happy and enjoying themselves.   They played numbers such as "Red Sails in the Sunset" and "Stormy Weather" and other currently popular tunes.   To this day I can't hear these tunes without feeling very emotional as obviously my Mother was desperately unhappy, and when a particularly sentimental tune was being played I noticed tears in her eyes.

Very occasionally Mother and I went to visit "Auntie Nellie" in Wallasey.   She was an old school friend of my Mother's who was a very embittered lady having been deserted by her husband.   He had been injured after the First World War, and reputedly lost his memory.   However, when Auntie Nellie was able to trace him through the Military Authorities, she found him in a Chichester boarding house in the arms of another lady!   This experience did nothing to soften her already somewhat hard disposition. However, one redeeming feature was that she appeared to be reasonably well off and obviously enjoyed having my Mother to stay, and it was good to see my Mother happy.

I was tolerated!  Aunt Nellie couldn't stand my father as she was well aware of his extra curricular activities, and she bullied my Mother over her subservient attitude towards him.

A great deal of Mother's time during these visits was taken up playing Bridge and so Aunt Nellie arranged for me to go to the cinema with the son of a friend of hers called Bertie. I really looked forward to this first visit as we didn't often go to the "the Flics". My enthusiasm soon waned however when I found I saw very little of the film as Bertie would insist on sitting with his arm round me holding my hand and trying to kiss me! I was covered in confusion and embarrassment and had no idea how to handle the situation. I did not understand his amorous approaches. I was only 11 at the time and had had little to do with the opposite sex of any age. You could say I had had a sheltered background and was very unlike the 11 year olds of today.

No one could understand why I refused to accompany Bertie to the cinema again and I was far too shy to tell anyone, so these visits to Wallasey became a nightmare.

My brothers had been brought up with a Nanny and a Maid, but this was before the family rift between my father and his family, which was never healed. I found it hard to understand, particularly in later life, why there was such a disparity in the way my brothers had been brought up and the change in our present life style. Neither of my brothers were at home after I reached the age of four so I was really an only child — something I would not recommend!

One of the contributing factors to the lack of funds was of course that my Father was running two homes, the flat in Scarborough, which he said was essential for his job, and our bungalow at Yeadon. Having been brought up in a moneyed family he took badly to restricting his own expenditure. I can never think of our home, which was a pleasant little bungalow surrounded by garden and lawns, with fields in front, without thinking of noise!

My father was an Amateur Radio fanatic with his own transmitter and he spent literally hours calling up similar radio Hams and having long conversations with people as far away as Australia, South

America and the Continent.  His call sign was G8FP.  It was amazing how excited these radio buffs could become once they had established contact and they then seemed to call each other up at regular intervals.  An interesting but very expensive hobby and for my poor Mother who had been left on her own for 4 days in the week  not a very sociable one.  The transmitter was normally kept in the attic which had been adapted with a Dormer window, wooden floor and walls, but in the winter when it became too cold to sit for hours up there, he would transfer the lot down to the Lounge which meant Mother and I had to sit in the Dining Room.

Anyone who has had anything to do with Amateur Radio Hams will be aware of the shocking noise incurred when calling up a station and trying to carry on a conversation when the atmospheric conditions keep interfering with the reception.  No one was allowed into the radio area in case the myriad of dangling wires were disturbed — so cleaning the room was impossible — and when spring came and the equipment was once again moved upstairs, my Mother had a major spring clean.

I wanted to learn to play the piano, but never thought for a moment that our finances would permit the purchase of such an expensive item.  However, my mother finally prevailed upon my father to buy a piano — a second-hand one of course — and this was presented to me on my 14th birthday and I was reminded it would also have to be my Xmas present as well!  The following year when funds were obviously very short again — my father reminded me that I had had a piano the previous year and this would have to do for this birthday as well.  Years later when I was getting married and my parents had split up, he wrote to say that the piano would be my wedding gift!  It was sold when I went overseas for the princely sum of £10!

Although this didn't seem a large sum the reason for this was possibly because my father decided during one of our visits to Auntie Nellie to drill two holes through the piano to accommodate some of his radio cables!  At the time I was mortified, but the piano still played — but of course had lost all value!

Another incident related to my Father's "hobby" was when he suggested we paid Auntie Nellie a further visit and when we returned home to find slap bang in the middle of our front lawn a 40' Aluminium Radio aerial.   It was hideous — as besides the actual aerial it had numerous supports which were equally hideous and took up even more of the lawn, which besides ruining the garden and destroying the fruit bushes — the neighbours were horrified and quite understandably VERY annoyed.   This didn't daunt my father who was delighted that his Reception had improved and he could now pick up Radio Hams in even remoter areas!

This was only beaten by the next incident when it was suggested that my Mother and I should again visit Aunty Nellie — (by now my Mother really should have been suspicious of this generous act) We returned to find the whole bungalow had been painted with the same aluminium paint — it stood out like a satellite — and when the sun shone it glittered!   You can imagine it did nothing to improve our relations with the neighbours!

I think my father felt that with the bungalow covered in aluminium paint that his 40' aerial would blend into the background better and the neighbours would have nothing to complain about!

Such was life with Father!

I had been attending the local Council School, but at the age of 10 my Mother was determined I should move to a Private School, as she maintained both my brothers had been to good schools and she saw no reason why I should not have the same opportunity.   My Father was not convinced — he thought  that the local school was quite adequate for a girl — but this time my Mother won.

I was enrolled at Lawnswood High School which was about 10 miles away from our home including a mile walk to catch the bus.

My uniform was bought, which I am sure was a terrific sacrifice for my Mother, who somehow had to find the money with little help from my Father.   The uniform was the usual navy gymslip with white blouse and school tie, a navy barathea coat and navy school hat with the school band and black shoes.   In the summer we had the choice of three cotton dresses and the school blazer and a Panama hat. I had never had so many new clothes and whilst they may not have all been of my choice — I felt quite smart.

The only thing I objected to was a pair of shoes my Mother bought, that looked as though they were two sizes too big, had square toes and were without doubt the ugliest shoes one could imagine. I was quite indignant at having to wear them. (I hadn't of course seen what the young schoolgirls wear in the 90's — these ghastly black boots with lovely summer dresses) but I remember how embarrassed I used to feel when we assembled in the Hall each morning in line for prayers. I felt everyone was looking at my big feet — and to this day vividly remember how upset I was. I think my Mother had bought them as they were acceptable as to colour and heel height — and most importantly, they were cheap!

I was very shy in those days — but when my Mother wanted to accompany me to school on the first day — I pleaded with her to let me go on my own. I later learnt that she had followed me to the bus stop which was a mile away and watched me get on the bus!

I was one of the first school girls to get on the bus — but at Horsforth a crowd of girls, also going to Lawnswood High School, got on and chatted away between themselves as to what they had been doing in the holidays and I felt very out of it. Two girls sat immediately behind me and were giggling and making references to my long hair, which apparently should have been plaited or tied back. They knew I would be reprimanded and have to do something about it. One of the girls actually pulled my hair which I ignored — but the same girl eventually became a very good friend and still is to this day — 60 years later!

I think I was either very lucky, or very naive, but I had a 15 minute walk to catch the bus to school and whilst waiting at the bus stop, I was approached by an elderly man who started talking to me and offered me a sweet. The following day, the same man was waiting at the bus stop and immediately started talking to me and just before I got on the bus he handed me a Mars Bar! I thought this was very kind of him and the following morning he was again at the bus stop, and again gave me a bar of chocolate. In the course of conversation with my Mother I mentioned this "kind man" and so the next day she insisted on accompanying me to the bus stop. The man made himself known to her — said his name was Fayres and he had never married but loved children, and thought I was a very sweet little girl! I couldn't understand why my Mother suddenly decided she would always accompany me on the walk to the bus stop! When I questioned why she wanted to join me, she made excuses about going to the Library, the Bank or the Butchers to buy meat.

In spite of my Mother being with me, Mr. Fayres continued to give me the odd sweet or Mars Bar before I got on the bus. He finally gave me a delightful book of poems and inscribed it suitably as being from "the friend at the bus stop"!

I have to admit that in this day and age I would have been very suspicious.

My younger brother had never got on well with my Father — they were too much alike. With the Depression, he seemed unable to get any long term employment and did not share my elder brother's determination to study. So when my Uncle in Canada was taken ill with T.B. — which in those days was usually terminal, — Eric went out to Canada at the age of 18 to help my Aunt run the ranch at Calgary.

Other than the occasional letters nothing was seen of him for 11 years. My Uncle died and the Ranch was sold and my brother went onto another Ranch and then became a Cowboy. Whilst very exciting it was not very lucrative, and he was unable to save sufficient money to return home. However, he took casual, but very demanding work, herding 5,000 head of cattle across the prairie with the help of two other cow hands. The money he received at the end of the trip was however stolen! So he was back to square one. He eventually worked his passage back to the U.K. on a tanker, and arrived in the U.K. penniless. He then had to walk the 16 miles from London docks to my brothers flat in Kenton — a poor reward for his 11 years of hard work in Canada.

My elder brother, who had taken an Apprenticeship with a Structural Engineering Company in Yorkshire, had gone to nightschool for the next 4 years and finally ended up with many following qualifications.

He then secured a position with a Company of Consulting Engineers in London.   After a few years he was made a partner and ended up as the Senior Partner until he retired.   Studying obviously DOES pay in the end!

When the Second World War started, both my brothers volunteered to join the Army in the Engineering Corps — my younger brother was in the 8th Army and had an exciting but rough war.   He was wounded and ended his Army career as Sergeant with a Mention in Despatches.

My elder brother, after a few weeks training, was sent out to Teheran as a Captain in the Engineering Corps and ended up as a full Colonel and Chief Engineer  and was subsequently awarded an MBE.(Mil)

Whilst very successful in business — my elder brother's domestic life was full of traumas.

Before taking up his London appointment, he married a local Yorkshire girl whom he had met through the Church.  I was one of the bridesmaids at their wedding and wore a yellow organdy dress which then became my party dress!   After the ceremony — the happy couple set off by train for Bournemouth which meant changing trains in London where my brother had a flat.   Very suddenly his bride of two hours collapsed and so when they got to London she was taken by Ambulance to Hospital.   It was discovered she had T.B. which was described as "galloping".   My brother sent for her parents who came down to London where they remained for the next 6 months — but Mabel never recovered and died leaving my brother shattered.

George worked long hours and after work had made a habit of

going into a restaurant on his way home, for a meal. Here he met a waitress who initially enquired where he had been eating as she hadn't noticed him coming in for his evening meal for about 6 weeks. She knew he had been recently married and that his wife had been ill, but had no idea she had died. Over the next few days she offered to come to the flat and cook an evening meal for him and this progressed to doing some of the housework, washing and ironing on her day off. My brother felt this would be a good arrangement and one year later he married her. They had two children, a boy and a girl. When the war came my brother volunteered for the Army and was eventually sent out to Teheran. He was away from home for about 4 years and had taken on a lot of responsibility and with it came a lot of socialising. The time came when he was discharged and returned home. With the money he obtained on his demobilisation he was able to buy into the partnership. But his return home was not the happy occasion it should have been — his wife was resentful of the time he had to spend at the office establishing what became a very successful partnership — she seemed to resent his success and found having to look after a husband after years of being on her own, not to her liking.

She was not prepared to entertain any of his clients, so he had to do this in restaurants on his own. To cut a long story short, after a particularly nasty exchange of words, he finally moved out and took a flat near his office.

I think Secretaries have a particular place in their employers' lives and in this instance my brother's Secretary took over not only the arranging of Conventions and his travel arrangements but also the arranging of business dinners, at which she would act as hostess, and these "duties" extended to arranging dinners at his flat for friends.

George was obviously very unhappy with the state of affairs at home and  eventually the inevitable happened and he and his Secretary started living together and my brother initiated divorce proceedings.

The girl (let's call her Iris) was one of twins — and after they had been married about 6 months her twin sister went abroad and Iris became very distressed and unhappy about this severing of a very happy relationship and seemed to go into a decline. She was continually weeping and finally the Doctor suggested that she get away from the rat race and go into the country.

George had bought a cottage on the Isle of Alderney some years earlier for holidays and so this seemed to be the answer to the present problem. They moved to Alderney where George spent every weekend, returning to London on Monday mornings and returning to Alderney Friday afternoon. Iris did not like being on her own so George engaged a young girl of 16 who lived on the Island, to be a companion to Iris when he was not there. She slept in the house — and did all the shopping and cooking. Iris seemed to be recovering with this new life style and so when George went over for the weekend they used to go out for dinner and socialise a little.

One particular weekend — they had gone out for a drink on Sunday morning and Iris suddenly complained of not feeling very well. They walked home and whilst George was opening the door Iris suddenly collapsed in his arms and was declared dead by the Doctor he called!

She apparently had had a heart attack. My poor brother really did seem to have more than his share of bad luck.

He didn't want to return to Alderney for some time, but felt he couldn't leave the house unattended — so he continued to employ the young girl to look after the property. This arrangement went on for several months until one particular week when he had had an extremely hectic time and had returned home to his London flat to find a pile of ironing to be done, and a meal to be cooked not to mention a spot of cleaning, he realised how foolish it was. He was paying this young girl to look after an empty house and he was having to do so much in his London flat. He didn't want to sack her so he suggested that she fly over to London and she could do the housekeeping in London.

On our next leave, my husband and I decided as we were

unexpectedly in the area where my brother lived that we would call on him and suggest he joined us for a meal. Imagine our surprise when we rang the door bell and a young girl in her jeans answered the door and when we told her we had come to see Mr. Kirkland she said that he was not in! I then asked her to tell him that his sister from India had called to see him and she would ring him at the office. Immediately we heard George's voice saying "come in — come in" and we found him in the kitchen cooking dinner! He was delighted to see us and explained the circumstances as to why this young girl was in the flat but as he seemed to still be doing the cooking we wondered if it had been a sensible move as he was now cooking for two!

We returned to India — and a year later we heard that they had married. You see why I say that George was a great success in his business life, but his domestic life was a disaster!

I was probably 14 before I realised why my Mother had bouts of depression. Frequently I would find her crying — but when asked what was wrong she would merely say "she was being silly".

I was very concerned particularly when one of my school friends mentioned she had seen my father in Scarborough teaching a lady to drive! My mother had often asked my father to teach her to drive, but my father explained that it was a Company car and was not suitably insured, and she accepted his explanation. I however found it difficult to understand why he should therefore be teaching another lady to drive! This unfortunately was only the beginning of many similar episodes.

When I told my father what my friend had told me, he said she must have been mistaken and became quite short tempered!

In 1939 the country was at war and my father who had served in the First World War was considered too old for active service. His Company decided to move their headquarters down to the West country which they felt would be safer — away from the possible bombings in the more built up areas.

My father accepted the transfer with alacrity and closed up his

Scarborough flat. My mother assumed that we would all move down to Yeovil — but was told that the war wouldn't last long and that it was essential I finish my Secretarial Course which I had started when leaving school.

Dull as I found this I have NEVER regretted it. No matter where I have travelled in the world the knowledge I acquired at this business College has held me in good stead and I have always been able to get employment, often when my friends who were better qualified in other fields — found it impossible.

I would have liked to study medicine, but in those days there were no Grants and obviously my parents could not afford University so — I was enrolled at Bradford Secretarial College. Whilst not a career that I would have chosen — in the circumstances I felt it was the best solution.

So my father moved down to Yeovil when I was half way through my course, and took a flat at Crewkerne, in Somerset.

My course finished and the War of course was far from over — so my Mother was making plans for us both to move down to Crewkerne at least for the summer holiday period and hopefully for good. She knew the flat my father had was small and therefore she thought by telling him early he would have time to look around for something slightly larger for us all. The bungalow at Yeadon could easily be let as it was near the Leeds/Bradford Airport.

Imagine the shock I had when my father wrote to me and told me I should discourage my mother from going to join him as he was living with a lady who had been his housekeeper in Scarborough for a few years AND had it not been for my birth he would have left my Mother years ago.

I really didn't know what to do as my darling Mother was quite excited at the thought of joining my father at last — it had been a long separation.

Obviously I could not put off telling her and thought the easiest way was to show her the letter — an unenviable task which I shall never forget. Obviously my Mother was shocked and very unhappy but think she had been well aware for some years that this could happen, as there had been similar situations which she had managed to overcome. But now she was faced with a fait accompli — the die had been cast.

Shortly after this, an official separation was arranged — and in retrospect I don't think my Mother was sufficiently avaricious in agreeing to the settlement. The deeds of the bungalow at Yeadon were to be transferred to her name on condition she made no further financial demands on my father as regards maintenance for either of us. What she didn't realise when she signed this Agreement was that my father had two Mortgages on the property which my Mother had to pay off!

My Mother was a truly wonderful lady and quite determined not to let this beat her — but at 60, with no income — the problem seemed insurmountable.

This was my first experience of what is now my conviction, that when one door closes, another quite often opens.

About this time the local authorities had decided that the little village of Yeadon had grown to such an extent that a second Post Office was needed.

During the First World War my Mother had volunteered to join the Post Office in Thirsk and eventually became Post Mistress. It seemed providential therefore, that 20 years later when a Postmaster or Postmistress was required for our village that my Mother should submit an application. Most men of course were either at the War or doing work in the old woollen mills which had been converted to ammunition factories. So my Mother was an obvious choice. However there were certain conditions she had to fulfil and one was that she had to provide the premises for the post office. We therefore converted our Dining Room into the office — which entailed knocking down a wall and making a separate entrance through the garden and installing a large Safe. She received help towards this of course from the Government, and my Mother was a very able, cheerful, happy and popular Postmistress.

I had never seen her as happy as she was during this period. She had a cheerful and helpful word for all the customers who loved coming to her Post Office to draw their pensions and buy stamps. She listened to all their problems — giving advice and most importantly, sympathy.

The job was not without a lot of worry and anxiety; she was no longer young — hadn't worked in business for over 20 years — so this was indeed a challenge and I am full of admiration as to how she coped AND remained so happy and cheerful.

For my part there was little to report of real interest in these early years. The College I went to would send you out on temporary assignments after you had attained a certain standard but before you had completed the course.

My first "work experience" was for two weeks at the local Aero Club at the Leeds/Bradford Airport, working in the Radio room on the Teleprinter for the local Manager. This was in the days of the C.A.G. (Civil Air Guard) formed and sponsored by the Government This meant that people could learn to fly for the ridiculous sum of two and sixpence for an hour's tuition. My salary for this two weeks was £1 per week so I obviously could not afford such a luxury, but it was very tempting. I was taken up on the odd flight a couple of times and well remember my first trip in a Tiger Moth!

After I completed my Secretarial course I applied to the Airport Manager referring to my Work Experience fortnight with them and to my utter amazement received a letter asking me to go for an interview. I was accepted — but still only on £1 a week — and returned to the Radio room.

One of my duties was to send a weather forecast in code each morning at 8.45 a.m. to the Weather Meteorological Office in Manchester. The information I gave them was subsequently relayed by the B.B.C. to all shipping channels. Having obtained the information from the various gadgets situated in or around the small Radio Station on the Aerodrome — I transcribed this into code and sent it off on the Teleprinter. This covered wind velocity, direction, cloud formation and the amount of cumulus and cirrus cloud, the visibility, the air pressure and the past weather, present weather etc. It was a numerical code and having established the correct information from the gauges, I then transcribed it numerically and sent this on the teleprinter.

On one epic occasion I inadvertently transcribed the information incorrectly and just before 9.a.m. the Teleprinter started up feverishly querying my code as I had said there was a sandstorm blowing over Yeadon at the time! Fortunately it had been noticed before being passed to the B.B.C. but I was covered in confusion at this stupid mistake.

It was here I fell in love with one of the Radio Operators — old enough to be my Father I might add — in fact I think it was the Father figure I had lost as there was very little real romance even though he made my heart race. He was very kind and helpful, had a super sense of humour and we shared many amusing incidents through working together. He was also very popular with the pilots who came in with messages to be sent by morse code and I marvelled at the speed he could rattle these off.

On our days off he would occasionally take me to Betty's Cafe in Leeds for toasted teacakes and cream buns! Then perhaps a cinema show. There was only one occasion when he obviously had more on his mind than "cream buns" — and he invited me back to his digs for a meal. His landlady was away on holiday — and so I suppose he felt this was a God sent opportunity to lure me to bed! A lot of effort was put into this manoeuvre on his part but the outcome was not what he had hoped for. I am glad to say this did not affect our friendship.

The Airport figured quite large in my life. It was within walking distance and a few years earlier (I was 14 at the time) I had taken my Airedale dog for a walk on the moors surrounding the Airport. On the way back home the dog was attacked by a vicious Alsatian — and I watched helplessly as my poor pet was being savaged. I was very relieved therefore when I saw two men in RAF uniform coming to my rescue, one picking up my dog, and the other warding off the Alsatian with a stick. I was so relieved that my dog Bill was still alive and these good Samaritans accompanied me on my walk home.

My Mother was in the garden so I explained to her what had happened to poor Bill whose ear was bleeding and she invited these boys in for tea. They both refused though one of them asked my Mother if he could take her up on this at a future date as they were then due back at camp. My Mother suggested they came round for tea on Sunday and they accepted with alacrity.

Only one of the boys turned up as the other we were told was on duty. After tea on this particular Sunday the airman called Harry, said he was going to a Church Social at Horsforth and asked if he could take me along and assured my Mother I would be home by 9.p.m. My Mother agreed and he was really a charming companion and very attentive and I thoroughly enjoyed these Church Socials which became a regular Sunday evening occupation. It was a nice change from going to my own church, St. Andrews in Yeadon, as it was full of young people. We sang, had a short talk from the Minister and then tea and cakes before coming home. At that age of course there was no romance — just good friends. I was always home by 9.p.m.

This feature impressed my Mother, who decided he was a very suitable companion. Added to which when picking me up on Sundays for these Young Peoples' Church Socials he would often arrive with a large bunch of carnations for my Mother who hadn't had flowers bought her for years!

About 10 weeks after we met, he told us that he had been posted to Aden and would be leaving the next week. This was before the 2nd World War and he was a Regular in the Air Force. I was sad to lose his friendship as he had been rather like a big brother, but he promised to write. During the next 4 years I was bombarded with letters from Aden. I was amused and of course flattered when the letters became affectionate saying how much he missed his visits to our home, and seeing me in particular. I never took these letters very seriously as by this time I had many friends of the opposite sex, — and in retrospect, — far more suitable.

I suppose though he was different — he was five years older than I with a flamboyance and confidence that appealed to me after my rather sheltered upbringing. In these letters he told me he loved me and was waiting for me to grow up! I thought it was all rather amusing as at that age no-one had mentioned romance, let alone love!

During my early teens I always had a sense of guilt when I went out enjoying myself when Mother was at home on her own, often trying to balance the post office accounts!

Marriage certainly didn't figure in my plans for many years. I enjoyed my job at the Airport, had lots of friends — therefore I still find it hard to believe the sequence of events when my pen friend returned to the U.K. (five year's later I might add) on leave. He immediately proposed marriage — not once but several times, which I thought was flattering and rather amusing, but when we went for a walk past St Andrew's Church and he bodily carried me up to the Vicarage and announced to the Vicar that we wanted to put up the banns for our marriage, I was mortified.

The vicar who knew our family well was as astounded as I and suggested that we went away and seriously thought about it before he would read the banns in the Church.

I went home and discussed this with my Mother. I had no intention as I said before of an early marriage.

I have to admit when discussing the church episode with my Mother, she did not discourage me, but said she thought he was a "nice young man". I realised subsequently that she was so worried she would become a burden to me as she got older — and with so many of my friends being called up into the services she was worried that I might choose to stay at home to look after her. She was without doubt the most unselfish mother.

We talked about this for hours and she pointed out all Harry's good features — the fact that our friendship had endured a long separation, he was far more attentive to us both than my Father had ever been, and having just returned from 4½ years overseas it was probable he wouldn't be sent abroad again for some time, and she felt that Harry was suitable. So I finally agreed to getting married the day after my 19th birthday.

What a disaster! Whilst my Mother was enthusiastic about the forthcoming marriage, she did confess to me years later of her concern that I would make the supreme sacrifice — avoid marriage in order to stay at home and look after her so marriage to Harry relieved her of these fears.

We were married five weeks later on the 18th October 1941 in St. Andrews Church at Yeadon. A small ceremony — no white wedding dress as of course the dreaded coupons had been introduced and to obtain the items required for a white wedding would have taken my year's supply of Clothing Coupons. In any case with the country at war and all our friends in the services — it was not possible nor for that matter appropriate.

I am sure that the young to-day would find it hard to believe that at the age of 18 I was still a virgin. I am convinced now that had I sampled the intimacies of marriage, that the marriage would never have taken place! However this was 1941 — before the introduction of the Pill and all young people were told of the shocking effects of V.D., the results of promiscuity — and the fears of having a baby out of wedlock were far stronger than the fear of acquiring AIDS to-day — or so it seems to me!

There is a lot to be said of to-day's life style where young couples live together for a while before taking the vital step of getting married. I am convinced that many divorces are avoided this way.

We had a disastrous honeymoon in Llandudno which put me off sex for months to come. The chemistry just was not right — and the five years on "the Rock" had given him a very odd slant on sex.

Harry had been transferred to Bebbington in Cheshire, so we rented a flat on the Wirral. I got a job at Lever Brothers at Port

Sunlight as a Secretary in the Soap Division which helped out with finances — but a boring job compared to the one I had left at the Airport.

I suppose to all intents and purposes we were happy — although I still found his excessive sexual appetite far too demanding and at times alarming. However, not having had previous sexual experience I had no yard stick by which to judge — so felt I had to accept what I later learnt was "abnormal" and often peculiar behaviour.

Whilst living on the Wirral I had my first medical disaster. I went for a routine check-up at the Company's dentist which resulted in my having a wisdom tooth removed, not because it was giving me any trouble but because the dentist felt that wisdom teeth generally were of little use and often gave trouble in later life — so he suggested an extraction.

I arranged to have the tooth out in my lunch hour the following day. In those days the taking of dental X-rays was not routine, so it was not discovered that the tooth was in fact impacted and growing under the jaw bone. After 1½ hours of pulling, tugging, levering and lancing the gum it became obvious that the tooth was not coming out! The dentist said I would have to go into hospital but there was no bed available for three weeks. So I returned to the office with this ghastly mess — and was immediately sent home.

When the anaesthetic wore off I was in agony and when I could stand it no longer I went to the Dr. who referred me to a bone specialist who diagnosed the problem that the tooth was under the jaw bone and that the jaw bone would have to be chiselled away. He agreed to do this immediately as he could see the pain I was in. The procedure though painful was simple and within a few moments the tooth was out. He stitched up the gap and away I went, still feeling very much below par.

Little did I know then that septicaemia had set in and six months later discovered I had lost the sight in my left eye through this, and was told I was in danger of also losing the sight in my right eye.

Obviously I was distraught and wondered how I could cope with no sight. It was suggested by the eye specialist that I changed careers and take up something that I would be able to do if the worst happened and I became blind.

I therefore resigned my job and started as an Assistant to a Doctor who had a Physiotherapy Department attached to his practice, and who agreed to train me. For weeks I watched and occasionally was asked to massage an arm or shoulder. Sometimes I had to practice on his back as he had a long standing back problem. He told me I was a "natural" in the art of massage and I soon progressed to having my own patients — referred by him of course and was doing this full time. In the cold north of England it seemed to me that everyone had back trouble of one kind or another or sciatica or stiff shoulders, and I seemed to specialise in shoulders and lower backs. Usually before the massage treatment the patients had some form of electrical treatment — carbon lamps, ultra violet, deep heat etc.

There was one terrible day after we had acquired a new piece of equipment to take the place of the old fashioned ultra violet lamps. The old lamps were used for ten minutes on the patients before starting the massage. No one had told me that the new Mercury Vapour lamp only required a three minute treatment. You can imagine the result when this particular patient received a 10 minute treatment! He was badly burnt on his back and the Doctor was so alarmed he visited him three times that evening to try to alleviate the pain! Fortunately the patient didn't sue and I learnt a very important lesson.

Occasionally I had male patients who obviously enjoyed the massage I gave them. They would be discreetly covered by a towel and I was slightly alarmed initially when at times I saw the towel covering the lower torso rising! The first time this happened, I excused myself and went to discuss this with the Doctor as I found it embarrassing and I am sure the patient did. I was told to put more pressure into the massage and not just stroke the thigh! Another lesson learnt!

However, in spite of all this preparation for the possibility of my going blind, I was very lucky and I retained the sight in my right eye.

I was not so lucky with my marriage!

My husband was posted to the south of England — where there were no married quarters and this transfer was for further training before proceeding on overseas service again. I stayed in Liverpool for a time and then returned to live with my Mother after the tooth incident and obtained an appointment with the Ministry of Food issuing Ration Books, — not mentally taxing, — but a job that had to be done.

I was given a few days leave — and decided at the last moment to surprise my husband by joining him for the weekend as he was living in Air Force billets. It was not an easy journey — many changes on the trains and a long wait at Crewe station and then of course the difficulty of finding the billet. When I found the house there seemed to be many airmen in this rather large house and a very ordinary but a very kind little woman invited me in, but looked very embarrassed when I explained who I was and why I had come. The various airmen that were in the kitchen promptly disappeared — which I suppose should have told me something!

It transpired that my husband was not in and he didn't appear for about 4 hours. When he did walk in with an attractive WAAF on his arm, I felt stupid and could understand everyone's embarrassment when I appeared. My husband seemed to recover from the initial shock — far more quickly than I or the landlady did. She immediately made herself scarce and left us in the kitchen.

I can't remember the excuse on this occasion — there were so many over the years. I suppose I wanted to believe there was nothing to worry about — and so I did. This was the first of many such experiences — and each time my husband came up with an explanation, an excuse or if he was cornered, he would break down and weep and assure me it would not happen again. In retrospect I cannot believe that I was so gullible. How stupid youth can be!

This typified my life for the next 6 years — heartbreaks excuses, — forgiveness — and more heartbreaks — the final years became unbearable.

Harry had taken his discharge from the Airforce and therefore I felt when he was living with me with no more long separations, there would be no cause for these extra marital associations. Can you believe my stupidity? We had discussed having a family and foolishly thought this might cement our rather precarious relationship and when I became pregnant I was truly thrilled and really felt this would sort out our marital problems. Another fallacy of youth!

For a time things seemed good — my husband was working for a London firm of paint manufacturers as Export Manager. It seemed plausible therefore that he would have to meet Overseas Buyers when they arrived in London and I could accept that occasionally he would have to go to the Airport in the evening.

However, even if I was blinded by love and excitement about the arrival of a baby — I found it hard to believe that there were customers arriving every night and that they had to be entertained until midnight — and sometimes 2.a.m.! I became very suspicious and eventually decided I would go to my husband's office and wait outside to see what time he left.

I took up a position in an arcade opposite his office and, as I feared, he came out with a gorgeous looking lady and they strolled off arm in arm together. That night he again came home around midnight with the same old excuse of going to the airport and I was so upset I blurted out all I had seen. I think in many ways he was relieved — and he admitted that he was no longer in love with me — he did not want the baby we were expecting and he wanted to marry this lady who was working in the same office. He suggested that I pack up and leave the house the next day as he was bringing this lady to live in the home!

Fortunately my brother also lived in London at that time and so I sought his advice as I really wasn't thinking very clearly. Although suspicious — I was not prepared for this turn of events.

36

As I have always been independent my first re-action was to leave. However my brother suggested I visit a Solicitor to assess the situation. This was my first experience of the peculiar idiosyncrasies of the Law. I was advised to remain in the house — uncomfortable as it would be — but if I left it was possible my husband could sue me for divorce on the grounds of desertion. I reluctantly returned home and removed all my personal things into the back bedroom from the master bedroom.

That evening my husband arrived home early, accompanied by this lady. She stayed in the house for two weeks only, but it was the longest two weeks I have ever known. Why she left I never knew as it certainly wasn't the end of the relationship and my husband reverted to returning home around midnight. This state of affairs continued until about a week before the birth of the baby when I found he came home early and was trying to be pleasant. I was pretty despondent — heavily pregnant and desperately in need of some support. Fortunately my neighbours were wonderful.

On the 16th November it was obvious that the birth was imminent. I went into labour and asked Harry to take me to the Nursing Home which was over 5 miles away. He kept telling me the pains were not severe enough and that I should go to bed and sleep! By about 1.a.m. on the 17th my waters broke and I rang the Dr. who told me to get to the Nursing Home immediately. I called a taxi and will never forget that whilst I was downstairs with my bag packed waiting for the Taxi, Harry was upstairs choosing which tie he would wear and applying After Shave! Doubtless wishing to impress the nurses if not me! The Taxidriver was very concerned — I think he thought I might give birth in his taxi — and as soon as I arrived at the Nursing Home I was taken directly to the Labour ward where a nurse examined me — and was then simply furious with my husband for not bringing me earlier. There was no time for the usual preparations as I was fully dilated. In those days there was no question of husbands being present at the birth.

At 6.30.a.m. on the 17th November, 1946 our darling daughter

Linda was born and I will never forget the feeling of joy and elation. I felt I was the only person to have given birth to such a darling baby.

I had always hoped for a little girl who I was sure would be a great friend and companion as my own mother had been. She was not only a source of joy she was beautiful, had a mop of curly dark hair and the most beautiful eyes, which at this early age she seemed to use to advantage. She weighed 7 lbs 2 oz was 21" long and I really felt that no one else in the world had been so clever as to produce such a wonderful little bundle. It made all the misery of the last 3 months seem worthwhile.

Harry was brought into the room to see his daughter, and it really appeared that he too was as emotionally affected as I was. He immediately broke down — knelt at the side of the bed and wept and pleaded forgiveness — he said he couldn't understand why he had behaved so badly and that if I would give him another chance all would be different.

Initially I felt this display of histrionics was purely psychological and that when he became accustomed to having a daughter — he would revert to his previous life style. But when I returned home this didn't happen and he was home every day by 6.0.p.m. and he seemed to look forward to the weekend when he could take Linda out in the pram and show her off.

I feel embarrassed to say that yet again, as I suppose I wanted to believe this, and as there appeared to be a complete change in his behaviour, I agreed during the next few days that we should start all over again, and that I was happy to forget the past. Little did I know.

My lovely neighbours who had been so supportive over the last few ghastly months, were quite shattered at Harry's complete change of attitude AND in their opinion at my stupidity in forgiving him! Harry was obviously not comfortable with these people who had befriended me and so suggested that we move. I gathered that the atmosphere in the office was equally fraught and he wanted a change in employment. So he started looking for a job and we planned to move to an area where his indiscretions of the past would not be known.

When Linda was 4 months old he applied for a job in Calcutta. The salary seemed attractive and the job interesting — the only stipulation was that he should travel out on his own and I could not join him for 3 months. This gave both he and the Company time to find out if he was suited to the position. This was not what I had hoped for and frankly the thought of travelling out to India on my own was frightening; up to a year ago I had hardly been off the West Yorkshire bus route — and here I was contemplating a journey of 12,000 miles with a baby!

This opportunity though seemed providential — it gave us the change of environment, away from the people who would not easily forget his indiscretions.

So he sailed for India on S.S.Strathmore in March, 1948. He wrote regularly, said he loved the job and had been put into Mrs. McDonald's Boarding House until such time as Linda and I arrived.

It was here he met another young man, Phillip who had also been booked into this boarding house until he could move into a "Chummery". This is accommodation owned by the Company for their young assistants — which was much cheaper than running their own establishments or staying in a Hotel or boarding house. They were able to share the expenses of the Cook, Bearer, Sweeper Dhobi etc., and divided the food bill.

He and Phillip shared a table in the dining room and obviously shared experiences of their first weeks in India.

During this time I received the same regular and loving letters from Harry saying he couldn't wait until our arrival. It was hard to disbelieve him and I really felt quite happy with the decision to go overseas.

My three months in the U.K. passed quickly. I had to sell up the contents of our home in Greenford, Middlesex — a hard task as most of the furniture and furnishings had come from my home in

Yeadon, Yorkshire, and there was a degree of remorse at having to part with sentimental items that had been with me for many years — even the piano would be missed!

With the proceeds of the Sale I was able to purchase items of clothing for myself and Linda for India.    I was told that I would require a largish wardrobe, including evening dresses as there was quite a social life — and even for the trip out I would require evening dresses as it was usual to dress for dinner except when in Port.

My biggest sadness of course was saying goodbye to my darling Mother.   She was now well established in her post office, had made lots of friends among the various customers and was well thought of and admired by all the village.    I had not disclosed very much about my own problems prior to Linda's birth as I felt she had enough worries of her own, but I think my brother George on one of his visits to Yeadon had indicated that all had not been well.   Therefore she was delighted for us that this opportunity had arisen and that the hints my brother had dropped about things not being very good between Harry and I were obviously ill founded.    I was able to spend the last few weeks with her which was a bonus and she so enjoyed having us to herself.    I felt she had not been catering for herself very well — living on innumerable cups of tea, so whilst I was home she enjoyed not having to think about food or the housework.

So I left with her blessing — and she was looking forward to our first leave in two year's time.

My old school friends were intrigued that I was back with a baby, and such a pretty one at that.   The fact that I was about to sail to India they found mind boggling — as people did not travel as they do to-day.

As a teenager I had had my fortune told by a gypsy who had knocked on the door asking for food or whether we would buy some wooden clothes pegs!    We didn't need clothes pegs and so my Mother gave him a sandwich and for this he predicted that I would travel to many lands and see many strange places.   He said that all my journeys would not bring happiness — but that in the end there was a great deal of love and happiness in my life. He also said that I would know poverty — and whilst I would never be VERY rich I would eventually be very comfortable — and I would never starve. Above all, my life would not be boring! How right he was.

I didn't take very much notice of this prediction at the time, convinced that he told all young people the same thing, but only in later life, when I look back, do I realise there was so much truth in what he said.

**Bustling Aberdeen Harbour and the floating restaurant**

**The hand-pulled ferry at Tai O fishing village, Lantau Island**

**Hong Kong Harbour at night:**
**Central and Eastern Districts and Tsimshatsui, Kowloon**

**Manila**
*No one lives in this village. It is purely a memorial to the departed.*
*Each "home" is elaborately decorated.*
*Some houses even have air conditioning!*

## The Caraboo Cart at Villa Escudero
### *(Another form of transport in Manila)*

## The Jeepney Factory
### *(Outside Manila)*

# Thaipusam Festival in Batu Caves, Kuala Lumpur
*(A major Hindu Festival celebrated yearly when devotees fulfil vows by bearing "Kavadis" up the 272 steps to the caves of worship)*

## Thaipusam Festival
*(Hindu devotees with long spears pierced through their cheeks whilst in a state of ecstacy, thus fulfilling a vow to Lord Murugan)*

**Saizkammergut-Druckerei**
**Church on the lake at Gmunden Austria**
*(where Fiona was married)*

**Turks and Caicos**
**Queen's Birthday Celebrations**
*(High Commissioner arriving by London taxi)*

## Singapore: National Day
*(Produced by coloured flags)*

## The Merlion: Guarding the Singapore river
*(A creature which is half lion and half fish)*

**Goodwood Park Hotel, Singapore**
*(Decorated for Xmas festivities)*

**A Dragon Dance**
**in the grounds of the Goodwood Park Hotel, Singapore**
*(To celebrate Chinese New Year)*

# A Rescue on "The Rock"
## *(Ayers Rock, Northern Territories, Australia)*

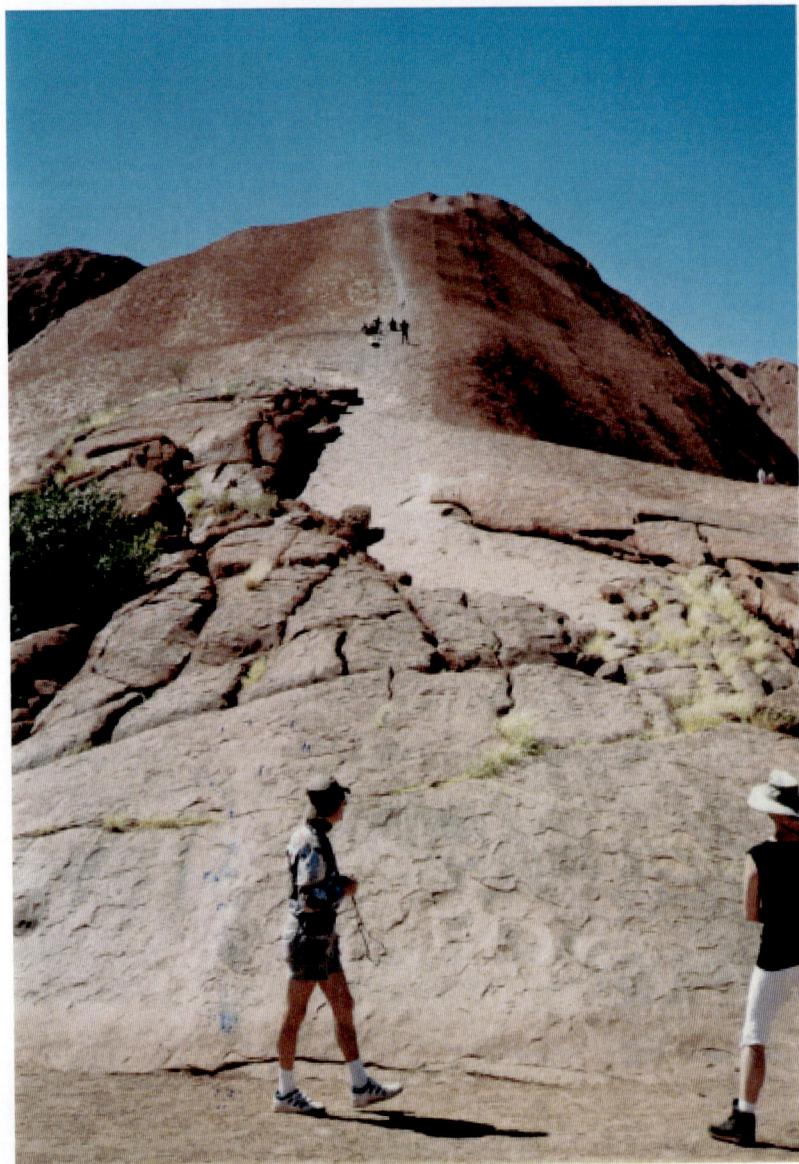

# Walking through the Olgas
## *(The easy part!)*

# Climbing "The Rock"
## *(With difficulty)*

**Sunrise over Ayer's Rock, Northern Territories, Australia.**
*(Sacred to the Aboriginals, it is known locally as 'Uluru'.*
*Like the nearby 'Olgas' it is the tip of a sandstone hill, half sub-*
*merged in a semi arid plain.)*

**Ancient Domes of the Olgas at sunset.**

**Shot Over Gorge, New Zealand**
*(Shooting the rapids)*

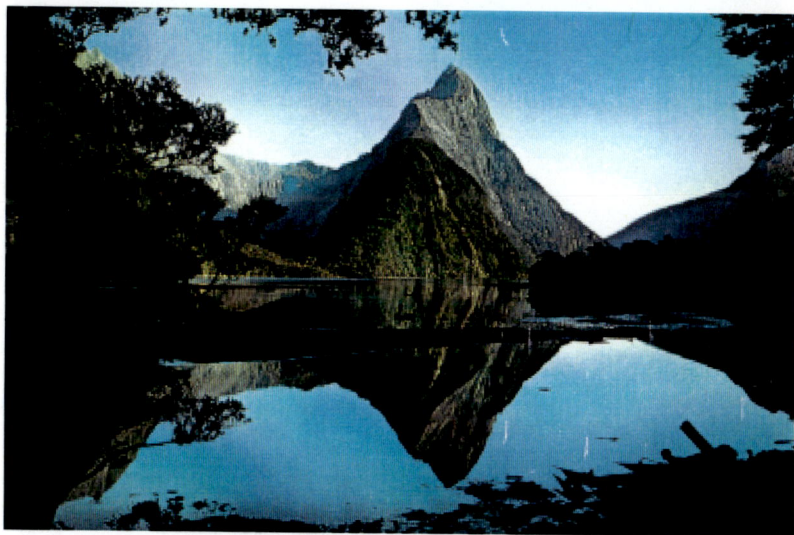

**Mitre Peak reflected in Milford Sound**
**New Zealand**

**Anchor Lines**
*(The m.v. Cilicia which brought us to India)*

**Port Said**
*(Centre: The well-known Simon Artz store)*

**Bombay**
**A reception for H.R.H. The Duke Of Edinburgh**
*(30th January,1959)*

**Karachi**
**Visit of H.M. The Queen and H.R.H. Prince Philip**
*(Reception at the State Guest House: 3rd February, 1961.)*

## The Saturday Club, Calcutta
### *(Known as 'The Slap')*

**Johore Causeway**
*(Links Singapore to Johore and the Highway to West Malaysia.*
*Beyond the Causeway is Johore town.)*

**Transport of pigs**
*(Chinese style)*

**Entrance to Changi Prison**

**A Haika family at Lok Ma Chau**
*(Overlooking the Chinese border)*

**Haika ladies in the New Territories**

# View of Kathing
## *(800 year old walled city in the New Territories)*

**Romance in the desert**

## Chinese Gravestone
*(First wife on the right, second wife on the left.)*

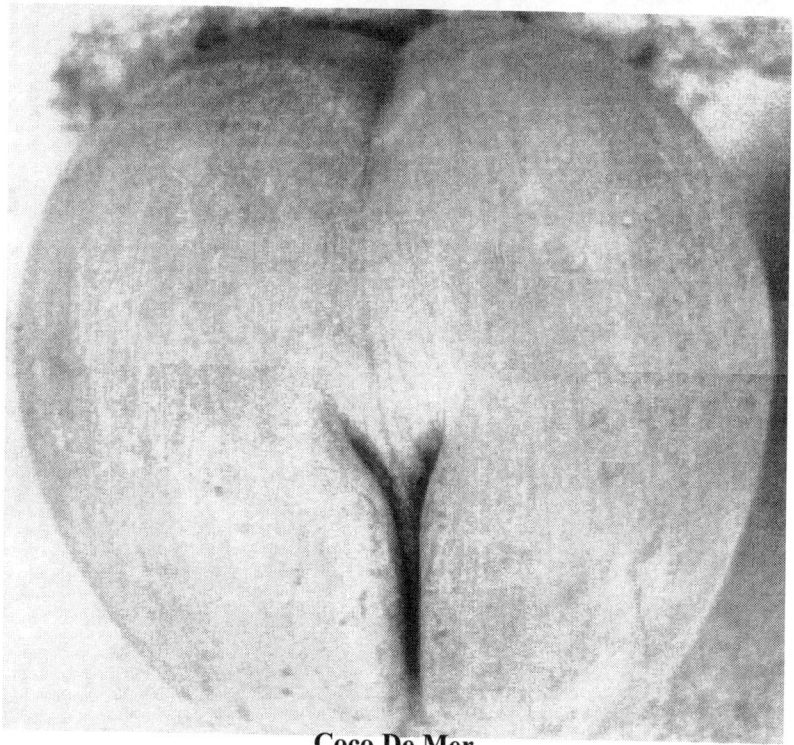

## Coco De Mer
*(The fruit of the Seychelles palm tree)*

# ONE
## *Starting Up A New Life*

I left home on the 24th June, 1948. My brother Eric drove me over to Liverpool where I was to board the m.v. Cilicia — one of the three sister Anchor Line Ships. He was living at home at the time and assured me that he would keep an eye on my Mother whilst I was away. Even so, I felt very concerned about leaving her.

Naturally, I was excited about the trip — and other than the disastrous honeymoon in Llandudno I had never had a holiday as such and whilst very excited, I was also nervous as to what lay ahead. It transpired later that I had every reason to be nervous!

I have always had, and still do, an apprehension about being late for trains, bus departures and now was equally concerned about missing the boat! As a result we arrived on the dockside about noon and went straight through Immigration and I had my luggage cleared by Customs and was waiting in the Customs shed to go on board. Nothing seemed to be happening and as Linda's lunch was well overdue, I asked one of the Port officials if I could now go on board.

The Port authorities had recently been on strike so in typical unhelpful British manner he told me I could go on board if I could carry all my own luggage, but that the Porters would not be on duty for another two hours! There was no way of course that I could carry all my Cabin Baggage, plus the pram and the baby plus the large bag every mother seems to need containing nappies, bottles and things for any emergency. I pointed out that Linda had to have her lunch and asked if I could go on board and return later to claim the balance of my luggage. I was told it would be very unwise to leave personal possessions on the dock side and the Port authorities could take no responsibility for them!

Standing near me in the Customs shed where we had been queuing in alphabetical order of surname, was a charming and very good looking man reading mail, which I assumed was from his wife or girl friend. He looked to my inexperienced eye to be about 42, and had obviously heard my conversation with the unhelpful Port official. He said he knew what it was like travelling with young children and asked if he and his friend could help as they had no hand luggage and were ready to go on board. I was very relieved at this kind gesture and had no idea how this chance meeting would eventually affect the rest of my life.

He called his friend who took my bags — and he took the pram leaving me with the baby and the baby items. When I got on board I handed my Boarding card to the Purser who detailed a crew member to show me to my cabin. He naturally assumed we were a family and this gentleman quickly assured him that we were not together and that he and his friend were merely helping me. I went into the cabin and was relieved to find my cabin had a port hole! I then changed Linda, and gave her lunch and we wandered on to the deck to watch proceedings — quite amazed and relieved that I had actually got on the right ship on time. When I left home that morning the whole venture seemed unbelievably difficult.

My feelings were not really helped at the Docks by mixing with all the passengers who it seemed had been doing this trip for the last 20 years; everyone seemed to find a great friend and were obviously delighted to be sailing yet again "back in the right direction" I was told! I really felt like a country cousin and was therefore doubly pleased to have got on board and able to look down on the chaos and confusion that was taking place in the Customs shed as more and more passengers arrived.

Afternoon tea was served on the sports deck and we sailed about 6.30.p.m. — children's supper time was at 5.30.p.m. so I had to find the dining room where I spent more than 6 hours per day having to attend children's mealtimes and then my own.    I saw a notice asking people to register for either First or Second sittings for meals. I decided that the second sitting would suit me best as it would give me time at night to settle Linda and leave her sleeping before going down to dinner.   The Stewardess was on duty and would call me if I was needed.

As children's supper time often didn't finish until 6.15.p.m. I realised there was no possibility of my changing and getting Linda to sleep before the first sitting at 6.30.p.m.   One was given a book of instructions when you purchased your ticket and from this I gathered that people dressed formally for dinner every night except the nights when we were in Port or the night we sailed.

My previous experience of "dressing for dinner" was for my Grandparent's Golden Wedding!   Naturally I kept this information to myself!   Having taken the second sitting — this enabled me to have a wander on deck to see what the First Sitting passengers were wearing!

I was fortunate enough to be seated by the Purser at a table with a Mr. and Mrs. Edwards who were from Assam where he was a tea planter and the two nice young men who had come to my rescue when boarding.   I soon discovered that my 42 year old who I thought must have a family — was indeed single and only 24!   He explained that he knew what it was like for a lady travelling on her own with young children as his sister had recently sailed out to Accra on the Gold Coast where her husband was in the Colonial Service.   She had complained bitterly in a letter home about the lack of help or support she had received and the difficulties she had experienced travelling with two young children.   With this fresh in his mind — he was happy to help another lady travelling on her own with a child.

I don't think he was very flattered when I said I thought his kindness was because he had children of his own and had experienced the joys of travelling with youngsters!

The other young man who had helped was the son of a Missionary who had now retired but had spent most of his life in India. Funnily enough his family were living in Horsforth, the next village to where I had been brought up.

Having been born in India, but leaving for school at the age of 6 — he was anxious to see once more the country of his birth and he and the other young man were joining the same company.

The first two days on board I spent confined to my cabin with sea sickness, and at times really wished I could die. The Bay of Biscay was living up to its reputation and this old Anchor Line boat not only swayed from side to side but it also had a top to tail motion as the Cilicia, along with its sister ships had been built long before the days of stabilisers which were then fitted to the modern ships. This continual motion was just too much for me and as soon as I lifted my head off the pillow in the morning it started and although I was determined to conquer this feeling of nausea, as soon as I got into the Dining Room at 7.30.a.m. for children's breakfast, I had to fly back to the cabin where I heaved my heart out and had to stay prone for the remainder of the day.

The motion seemed to have no effect whatsoever on Linda and so she played happily in the cabin, but of course wanted lunch, tea, and supper, so I made this ghastly trip down to the Dining Room four times a day — sometimes I made it — and sometimes I had to leave hurriedly leaving her in her high chair with the Steward promising to keep an eye on her until I could re-appear. The thought of requesting cabin service of course never entered my head — I really had a lot to learn!

I am glad to say that I was not alone in my dilemma and many of the hardened travellers I later discovered had been confined to their cabins. The Dining Room was pretty deserted for those three days, though I did learn that my two "helpers" and now table companions, never missed a meal!

After the third morning I decided I would perhaps feel better up on deck in the fresh air — and Linda most certainly would have a change of scene.  I bumped into my table companions who seemed surprised to see me and said they had begun to think that I had disembarked before sailing!  I explained the problem and by this time had again found the corkscrew action of the "Cilicia" was having its effect — so I made my excuses and said I would have to retire to my cabin.  They very kindly offered to take the pram and push Linda round the deck and when they brought her back to the cabin at lunch time they brought down with them a "sure cure" for seasickness in the shape of a Port and Lemon!  I was feeling pretty desperate at this stage, so happily took anything that might help the situation.  However, this "sure cure" stayed down precisely two minutes!  They meant well!

The further we sailed into the Mediterranean,  the calmer it became and I awoke on the 4th morning to find that at last the lurching, rolling and corkscrewing had actually stopped — and indeed I felt a new woman and began to enjoy life.

I soon discovered that life on board  was very pleasant.  There was the Nursery for the children of course which one had to use during adult meal times as no children were allowed in the dining room other than at children's meal times.  It was also open for 4 hours in the morning and 4 hours in the afternoon.  I still didn't like being parted from my baby for very long, but I soon discovered when she was at the Nursery during my meal times that she was very happy and enjoyed the company of the other children, and all the different toys that there were — so — I was then able to participate in the morning deck sports.  I was amazed at the number of games that could be played in such a confined space.

A few of the old timers had formed Committees to organise various tournaments and everyone was approached and asked to participate.   For people like myself travelling alone this was a wonderful way of getting to know people and I soon found there were not enough hours in the day for all the activities.  At 11.00 a.m. daily, soup was served on the deck and at the same time tickets were sold for a lottery on the ship's Daily Run.   The Captain announced at 12 noon each day the number of miles travelled in the last 24 hours.    I won this during the last week on board and was given a voucher which I could spend at the Ship's Shop — which was well stocked with luxury items as well as necessities.

There was a "quiet time" between 2.p.m. and 4.p.m. when no games were allowed and parents were requested to keep their children quiet.    The library was open and there was usually an afternoon film show.    At 4.30.p.m. tea was served on the deck or you could go into the Lounge.

Although we stopped at Gibraltar, for some reason we were not allowed shore leave — possibly because we were there for so short a time.    Our first shore leave therefore was Port Said where we arrived early in the morning.  We docked along side, and it became clear that the arrival of any ship was a cause of celebration for the shopkeepers and the dock side was seething with vendors.   Guides were anxious to show us around (for a fee of course) and Arabs wandered around anxious to see who was on board and whether the Captain was going to allow them on board to display their wares or entertain the passengers.    Every lady on board was referred to as "Mrs. Simpson" as the abdication of Edward the VI who wanted to marry Mrs. Simpson was fresh in everyone's mind.

We were finally told we could go ashore and had to assemble in the Lounge with our Passports to get our Landing Card and deposit our passports.    I remembered the note that was included in my Passport when it was issued, that one should NEVER part with your Passport —  so I was not at all happy about this — but — like a sheep — I followed the crowd.    We apparently had to wait for about 5 hours for the remainder of the convoy that would accompany us down the Suez Canal.    I and  some new friends I had made on board decided we would make for Simon Artz, the departmental store that was so well known.   It seemed to be completely deserted other than the passengers from the "Cilicia" and I gathered that the shop only opened when ships were in port as otherwise there was little or no business from the local community.    It was a poor substitute for a department store, which is how it was advertised — and other than a lot of oriental items of a poor quality, it had very little to interest us — but it was an "experience" and in the future whenever I passed through Port Said I always made a point of visiting this well known store.

Most of the passengers seemed to be buying cigarettes, watches, perfume and toys from the vendors who had set up stalls along the quay side. When we got back on board we found that some of the vendors had been permitted to come on board and were also selling similar items. The nearer to sailing time the lower the prices became. I had noticed the displays of genuine leather bags and "pouffes" — and I decided that when the prices dropped I would buy one of these "bargains" — a genuine leather pouffe for a little over a £1! I subsequently realised why it was so cheap — the leather had not been cured and it smelt to high heaven! On the dock side I thought the smell was just Eastern odour and didn't realise it was my leather pouffe until I was in the cabin! I hasten to add that it did get better after a few days in the sun and I transferred it from my cabin to the Hold for the remainder of the journey and it stayed in the family until a few years ago so I suppose it was quite a bargain.

It was here on board that I had my first experience of the "Gully Gully Man", who I think could be described as an Eastern Magician with an amazing sleight of hand. He was surrounded by a crowd of passengers listening and watching his antics — he really was very entertaining. He produced live chickens from everywhere, people's pockets, their ears and from their sleeves and repeatedly he would produce two or three chickens from the depths of some well proportioned lady's bosom — to the horror of the lady — and great amusement of the crowd. A couple of trips later I was the victim and besides being horrified when I felt this furry little chick snuggling in my décolletage — I was even more amazed when the Gully Gully man produced two more!

He was very gentle with the children and having produced a simply delightful little fluffy chick from the pram where Linda was sitting, he gave it to her to play with for a few moments. How these poor chicks survived I will never know — I have seen him produce no less than 8 chicks from someone's inside pocket, and these must have been stowed away amidst the flowing robes he wore for well over the hour that the show lasted. I have often thought in recent years when one's wallet can disappear out of a closed handbag in a crowded English city, that the thieves must have been trained by the "Gully Gully man"!

I think the day and a half that it took us to sail through the Suez Canal was for me perhaps the most memorable. I could hardly tear myself away from the deck — even for meals. Although in retrospect — a lot of the scenery is very repetitive. When it's your first time through the Canal though you are very anxious not to miss anything, so I spent the day, and half the night, standing on the deck with binoculars watching the very spasmodic activity on both banks. We dropped anchor in the Bitter Lakes — of which there are two, the Great and Little Bitter Lakes which are between Ismailaya and Suez. This stop was to permit the northbound convoy to pass — and there must have been about 16 ships in this particular convoy — whilst we were a mere 12. It was extremely hot in the Great Lakes, not a breath of air, and the swimming pool was closed! Around the towns of Jidda and Jizan I could see trucks driving along both sides of the canal, often filled with soldiers who waved as they passed. After about 12 hours in this blistering heat we emerged into the Red Sea from Suez and it was odd not to be able to see land on both sides as one could in the Canal.

Our next port of call was Aden where we spent the day and were allowed ashore. It was exactly as Harry had described it in his letters to me — barren, dusty with little if any sign of vegetation and as we wandered around the shopping area which was very sparse and primitive I realised how desperate my husband must have been spending 5 years on this rocky desert. The Arabs in their long flowing robes and banoos obviously caught our eye and they in turn were intrigued with my fair curly headed daughter I was pushing around in the pram. There were very few Arab women to be seen and those that we did see were covered from head to foot in black burkas.

A couple of us took a taxi which looked as though it had been in a terrific accident and judging by the springs and the play on the wheel — I think it had! We explored a little further into the Protectorate — but all we could see was desert with a few run down shacks which the majority of the population appeared to live in. All in all we were glad to get back to the boat, have a shower and get ready for dinner and the evening activities.

Evening entertainments of course were equally varied as the day-time sports — and after dinner one had the option of playing "Housie" on the Sports Deck, dancing in the Lounge or perhaps Horse Racing or yet another film show. The dances were very popular with all age groups either as spectators or participants as all crew members were detailed to dance with the ladies, and with the practice they obviously got, there were some excellent dancing partners amongst them!

The children also had their share of entertainment, Sports, Films, Deck Games and a Fancy Dress Party. The ship's Entertainment Committee asked that no costumes were used that had been brought on board, so — I was quite delighted when young Linda won the first prize in the toddlers Fancy Dress. I put her in little bikini pants and stitched lettuce, cucumber, spring onions onto the bikini and made her ear rings out of 2 carrots with a necklace made out of slices of radish and the caption on her card said "Salad without Dressing". Even at such tender years she seemed to know she had done well and she beamed at everyone.

For the adult Fancy Dress party, I was not inspired and felt quite guilty when I saw some of the hilarious costumes that had been concocted in the cabins in the afternoon. Obviously the passengers who had done this trip before were well prepared — though this in no way detracted from their ingenuity.... as the same rules applied and no one was allowed to use anything that had been brought on board specifically. Borrowing from the stock of linen on board was permitted — and there were many Gandhi's, Nehru's, Greek Gods and Goddesses and some of the funniest, large hairy chested babies with moustaches, in nappies — one soiled with Worcester Sauce! Another appeared in a Baby's pram complete with dummy made of cardboard, being pushed around by a supposed Ayah dressed in a tablecloth as a Sari.

A very amusing evening for spectators and participants alike, particularly when the Ayah lost her Sari!

The Fancy Dress party was the last evening on board and we were reminded to pay our bar bills before leaving the ship and that gratuities could be accepted by the Purser or handed to the Stewards. I discovered there were quite a lot of people one was expected to tip. Obviously my Cabin Steward and Stewardess and the Table Steward, the girl in charge of the Nursery (who really earned a gratuity) but then I found the Wine Steward expected a donation even though I personally had not used him, the Bar Steward round the Swimming Pool, who had occasionally produced orange juice, there seemed to be no end to the tipping and gratuities. As I was on a very limited budget I probably did not include all that I should have done!

The three weeks on board was a very happy time, and without doubt the best holiday I had experienced, which of course was not difficult when I cast my mind back to the dreary days spent in Scarborough on the beach in the rain! It is sad that nowadays it is cheaper and of course much quicker to fly Expats to and from the U.K. on 747's, 737's as these trips are fast becoming an endurance test and a far cry from those happy lackadaisical days spent at sea either on Anchor Line Ships or the larger P.& O or Lloyd Triestino vessels.

I was indeed sad when this happy three weeks came to an end — not to mention slightly dubious about the new country which was to be my home for the next few years. However, I was looking forward to seeing my husband after all this time. He was to meet us in

Bombay and then we were to fly to Calcutta, sending our heavy Hold luggage by train.

We were due to dock at Bombay about 7.a.m. and disembarking was to start at 9.a.m.. We were told breakfast would be served from 6.30.a.m. and then we should gather in the Lounge at 8.a.m. for Immigration where our passports were examined and stamped — leaving only the Customs formality for the Docks.

There was an air of excitement all over the ship, the hatches were open as early as 4.30.a.m. and the cranes started to work and got themselves into position squeaking and making odd metallic noises which meant no one had much sleep after 4.30.a.m. and most people were up and about and leaning over the rail on the deck peering into the distance long before Bombay could actually be seen.

Out of the early morning mist it slowly took shape and one could see The Gateway of India and the Taj Hotel. I later learnt that when the Taj Hotel was built, the architect's plans were misread and it was built back to front and although they have enhanced what was the back of the Hotel to make it more prepossessing, they never did change it, so the back of the Hotel is facing The Gateway of India.

India in the morning was always covered in mist or smoke which came from all the hundreds of chulas (fires) which were lit early in the morning to boil water for tea and seemed to produce more smoke than a steam train. These fires were fuelled by "cow pats" — (dried cow manure which was mixed with straw and shaped by hand!) They were dried in the sun and then used to start the fires — hence the smoke and I suppose the smell!

Bombay slowly appeared in the distance and I remember seeing it first when I was in the Dining Room having taken Linda for breakfast and I remember trying to peer out of the port holes to see what was ahead.

We finally tied up about 6.30.a.m. and there was, even at this early hour, a sea of faces gazing up from the docks looking for loved ones — (and not so loved ones!) I spotted Harry who waved frantically and appeared, to all intents and purposes to be excited and pleased to see us. I held Linda up so he could see her as of course she had grown considerably from the 6 month old he had left in Yeadon, to the present 9 month old.

I suppose it was well over an hour and a half before guests were allowed on board. Everyone was bustling around looking in the Lounge and then the Cabins trying to find each other. There was great excitement — tempered with a little sadness, saying goodbye to people who had become great friends in the three weeks we had been at sea. Addresses were exchanged, and telephone numbers given to people who were to end up at the same destination.

Linda and I were at the top of the gangplank when visitors were allowed on board, waiting excitedly to meet Harry. He seemed equally delighted to see us and was amazed how much Linda had grown. I was able to introduce Harry to my travelling companions. The Edwards were off to Assam — other friends were taking the train to Madras, quite a few people were to stay in Bombay and then of course there was the Calcutta contingent. I realised I had made more friends in this three weeks than I had in the last three years.

I think the "smell" of India was the first thing I noticed — a smell I grew to love, but initially it seemed very strange. I couldn't get over the number of dark skinned Indians dashing up and down the gangways with our luggage balanced precariously on their heads, cushioned with a rather grubby looking cloth which they wound round the top of their head. They would often have 2 or 3 suitcases on their heads and another two under each arm and skilfully manoeuvred the gangway. I hadn't seen anything like this outside a circus and was truly amazed at their balancing acts and their stamina as they appeared painfully thin and emaciated.

As soon as they had delivered one consignment to the Customs shed they dashed back up the gangway for the next lot. With knees slightly bent they would even charge up and down with huge tin trunks on their heads. I couldn't believe the strength of these skinny little men, all dressed in off white dhotis (a type of loin cloth) who were so active. I subsequently learnt that hunger is a great incentive of course, and they were anxious not to be replaced by younger and fitter Porters.

Having seen this performance I was still rather stunned when one of these little men arrived in my cabin and started helping himself to my luggage! He gave me a number and said he would see me in the Customs shed. At least that is what the Cabin Steward told me he said — as I hadn't yet learnt to understand the sing song voice, the pidgin English and the Anglo Indian patois, nor to comprehend that when an Indian shook his head from side to side he meant "yes". There was a lot of Aitcha Sahib — Tikai Memsahib — none of which meant very much to me.

Finally we were told we could proceed to the Customs shed so the three of us staggered down the gangplank and it was odd to be standing on terra firma once again although for some time I continued to feel the motion of the ship.

It was a shock to see a whirlpool of frantic bodies shoving, scurrying, shouting and darting here and there amidst a jumble of trunks, cases, valises, old fashioned hat boxes etc., trying to find a spot to deposit further luggage off the ship. There appeared to be no sort of order and having deposited one lot of luggage the porters dashed off for a further lot. The heat, the dirt, the smells and the continual shouting of the Porters, which to me sounded as though they were about to have a fight, but was in fact their normal tone of voice, completely confused me.

The mass of humanity on the docks, were all dressed so very differently, the very smart bejewelled Parsee ladies in their colourful saris with a bare mid-riff and gold bracelets on their wrists and ankles and numerous gold chains around the neck were an incongruous contrast to the apparent poverty of so many Indians on the docks. The more affluent had come down to the docks in their smart cars to meet friends or relatives and were indeed an odd contrast to the dock labour, the coolies, the deformed children and beggars thrusting out their stunted limbs for bukhshee.

I loved my 23 years in the Indian Subcontinent — but at this stage it's hard to remember my true initial feelings. I had associated dark skinned people with the slum areas in Leeds, Bradford and Liverpool — where so many migrants had settled — and therefore to arrive in Bombay which was seething with people who were obviously quite different to the ones I had seen in the U.K. , bewildered me. Bombay is very multi racial, industrious Sikhs, Religious Jains, Orthodox Jews, hardworking Hindus, Moslems, Christians, and Arabs who tipped the porters more than many of the people earned in a month, and of course Parsees.

The Parsees are very light skinned — and their ladies extremely beautiful. It is said that their influence has been out of all proportion to their numbers, and that it was the Parsees who had made Bombay such a successful city. The men all seemed to be running their own highly lucrative businesses, or were in commerce and they all appeared to be very wealthy. I found it quite mind boggling and felt very lost and unsure of myself, I suppose frankly, quite terrified.

Whilst standing in the Customs shed waiting to clear our luggage, we were again requested to wait in alphabetical order as all the Hold luggage had been stacked that way. So once again we were standing next to Ken, this delightful young man who had helped me on board in Liverpool and had been a great friend during the trip. Harry was explaining that there had been a recent change in the regulations regarding unaccompanied luggage on the railways, which meant that we would be unable to fly over to Calcutta. Therefore we would have to go down to Victoria Station to see if we could obtain a Sleeper for that night's Calcutta Mail train. This would mean having 3 days on board the train — not ideal with a young active baby.

Again this very nice young man with his friend came to our rescue. He said that they would be going over to Calcutta by train in 3 days time and were quite happy to have Cox and Kings load our tin trunks on the train in their name. This was indeed a stroke of luck and Harry accepted this kind offer with alacrity.

We were able to get seats on the afternoon flight and arrived at Calcutta's Dum Dum airport in the evening, and took a taxi to Park Street where Harry had rented a flat in Gallstone Mansions (known locally as "Gallystony Mansions). I can't say I was very impressed with the flat — I had never lived in an apartment block — and was shattered when the taxi drew up to find we were surrounded by beggars who all seemed to chant "No Mama, No Papa, Bukhshee Munkta" — which I learnt meant "I have no Mother or Father and want some money". There were many young children among this crowd and one or two mothers carrying children who were badly deformed. I was appalled, and felt I would never be able to live in this apparent squalor in such an uncaring society.

I soon learnt that begging was a profession in India, and that the badly deformed children — some minus arms or feet — had been deliberately disfigured by their parents as this made more impression on the public and made people more generous! Sometimes these children were lent to other adults, for a fee, as their potential for begging was so great.

On entering the flat it seemed incongruous that there were no less than 4 servants to greet us, an Ayah to help look after the baby; (I didn't want anyone to look after my darling daughter let alone a strange Indian girl), and when she made a grab for Linda to take her to her nursery, Linda immediately let out a high pitched scream. Frankly I could have joined her. There was also a Khansama (Cook), whose duties were to do all the food shopping and cooking and a Khitmagar or Bearer to do all the housework, a Hamal who didn't speak a word of English and whose duties I was told were to help the bearer do the dirty work. In addition we had a sweeper who came in around 6.30.a.m. and again in the early evening. His particular duty was to brush and wash the floors, clean the toilets — but he must not touch anything else above floor level! He worked for about 4 families — and worked for a pittance, as they all did. How else could we afford all these staff? Our laundry was picked up every morning by the Dhobi and returned beautifully ironed and starched in the early evening.

I really felt we could do without all this entourage; in the U.K. I had managed quite well to run a home, shop, cook, wash and iron, look after the baby and even did the garden!   However, it was explained to me that I would be depriving about 6 families of their only income if I was to dispose of them — and — I would be looked down on by the Indian community and the Expats.   So.... they stayed and I just had to get used to this new life style whether I approved of it or not.

The Bearer, when he had been introduced to the new Memsahib disappeared and I subsequently found he had unpacked all my cabin luggage, had neatly arranged all my underwear in drawers, hung up my dresses, put my toilet things in the bathroom along with the rather intimate items ladies have — and I was quite shattered at such familiarity.   He then disappeared into the kitchen while I was recovering!

A few moments later the Bearer appeared from the kitchen to tell us that lunch would be served in 15 minutes!

As you can imagine I found all this quite unbelievable, and with all the servants, felt we had permanent house guests and had no privacy whatsoever.   Only the Bearer spoke English so all conversations had to be directed through him.   The Ayah, a little Nepali girl, seemed to have limited English, but had a very sweet face and she already seemed devoted to Linda — (whom she referred to as Linda Baba) though at this stage her devotion was neither appreciated or reciprocated.

All the furniture in the flat seemed old fashioned and very dark; the rooms large and the ceilings were exceptionally high compared to homes in England.   It was not a warm welcoming apartment and when I finally went into the kitchen, which the Bearer seemed to take great pains to ensure I didn't see, I was appalled — and decided there was no way I would have been able to cook in this kitchen.

The cooker was a black monstrosity called a chullah which

devoured cow pats as fuel! I have to admit that the cook or Boatchi as he was called — worked wonders on this Heath Robinson type apparatus. To this day I never discovered how he lit the thing or how he controlled the temperature. There was no Refrigerator, but an Ice Box and this was supplied daily when the Ice man called with large lumps of ice which seemed to last 24 hours — though one wondered how! The legs of the ice box were standing in little pots containing kerosene, which I was told was to keep the ants and cockroaches out!

I was simply terrified at the enormous size of the Calcutta spiders, which seemed to race around the room making it quite impossible to kill them. It was useless enlisting the help of the Bearer to dispose of these huge creatures, which were the size of afternoon tea plates, as they seemed to practise "out of sight out of mind" and would cheerfully chase them behind some piece of furniture and then beam at you and say "Spider gone Memsahib". Obviously it would re-appear and until it was killed I could not rest. A good job I wasn't attracted to the Buddhist faith, as the necessity for slaying all these creepy crawlies made me realise I could never subscribe to all the tenets of Buddhism!

We invited a very pleasant couple for dinner, only to discover they were Jains, which did rather "phase me". Particularly as the Cook gave me a list of all the things they were not allowed to eat or drink, and I was left wondering what on earth I was going to give them. I ordered Pineapple and Tomato Juice, as I knew that alcohol was OUT but the Cook explained that Pineapple would not be acceptable as it grew IN the earth — but the Tomato and Orange juice could be offered. Fortunately the Cook was very knowledgeable about the Jain religion, so I left the ordering of the meal to him.

In the rainy season we would have huge cockroach type creatures with hard backs fly into the flat and literally flop onto whatever took their fancy. If it happened to be you, then you were unlucky, as they would cling to you, and all attempts to brush them off were useless and I was far too scared to touch them or pluck them off! I soon discovered that standing on them was a waste of time — as they merely walked off afterwards giving you a shock as you were convinced that your weight must have killed them.

Then of course there were the big cockroaches which seemed to breed in the thousands — and would fly into the flat when the lights were on — and disappear. I had never seen a cockroach — and was terrified when these things appeared out of every nook and cranny. I got through cans of Shelltox as it was the only thing that seemed to have any effect. Writing about these ghastly intruders makes me wonder how on earth I survived. Prior to leaving the U.K., I thought a blue bottle was about the worst invader I had had to cope with!

There was so much to get used to and I wondered how I was ever going to adjust to a life style that was so alien in every respect.

At this time my domestic responsibilities appeared minimal; I was told by other Memsahibs in the Company that I should keep a Cook's Book which the Boatchi produced every morning along with his purchases. This should be "vetted" they told me, as the general feeling was that if the Memsahib was checking the Cook's accounts — they would be a little more realistic or should I say — honest. As I had no idea of the cost of anything at that stage, it was rather a futile exercise. I merely looked at the purchases saw they were entered in the book with the costs and looked to see that no extra items were added — signed the book and returned it along with another 30 Rupees for the following day's marketing. There never seemed to be any left overs!

None of this really made very much sense to me — but one of the Company wives who had obviously decided to take me under her wing gave me a run down on how a "Memsahib" was expected to behave! It appeared that the Company had not just hired my husband, but I too had my duties. I assume that initiating me into the ways of life in India was considered the "duty" of this particular wife!

My first days were very confusing. I remember wandering from room to room looking for some household chore and trying to avoid the army of servants who seemed to pursue me, and all very anxious to convince me that they were working hard!

There were many frustrations.   It appeared that the Bearer's idea of dusting was to flick a large feather duster around — but this merely moved the dust to another area and I could not get him to use a duster which would retain the dust.   He seemed to love brandishing this darned feather duster with as much vigour as a maestro would have shown, but the dust was never eliminated it just moved from one item to the next.   This probably explained why the dusting was done twice a day and all the floors washed at 6.a.m. and 3.p.m.!

My day started at 6.30.a.m. when there was a knock on the bedroom door which was immediately opened before anyone had time to say "come in" and the bearer arrived with a tray of fruit and tea.   This was known as "chota hazri" — and although I have never enjoyed "bed tea" — when we managed to stop the "char" he still brought the fruit!   Having deposited the tray on the bedside table, he drew the curtains and then disappeared into the bathroom to run the bath for the Sahib.   He then darted into my husband's almirah (wardrobe) and chose the items of clothing he decided my husband should wear that day.   These were laid out on the Dresser and then he finally disappeared, only to reappear with the daily newspaper in a few moments.   Not much privacy! I found I had to choose my moment to get out of bed between all these various visits!

I just could not believe this ritual which my husband — who had been in India over three months — seemed to accept.   When I commented about this to one of the wives at a later date saying how decadent I found this, she said that the laying out of clothes and drawing the bath were very minimal and that some Sahibs who had been out East for many years actually had the Bearer shave them, then wait until they were bathed in order to dry them and help them dress!   This was quite repugnant as far as I was concerned. Certainly when I finally got into the bathroom I found that the toothpaste had been spread onto my toothbrush! I soon stopped this.

Breakfast was served on the Veranda at 8.a.m. by which time Linda had returned from her walk on the Maidan (equivalent to a Park). There was a general meeting of Ayahs at this hour as of course it was too hot later in the day. No matter how early I awoke it appeared that the Ayah had already left with "Linda Baba". Presumably this was also intended as a favour to the parents who could also sleep or whatever, a little longer! It was indeed a big change from getting up two or three times in the night to change Linda or give her a drink as I had done whilst living with my Mother in the U.K.

We all had breakfast together with the Bearer hovering around waiting to pour tea, pass the Cornflakes and make the toast so it was freshly toasted, and the Ayah stood behind Linda's high chair to attend to her every need and guide her in good table manners. I truly hated this intrusion into our privacy — but if I was to live in India I realised I had to accept it.

Harry left the house about 8.30.a.m., being picked up by a chauffeur driven car which he shared with another young assistant from the same company. He said he would be back for "tiffin" (lunch) at 1.p.m.

Sahibs and Memsahibs did not use public transport, but when I saw the way the local populace clung onto the roof, and hung from the windows of the local buses I could understand why! I used Rickshaws for short journeys — but always felt uncomfortable that some poor little wizened man should be pulling not only the Rickshaw — but me and the baby as well. If we were going a long distance then I would use a taxi, but one really took one's life in one's hands then.

On one trip I found the taxi driver looking in the mirror and masturbating — so after this experience, when ordering a taxi I would ask the Bearer to take down the number before I left the premises — and I would keep the taxi until I returned.

The price of cars — and of course taxis — was astronomical and so the cars were really run into the ground and never seemed to be replaced. The springs were usually non-existent, they often had wheel wobble — and all the drivers seemed to ride the clutch — and drove like bats out of hell!

After breakfast I found that the beds had been stripped and the sheets and pillows were already on the back veranda in the sun being aired. The Dhobi had arrived to take away the washing and was waiting for me to check the items he was taking. He also had a little book, but as he had written everything down in Urdu, there was little point in my checking the book, so the Bearer did this. I decided I would keep my own Dhobi book in English that I could understand. This didn't work terribly well as of course the Dhobi didn't speak English and although I was struggling to learn Urdu I certainly could not argue as yet — and when things were not returned I could never find out why. So eventually I admitted defeat and reverted to the Dhobi's Book and the Bearer checking it. I did however, have the occasional check on sheets and towels as they had a habit of disappearing or, worst of all, being replaced by really worn out towels and sheets, which the Dhobi swore were mine! Mind you when I saw the Dhobi Ghats where the clothes were literally thrashed on the rocks to remove the dirt and very little soap used — I felt perhaps they could even wear out overnight!

One amusing story I discovered through the Bearer was that when the Dhobi arrived in the morning to collect the laundry, besides being dressed in this drab dirty looking dhotie — he had a piece of string dangling round his neck which was sometimes hooked over his left ear. Curiosity — although I like to refer to it as "interest" prompted me to enquire why he had this string looped over his ear as I felt it must be very uncomfortable. I was told that it was to remind him that he hadn't answered the call of nature that day! Once he had — then the string was removed!

Each morning I was approached by the "Cookie" with his numerous little tins, asking for supplies of rice, sugar, flour, cooking oil, butter, or anything else he might need for the day's menus.

In the early days I merely gave him everything he asked for from the store cupboard — as I felt it was quite wrong to have to lock up one's dry stores — it looked as though you didn't trust them.

However, I tried leaving the cupboard unlocked and telling him to help himself — but when I discovered we had used 110 lbs of white sugar, an equal amount of flour and 30 lbs of butter in one month, I decided that perhaps the locking method was after all the best. Neither Harry or I took sugar — and the scraping of butter on our morning toast was about all the butter we had — other than any that was used for baking cakes for tea or the odd sweet.

I started asking what he wanted the various items for — and then I found he was doubling the quantities that one would normally use. His excuses that the sugar wasn't very sweet this month or that because it was hot one needed more butter — were, I have to admit, amusing and as all this had to be translated through the Bearer it became a marathon task.    I finally gave up the struggle and when he asked for 3/4 lb. of sugar I would give him 8 oz and he would twitch his head — and I never found out what this meant — but at least we still ate and the sugar consumption went down.

I should explain of course that every month each member of the staff received 20 lbs of sugar, 20 lbs of rice, 5 lbs of milk powder and a bottle of cooking oil on top of their salary.

Although I was still uneasy about this strange life style, I found it interesting — and I suppose my natural curiosity has been my salvation as I can honestly say that except for the first few weeks in Calcutta, when I felt homesick and "confused", friendless and a stranger in my own home, I have thoroughly enjoyed every moment of my life in the East.

Although all the servants obviously had names — everyone referred to them according to their occupation — so it was never Ahmed — but Cookie or Boatchi, similarly the Bearer was never called Mumtaz — but Bearer — and I don't think I ever discovered the Hamal or Sweeper's names — they merely answered to their occupation.

It's hard to remember the sequence of events, but the morning "Chota Hazri" was stopped, though the Bearer still knocked on the door to draw the bath. The laying out of clothes was fortunately stopped — as nine times out of ten Harry never wore what had been chosen by the Bearer. I had a sneaking suspicion however that he rather enjoyed the attention — which I found nauseating.

I should perhaps also mention that every other day the "flower wallah" would arrive and for the princely sum of Rs20 (£2) per month he would fill two or three flower vases and arrange the flowers. Obviously sometimes the flowers would last longer than 2 days in which case he would fill further vases which meant that the apartment was always full of flowers. Quite unbelievable in a country that had so little vegetation and what they had appeared to be devoted to rice.

I soon became familiar with the market prices as I made one or two friends who took me to the early morning markets every few weeks. This was indeed an experience in itself — the fly blown meat stalls — cut fruit left open — and the noise and congestion not to mention the filth on the floors — no wonder there was so much dysentery in the country. Chickens were sold live and you were asked if you wanted them plucked! I was simply horrified when I found that the chickens throat was cut in front of me, and then the chicken was plunged into boiling water for a couple of seconds after which all the feathers came off easily!

After this memorable first visit to the market I soaked all vegetables in "pinky" (Potassium Permanganate) and would not allow the Cook to purchase any fruit that was not entirely whole. All our water was boiled and filtered — and I would personally check that the water was actually boiling for 25 mins which the Doctors said would kill any bacteria in the water. I also checked that the fruit and vegetables were being soaked in "Pinky". Mind you no one told me that fruit such as Water Melon was highly suspect as the farmers would soak the water melon in the local streams so they absorbed water through the skin which added to their weight! There were so many ways one could contact the various Dysentery's and I don't think I ever went 6 weeks without getting either Amoebic, Bacillary or Gardia Dysentery.

When the Cook knew you were familiar with the current market prices then he would add only 20% to the Cook's book prices, instead of the usual 50% he was trying to get away with.     Mind you the salaries these people earned were so small and they all had large families they were supporting.    Most of the families were kept in the Mofussil (the country) and not in Calcutta which was considered expensive, — so one had a degree of sympathy and tended to shut your eyes to things that disappeared so long as they left one's personal items alone.

The second week we were in Calcutta Harry came home and told me that the two friends, Ken and Harold, I had met on board the Cilicia who had kindly brought my tin trunks over from Bombay, had phoned to say that Cox and King's would be delivering the trunks the following afternoon.    He had invited them round for dinner the following night and they had asked if they could bring the friend with whom they worked and were sharing the Chummery. I was delighted to have the opportunity of meeting up with someone I felt I knew, who spoke English, and doubtless would be sharing my doubts and difficulties in adjusting to this new life style.

This was to be my first dinner party, as up to now we had been entertained by other Company wives, but had hardly had time to reciprocate.    The Boatchi discussed the menu and suggested Soup, Chicken a la Kiev with a mixture of 4 vegetables and a mixed fruit dessert.    The table was laid beautifully with two lovely flower arrangements — and the Bearer had changed his uniform and looked very resplendent in a flamboyant pugri (head gear) and even Cookie sported a clean apron — even though he never appeared in the Dining Room.

The guests were invited for 7.30.p.m. and when the Bearer brought them in I was so delighted to meet someone that I actually KNEW that I failed to notice the horrified look of recognition on my husband's face when Phillip, the third member of the Chummery, was introduced. It later transpired that Phillip had been his table companion at Mrs. McDonald's Boarding House where they had both been living for the past 3 months. Apparently, I learnt weeks later, that Phillip was equally embarrassed at meeting me as he obviously knew so much about my husband and his promiscuous life style. Now he had met the wife of the philanderer and told the other two boys when they left that he felt very sorry for me and explained to them the details of my husband's excessive night life.

At breakfast each morning, it appeared that Harry had regaled Phillip with the most intimate details of his previous evenings liaisons. I was of course quite oblivious of this at the time and it was months later before I learnt what had been said, and what had been taking place before my arrival.

As far as I was concerned this was a very successful dinner party, everything went very smoothly and although I popped into the kitchen from time to time to see that the food was being prepared in a way I felt was acceptable, I very soon realised that the Boatchi's expertise was far far greater than mine — and the meal looked and tasted delightful. A great deal of care had been taken in decorating each dish with tastefully cut vegetables — this is indeed an art — and to this day I am filled with admiration at the way carrots, tomatoes, peppers etc., can be turned into beautiful looking roses, daisies, ducks and swans.

The table had been laid beautifully but I was shocked to see that half the serving dishes and some cutlery did not belong to me! It seemed that "borrowing" between the servants was very much accepted as normal procedure and many times have I been invited out for dinner to find my cut glass water jug or my avocado dishes were in use! The Memsahib was never consulted about either the borrowing or the lending and it seemed to be a custom — so — I felt if you can't beat the system you might as well join it! Perhaps this is why our breakages seemed so excessive and one was for ever trying to replace the odd tea cup or glass!   Often this meant waiting until your home leave as these items were not available in India.

I think the only disaster was that when the boys pierced their Kiev's the butter spurted out and both their suits had to  be cleaned afterwards.   This at least proved the Kiev's were piping hot!

After this dinner party, I was not afraid of entertaining, and consequently our social life improved.   The first few weeks it had been virtually non-existent.

Every Sunday evening was "cinema night" which I gathered was quite an occasion.   It was usual for the men to wear black tie and the ladies to don evening dress and go to Firpos for dinner followed by a visit to the cinema.   This dressing up to go to the cinema seemed very peculiar to me though it did make it more of an occasion.   We were invited to join the three boys from the Chummery and sometimes there were other friends of theirs.   We all had dinner together and then went along to the cinema.

Harry often had to go to Dum Dum airport to meet clients and would not return home until late!   I was not entirely happy about this — but — as Export Manager, which was now his title, it made a degree of sense that he would be responsible for meeting overseas visitors.   But surely not as frequently as he made out?   As for any doubts about his promiscuity I convinced myself that there were so few European ladies — that it wouldn't be easy for him to continue his previous life style, and of course one never thought for a moment that anyone other than a European would be of interest.

One was very conscious from the moment you arrived in India that mixed marriages or mixed affairs were definitely "taboo"   Many a young man had been sent back to the U.K. because he had been seen in the company of an Indian or Anglo Indian lady, so on contemplation the thought of him being promiscuous again really seemed ludicrous.

On one or two occasions — when going to the Airport on Sunday evenings — he rang the Chummery boys up to tell them that we would not be able to join them at the cinema on Sunday. I was told that they had suggested they pick me up — and we could all go along together. I subsequently learnt this was far from the truth, Harry had in fact suggested that I accompany them to the cinema as he was unable to go and I already had my ticket! Be that as it may, there were quite a few occasions when I went along with the boys. I think they enjoyed some female company and I found it a very acceptable alternative to sitting in the apartment on my own. I suppose one could hardly call a household with 5 servants as "being on my own".

Curry lunch parties on Sunday were also part of the norm — sometimes at friends houses — other times at the Saturday Club. I was not terribly keen on these Tiffin parties as Linda was initially too young to take along and I hated leaving her, so we would often decline. If we did accept then we would leave early and try to be home before Linda woke from her lunch time nap.

The Saturday Club (known as the SLAP) was really very impressive and next to The Bengal Club — rated as one of the best Clubs in India. Entry was formidable. Usually one's Company submitted an application on your behalf — and after a month or so on the waiting list you were requested to attend the Club on a particular evening, in Black Tie of course, with your spouse for what really was "vetting". One was introduced to each member of the Selection Committee, who offered you a drink and had a general chat as to what other Clubs you were a member of, asked if your father had been a member of this or any other Club, what other overseas postings you had had and what sports you were interested in and what hobbies you had! There was general small chat whilst they summed up whether you would be a suitable member. At the end of the Meeting each Committee member had to cast their vote on the "Black Ball" system, by depositing either a white or black ball into the box with the applicant's name. Anyone receiving even one Black Ball would be refused membership. A small number of wealthy Indians were members, but no Anglo Indians or people of mixed race appeared to pass the test!

I was not particularly enamoured with the apartment we were living in or the location, and therefore when I heard that there was a flat available in a much superior block of flats, actually on Chowringhee the main thoroughfare, overlooking the Maidan — I went along to investigate.    I saw the Manager of Whiteaway Laidlaws whose building it was — they were the biggest if not the only large department store in Calcutta at that time.

The rent was the same as we were paying — the ambience so much better and obviously the Manager approved of these possible tenants and so we were able to move at the end of the month.

Most of the tenants appeared to be European or well educated Indians and consequently the building was kept in an excellent condition and well supervised.    There were Chowkidars (watchmen) on duty 24 hours — and a Sweeper for the whole building who kept the approaches washed and clean.    I was much happier.    Next door was a charming English girl with two children — and she took me around and introduced me to the new area.

Harry continued to have the odd business appointments which sometimes kept him out in the evenings — and whilst I wasn't entirely happy about them I had met other wives who confirmed that most planes seemed to arrive around 9.p.m. or 10.p.m. and it appeared usual for someone in the Company always to meet visitors and take them to their Hotel and settle them in.

I found my girl friend next door had similar problems — and so we would often spend these evenings together.

It transpired that she was just about as naive as I — as her husband was bi-sexual — and nearly every evening after dinner he would go out — reputedly to play squash or meet a business friend.

Harry and I had noticed that he always carried a mackintosh over his arm — which puzzled us as it rained very rarely in Calcutta, after the Monsoon was over.    We later learnt that he had made many friends in the Sikh community — and would meet these friends on the Maidan after dark.    I don't need to explain why he took the

Mackintosh! He was like all AC/DC men — VERY amusing with a dry sense of humour and obviously quite oblivious to the fact that anyone would guess his double entity.

I remember one evening I was in my friend's flat playing cribbage and he came home earlier than usual very upset that he had had his watch and wallet stolen whilst walking on the Maidan! Whilst I felt it was a very peculiar place to be walking and wondered why he would not advise the police — far be it for me to sew seeds of doubt in my friend's life.

A few weeks later however, I was returning to the flat in a Rickshaw around 4.p.m. when I heard screams from above and on looking up saw my friend in a terrible state on their large Veranda, with torn clothes, fighting off the Bearer!

I thought the man must have gone berserk — so rushed up to the flat taking the two Chowkidars (watchmen) with me. When we finally got into the flat through the servant's entrance, found my friend hysterical, badly scratched and her clothing ripped — there was little doubt what her Bearer had had in mind.

The Bearer appeared to have been drinking and ran off to the Servant's quarters when we arrived. The Chowkidars chased him and I told them to keep him locked up until her husband arrived. I rang her husband and suggested he came home immediately as his wife had been attacked — and then I stayed trying to comfort her. I told her husband when he arrived that I hadn't as yet called the police, but was leaving that to him as his Urdu was considerably better than mine — and off he went to see the Bearer who was under lock and key.

Imagine my indignation and confusion when I discovered that he had unlocked the door and told the Bearer to leave. No one could understand this ridiculous behaviour, but it later came to light that the Bearer knew very well that my friend's husband had peculiar tendencies and he assumed therefore the wife would be neglected sexually and would be quite pleased to have his attention! As the Bearer had been drinking — (the Sahib's whisky of course) he had acquired sufficient courage for this attack. Fortunately I had seen this so "his gas was put to a peep" so to speak!

Joan, this friend, had been married 12 years and had no idea that her husband was bi-sexual — and that he was a practising homosexual. She was mortified. It appeared that because he had two children he looked upon this as a cover and that no one would suspect he was anything but "straight"!

Joan approached the family Dr. saying she wanted the children and herself checked for V.D. as she felt she now knew the reasons for her husband's repeated visits to the Dr. She had learnt her husband was being treated for V.D. in a place that only a practising Homosexual could acquire it! She felt this was in itself grounds for divorce — so returned to the U.K. with her children and started divorce proceedings.

However, this was not so easy as when the evidence was produced in Court her husband's Counsel produced a certificate from a London Hospital which proved that he had been treated for the same condition four years prior to their marriage. His present condition therefore was NOT a new infection but merely a return of the original problem and did not prove conclusively that he was still practising. As she had married him AFTER this treatment, the Court said she MUST have been aware of it and therefore had condoned his behaviour and there were no grounds for divorce.

I was naturally very sad when Joan left, particularly as I couldn't help having doubts, bearing in mind my previous experience, about Harry's business meetings. I tried to reason with myself that there was no way my husband would risk the misery we had been through previously — and after all — hadn't he travelled 12,000 miles to make a fresh start?

Joan did eventually get a divorce on the grounds of their three year separation, but it seemed hard that she had to wait so long in the circumstances.

I have always been concerned about getting into debt and whilst our Indian salary "sounded" good — I wasn't convinced that our expenses were not exceeding our income.  So, I used to examine the bank statements just to ensure that there was a credit balance at the end of the month — or at the worst — a small debit.  On one of these checks I discovered an amount of Rs2,000 had been paid to Whiteaway Laidlaw's Jewellery Dept.  As this was 3 weeks before my birthday I felt I should not spoil Harry's surprise by commenting on it.  My birthday came — but no jewellery,  I think I received a set of dekchis (Indian cooking utensils), which were badly needed in the kitchen!  I therefore felt quite justified in questioning this payment of Rs.2,000 — but was told he had allowed a friend in the office to buy his wife a gift on our account for which he had received cash!  A likely story I thought and this made me doubly cautious.

Shortly after this Harry went on a 10 day business trip to Delhi, and I noticed a great change in his attitude on his return.  He appeared very pensive and would spend hours playing sentimental numbers on the Grand Piano we had rented.  He played by ear beautifully but appeared to be introspective and MILES away!  On one occasion Linda and I returned from our afternoon outing on the Maidan and found him playing the piano with a photograph of an Indian lady on the top of the piano!  His explanation that she "inspired him" naturally greatly disturbed me.  Not half as disturbed as I was when the next bank statement arrived!

I found a payment of Rs2,500 to a Mrs. Goldstein!  This was a fortune in my mind.  Naturally I questioned Harry about this and initially he made some feeble excuse but was obviously embarrassed and told me in future I had not to open his bank statements!  On further questioning he said that this Mrs. Goldstein, who worked in the Delhi office, had lent him money on his last Delhi trip and this was the re-payment!  Naturally I continued the questioning and wanted to know what on earth he had spent this amount on!  He was on an expense account whilst on Company business, and therefore this amount must have been for personal expenses.

I got no satisfactory reply.  Not only was I upset about this large debit, but after my past experience, was very suspicious, though still couldn't bring myself to believe that he was reverting to the status quo of our London days. How very stupid women can be — as I still did nothing. Possibly because I could really see no alternative.

Things between us went from bad to worse — even though his demands and ability in bed did not seem to be affected by my coldness — I was a very unwilling bed partner — and I suppose in this day and age his advances could be classed as rape!

I decided that I must make some plans for the future as this state of affairs could not go on much longer, but I was a long way from home, and had no one to turn to or anywhere to go.

To cut a long and sordid story short. After yet another harrowing confrontation with Harry about expenses and his inability to explain the debts, he became quite violent and finally confessed that he had fallen in love with an Indian lady who had recently been divorced by her American husband called Goldstein. She was the Company Secretary in Delhi which he visited frequently on business.

It was this same lady whose photograph had adorned the Grand piano. The Rs2,500 had been to pay for an abortion! Whilst I had had certain "doubts" during the last few weeks, this information really shattered me, but this was not the end of my husband's callousness.

He then insisted on reading a love letter he had received from this lady that morning in the office. It was a very explicit letter and left no doubt whatsoever that they had spent his last 10 day visit to Delhi, together and from all accounts a great deal of this time had been spent in bed! The most intimate details of their love making were referred to and my husband seemed to get a sadistic pleasure in reading this letter to me. Again he became quite violent and I ended up with a bruised eye.

I just could not believe that I had travelled all this way — merely to be presented with the same problems I had had in the U.K. This time of course I had no close friends or relatives to turn to for advice.

It is surprising though, how quickly one can mature when there really is no one to turn to and you are on your own. Every time I was beaten up, I had gone to the Dr. which as things turned out, was very wise.

I realised the love letter that had been read to me which had subsequently been torn up and thrown into the waste paper basket, could provide sufficient evidence of adultery, but more important, sufficient evidence that my husband was warped where sex was concerned and quite unsuitable to be considered a suitable parent where custody of Linda was involved. So, I was determined to retrieve this if possible!

After the disclosure about his love life, I had moved into the Nursery and slept with Linda, even though the Ayah was more often in the room than out of it. This in itself caused more violence as in spite of his declaration of undying love for this lady — as she wasn't available he expected me to sleep with him! I naturally refused, but Harry then went into the room where Linda was sleeping and told the little Nepali Ayah to come to his room. He told me that if I wouldn't sleep with him then he would rape the Ayah!

This particular evening, after I had been subjected to the love letter reading, I awaited until about 3.a.m. when I thought Harry would be in a deep sleep, and crept out into the Lounge and rescued all the pieces of the letter which I assembled the following day.

The following morning I went to the Dr. before I went to the office and told the Dr. of my problems and asked if he thought it likely that I could have contracted V.D. as my husband had been sleeping with an Indian woman. The embarrassment of having to go for a V.D. test was bad enough, but when the Dr. asked me to take Linda in for a check — I felt humiliated beyond words.

At this time I was badly bruised and the Dr. had a record of my previous visits and saw that again I had a black eye. This was one of many I received before the saga was over and each time I went down to the Dr. as I felt this was more evidence of my husband's instability.

This was my insurance policy in case he tried to take Linda away from me, on the grounds that I could not provide her with all that he could.

The same day I made an appointment with an English Solicitor, practising in Calcutta. I took the patched up letter with me and he confirmed that this was quite sufficient evidence for a divorce on the grounds of adultery AND he felt very strongly that no Court would give him access to his daughter after reading the contents.

The big problem now of course was money. The Solicitor pointed out that he was not a philanthropic society and that if I wanted him to handle my divorce, he would want an initial deposit of at least £200. I would also require a U.K. Solicitor to represent me at the hearing in London, as our marriage had taken place in the U.K. So I left the letter with him and went away to think how I was to achieve this.

I decided to go to the British High Commission and applied for a job on their staff. I initially had an interview with a Clerk, and then a First Secretary and finally with the High Commissioner himself. He was a dear fatherly type of man — who wanted to know why I wanted to work!

Most of the staff were employed in the U.K. and brought out in the then Diplomatic Service. They did have one or two locally employed staff, but for Security reasons these had to be well and truly vetted. Even though they had to sign the Official Secrets Act, personal references were required. I was of course unable to provide immediate U.K. references from this distance, and no one locally had known me long enough. I could not supply the name and address of any Company that could vouch for me. Certainly not my husband's Company — who knew nothing of the divorce at this stage.

Obviously this made my application seem suspect as I particularly asked that they did NOT approach Harry's Company. If the reasons for the divorce were to come to the knowledge of his office, he would be sacked and sent home — so long as he was employed I would be eligible for support!

However, it became obvious that I would not be employed unless I gave the High Commission the name of my husband's Company. I found H.E. (His Excellency) so kind and fatherly that I broke down and explained to him why it was important for me to have a job and why it was equally important that he didn't contact my husband's company at this stage. I was saving up for a divorce which my Solicitor had assured me would also give me costs, custody and maintenance, and make my return to the U.K. possible, and safe.

After these interviews I was told that they would employ me on a temporary basis, but I could not touch any of the Top Security files until Security Clearance was received from the U.K. So I started work in the Nationality division with restricted responsibilities initially. The Security Clearance came through in about a fortnight and I then felt reasonably secure.

The salary certainly was meagre and I could not live on it — but I was assured by H.E. that I would be considered for an increment once my U.K. references had been checked. This did help of course, but my expenses were still more than my income! But, it was a start and gave me a certain independence.

I enjoyed the job which had its humorous side, and helped me forget my personal problems during office hours — I didn't feel particularly guilty leaving Linda as I used to go home for lunch — she had a sleep most afternoons and I was home at 4.30.p.m. and able to take her swimming or out on the Maidan.

However, this state of affairs did not last for long. When Harry found I had started divorce proceedings he again became very violent and really went berserk. He attacked me with a carving knife and I had to run into the next flat to ask for assistance. The neighbour came back into the flat with me. This seemed to have a salutary affect on Harry who became subdued and then started to cry and plead forgiveness. There was no way now that I would drop the proceedings. I had become very hard, very bitter and very much wiser, and having a job gave me a degree of confidence I had to date lacked.

When I refused to drop the proceedings, Harry became very agitated and unbeknown to me, later that night, tried to commit suicide by putting his head in the gas oven!   I didn't think he had the guts to have gone through with this, but he was discovered by the Bearer who woke me up.   A sleepless and miserable night ensued.

The next morning I again went down to the Dr.   When he saw the condition I was in and I told him what had happened, he said he could not take the responsibility of ignoring these attacks any longer — and therefore rang Harry's Burra Sahib (Boss) and told him of his fears for my safety.   The Company asked me to go and see them — and wanted to know the reasons for these attacks.   I told them they had been initiated when Harry found I had been to a Solicitor and had started divorce proceedings.

They then wanted to know the grounds for the divorce — and as it appeared the cat was out of the bag I gave them the details of Mrs. Goldstein's abortion.   They didn't seem convinced that this was related in any way to Harry even when I told them that it was a result of Harry's visit to Delhi when he was on Company business — and at the same time gave them the address of the Nursing Home where the abortion had taken place.  I suggested that if they checked they would find that the Secretary was absent on these days.

I still felt at the time that they were not very convinced that I wasn't making up this saga but to be on the safe side sent one of the Company wives and her husband to spend the following night with me to ensure there would be no further attacks.  Harry had been told that he was to return to the U.K. immediately and his employment with the Company terminated.  I suppose this prompted the suicide attempt.   I realised that with his dismissal — so went any hopes of maintenance or support.

His Company wanted me to return home the following week as, having brought me out to India, they were of course responsible for me so long as I remained in India.

This did not fit in with my plans at all.   I had anticipated this happening but not for a few more months when the divorce would have been heard. I was very reluctant to leave India; I had a job with a promise of promotion once my divorce was through — I still remembered Harry's threat that he would take Linda away from me as soon as I set foot in the U.K., NOT as he said, that he wanted the baby — but he would see that I didn't have her.

So until I had that piece of paper from the Courts giving me custody and hopefully denying Harry visiting rights to my darling daughter, I wanted to stay in India. Linda really was a beautiful baby, and I might add grew into a beautiful woman.

I went to see H.E. the following day to advise him what had happened and that the Company wanted me to return to the U.K. He rang Harry's Burra Sahib and found out that one of the main problems was that if I got into debt — the Company would be responsible for my debts, as they had brought me out to India — and they could not hold my return fare once Harry was no longer an employee.

H.E. told them that after 2 year's employment with the High Commission I would be eligible for a return fare to the U.K. and he was prepared to guarantee my return passage as in those days I would be eligible for repatriation if everything went wrong, but he felt after talking to me that I was determined to support myself and child by taking in P.G.'s (Paying Guests).

I had established with Whiteaway Laidlaws that the lease on the flat could be transferred to my name. Obviously quite a few people had faith in my ability to support myself — though I confess I wasn't completely convinced — but I was determined to give it a go!

The Solicitor was also approached by the Company and he assured them that I had very good grounds for divorce and that once it was granted I would be eligible for, Costs, Custody, Maintenance and Child Support. The Company finally agreed that I could remain in Calcutta, but that they would no longer be responsible for me in any way. This was indeed a victory, but I still had to find the money to pay the rent and support us.

I do sincerely believe that when one door closes finally and irrevocably that another one often opens!

A Company car came to collect Harry to take him to the Airport the following evening.    Seeing him leave was traumatic — as I couldn't help thinking of "what could have been" — and naturally was worried how I was going to cope.   I have never seen him again.

Where there's a will — there's usually a way — though at the time I needed a lot of convincing!

My first stroke of luck came reasonably quickly.   I had put an advert on the notice board of the Calcutta Swimming Club the day Harry left,   saying P.G. accommodation was available.   At the weekend I received a telephone call asking if the P.G. accommodation was still available and I assured them it was — I'd hardly had time to receive any more enquiries, and so this couple arrived to look at the flat.

He was American and his wife English.   She apparently had been suffering repeatedly from Dysentery and even now had Amoebic Dysentery and as she was pregnant her husband felt they must get out of the Boarding House they were living in and would like to move in immediately!   They, or at least the husband, made one request to the effect that as his wife had been so ill — she did not wish to be worried with running a home and coping with servants which were obviously as new to her as they were to me!   So was I prepared to do this and arrange any dinner parties they had to give?

This was an ideal arrangement as far as I was concerned as it meant I would not have to get rid of the servants — which had been worrying me — as I knew they needed the job and let's face it — I now needed them!

I was then asked about the rent?   Well I really had no idea — but I did know that I NEEDED Rs.750 per month to meet the overheads — but this seemed a lot of money.   While I was plucking up my courage to tell them the figure I had in mind — the American pipped me to the post and enquired whether Rs.1350 would be sufficient?   This was the figure they had been paying at the Boarding

House.   I was speechless as this was way beyond my wildest dreams and would mean that Linda and I could also live on this amount — and I would be able to save my salary to pay for the divorce.   As explained, I had been assured by my Solicitor, that once my Divorce was final, not only would I receive the costs and maintenance (which by now were quite considerable) but the High Commission would be able to increase my salary and I would get an allowance for Linda.   I could then acquire a little nest egg which I would need to start up a home in the U.K.

So Frank and Renee Drew, this very nice couple, moved in the same night and they were quite delightful and included me in their dinner parties and would ask me to join them for a glass of wine before dinner.   I thought they would wish to eat alone — but they insisted that we all ate together as a family — so Linda also was included which was super.

Unfortunately this state of affairs only lasted 3 months but it did give me time to adjust and build up some savings, which regrettably would have to go to the Solicitor!   This very nice family who had now become friends came home with the news they had been posted to Karachi!   I was really sad and realised that life would not be so easy from now on.

I advertised once again for P.G.'s — and a rather reserved, but very pleasant Irish couple applied.   Unfortunately their financial position did not permit them paying any more than Rs750 per month — and they did not want me to do the catering — and they did not want my Bearer as they had their own.   Obviously I could not afford to keep him nor for that matter would there be the work for him — but I was lucky and obtained a position for him with one of the Expats working for a Bank.

This young couple obviously wanted to be alone in the evenings and so I felt banished to my bedroom with the baby and the Ayah — which presented problems in itself.   If I had the light on to read, Linda would wake up — the Ayah who enjoyed sewing and had been in the habit of doing this in the Bearer's quarters whilst he was busy in the evenings, was unable to pursue her little hobby. However, we coped, but obviously we didn't eat so well and I found I was making inroads into my savings as we could not always survive on my High Commission salary.

It had been my plan to return to the U.K. once the divorce was through — but obviously at this stage if I kept dipping into the little I had saved and was not able to add to it, I was not going to have any spare funds to help me with the move and settle back in the U.K.

However, I had written to the Child Care Organisation in Greenford, the area where I had been living prior to going overseas, asking if they would accept Linda on our return. This at least would enable me to work — as I really had no one with whom I could leave her. My darling Mother — who had had her own share of problems and worries, most certainly did not want mine — or at least I was determined she should not have them.

In fact in order to spare her worrying I had been in India 6 months on my own before I told her Harry was no longer with me. I was able to put her mind at rest by saying I had obtained a job with the British High Commission and that I would be returning home after I received the Decree Absolute. Obviously she was concerned, but not half as concerned as she would have been if she knew the full facts.

As though fate had stepped in yet again, at the same time I received a letter from the Child Care Centre saying that they would not have a vacancy to take Linda full time i.e. 8.30.a.m. to 4.30.p.m. until she had turned 4. She was then 19 months old! At the same time there had been no progress with the Divorce — and I couldn't help thinking that if I had more finance available the results might have been different and the Solicitor would have taken a little more action to speed things up. Everything had to go through this U.K. Solicitor — and I can only assume that letters had been sent Sea Mail (or by pigeon) as there really seemed to be no progress.

The U.K. Solicitor said one problem was trying to find Harry to serve the papers on him — his family insisted that they had no idea where he was, and seemed quite surprised apparently when they heard of the divorce.

All things considered therefore, I decided that perhaps it would be to my advantage to stay with the High Commission until at least the Child Care Centre had a vacancy to take Linda full time.

My new Paying Guests obviously wanted to be on their own — and I was acutely aware of this which made me feel very uncomfortable. This state of affairs was unsatisfactory for everyone and, to add insult to injury, I was getting into debt.

In Calcutta, at that time, there was a system for getting apartments which was referred to as "paying key money". This meant that anyone who held a lease could transfer it to whomever they wanted — and were quite justified in asking a payment for this. This system unfortunately was abused by money grabbing landlords as there was a dearth of accommodation. I thought I would look into this possibility as it would enable me to get out of debt — would give my paying guests the privacy they so obviously wanted.

As I didn't want to get into any legal problems — I went along to see the Landlord, a delightful European elderly bachelor, who reputedly was rather feminine, but a gentleman and very kind and understanding. I explained my problem about my debts and the difficulties I was experiencing and asked if he would permit me to transfer the lease of my flat to my paying guests who in turn would pay me a minimum to enable me to clear my debts.

Not only did he agree, but asked where I planned to live once the transfer had taken place. I said that I planned to look for a room with cooking facilities in a cheaper area — whereupon to my amazement he offered me an apartment in the same building. It had just two large rooms with a bathroom and he was prepared to put a cooker in a corner of one of the rooms which I would use as a dining room.

I couldn't believe my luck — this solved so many problems — and I would still be able to live in the same area where I had made one or two friends, and still have a lovely view over the Maidan —

and I was well known to the Chowkidars and many of the residents who were all so charming and helpful. Linda had her own little circle of friends that she met with their respective Ayahs on the Maidan each morning — most of them from the same block of flats — and it was reasonably near the Calcutta Swimming Club where I still had a Membership which unfortunately was due to expire very shortly.

I really felt that life was being good to me, or at least, the friends I had made were so genuine and kind.

My paying guests were as delighted as I was — at last they could have their privacy — and were agreeable to the very minimal "key money" I requested. My debts were Rs2.000 — so I had asked for that amount — and I know that some of the tenants had paid as much as Rs.20,000 for the transfer of the lease of their flats.

I moved into this new apartment at the end of the week, paid off my debts and rented the very basic amount of furniture. I chose two very large Almirahs (wardrobes) and used them as dividers in this very large room — so out of this one room I virtually had a bedroom and a lounge with a small patio off it. The Ayah when I was at home made up a bed in the Dining Room after supper. When I was out she made up her bed on the Veranda which enabled her to keep an eye on Linda.

Naturally, although I could just balance my budget — there was no allowance for emergencies — and certainly no way I could save. Again — wonderful friends came to my assistance.

Living entirely on my own with Linda was a new experience and I remember we had several moments when I wished we had someone to turn to. We frequently had bats that flew into the apartment at dusk — and besides the natural fear of them we were told they often housed fleas — and would cling to one's hair — even though they are reputed to have a sensory system that would prevent them from doing this. It obviously didn't always work! Unlike some flying insects that follow the light and would therefore disappear when the lights are turned off — this had no effect on bats! They just clung to whatever they could find and when the lights were turned on would often start their evening escapades again. I often had to send for the Chowkidar and tip him to remove the offending bat — as I was as scared of them as Linda was — and certainly could not sleep with them in the room.

Then there was a night when we saw a rat in the room, but we had acquired a little Dachshund that very quickly caught the rat and obviously broke its neck. Whilst we were grateful on this occasion there was a time when the little dog didn't know the difference between a rat and a cat — and there was a horrible incident when we had to rush to the cat's aid; the owners were not amused!

The receptionist at the High Commission had been in Calcutta a number of years and was well known, and proved a very good friend. She had a mutual friend who was wanting a part time Secretary. This gentleman, although employed full time in one of the large Trading Companies in Calcutta, had three small business ventures in the U.K. as a side line. These had grown to such an extent that he felt he could no longer give his office secretary the letters appertaining to these businesses. He therefore decided he needed an additional Secretary who would work at night and was given my name (and doubtless told of the dilemma I was in — waiting for my divorce). He asked me to go for an interview — and it seemed that the job would be ideal.

He could only work in the evenings after business — and so it was arranged that I would work for him three evenings a week at his flat — a car would be sent to pick me up after I had given Linda her supper and seen her into bed. Whilst the Ayah would have done this — I felt it essential I spent this quality time with her — and so as soon as she was in bed — around 7.p.m. I would leave in the car and would take dictation for about 3 hours. The following evening I would type these letters at my flat and take them with me the following evening when I went for more dictation. This worked well — but in addition — the most attractive feature as far as I was concerned was that around 9.p.m. we would stop for dinner, or if I was late arriving, have dinner before I started work.  This was a wonderful perk as it cut down on my housekeeping — and as though that wasn't enough he would always ask his cook to put the remainder of the meal into a "doggie bag".  These "left overs" provided a delicious lunch for Linda the following day — and sometimes there was so much "left over" that it would do for us both the following evening!  He was so very kind and thoughtful and the way he handled the "doggie bag" — I never felt embarrassed.  I admit I never confessed to the Cook that the dog didn't even SEE the "left over".

The car and driver took me home around 10.30.p.m.  The pay was good and although I had to work very hard, often transcribing the previous day's shorthand until late in the evening — I felt fate had again been more than kind.

Obviously my social life at this time was just about nil, although my companions from the ship continued to come round, and at the weekend would take Linda and me out on picnics and sometimes I'd go to the pictures with them.  They were indeed great friends as were all the Staff in the High Commission.  I have never known such kindness and thoughtfulness.

Parcels would arrive on my desk with a little note saying that the enclosed dresses, shoes etc., would no longer fit their little girl and they hoped I wouldn't be insulted but perhaps Linda would be able to wear them!  I swear that sometimes the dresses had been bought especially — as they appeared brand new.

I can to this day still shed a tear when I think of their kindness at Xmas!  I happened to say that I had made Linda a rag doll and although she had hoped for a pram I hoped she would be pleased with "Moppity Ann"!  I had been looking in the local paper for "House Sales" hoping to find someone disposing of a cheap pram. I was always the first to read the local paper — so the staff knew that I was anxious to get her a pram which was obviously a much wanted toy, and she was always borrowing doll's prams from the friends she played with on the Maidan, and was sometimes very reluctant to return the pram to its natural owner!

On Xmas Eve there was a party in the office when everyone brought in bottles of Sherry and Mince Pies. I decided I would give this a miss as there was no way I could contribute BUT — they pleaded with me to attend and said they fully realised why I had refused.

So — I decided I'd go along and when I came into the room where the party was I found a pile of presents all beautifully wrapped. I was immediately worried as I thought to myself that everyone was exchanging gifts and hoped they would understand why I had not been able to contribute. How wrong I was! All these beautifully wrapped parcels were for Linda — and the largest one was a brand new pram — with the most delightful and touching note, signed by all my work companions, which I still have today, saying how much they admired me and wished they could do more. I had a surprisingly wonderful Xmas watching Linda open all these interesting little parcels — even my rag doll was appreciated and was promptly pushed around the apartment in her new pram.

There was even more kindness to come. My companions from the boat, Ken and Harold, presented me with a year's subscription to the Calcutta Swimming Club as a Xmas present — which meant I could continue to take Linda swimming and use the Club myself. I was thrilled — such a thoughtful and much appreciated gift, which made life for us both so much more pleasant.

Mind you I had to ensure that I didn't run up any Club bills which, as we all know, is so easy to do — bottles of coke, sandwiches, cookies not to mention a meal occasionally. On my strict budget a Club bill at the end of the month would have put me back in the red. I therefore went down to the Club with a flask of juice for Linda and one or two home baked cookies, and, although bringing food into the Club was strictly taboo, I felt they couldn't object to the baby nibbling on a cookie! On my part I had to ensure that I didn't accept offers of drinks from friends, as I would have found it impossible to reciprocate, so I was never thirsty or hungry when at the Club!

It was a difficult time and even to-day Linda remembers all this though I sometimes think she doesn't appreciate why she had to be deprived of these daily treats other children took for granted, particularly as she got older. In to-day's world it is quite incongruous that anyone's budget would not permit the purchase of a daily Coca-Cola or perhaps an ice cream! I still cannot adjust to the changes in today's world, and am mortified at the pocket money that is now given and the presents children ask for — the cost of which would have supported Linda and me for a month!

Although these were worrying days, I loved the job I was doing in the High Commission — as I said before it meant a lot of contact with people, and I enjoyed this, and learnt a great deal.

I never realised the difficulties that confronted children born abroad, particularly if their fathers had also been born overseas. This was the time that people had to apply for U.K. Citizenship and register their applications before a certain date. To obtain Citizenship you or your father had to have been born in the U.K. or been Naturalised. This had to be proved by production of birth certificates and marriage certificates to prove the applicant was "legitimate"! It was amazing how indignant people were when asked for these documents and obviously found it embarrassing. Many people were unable to produce these documents, as there had never been a marriage ceremony! Reference to Somerset House which should have had the records if a marriage had been registered — often came back with a "no trace" comment. In to-day's world that would have been a common occurrence, but way back in the late 40's, it was to say the least "unusual" and certainly something people did all they could to hide. De facto relationships were not recognised — and so there were quite a few red faces when we insisted on production of these documents.

I felt rather sad for people whose families had been in India for 2 or 3 generations and were so obviously British in every sense. Tours of duty in those days could be anything from 4 — 5 years so it obviously was not possible for all one's children to be born in the U.K. as that would have meant long separations as most Contracts permitted only one return passage per tour. So if their ancestors on the male line had all been born in India, they now had no official claim to U.K. Citizenship under this section of the British Nationality Act. They then had to apply for Registration or Naturalisation and this in itself often meant producing birth and marriage certificates for three generations — which offended many.

People who had been born in British Protectorates presented further problems.

In the meantime my Solicitor seemed to have completely lost interest in my Divorce — or so I felt. He had my £200 and knew I had little more until I received my costs, maintenance and child support which he had been so confident I would receive.

I repeatedly rang him to ask when the case was being heard — and he would make innumerable excuses that he had not heard from the U.K. Solicitor — but had sent the "evidence" off to him weeks before and he wondered if his clerk had make a mistake and sent it sea mail instead of air mail! Anyway the London Solicitor said it had not arrived in time for the case to be submitted before the Courts closed for their summer recess — so it would be another few months before he could guarantee a hearing. However, he said that as I appeared anxious to get this heard as quickly as possible, IN CASE the evidence had been mislaid or lost, he suggested that we send further evidence in the form of medical certificates from the Dr. who had been treating me for the abuse I received, and a certificate from him regarding Harry's attempted suicide.

This seemed to me to be quite an unnecessary procedure — and meant yet a further bill from the Dr. and from both Solicitors dealing with this extra paper work. Looking back I am now sure that the initial evidence — the letter — had been lost — otherwise why would they pursue this other line of attack. Surely copies of the letter would have been kept though, very foolishly now, I realise that I hadn't kept a copy but when you are paying for legal advice, you feel that all these eventualities would have been covered.

My divorce was finally heard and my brother went along on my behalf to the hearing in London.   Afterwards he said he was shocked at all he had heard in Court — and he was very relieved that I was free from this maniac at last.

As the Solicitor predicted, I was awarded Costs, Custody, Maintenance and Child Support.   I felt elated as once my decree Absolute was granted and the monies owing were received I would be able to plan my return to the U.K.   I had been with the High Commission by then over 2 years and therefore they would pay the return fare for myself and Linda.   This would give me a reasonable amount of security until I was able to get employment in the U.K. I was now awaiting to hear from the Child Care authorities in Greenford.

The weeks passed by — the decree Nisi was received and subsequently the decree Absolute but still no sign of the monies due me.   It appeared that Harry had disappeared after the hearing (which he didn't attend) and all attempts to contact him at the addresses his Solicitor had were to no avail.   He had left the Company he had been working for and they had no forwarding address.

The London firm of Solicitors then suggested that I employ a private detective to trace his whereabouts — as by this time he owed me a considerable amount of money.   The Calcutta Solicitor recommended this  — and so he authorised the London Solicitor to go ahead.   This meant that both Solicitors required more money — and I had very little, only the monies I had managed to save with my two jobs.   Even so it seemed a sound proposition to spend £100 in the knowledge that I would be getting at least £3,000 in return!

Harry was apparently traced to a London address and papers were served on him and he had to start paying the Maintenance immediately and of course attempt to pay off the monies that were due to me over the last two years.   The alternative was a jail sentence — which would not help my cause whatsoever.   I was optimistic however, as I didn't think that Jail would be an option — even though he had proved so dishonest in our relationship. Of course I should have known, he was far smarter than that, not only did he fail to appear at the Court for the hearing — but he managed to disappear yet again!

Why I didn't call it quits and accept defeat at this juncture I don't know, but the thought of the monies that were due to me — with encouragement from the Solicitor — did spur me on and I felt determined I was not going to be defeated. So the whole charade was repeated yet again — and with the same results as last time.

I have never quite been able to understand our legal system — but I did feel that on the last occasion he should have been jailed when he was found, but I wasn't the only one that would suffer if he was unable to work, and therefore think the Solicitors were keener than I that retribution should be made. I had not been able to pay them for the last "search" — they said they would take this out of my costs when received, so presumably they were anxious that I should receive what was owing to me and were optimistic over the outcome of the searches.

On the last search however, the London Solicitor said they had reason to believe that Harry had gone overseas again and therefore was out of the jurisdiction of the British Courts — and they thought it very unlikely I would receive any of the monies that were due!

I was really at an all time low, as I could not see how I could return to the U.K. with no job to go to, and now with no financial security, even if Linda was accepted into the Child Care scheme, I didn't know how I could cope.

At no time did I consider it feasible to return to live with my Mother, she could not possibly look after Linda and I was most anxious that after the ghastly life she had had, that she had no more worries, certainly not on my behalf.

However, there were bright spots — once my decree Absolute was granted (which was 6 weeks after the Nisi) my salary at the High Commission was substantially increased and I was allowed a small allowance for Linda.    Medical bills for us both would also be met — so that was another great burden off my shoulders.    I still had my evening job — but that had been cut down to two nights per week — and even so there was far less work involved than there had been initially.    I think the businesses in the U.K. were not exactly thriving at that time, and in retrospect I really think my services could have been terminated.    Perhaps because of my financial position, my boss, who had also become a friend, decided to keep me on — and there was always the hope from his angle that his business ventures would improve when my services would be needed again.

Being a fatalist, I decided that all things considered I would be well advised to stay on in Calcutta until I had been able to save a little — and I was still waiting to hear from the Child Care Centre.

Having made my decision, I felt much happier — though still damned annoyed (and still am to this day at the way Harry was able to dodge the law) — and really would have thought he would have been very concerned as to how his lovely daughter was living.

# TWO
## *A Second Chance Of Happiness*

All through these miserable and worrying months, I had had the support and very valued companionship of the two friends off the boat, Ken, Harold and their Chummery companion, Phillip. The three of them would often come round at the weekend and take Linda and me for picnics — to the swimming club where they would play with her in the water for hours, or to private lunches with friends of theirs who also had children. I don't know what I would have done without them — and I think, having heard from Phil the background of my marriage to Harry, they had more than a degree of sympathy.

I remember vividly the first time they came round after Harry had left and they found me in tears and they said they knew exactly what was wrong and would do all they could to help if needed. They then told me HOW they knew of my distressing marital position and assured me that I was doing the right thing. They had nothing but contempt for Harry.

Even so, Phil was obviously of the cautious type and not only cut down his visits after a while, but apparently advised the other two boys, Harold and Ken, that he thought they should "play it cool". He warned them that getting involved with a married lady might spell disaster not only with their Company who would not approve of any liaisons, no matter how innocent, but most of all he thought they might find themselves involved in the divorce as he knew there was no depth to which Harry would not stoop.

Fortunately for us, Harold and Ken continued to come round and we both grew to look forward to their visits.    They were good company — and would always listen to my latest trauma and offer advice — and I really grew to depend on them for support.    On Saturday afternoons we would go down with Harold to the C.F.C. (Calcutta Football Club) to watch Ken play Rugger, I was always terrified he would get hurt, particularly when they played the Armenians who could be very violent and were continually being sent off.    I became friendly with some of the Rugger wives who would include us in Rugger parties though I was aware that a lot of them found my presence in India as a Divorcee with a child a little "way out".    However, they soon accepted us — and I began to learn a little about the game — and enjoyed these Saturday afternoon trips.    Often they would be followed by Rugger parties in the evening, to which I was included after putting Linda to bed.    Harold did not share Ken's enthusiasm for Rugger so he would give these parties a miss, and therefore it seemed natural that it was Ken who would be the one to accompany me to the evening parties, picking me up and bringing me home.    He was the most charming, good looking, kind and delightful gentleman I had ever met, great company, and I grew to look forward to these outings.

Sometimes we would go to "Princes" after a dinner party — this was a disco in the Grand Hotel.  I couldn't remember dancing other than on the boat coming out — and so was rather rusty, but Ken was a wonderful dancer — and I soon felt relaxed and not embarrassed at getting on the floor, as I was initially.

On Sundays we would go on picnics, either down the Hooghly where the jute merchants lived in their colonial homes or, towards Chandernagore (an Ex French Colony) where there was a Monastery surrounded by rather lovely grounds.  The Monks here were of a silent order, but I understand they would accommodate some of the itinerant travellers for the night.  They had to sleep on the ground and the Monks would give them a bowl of rice in a soup mix.

One particular afternoon when sitting on the sides of the Hooghly, Linda whispered that she had to go to the bathroom.   So she and I disappeared behind some trees, but I had no toilet paper — so not to be outdone I decided to use what looked like a Dock Leaf! Poor child — it was an Oriental stinging thistle type plant and not the innocent dock leaf we had at home. She was screaming in pain — and so we rushed up to the Monastery to ask the Monks assistance. I don't know who was the more embarrassed. Even though they didn't speak I think they "caught on" and gave me some water to wash her and some camomile lotion — even so the poor child was far from happy. We returned home immediately though by this time the irritation had disappeared and she wanted to go back to the picnic spot — so obviously the Monks knew what they were doing.

Again Ken was simply terrific.

The girls in the office used to tease me about him — but I can honestly say that I never assumed our friendship would develop into anything of a serious nature. We were having a great time together, and I found he was spending more and more time with us. I put this down to the fact that he was getting fed up with Chummery life — and whilst I felt he enjoyed our company, he'd often joke about the number of girls back home — and how he would not get married until he was at least 35 and then only to someone with money! I had seen photographs of his girl friends and they were all very attractive — and all younger than he was. I was 2 years older than Ken — divorced with a child, no money, and wearing glasses, so one could hardly say I was an attractive proposition!

I was so sure that there could never be anything of a serious nature between us, so that when a very attractive Scots girl arrived to work in the High Commission and was put into my section, I thought she would be a very suitable partner for Ken, also a Scot. I therefore manipulated a date for them both, but whilst I think they enjoyed each other's company, as far as I knew, there were no more dates! I tried!

I was very happy during these months, I was able to save a little, had the security of a reasonable job, and had made some very good friends, but to be honest, I suppose, the greatest attraction was the time I spent with Ken.  I thought (and still do) that he was terrific — he was so kind to Linda who missed having a Daddy around (even though she could not remember him).

However, about this time when she was 3½ she became very difficult, had tantrums for no particular reason which I could never fathom.  Could it be that I had spoilt her trying to over compensate for not having a father around, or did she resent the time I was now spending with my friends, although she was always included in any outing which took place before her bedtime.  I had an excellent Nepali Ayah who had been with me since I arrived in Calcutta.  She was a sweet and devoted helper and obviously had Linda's interests at heart, nearly as much as I did.  She and I were at a loss to understand the change in my daughter's temperament, but she was being very difficult and unco-operative, and at times rude.

Even this didn't seem to daunt Ken and Harold who continued to take us out to the Zoo, trips on the river and picnics.  To take one's own food was so much safer than risking eating out in the Mofussil where Dysentery, Cholera and Typhoid abounded.

Being a Divorcee in any country at that time caused one to be viewed with suspicion;  but to be divorced, with a child in India, was without doubt a social stigma and there were quite a few raised eyebrows amongst the Memsahibs, particularly those recently arrived, who were not aware of the circumstances related to my remaining in Calcutta.  Consequently there were times I felt uncomfortable and self conscious and so when I received the letter from the Child Care Centre in Wembley saying they would have a vacancy for Linda in the Spring, I decided it was time I returned to the U.K. as there really could be no long term future in India for us, and much as I loved the country and the wonderful friends who had stood by me through thick and thin, I didn't feel I should push my luck any further.

I therefore accepted the vacancy for Linda and started to plan our return.  It all seemed rather formidable, but no matter how I argued with myself over the pro's and con's of staying longer — I realised — the move had to be made.

All this happened mid-week and on the Saturday afternoon I brought out of store the old tin trunks that had brought my possessions out here. I thought if I packed the nucleus of the linen and the few things I would not require in the immediate future, — and perhaps get at least one trunk despatched to await our arrival in the U.K., I could pack our clothing at the last moment.

Whilst doing this Ken arrived to take Linda and me out for tea, a very popular pastime in India. People would go to Firpos or a cake shop in Park Street that served delicious cakes — and one would be sure of meeting lots of friends similarly gorging! He was obviously taken aback to find me packing, even more so when I explained that I was planning to return to the U.K. in early January. He sat down, became very moody and disgruntled — said absolutely nothing and any idea of taking us out for tea seemed to have been forgotten!

I was pretty irritated as I had so many niggling doubts about this decision I had made and really needed support and not apparent disapproval and certainly not moodiness.

Whilst during the last few weeks we had become more than just good friends, there had never been any thought in my mind that there could ever be anything serious between us.

Also I had a very strong inferiority complex which had been accentuated by the fact that Harry had not just found one lady he preferred to me — but several. Lack of money had not permitted me to dress particularly well or to spend money on hair do's, manicures or the like. I had had to wear glasses ever since the dental incident in Liverpool which had taken the sight of my left eye — and as I was told — "men never make passes at girls who wear glasses" — so — I felt I really was not an attractive marriage prospect and most certainly marriage did not enter into my future plans in any way.

Ken continued to come round and, though sometimes a little moody, we both had some very happy times together.

Imagine my surprise therefore when a couple of weeks after

this incident he asked me if I had any idea what basic salary a married man would need to survive in Calcutta. I was surprised at being asked this question on two accounts, the first being that, as he had been spending so much time in my company, I couldn't see how he had had time to meet anyone that might make him think of marriage. As far as I knew he hadn't seen the Scots girl again — but then perhaps he had. Maybe one of the many ladies he corresponded with in the U.K. was prepared to come out to Calcutta. The second reason of course was that I really didn't think I could be looked upon as an authority on cost of living. I had lived on a shoe string for the last two years so was hardly the person to ask about normal living costs.

However, I gave him a conservative figure, but stipulated that he would have to ensure he had no children for at least two years when he could expect an increment from the Company.

I was completely confused when he replied that the lady he was thinking of marrying already had a child! I confess that I wondered briefly if he could possibly mean me, but as I said, I had a monumental inferiority complex, so dismissed this.

Finally his proposal came, and I really could not believe what I was hearing, nor could I believe my good fortune, and even to this day, 44 years later can I completely understand why this delightful, kind hearted and very good looking eligible bachelor would want to marry me! I knew that I was more than a little in love with him — who wouldn't be? However, I had not allowed this emotion to register — not wishing to be hurt yet again and feeling that any question of marriage was completely out of the question.

Looking back on this fairy tale type of love story, I am still amazed, and feel that yet again fate had played quite a part. Had I not married Harry and gone to India where I was so miserable initially, I would never have met Ken. Perhaps I was supposed to go through all this abject misery to make this all possible. If so, then all the misery was worth it and although we have had our share of worries in our marriage, never have I regretted sailing for India, meeting this wonderful friend who helped me through so many of my problems, became my lover and then my husband — and is still all three. To sum it up — the best friend anyone could have.

Having asked me to marry him and my saying Yes — was not the end of all our problems in that direction.

Ken was on a five year contract and one of the conditions was that he could not get married on his first contract, so he had to get permission from his Head Office. His Burra Sahib was rather shattered at his request and doubly shattered when he heard I had a child. Initially he said it would not be allowed as they did not consider his salary was sufficient to support a wife in the life style to which the Company would expect one of their Assistants to live. He also pointed out that he was really too young for the responsibilities of marriage at the age of 26! Ken suggested that as he had been old enough to fight a war —(he had been in "D" Day) that he felt he was old enough to take on the responsibilities of marriage. As for his salary, he pointed out that I was working at the British High Commission and earning more than he could expect in increments for the next five years — therefore his salary really should not be considered.

He was then asked what would happen if any more little Campbell's appeared in the next year or two, and Ken assured him this would not happen, which seemed to surprise his boss, and one was left wondering if he had even heard of birth control!

Even so the Burra Sahib said it would have to be referred to Head Office in London but in the meantime he and his wife would like to meet me! We knew quite well that this meant I was to be vetted — I must not be of mixed blood or of Indian origin — I would have to be socially acceptable — and know how to hold a knife and fork and contribute to a conversation. I was quite nervous of this ordeal — but it would appear I passed the necessary criteria and Ken's application to marry was sent to London.

We waited anxiously for the reply and with my usual pessimism, I had my doubts that permission would be granted but, finally Ken was called into the Burra Sahib's office and told that he had permission to marry — BUT — they would not be responsible for any medical bills for myself or Linda.    This actually was not too unusual at that time.

All this happened in November 1950 — and we were officially engaged on Xmas Eve.   Ken gave me the most wonderful 5 stone diamond ring, which I knew he couldn't afford and I think he was paying for months after we were married!   It was and still is beautiful and I am very thrilled with it.

I had to advise the High Commissioner of my proposed forthcoming marriage and, I have to say, there were no doubts on his part and he and the Staff were all thrilled for us.

The wedding was planned for the 10th January, 1951, and in the meantime once permission had been granted for this marriage, we both wrote to our respective parents.   My mother was delighted though really had no idea of the problems I had been through.   Ken's mother who had been a widow for many years must have had many misgivings about her only son marrying a lady in Calcutta who was a divorcee and who had a daughter.   Not what the average mother would desire for her son and I am afraid she must have been very concerned and doubtless unhappy about it.

Bless her though she did write a lovely letter saying if this is what Ken wanted we both had her blessing.   My only regret is that she didn't live long enough to know that the marriage would last, and to know how happy we both have been.

At first it seemed doubtful that we could get married in Church; Divorcees were frowned upon and the Church of England obviously felt that God could not bless a second union.   We went to St. Andrews Scottish Church and met the Rev. Andrew Bailey, who having established that I was not the guilty party in my divorce or had broken my marriage vows, said he was very happy to marry us.

When discussing where we would go for our honeymoon — my biggest worry was that Linda would be happy for the time we were away.   I didn't really think with her "moodiness" of late that she would be an asset on our honeymoon and felt we deserved a short time together. Great friends of ours, who had two children of a similar age — were most anxious to have Linda, and she seemed very happy at the prospect of going to spend some time with these children in this wonderful family.

So we had Linda fixed up and had the Church and the day, but neither of us had the money for a large wedding, and neither of our parents were in a position to help as we were both helping them out financially to a small degree. We each had a large circle of friends, having been in Calcutta for 4 years, but we really could not afford to invite them all to the Wedding or Reception. Ken's Burra Sahib had kindly said we could hold the Reception in his home, so long as it was kept to reasonably small numbers, and of course we financed the occasion.

This was wonderful as it saved us having to hire a Hall, and his wife, who was very much the Burra Memsahib but still a great friend to this day, offered to help with the catering, linen, crockery, glasses etc. Indeed on our wedding day her home looked simply beautiful with wonderful flower arrangements, and the most appetising food laid out so tastefully as though it had been provided by a first class hotel. My friends in the High Commission were again very understanding and our wedding present from some of the officers who enjoyed Diplomatic Privilege, was a crate of Champagne! The price of this in Calcutta at that time was prohibitive — so we were very thrilled. A three tier cake was duly ordered so that there would be sufficient to send in those silly little cardboard boxes to friends who were unable to attend the wedding. I am sure by the time the boxes arrived in the U.K. the cake would be quite inedible.

We decided that it would be a good idea to hold the wedding during office hours when few people would be able to attend! In those days people were very conscientious and would not dream of taking time off unless they were very ill, or they were taking a day's leave. By doing this we were able to restrict the guests to the 30 Ken's boss had suggested, and hopefully no one would be hurt. If a few people came along after the offices had closed — it would be near to the time we would be leaving on our honeymoon.

Harold Whittle who had been on the Cilicia with us in 1948 and shared the Chummery with Ken, was the Best Man, and a friend of mine from the High Commission, Molly Edwards was my bridesmaid.

I felt it would be quite inappropriate for me to get married in white so I ordered a Navy and Pale Blue Water Taffeta dress and had a hat made of the same navy material with a pale blue ostrich feather.

The church service was delightful, but during the service we realised that the Church was packed!   There were at least three times the number of people we had expected.   It was not until we left the Church for the Reception that we realised that nearly all the staff from the High Commission had come to the Church.

The High Commissioner — who I have said was so kind and helpful to me, had closed the office early, leaving a skeleton staff on duty!   A delightful gesture, but you can imagine the anxieties our poor host and hostess had — not to mention the Bride and Groom — where were we going to put all these people?   Not least of our worries was — would there be enough food and drink?   We had assured Ken's boss that the Wedding would be small with no more than 30 people and here we were with what appeared to be 90! However, once they knew the reason for this surge in the guest list they joined in the spirit of things.   Ken's boss lent us more liquor from his private store and the food, like the five small loaves and twosmall fishes somehow seemed to stretch, and consequently we had a very memorable and happy day.

For our honeymoon we were taking the early evening train to Puri — a night's drive from Calcutta — and were staying at the B.N.R. Hotel (Bengal, Nagpur Railway Hotel) on the beach.   Our departure time was around 9.p.m. so it was planned that the immediate participants would have dinner together at Spencer's Hotel.   This was indeed a merry and happy occasion — so much so that no one really noticed the time until we suddenly found we had about half an hour to get to Howrah Station and onto the train. With Calcutta traffic, half an hour was hardly enough, but the driver realising the urgency of the situation drove like a maniac. I was terrified.

The Bearer had been sent down to the station early with our luggage and to lay out the bedding rolls, which was the custom, put in the ice box with supplies of Beer, Orange Juice, Tonic etc.

We arrived at the station on the dot of departure time — were hurriedly whisked through the turnstile and ran towards the train. We seemed to have run half way down the train looking for the First Class Sleeper B4, when suddenly the Best Man realised we were on the wrong platform and this train was for Delhi not Puri! There was another mad panic — back along platform 3 — through the turnstile then dashing to platform 13 where the Puri train was starting to move! We spotted the Bearer hastily pulling out the bedrolls, ice box etc., as he realised we were not coming. The Guard blew his whistle — I never knew if it was to stop the train or to let the driver know it was all clear to move — but the train kept on slowly moving down the platform — we were fortunately overtaking it in the hopes of reaching our compartment before the train gathered speed.

Suddenly the Bearer spotted us- and he immediately gathered up the bedding rolls, threw them into the compartment — went back for the ice box, which by now had been left 20 yards back on the platform, he staggered into the compartment and actually jumped in and hurriedly tried to lay out the bedding rolls. We caught up with the particular part of the train he was in and as he jumped out Ken jumped in and literally I was pushed by the Bestman and bridesmaid who continued to run hysterically along the side of the train waving goodbye and doubled up with laughter.

I suppose I should tell the whole story. Because of our hurried departure from the Hotel, I had been unable to visit the washroom and, as it had been a long and thirsty day and my fluid intake had been high, this was very necessary.   What goes in — must come out!!   All this running and laughing was too much for me — and there were disastrous results as I had a wee accident!   Not many brides I am sure start their married life with wet pants!

For those of you who haven't experienced travelling by train in India — I should perhaps mention it is an unforgettable experience. There seemed to be more people travelling on top and around the train than IN it — really just like ants on a green leaf and one was left wondering if as many bodies arrived at their destination as initially set out!

The train seemed to stop at every station en route to Puri — and there were a lot of stations I assure you, and on each occasion people banged on the doors shouting "Cha" (tea) and as we peeped out of the closed blinds we could see a dirty turbaned little man pouring tea into paper cups — (which looked as though they had been used before) — from his very handsome brass samovar.   There were other people banging on the door, hoping that if we opened it they would be able to force their way in and travel INSIDE the train instead of on top of it.   We had been advised not to open the door under any circumstances unless one of the B.N.R. staff was outside. Obviously with all the thousands of bodies sticking like leeches on the train — it would have been foolish to agree to anyone entering the compartment.

We did on occasion get out and stretch our legs, but only when the Guard approached us and told us there would be a ten minute wait and asked if we would like to get out and he locked the compartment behind us.   With the mass of humanity barging up and down the platform — we soon decided we were better to return to the carriage, which we had entirely to ourselves.

It had a bathroom attached — which was not over clean — and the presence of some rather large cockroaches did not encourage me to spend much time there!

All in all we were delighted to arrive at Puri station and to be met by people from the Hotel who drove us in a horsedrawn carriage to the famous B.N.R. Hotel.

Puri was delightful — lovely beach — the sand far too hot to stand on without slippers; the Hotel was old and full of history having been used by the British Raj for many years as a holiday resort.

We were more than a little "shattered" though amused when shown the bathroom! No flush — no running water — and we were told this was brought in by the Hamal early morning and evening in large containers and poured into the bath when you wanted it — the system worked well as it kept people employed. But the actual toilets were out of this world. To begin with there were TWO — side by side if you please — and they consisted of a wooden seat with TWO spaces to sit on — over a big drop! These were emptied from the rear by the Sweepers twice per day. I didn't think however, that they would do this whilst the toilet was in use!

One morning I was sitting on this contraption when I was conscious of a rustle and scraping beneath me — and I shot up — to find that the container had disappeared and the Sweeper was trying to return the empty one whilst the toilet was still in operation! I got into the habit of looking IN the toilet before I sat on it, and quite expected to see a pair of brown eyes looking up at me! A ghastly form of employment for anyone, but it seemed to work though I could never understand what method the sweeper adopted — as it always seemed that the toilet was emptied very shortly after use — or as in my case — during!

Whilst the sweepers looked very dejected, dirty and literally were in rags — the Bearers on the other hand looked really magnificent in their ornate Pugris (type of turban) and crisp white starched uniforms. But they all paddled around in bare feet and were exceedingly quiet in everything they did.

Our bedroom in the Hotel had been advertised in the brochure as having its own large balcony — which was technically correct, but the balcony stretched in front of four adjoining bedrooms. When I tell you that all the rooms had stable like doors, you'll appreciate that we didn't have quite the privacy a honeymoon couple hoped for!   The other rooms were all occupied by couples who had been married for years and obviously knew each other well.

We were a little daunted when we found they retired to the veranda after dinner each night and played Bridge until well after midnight. Anyone who has had anything to do with bridge players will know of the long discussions that are liable to follow once a game has been played.   Long arguments would follow as to why someone trumped her partners ace — or why on earth they had called 4 spades with only 10 points.   Some of these arguments became quite heated — altogether a little off putting for a young bride!   However, in view of what happened next — this was not to matter very much!

For years I had admired people who could surf — but had never been anywhere where there had been an opportunity to try this sport. The U.K. was far too cold and the River Hooghly didn't even have a ripple.   So, when I saw people leaving the Hotel with their Surf boards and the Hotel told us that the surf was good  — it seemed an ideal opportunity for me to experiment.   The Hotel provided the boards and it all seemed rather easy.   As a complete novice it seemed to me that all one had to do was swim out with the board to where the waves were breaking — wait for a big wave — lie on the board and you'd be swept onto the beach riding the top of the wave. No one told me that I should keep the head of the board slightly out of the water — so when I found my first big wave — off I went but in seconds found myself turning somersault after somersault over and over the board until I let go of the board and then it hit me!   By this time I was completely stunned and had lost my sense of direction — and didn't know if I should be trying to swim UP or DOWN. However, just as I decided I was going to drown, I was dumped on the beach breathless and grateful, but I was black and blue all over, but chiefly down the front of my legs, my tummy and ribs.   I felt very sorry for myself and decided in future I would sunbathe and would never try surfing again!

Ken was very adept on the surfboard, but eventually came to join me on the beach.   Neither of us realised how strong the sun can be so much nearer to the Equator and, although I had covered myself with sun oil and a towel — Ken had been too busy surfing and he received the most ghastly sun burn and he had to keep completely covered for the next 3 days. My front was very sore with the bruising, and Ken's front was blistered — not exactly what one would hope for a honeymoon! At least the Bridge players didn't upset us for the next three nights as even lying down was agony for us both!

The next day we were able to explore Puri village and watch the beautifully decorated elephants in gold and scarlet with their Howdahs similarly decorated — wandering from stall to stall collecting "bukhshee" (gratuities) from each stall holder for some religious festival. The elephants seemed to have been trained not to leave the stall until they had received a contribution — and no one was prepared to try to dismiss the elephant!

We explored the little bazaar type shops, full of curios — we hired rickshaws and went to the nearby country side — and after a couple of days rode an elephant to the local temple. By that time we both had recovered sufficiently from bruising and sun bathing to go swimming early morning and after 3.p.m. when we were assured we would not be burnt! Puri really was an ideal spot for a honeymoon in spite of the Bridge players, the sun and the bruises!

The ten days passed all too quickly though we were anxious to get back to Linda. Right from the start of our marriage, Linda was always referred to as "ours" and in fact for some odd legal reason she had her name changed to Campbell a week before we were married and immediately started calling Ken "Daddy"— which caused a few raised eyebrows from people who had known her for some time and didn't know we were about to get married.

The trip back to Calcutta was more organised than our trip down to Puri — we were at the station on time — we were used to the shouting and banging on our door at every station — and much as we'd enjoyed Puri we were looking forward to starting married life as a family.

Linda had obviously thoroughly enjoyed staying with our friends

— in fact I was afraid she wouldn't want to come back home — but this did not happen, she was thrilled to see us. She had often asked me why everyone had a Daddy but her — and when she went to the Park every afternoon with her friends — they too had apparently asked her why she didn't have a Daddy. So now at last she was the same as everyone else and could boast about her Daddy.

It was in Calcutta that I developed my enthusiasm for Rugger — Ken used to play for the Picts — and went down to Ceylon and Madras on a couple of All India matches.

At the C.F.C. (Calcutta Football Club) where the rugger matches took place, we met an amusing individual, John Andrews, who always had some anecdote to relate. He was a Hockey player and had played for West Bengal and had a girl friend who was a BOAC air hostess. She usually had a two day stop over in Calcutta and the crew stayed at the Great Eastern Hotel.

John was expecting her on a flight that weekend, so rang up the Hotel to enquire if Miss Turner had arrived, and was assured she had and they gave him her room number. He told the Receptionist he didn't want to be put through to her but would call round later.

He had a Hockey match that evening but obviously was very anxious to spend as much time as possible with her — so went round to the Hotel and went straight up to her room. He hoped she would come with him to the Hockey match and they would then go out for dinner afterwards. When he got to the room he found the door was not locked so he went in hoping to give her a surprise (which he certainly did!) He found she was sleeping — so he tiptoed over to the bed, pulled the bedclothes off and gave her a playful smack on the rear end. I think his exact words were "get up gorgeous — we are going for dinner".

This prompted screams from Miss Turner who was obviously quite upset — as well she might be. John had got the wrong Miss Turner who was also an air hostess.

The screams brought the rest of the air crew running to her room — and seeing John in his shorts, long hockey socks, and brandishing his hockey stick — they assumed the worst and frog marched him out of the Hotel!

John worked for a Tea Company which had a bungalow down at Puri where we had spent our honeymoon. He subsequently married the air hostess — and we had a couple of enjoyable and amusing weekends with them down there.

One of the popular Clubs in Calcutta was the Light Horse Club, and a group of young assistants were sitting round the Bar one evening when one of them suggested adding a little excitement to what appeared to them as a rather dull existence.

Around Calcutta were numerous statues of various dignitaries who had played a part in Calcutta's history. The majority of these were mounted on horse back and this "group" decided they would liven things up a little. Doubtless the demon drink had something to do with their decision. With military precision they divided themselves into groups of five and each group was allocated one of the statues, and provided with a chamber pot, a piece of wire — and some red paint! The operation was to start at 2.a.m.

They decided that one person in each group would act as look-out — and warn the other four in the group if the police or any strangers were approaching. The second man, who had to be the strongest, was to be the main support and the idea was that the third man would stand on his back and then allow the fourth man to climb onto his shoulders. He would then be handed the chamber pot which he had to secure with the wire, on to the head of the statue!

In the meantime the fifth man was to paint the horse's posterior with red paint.

Speed was of the essence, and I believe five minutes was allowed for "Operation Chamber Pot" to be completed.

The following morning, of course, people driving to their offices were astounded. The diplomats felt that it was an anti-British demonstration and were very concerned — but I gather one or two of the Burra Sahibs (bosses) called in their young assistants and asked them what they knew about this incident — and made it quite clear that if they were involved they would be sent back to the U.K. and would lose their jobs.

Those involved had all been sworn to secrecy and were even threatened not to mention the episode to any family or friends — and as far as I know, no-one has ever admitted they knew anything about this although it was the favourite topic of conversation for some time!

# THREE
## *Calcutta*

Having explained what brought me to India — I should perhaps elaborate a little on the country as I then saw it.

We came to India in 1948 — one year after Partition and people were still talking about the Calcutta riots and the atrocities when Hindus attacked Muslims and Muslims attacked Hindus. We were told that the year before, Park Street, where we were living, had been flowing with the blood of followers of both religions.

One horrific tale is that subsequent to a serious attack on Muslims by Hindus in Calcutta, that later in the week on the arrival of the train bringing in fresh frozen fish from what was now East Pakistan, on opening the boxes which should have contained fish packed in ice, to the horror of all, the boxes were found to contain the bodies of dead Hindus.

Calcutta was predominantly a Hindu city, but with a large community of Muslims and, to a lesser degree, Parsees. Many Muslims left Calcutta at the time of Partition to live in East Pakistan which today is known as Bangladesh, while many Hindus left what had become East Pakistan, say from Chittagong or Dacca, to live in West Bengal and particularly Calcutta, and it was they who suffered in the riots, and indeed a number were killed as they made their way as refugees to East Bengal.

To explain, Bengal at Partition had been split into East Bengal which went to Pakistan and West Bengal which remained in India. A split society such as this could never be a happy one and whole families were frequently split with some becoming refugees and transferring from West Bengal to East Bengal and vice versa, leaving the rest of the family in the country in which they had been brought up.

During our time in India and later in Pakistan, there was spasmodic fighting — and sadly two Wars. Independence had not brought the peace and satisfaction that residents of the Indian sub-continent had hoped for, as Partition created problems never foreseen, and still remains in the sabre rattling which persists even to-day over the Kashmir question.

Many times during our stay in India we were asked why Britain had agreed to Partition and, in certain instances, why Britain had ever agreed to grant India Independence, as life had been so much easier and progressive under British Rule. In later life I came to the view that wherever the British had colonised, it had in general been to the benefit of the country and of it's residents and that when granting independence and leaving a country the Colonial rule was sadly missed.

Calcutta is the fourth or fifth largest city in the world — but no one knows for sure just what the population really is as it is impossible to count people who live on the sidewalks. The 12 mile ride from Dum Dum airport makes you think Trafalgar Square on New Year's Eve is rather a lonely place!

The British made Calcutta the capital of the Raj for 120 years but transferred the capital to Delhi in 1911. Incidentally the term "Raj" refers to the period of the British rule of India!

Calcutta was once looked upon as the most glamorous city in the East, and it still retained the majesty of its past. The 19th Century elegance of Calcutta was as real as its poverty and the two seemed to exist harmoniously. It was also referred to as the "most horrible or revolting" city in Asia.

Sir Percival Griffiths referred to it as "a city of gulfs" where nobody knew anybody outside their own particular sphere. The Civil Servant didn't hobnob with the business man whilst the Indian business man did not hobnob with the British business man. The

Bengali business man didn't mix with the Marwari businessman. It was a city of four or five quite separate communities which hardly mixed at all.

The extremes of Calcutta really began at Howrah Railway Station which was smothered with human forms all in very primitive attire, sitting, and sleeping, just a mass of humanity. At dusk the pavements were rather like large dormitories with row upon row of "bodies" lying covered with a dhoti or loin cloth and for all the world looking like corpses. It was difficult walking at night without stepping on these bundles and the Railway Station was packed with bodies as here they got protection from the elements in case it rained and in the cold weather it was much warmer.

When doing voluntary work I was taken to a "bustee" area — the term used for a registered slum area — not just a slum but an acknowledged one! Here I saw again poverty beyond belief — which made it hard for me to reconcile with Calcutta being the wealthiest city in India and having more rich people than any other city in the country.

I discovered that so many of the young boys, say from 5 to 13 years of age who pursued us, offering to do various services, run errands and so forth, are called kanalis and almost never have any parents, perhaps having been born on the sidewalks and deserted immediately. They were not beggars but wanted to earn small change for services, carrying parcels, getting you a taxi, showing you the way to certain shops and they spend the night sleeping on the pavement. They could be found scavenging in the refuse bins, particularly outside restaurants, for food that had been discarded by the rich overfed patrons. Although at times you felt they were a pest — one had to be sympathetic — but what is the answer?

On the other side of the Hooghly River, "British" India was a world apart; its splendid Maiden flanked by palatial Government Buildings, a Racecourse, and a Cathedral. Then there were the Army and Navy Stores, Hall and Andersons, and the Great Eastern Hotel which was the first place in Calcutta to be air-conditioned, and the Grand Hotel which was said to be over run with rats.    I personally had a rat run over my feet whilst having a drink in the Hotel.

Then one must not forget the famous "Firpo's" where if you ordered a whisky the bottle was put on the table!

The heart of Calcutta is the Victoria Memorial, an ostentatious monument in white marble built to commemorate Queen Victoria's rule as Empress of India.    Lord Curzon, who conceptualised it in the early years of the present century, meant it to rival the Taj Mahal, which of course it never did.    Government House rivalled the President's house in Delhi.    It had a throne room containing the throne of a former Muslim ruler, Tippu Sultan, a dining room with marble floors and a ballroom with polished teak floors.    No other State had such a grand Governor's Palace, yet it looked deserted and most of it's many rooms were locked including the throne room and the ballroom.    It was rather like a Museum with the Governor using only part of the building.

Nowhere did Victorianism thrive more than in the Clubs of Calcutta.    The best Calcutta Clubs such as the Bengal Club, the Tollygunge Club and the Saturday Club were closed to Indians during the days of the Raj but slowly non-Europeans were being accepted. There were some equally grand Clubs such as the Calcutta Club, the 300 Club (named because it could have no more than 300 members) which had mixed membership.

I understand it is now the Indians who run the exclusive English Clubs and British residents have to apply to an Indian Committee to gain admission.    Historical justice one might say, though the Indians have maintained standards and kept the 19th Century character of the clubs intact.

Slowly all the street names over the years have been changed from their old English ones to Indian, but Calcutta is still the only Indian city where people still refer to the streets by their old English names.    Obviously the British sun has never set in Calcutta.

The start of winter in Calcutta coincides with Durga Puja in

October, the most important festival in Bengal. According to Hindu mythology, all gods and goddesses of the Hindu pantheon endowed Durga with a portion of their own energy to give her strength, or shakti, to destroy evil forces. Over 2,000 Pandals are erected throughout the city. The image of Durga shows her slaying the most powerful demon, Mahisasur. Another season for gifts, new clothes, and the shops overflow with the latest goods.

During our time in Calcutta we visited many Puja Pandals which seemed to have sprung up at every street corner, all very decorative in their individual styles.

Kali Puja is another popular festival. Kali is the Goddess of Destruction according to Hindu mythology, and having rid the earth of demons, Kali went on a rampage of destruction. Again, Calcutta had Pandals at every street corner, though the actual Puja takes place at midnight on the day of the new moon.

Twice we saw the Muslim festival of Mohurram, a Muslim (Shiah) celebration which takes place during the first month of the Muslim New Year to mark the day of the death of Imam Husayn.

To Western eyes it appeared more like a gruesome carnival! During the parade, young men flagellate themselves with ropes in which knives or razor blades have been attached. Obviously they end up dripping in blood, but seem to be in a trance and do not appear to feel any pain. Occasionally, someone will faint or collapse and they are taken off by their friends — but it really is a barbaric custom. We viewed this again in Bombay from a Parsi friend's office window — something I would not want to see again.

After the rains, came Diwali, the North Indian New Year, a Hindu Festival referred to as The Festival of Light which marks Rama's return from exile and is quite delightful. Households thoroughly clean their houses, put on new clothes and light up the little clay dishes with oil and a twist of cotton in them, which are placed on the gateways, along the walls, along the sides of the houses, windows, steps, anywhere. These are lit at sunset and this is accompanied by a feast when family members and friends get together for the evening meal.

Traders go to the Temples to pray to Ganesh and Lakshmi and bring new account books for blessing. Our servants who lived in quarters with us — would decorate the area around our flat with hundreds of little candles — which at times we felt were a fire hazard but admittedly were very pretty.

Two days after Diwali we saw Chhat Puja, a Bihari festival in celebration of the sun. Untouchables with transvestite dancers accompanying them, come to the Ghats to make offerings of fruit and vegetables. Often when on our way out to some dinner we would see these festivals — and I would persuade Ken to stop and watch them for a while. How else would we learn all about these festivals?

Ramadan is a Muslim Festival — when adults and some children, have no food from sunrise to sunset. This means getting up early to cook breakfast before the sun rises, and in the heat, not being able to drink is quite a problem. When we employed Muslim servants one felt very guilty eating lunch when you knew they could not — and it was very obvious that their work power naturally diminished during this month. Once the sun had set they were allowed to eat — so we tried to arrange our mealtimes so that the servants were free to eat as soon as the sun had set.

As a celebration, at the culmination of the month of fasting we had Hari Raya Puasa — Idul Fitri — these celebrations start with prayers in the morning and Muslims also pay a visit to the graves of their departed loved ones after prayers at the mosque. Hari Raya is a time for family get-togethers, and also a time to forgive, forget and make merry and homes are open to welcome and treat relatives and friends with special festive dishes.

There are so many festivals therefore I find it difficult to remember them all — but obviously we were very aware of the ones we had seen which I have mentioned. We were invited as guests by certain families with whom we had become close friends — and I think the

30 York Court,
The Albany, Albany Park Road,
Kingston upon Thames, Surrey KT2 5

My dears,

Just a wee note to thank you for t
 - just hope you don't think it a
I said it has given me something t
"cancer".   Compiling this "epistl
masterpiece - helped fill in all t
has given me an interest as Ken ca
life can be rather lonely.

Unfortunately - my sight which has
and I found it quite impossible to
have since been registered as "Pa
having to write on the computer -

Sorry to say Ken is deteriorating
has fought the cancer for 5 years
from the results of the Chemother
the cancer.   doing the book ther
cancer.   All our good wishes.

Love
Walt

thing that stands out in my mind more than anything else is the amount and variety of food that we were offered — and the number of guests there would be. As newcomers to India, it was all very fascinating, but trying to cope with all the food that was placed on your plate — (or often a banana leaf), was difficult and you didn't want to offend your hostess or appear rude by leaving it!

I believe that Rudyard Kipling said that Maharajas had been created to offer a dazzling spectacle for the rest of the world to marvel about. When we arrived in India the Maharajas were much fewer in number than they had been, but I can remember being enthralled with stories of their extravagances and eccentricities

For instance we were told that the Maharaja of Baroda worshipped gold and precious stones. He had in his collection the Seventh Biggest diamond in the world which was offered by Napoleon III to Eugenie.

The Maharaja of Patiala had a pearl necklace insured by Lloyds for one million dollars. But the most talked about event was that once a year he appeared naked, with the exception of a breastplate containing over 1000 diamonds. He was apparently "well provided for" and his subjects applauded this act — as rumour had it that the "organ" had certain powers that drove evil spirits away!

The Maharaja of Gwalior decided he wanted a chandelier in his Palace larger than any in Buckingham Palace. He ordered this in Venice, but there were doubts at the time that the roof of his Palace would support the weight of this fantastic chandelier. He resolved this by having one of his heaviest elephants hoisted on to the roof of the Palace, and when it was proved the roof could support the elephant — he then went ahead and had the chandelier fitted. The mind boggles as to how this would be cleaned!

Also, it appears that the Maharaja of Gwalior had a hobby of collecting electric trains — and he had over 250 feet of solid silver rails set around his Dining Table — with branch lines into the kitchen from where all the guests were served! There was an occasion when the control panel, which the Maharaja controlled, short circuited, and the trains all ran amok splashing food all over the Maharaja's guests! I understand he was entertaining the Viceroy at the time!

We have all heard of the sexual excesses of the Maharajas — about the size of their harems and the eroticism they practised. There were numerous other stories about their rather odd behaviour and, whilst I found all these stories fascinating, I was distressed that with all this opulence, along side it, there was so much poverty. How could any human being ignore the abject misery of his subjects whilst wallowing in such luxury?

In striking contrast to this opulence we found the various festivals that form such an important part of the lower caste Indian's life — quite mind boggling. For instance Holi is a Hindu fertility festival, celebrated in the Spring. Red powder and often red water is thrown and sprayed — on anyone and everyone — and this denotes the coming of age of young girls!

Effigies of Goddesses were paraded around on carts, some beautiful and some terrible.

One often saw them being made in the villages prior to any festival — they were comprised of wire, straw and clay very cleverly modelled, and quite beautiful, with the exception of Kali, who was grotesque.

To continue with this narrative, shortly after we were married Linda developed Whooping Cough and nothing seemed to relieve her continual coughing. The Dr. said he felt that the sea air would help her — so Ken made arrangements for Linda and I to go to Gopalpur — the nearest seaside resort. We travelled down by train having been told, yet again, to keep the doors and windows locked at all times, a wise precaution because again, before we left Howrah Station there were more people clinging to the sides and the top of the train than were actually inside. At every station there was a hammering on the doors and windows — people trying to get into the compartment — and of course this meant we could get no fresh air as it was out of the question to open the windows.

We travelled overnight arriving in the morning where we were met by a horse and cart and driven to the Hotel.

There was a lovely beach and we could step out of our room onto the beach. This sounded delightful, but the first morning we woke up there was a terrible noise outside our door and lots of little men rushing around with poles. It transpired a Cobra had been seen curled up on one of the reclining chairs outside our room — and all attempts to catch this creature appeared to have been in vain. They assumed therefore it had moved on — which didn't fill me full of joy as I wondered WHERE it had moved to!

We spent the day swimming and on the beach though I can't say there was any sign of Linda's cough improving — but it was early days. The next morning — there was again a lot of scuffling outside our bedroom — but this time the evening Chowkidar had found a dead body on the self same chair that the snake had been reclining on the previous night! They said it wasn't the snake — but I was waiting for number three catastrophe in my usual pessimistic manner.

The following day it was obvious to me that Linda seemed to be getting worse — she had a high fever and didn't want to leave her bed. I called the local Dr. who didn't inspire me by telling me after examining her that "she has high fever" in the usual sing song voice which hit the highs and then the lows — and of course this was the whole reason I had sent for him. He suggested that we returned home as he didn't have any suitable medicines in this very primitive place so arrangements were made for our return the next day.

In the meantime another of the Assistants from Ken's office had arrived, as he too had been very ill for a long time and again it was suggested that he took a holiday in Gopalpur. One couldn't help wondering if the Dr. had shares in the Hotel! Anyway I was very pleased to see him as at least I had someone who spoke English to share my worries with — but as we had to return two days after his arrival — I think he too began to wonder if the holiday and sea air would do him any good. I'm glad to say after 2 weeks he returned to Calcutta and did seem better.

This little holiday had been an expense we had not anticipated and any spare cash we'd managed to save had gone on medical bills. Therefore we decided we MUST have a month of the "short shirt" and really economise on food.    I assured Ken at the end of the month that our bills would be very low as I had cut down on so many items.    Imagine our surprise when the monthly bill arrived from the Stores to find it was the most expensive month we'd ever had|.

On examining the bill we discovered items that we had never ordered like 5 bottles of Gin and four 12 lb. tins of Powdered Milk, 2 Bottles of Vodka, 6 large tins of tea — an amazing list.    We immediately went down to the Stores and saw the Manager who showed us our signed chits to say we had received these items.

I should mention that it was the practice for Memsahibs to give a signed list of shopping required to the Bearer who took it to the store and brought back the items.    The store then sent their bill at the end of the month. The Bearer we had at that time had left suddenly as his Mother had died up country  (I was sure she had died the previous year as well but had become used to these elaborate stories — which basically meant they didn't want to work for us anymore or — they wanted a holiday.)    However, when I first examined the chits — they all appeared to have my signature on them — but on further investigation — I realised that some of the signatures had been forged — but were excellent forgeries as at the first glance I really thought they were mine!    No wonder the Bearer's Mother had died!

Whilst Ken was obviously distressed he did have a private chuckle as I had only that week told him his signature was terrible — no one could possibly read it — but — I have to admit — no one could copy it either!

So much for an economical month — though on paper we should have been able to save — every month there was some unexpected expense.

In 1953, whilst working at the British High Commission we had the thrill of meeting Sir John Hunt, Sir Edmund Hilary, Tenzing, and the team. They came round the office and talked to all the staff and Edmund Hilary (not then Sir) told us about the trials and tribulations they experienced in reaching the summit and conquering Everest. This coincided with the Queen's Coronation which they obviously were delighted about. All the Staff received their autographs — which although now rather faded, I still cherish.

Besides our life style changing considerably I'm glad to say Linda, when she recovered from her whooping cough, also had her own little social life. She still went to Loretto Convent — which was a mixed school but the medium for teaching was English. The uniform was a white cotton dress with pleated skirt and a little pale blue tie — she looked very cute.

Birthday parties in Calcutta were out of this world and Linda was continually being invited to parties — the like of which I had never seen. They hired entertainers — the Monkey Man was booked and came along with his small drum and emaciated monkey who had been trained to do various tricks.

One of the most popular events was to make a coir bag — which was filled with small toys and bran and then covered with coloured tissue paper and hung from either a tree or the ceiling. The birthday girl or boy was given a stick with which to break the tissue on the coir bag — whereupon all the bran and toys spilt on the floor and the children scrambled to pick up as many small toys as they could. You can understand why this was so popular!

It was normal for both the Ayah and the Mother to attend these birthday parties — so they became very social occasions and gave the children and mothers the opportunity to meet new friends.

I'd managed to arrange Ballet Classes for Linda — I "think" she enjoyed them — but — I think in all honesty I wanted to over compensate for the things I felt she had done without. Even so, she looked delightful in her Tutu — and along with all the other parents — we felt very proud when we went to the end of term concerts.

# SIGNATURES OF JOHN HUNT'S EVEREST TEAM
# THE FIRST TEAM TO CLIMB EVEREST — IN 1953

OFFICE OF THE HIGH COMMISSIONER
FOR THE UNITED KINGDOM.
I, HARRINGTON STREET,
CALCUTTA,-16.

JOHN HUNT — *LEADER*

E. P. HILLARY

JOY HUNT

TENZING NORGAY —
*THE SHERPA GUIDE*

A. GREGORY

I had been feeling decidedly "below par" and blood tests showed I had Infective Hepatitis, and this was 5 weeks before we were due to sail home on our first leave.  It was thought we would have to cancel our plans to sail on the Lloyd Triestino.  However, the Doctor finally decided that perhaps the sea trip and change of environment would be a good convalescence and he declared me well enough to take the trip.

As we were getting off the ship in Venice we planned to spend a few days in Kitzbuhel.  Linda needed a holiday as much as we did and we thought these few days would be beneficial for us all.

Unfortunately we had only been at sea a few days when it became very obvious that Ken had contracted the Infective Hepatitis.  He was yellow, lethargic and nauseous — all the symptoms I had had. The Doctor on board besides speaking very little English, was so behind the times that he actually used a trumpet like instrument instead of a stethoscope!  This did not fill us with very much confidence, and when he said that Ken was suffering from sun stroke — we tried to tell him that Ken had the same symptoms that I had had prior to getting on board, and that it was diagnosed as Hepatitis. Ken was as yellow as a Buttercup and that alone, I would have thought, would have been sufficient to convince him it was not sun stroke!

We knew he should be on a fat free diet as I was — but trying to get a fat free diet on an Italian ship was just about impossible.

When we got to Djibouti I decided to go ashore and try to find a chemist to get the same medicine that I had been treated with.  This was a bit of an ordeal, as no one spoke English, I didn't know the Arabic for Chemist Shop, but finally found a shop that looked promising.  Then trying to get the medicine was impossible, but I did end up with a large tin of Glucose and some medicine that I was assured would help.

A little man who had entered the shop to see what I was doing and who spoke very basic English tried to come to my rescue.  I got back on board half an hour before we sailed — very relieved to have made it!

Unfortunately, Ken didn't improve and after 4 days in Venice staying at the Piazza San Marco where we tried to do all the touristy things, sailing in a Gondola, going to a Venetian Glass Factory etc., but decided we must cancel our holiday in Kitzbuel and go straight home.    A wise move as Ken was quite ill and spent more than three quarters of his leave in bed — rest being the only real cure for Hepatitis in those days.

We were very sad not to have this ski-ing holiday in Kitzbuel but obviously we had to cancel our plans and we travelled back to the U.K. on the Oriental Express disembarking at Tilbury where I had my first brush with Customs — which even to this day irritates me.

A couple of days before landing in Venice there was great activity in the Hold — passengers packing their light weight clothing and taking out their warmer clothes for Europe.    As we had not planned to go directly to the U.K. — we arranged with Cox and Kings to clear and deliver the heavy trunks to us in England.

The Hold was dark and crowded — everyone having their final sort out and there seemed to be no room to re-pack — so I literally pulled out the warm clothes and jammed in the swim suits and cottons we had worn on board.    It all became rather too much for me as I still wasn't feeling on top of the world after my bout of Hepatitis.

When we were going through Customs at Tilbury — I was asked what I had to declare, and I reeled off all the items I thought they might want to charge duty on.    For instance I had 6 Snake Skin handbags as gifts for family and friends — which in India only cost about £1 each.    I'd brought a bottle of Drambuie as a gift for my brother and a few other small presents — none of very much value, and 6 pairs of tights for my personal use.    Without even opening my suitcases — the Customs officer stamped my form and we got on the train for London.

I hadn't thought of mentioning — or for that matter I didn't know, that a lot of the items I'd declared were not actually in the suitcases which we were taking with us, but were in the trunks and would be coming later with Cox and Kings. I really didn't think this mattered as everything dutiable I had declared at Southampton and it had all been cleared.

As Ken was far from well, I tried to relieve him of all this paper work and harassment — and never gave the remainder of our luggage a second thought.

We'd been home about three weeks when we received a letter from Cox and Kings asking for the keys of the trunks as Customs would possibly want to examine them. I was horrified when a few days later I received a letter from the Customs saying I was being fined £500 for trying to avoid Customs Duty! In addition they were charging me £10 duty on each handbag plus VAT — £4 duty on the Drambuie plus VAT, AND they even charged me £6 duty on the tights I had bought for my own personal use plus again VAT There were other charges on every small gift — and we were both mortified as we did not have that amount of money. I tried to phone Customs — but all to no avail, they said they would release the items once I had paid the charges.

I was so upset, as we didn't have sufficient money to pay the fines, so I decided to go down to London to see the Customs people and explain that I HAD declared all these items on arrival at Dover and they had been cleared. I told them I hadn't realised what was in the suitcases and what was coming in the trunks — and we'd had to change our travel plans at the last moment as my husband was ill. As I had declared them ALL on arrival at Tilbury — I really didn't think the fine for non-declaration was justified.

One of the questions they asked was how long it was since we'd left the U.K. I told them we'd been in Calcutta nearly five years — and this shattering piece of information seemed to change their attitude slightly and they let me off the fine. They refused however to let me have any of the items they considered I owed them duty on — but did offer me the alternative of putting the trunks in Bond and saying they would be returned to me in 6 months' time when we sailed once more for India!     This left us short of clothes in the U.K. and all the gifts I had taken home for the family were of little use back in Calcutta.     Who needs 6 Skin Handbags in stock? Infuriating as this was, it was a whole lot better than having to pay all the charges.

This was the first of many brushes with Customs officials over the years — and ALL quite unjustified.     I think I was particularly annoyed as when going through Customs at Tilbury, one of the passengers who had obviously done a lot of travelling, had hidden no less than 3 small transistor radios down her well proportioned bosom!     Her son had also brought a bike in from Aden, which he had dismantled and distributed various parts in their luggage — which he didn't declare.     It began to look after my experience that it doesn't always pay to be strictly honest!

Our first leave was I suppose a bit of a disaster.     Like most things one looks forward to for a long time — anticipation is often better than realisation.     Ken's Mother had been very ill with cancer which had left her slightly disfigured which was a great embarrassment to her, and she was in quite a lot of pain.     I think meeting her new daughter-in-law and her child, was also a bit of a shock as it would be to any loving Mother.     We actually discovered that she hadn't told anyone that I had been married before — or that I had a child.

A few close friends of hers asked us on being introduced "who Linda was?" I was upset and felt embarrassed at having to tell them.

Ken was still very sick and I hadn't fully recovered, and my own Mother was obviously finding running the Post Office, more and more of an ordeal.     The weekly balance was always out — and she was always up late into the night on Fridays trying to trace her mistakes.     She was determined to be independent and refused to consider giving it up.     She had a fear of ending up in the Workhouse — or accepting charity — and so she continued to work and obviously worried about the weekly balance.

She was respected and loved by all the customers who looked

forward to coming to collect their Pensions each week and have a chat to "Curly" as they called her.

The six months' leave which we spent with my Mother and Ken's Mother, passed very quickly, and whilst we were both very sad to leave our parents, we were delighted to be going back to what we now considered to be "home". This time we returned on m.v. "Circassia" — the sister ship to the "Cilicia" that we had originally sailed on in 1948.

What changes there had been in my life since then — and I was so very happy. We had two adjoining cabins which gave us space to breathe. Linda was now a more seasoned traveller and went off to the ship's nursery very happily. She took an active part in all the various sporting events that the Ship's Nanny arranged for them — and got two prizes in the Ship's Sports at the end of the trip. We met up with friends from Calcutta and other friends who had been on the Cilicia five years before who seemed slightly confused at my change of name appearing on the passenger list.

When we got back to Calcutta we found the Company flat at Alipore, which was being built prior to our leaving, was still not finished and therefore we moved in with some friends to Alexander Mansions on Chowringhee, as Paying Guests. A lot of our time was spent in choosing curtains, bed covers, furniture, refrigerators, cookers, and rugs for the new flat, as it was now Company policy, along with many other Companies, to provide furnished accommodation for their Assistants. We couldn't believe our luck, not only were we going to live in a modern flat, but would have up-to-date furniture instead of the old items we had hired in the past.

Linda returned to the Convent school — and seemed to do very well. The Nuns had been so good to her when I was on my own and took reduced fees at one time — the majority of the children were European so she did not acquire the sing song accent that was so prevalent.

It was brought home to me very acutely whilst living here, how

147

our life sometimes hangs on a thread. One of the ladies I worked with at the High Commission in Calcutta was out for lunch, but as she suddenly started to feel unwell — she left the lunch and returned home. None of her servants apparently were on duty in the afternoon and she became so ill and was violently sick for what must have been hours. She was obviously too ill to call for help, and when her servants came on duty at 4.p.m. they found her collapsed and they then rang for help. Unfortunately when help arrived it was too late, she was taken to hospital and had died of Cholera by 7.p.m. As we were living in the same complex I just wished I had had reason to call round and see her — but our association was basically at the office.

My niece came out to Calcutta to visit us en route to Malaysia , she was really a very naive 23 years old, but had qualified as a teacher. Whilst training she had met a lot of Malaysians and became very friendly with some of the girls and would take them home for the weekend and the odd holidays. Therefore when she was asked if she would go overseas to teach British Army Personnel's children she agreed but said she had a preference for Malaysia. So en route to Ipoh to take up her first appointment she came to stay with us and we were delighted as she was really more like a sister than a niece there being only 14 years difference in our ages. She had a wonderful time — we took her to all the tourist spots in Calcutta during the day and included her in the Company cocktail parties and dinners we had to attend at night. She was really wide eyed at this way of living.

My brother had expressed a certain concern that she seemed to have so many Malay friends — and so before she left Calcutta, we wished her well but I said whatever she did, she really should not contemplate marrying a Malay! I pointed out that marriage was jolly hard work when you married your own nationality and religion, but to expect a mixed marriage to work with a change in religion and language — would spell disaster!

She proved me wrong and about four years later she wrote to say she was marrying a Muslim, the brother of one of her College friends whom she had entertained in England. This girl, anxious to reciprocate the hospitality she had received from Diane, invited her home for a weekend — and — the result was a romance with her brother and she agreed to marry him after several weeks' of courtship.

She invited us to the wedding and of course we would have loved to attend, as at that stage we had not experienced a Muslim wedding but funds did not permit a trip to Malaysia. We saw a cine film of the various ceremonies connected with the wedding afterwards — and I think she had no less than five changes of clothes for the five ceremonies. All this took place over a period of 5 days!

We have since been to several Muslim weddings — but — for a young English girl this must have been a gruelling experience. During the five days, she was kept in her bedroom for most of the day — only appearing for the various ceremonies which seemed to take place in the evenings. The bridegroom's mother and his sister's bathed her, dressed her and said a series of prayers, bestowed her with the most wonderful gold and diamond jewellery — some she was allowed to keep. She had to wait in her room whilst the bridegroom arrived on an ornately decorated horse from his home to the house where my niece was staying. This procession was accompanied by drums and typical Eastern music — and she was eventually allowed downstairs. But after each of the 4 ceremonies she had to return alone to her bedroom and only after the fifth ceremony in front of the Mullah, was she permitted to stay with her husband.

She subsequently told me that the wedding sheet had to be produced the next morning for proof of her virginity. I can't quite understand why, as at that stage it would be too late to do very much about it if the parents decided she was not suitable because of previous liaisons!

As I wasn't present at this particular wedding I only gathered this information from her letters and photographs she showed us. They did have one ceremony when she was dressed in the normal

European white wedding dress and veil — but the other four ceremonies she was dressed in various Bajus, or Shalwar Kamiz — with matching veils — and ornate slippers — looking subdued and of course could not look happy.   All brides have to look demure — which to the Western eye so often looks like sadness.   Her poor mother and father, who could not attend the ceremony so far away, were appalled when they saw the photos of her looking so miserable!

Linda was now nearly 6 and we felt that it was time she had a baby brother or sister while she was still young enough to appreciate an addition to the family.   As we were no longer under an obligation to the Company not to have a child on Ken's first tour of duty, this seemed an opportune time.

I was naturally very excited when I thought I was pregnant but equally despondent when the Dr. said he thought it was Dysentery. How there could be any resemblance in the symptoms I don't know! He suggested that in view of the time since Linda's birth, that it would be a good idea if I had a D. & C. which would ensure my conceiving more easily!   So into hospital I went — had the D.& C. and hoped.

A couple of weeks after this when getting ready to go out to an important business dinner being held for a Head Office visitor from the U.K., I collapsed with the most terrible pain whilst getting out of the bath.   The next thing I was taken off to the Nursing Home where the same Dr. who had performed the D.& C. said he thought it was probably a cyst which he would remove the next day.   I was apparently haemorrhaging severely and my condition deteriorated to such an extent that I was barely conscious. The nursing staff kept coming into the room and taking my blood pressure and according to Ken, who stayed with me during all this, told him my Dr's partner was in the hospital having been called in for another emergency — so Ken asked if he would come and have a look at me.

As soon as this second Dr. came into the room he was obviously alarmed — examined me and within two minutes diagnosed a ruptured ectopic pregnancy and said if he didn't operate within the next two hours, I would be dead.    When I tell you it took the hospital 1½ hours to get hold of an anaesthetist — you can imagine how poor Ken suffered!    How the first Dr. could perform a D.& C. without noticing I was pregnant, I don't know!    To cut a long story short — I was operated on — and needed a transfusion of 10 pints of blood.

There seemed to be no difficulty getting this, but, even when the blood arrived, the Indian Haematologist wouldn't connect it to the drip I had — until Ken had paid for the blood — and it was very expensive.    Obviously he didn't have this amount of money but arranged with someone in the office to provide the cash — no cheques were accepted of course!    The blood was then connected.

This blood transfusion has played a major part in my life — and still does — but more of that later.    The blood in India at that time was not tested for anything — and so 10 days later I developed Typhoid Fever — and as I was already very run down, the drug they gave me for the Typhoid Fever apparently caused an abcess on the liver from which it has never recovered.    I was ill for over a year before I was anywhere near normal.

The Dr. used to call in to see me in the Nursing Home everyday and I can remember on one occasion bursting into tears as everytime he came through the door, I knew it was costing another Rs.68 which we didn't have.

We finally got a loan from the Company so were able to pay all these astronomical medical bills but of course we were paying this back over the next 2 years!

The Company flat was eventually ready and we moved to Alipore Estates into this very nice Company flat.

One evening Ken and I had been invited to our Doctor's yearly Cocktail Party — which I remember as a "fun" evening as in no way was it the usual business cocktail party but a gathering of old friends.    Normally Cocktail parties started round 6.30.p.m. to 9.p.m. but if there was no departure time indicated on the invitation — then people did tend to stay on a little longer and usually small chop

— like Roast Beef, Chicken, or Ham open sandwiches were passed around.

This particular evening people did not start to leave until around midnight — a truly good party!  By the time we got to bed it must have been around 1.a.m. and we were therefore both surprised when we woke up around 3.a.m. and on the way to the toilet looked out of the window and we were mortified that the landscape seemed to be rippling!  "That was a good party" said Ken but then we noticed that the fan was swinging backwards and forwards, and within seconds our Nepali Ayah came dashing into the room with Linda in her arms very distressed screaming that this was an Earthquake!

She had been in Darjeeling when a rather vicious Quake had destroyed her home and her father had been killed.  We were on the 9th Floor and it would have been foolish to use the lift and equally hazardous to join the rush of people trying to get down the stairs, so we stayed where we were taking shelter under the load bearing beams, and saying a wee prayer.  No sooner were we settled than the trembling stopped — but in case there were any "after quakes" we stayed put for a little longer and tried to comfort the poor Ayah.

The next morning we discovered that about half the occupants had fled down the stairs in nighties, dressing gowns, some with curlers in their hair — oh the shame of it all!  Then there were the people who slept "nongo pongo" because of the heat — and they tried to appear decent with a sheet wrapped round the bits that mattered!

Not a nice experience — though we had had a similar experience when living in Whiteaway Laidlaws Building, though the strength of the Quake had been much less, but at the time quite alarming as you didn't know how it would escalate.

It was not long after this incident that the little Nepali Ayah who had been with me since I arrived in Calcutta was taken ill.  I nursed her for a few days, but she was making no progress and so I called in a Dr. who took some tests and gave us the shocking news that she had T.B. of the most virulent type.  Obviously we could not keep her — and in any case the Dr. advised that she should return to Nepal, as her chances of recovery would be much better than in Calcutta.

We were all very sad, but gave her six months' salary, provided six months' supply of medicine, put her on the train and reluctantly said "Goodbye".

Linda and I went for tests and X-Rays and fortunately were all clear. Ken decided he really didn't need an X-Ray — he had little to do with the Ayah, — he was 14 stone — a keen rugger player and certainly didn't LOOK the T.B. type — so he didn't join us in having X-rays. By doing this we saved Rs.80 which at the time seemed a big saving, but in point of fact proved both expensive and foolish!

I had been doing a lot of voluntary work since resigning from the High Commission, when I was so ill for so long. I had joined the British Women's Association and through the voluntary work I did for them came into contact with that wonderful woman Mother Teresa — about whom we have heard so much in recent years.

In those days she was not quite so well known, except amongst the poor and the social workers in Calcutta who were all full of admiration for all the dedication and work she was doing.

She ran several homes for unwanted children — orphans and Homes for the aged. She seemed to house more unwanted children than anyone could imagine — and without exception they all seemed happy and well fed. When I first met her, I was doing this voluntary job for the B.W.A. who every year donated monies to various deserving charitable organisations. Mother Theresa's Home was always one of them. This particular visit I was supposed to report on how the monies that we had donated the previous year, had been spent So I had my first tour of the Home — during which time she gave me a run down on many of the children, what their background was, where they had been found, what she planned for them etc. She knew the names of every one of them and why they were in the Home — and there were literally hundreds of inmates.

When we came to one of the rooms, which was occupied by

older girls — one of the girls was obviously very pregnant. Mother Teresa introduced her to me and told me she was Marie who was very helpful but also very forgetful — and she had forgotten to get married before she ordered her baby! It struck me as a very sweet way of explaining the girls predicament.

Whatever one could do for Mother Teresa was not by any means sufficient — her family grew daily — I don't think she ever turned anyone away — but her resources were minimal. How she managed to do so much good for so many people with so little, is truly amazing. She was indeed a wonderful woman, it was a privilege to have been associated with her.

One can't be in India long before you realise that Anglo-Indians (people with one European parent and one Indian) seem to be looked down upon, both by the Indian community and the European.

Whilst I was involved with the various charitable organisations, I came across a young Anglo-Indian girl who was about to be moved out of the Home she had been in since a baby as she was now considered old enough to take up employment. She had helped the Rev. Mother in this particular Home with the babies and young children — and she was well thought of by the staff. I liked the girl — and so when our Nepali Ayah had to return to Darjeeling, I thought it would be a good idea to give this girl the opportunity of working for us. I was a little dubious about the arrangement, but she was very willing to learn, and seemed dedicated, and determined to give a good impression — after all this was her first employment.

I knew a lot of people did not share my views, but I had always had my Ayahs, Amahs, Nannies sleep in the bedroom with Linda whenever we were out. This ensured that they would hear if Linda woke up and needed attention. She would sleep in her quarters when we were at home; when we were out late, I would not of course wake her up and she would stay in the room all night. Many of my friends could not understand this — but I wouldn't have employed her unless I felt she was reliable, trustworthy and clean — and this arrangement suited me and obviously suited Linda.

Most people had their servants pass a medical before employing them — and naturally, I had done this — so really had no worries on that score. Linda enjoyed her company and as June was little more than a child herself — she enjoyed playing card games, doing jig saws — and was a very good companion for Linda. June was very much more English than any of our Ayahs had been, though she did have the usual Anglo-Indian sing song voice.

One particular night when we returned home from a Company dinner, I was going in to see Linda as I did every night just to ensure she was alright. This particular night I found the Nursery door locked — so I couldn't get in — and I was very concerned. I didn't want to knock on the door and wake Linda — but I was puzzled as to why the door was locked! Initially I decided to forget my evening visit, but would certainly reprimand June the next morning for locking the door. So I went to bed, but suddenly realised how stupid this was — and even if it meant waking Linda, I was going into the room.

So I returned to the Nursery — and was horrified when I heard voices. Whilst one of these voices was June's, the other was certainly NOT Linda's. I was frantic — assuming the worst, that June had got a boy friend in, so I banged on the door and demanded that it be opened immediately. After what appeared to be about half a minute the door was opened — and all seemed well. Linda had slept through the commotion, June was in her nightie and there was no sign of anyone else. I looked in the bathroom I asked her who she was talking to and she said she was talking to herself! I wanted to look under the bed, but by this time I was feeling rather stupid — so said goodnight and left, telling her not to lock the door in future.

When I got back to my bedroom I was still very concerned and thought how silly I had been in not looking under the beds. I HAD heard someone talking and it didn't sound as though she was talking to herself. If my worst fears were correct and she did have a boy friend in the room, obviously she would hide him — so — back I went into the bedroom.

I turned on the light and all seemed in order; June was in bed and there seemed to be nothing untoward. Even so I was determined to satisfy myself, (even if I looked foolish), so I looked under the beds, went into the bathroom, and then I decided to look in the Almirahs. I got the fright of my life, as there, peering at me through all the clothes, were a pair of deep brown eyes which on further investigation I found belonged to a little girl, aged about 9 who burst into tears when she saw me. I don't know who was the more shocked! This apparently was June's sister, who also had lived in the Home, and had never been inside a European house.

June had told her she could come and see the Nursery but we had returned before June could get her out. I felt very guilty after all my wicked thoughts — and allowed her to spend the night with June — and cleared it with the Home by saying she had been invited to stay the night — which technically was correct — but not invited by me!

Regrettably I didn't keep too well in Calcutta. No doubt living on a shoe string for four years and the frequent bouts of Dysentery, had not helped. I refused to admit it at the time, and it is only in recent years that I realise how I was "pushing my luck" in remaining in India. Mind you, Ken's first tour was nearly 5 years and that was a long time in "the Black Hole" without a leave. The repeated attacks of Bacillary, Gardia and the dreaded Amoebic, obviously had taken its toll.

We were not eligible for National Health Benefits in India and Companies still did not include wives in their medical schemes, so naturally I avoided going to the Doctor whenever possible. I was hospitalised on several occasions for Bowel Washouts and Emetine Injections — and on one occasion Ken was admitted to the same hospital — in fact we were put in the same room!

Ken had acquired a Tape worm which had become very "attached" to him in more ways than one and appeared to have no intention of leaving, and to date had managed to survive all six previous treatments — (the worm not Ken!). Each treatment the worm lost yards of himself — I kid you not — but the head never appeared and so the worm continued to grow yet again. We fondly referred to this worm as "George" — and he was obviously very happy in his environment — but he had to go! The hospital was going to have yet another attempt.

This hospital was really first class and we shared this very pleasant room and had it not been for our peculiar complaints it could have been a second honeymoon!

It was by now about a year since I had had the ruptured ectopic pregnancy, and we felt if we were to have an addition to the family we shouldn't delay much longer. This time when I thought I was pregnant the Dr. sent me to the local Pathological Dept., which took a sample of my urine which they injected into a rabbit! This was the way they tested for pregnancy at that time in India! I was to ring up in two days to get the result — and so was very excited, but imagine my concern when they told me my rabbit had died! So all this had to be repeated but I was thrilled when this time they assured me I was pregnant!

I kept quite well during this pregnancy after the initial morning sickness. We felt pretty convinced that it was a boy and had numerous boys' names on a short list. Some of which, in my opinion, were horrific, like Lauchland Mclauchland which Ken insisted was his choice, though I felt he was pulling my leg! But during the pregnancy we always referred to the new baby as "John Michael".

About a week before the baby was due, Ken acquired a shocking cold, and we were anxious to get this cured before "John Michael" appeared. He agreed to go to the Dr. and made an appointment for the 1st February, 1955. Because he had seen traces of blood in his handkerchief when he coughed, he asked for an X-Ray and was to get the result of this on the 2nd February. However, that night my labour started and I went into The Elgin Nursing Home in Calcutta. At 8.30.a.m. Fiona Deidre was born weighing 7 lbs 5 ozs — and in those days Daddies were not allowed to be present at the baby's birth, though he had been with me until I was wheeled into the Labour room, so I had no cause to think he was anywhere but in the waiting room.

Unbeknown to me, when I went into the Labour Ward, Ken had then gone off to the Dr. to get the result of the X-ray he had had taken the previous day. I think the Dr. thought he was unduly anxious requesting an X-ray — but he arranged for this the same day and he was to get the results the following day which was the 2nd February, 1955.

The Dr. was so convinced that all was well, that as Ken walked into his consulting room, he said that he hadn't had time to look at his X-rays, but he was SURE that all was well. He then put them onto the screen — and declared he was SHOCKED — Ken had "inoperable T.B."!

He was then told he had to go into Riorden's Nursing Home the next day — and when Ken told him he had left me in the Labour room at the Elgin Nursing Home, the Dr. said that under no circumstances could he kiss me or the baby and shouldn't get too close, as it was highly infectious!

I was in my seventh heaven having produced such a perfect baby — and for my part delighted it was another girl! From past experience it seemed to me that girls remained as family members after they were married and were good friends with their Mothers sharing the same interests. I really didn't think I would be much good discussing Rugger, Cricket etc. with a son! Mind you I have since learnt to discuss all these topics including sex with my grandsons, so doubtless I would have learnt!

When Ken came into the Elgin Hospital and told my Dr. the news, he suggested that he didn't mention this to me at this stage, as it might affect my milk supply. What stupid advice! Can you imagine my feelings when Ken popped his head round the door and said "well done darling" then said he had to leave but would be back later in the day! I immediately burst into tears, thought he was either disappointed that he didn't have the son he hoped for to play rugger with etc., or he just didn't love me! At least my first husband who had been such a lout and philanderer had at least been enthusiastic when Linda was born.

I was mortified and of course the nurses very soon knew why I was so upset. They told the Dr. that my milk was far more likely to be affected through worry that my husband didn't love me than it would if they told me the truth. How right they were! So that afternoon Ken came back and whilst he stayed quite a distance from me, and didn't go near the baby, he told me of the events that had led up to his having the X-ray.

I was shattered; we had waited so long for this lovely baby, and now Ken was not to be allowed to hold her, or even see her for at least 2 months. He was such a wonderful daddy to Linda, but had missed her first few months, and he was now going to lose the first few months of this baby. We had no time together to discuss a name, and as I told you earlier, had referred to the baby during my pregnancy as "John Michael"!

The nurses got quite worried that we hadn't decided on a name and threatened to give her a number!

My own fears about the T.B. were accentuated by the fact that, as mentioned earlier, my brother had lost his first wife with T.B. — she died within six months of having it diagnosed! I didn't appreciate the significance of the expression "inoperable T.B."

Some good friends, when they heard of Ken's illness, had offered to look after Linda whilst I was in hospital They told me that she wasn't at all well and they had sent for the Dr. who decided she had Chicken Pox. With a new baby he suggested I stay in hospital until Linda's infectious stage was over. Poor little soul — her Mum and now her Dad in hospital — but she did have June who was a great companion and had been with me long enough for me to feel confident that she would really look after her.

Linda wanted to see the new baby — but our friends explained the problems and she realised that if the baby caught Chicken Pox she would be very ill. It really was a heart shattering time for us all. It was particularly hard for poor Linda to understand what was happening and I think her little world must have crumbled, though the friends that acted as postmen made light of how upset she was, — as after all there was little anyone could do.

We finally decided, to call this new baby Fiona Deidre — and this decision was made through the little notes we were able to send to each other via the friends who visited both hospitals.

By the time we were all together for the christening, Fiona was 11 months old and could just about walk into the church!

Once again in my life, friends were fantastic — they would visit Ken and bring the lovely letters he had written which helped a lot — they would then return to Ken's hospital and deliver the letters I had written. We both dropped little notes to Linda and she sent us sweet little notes back again which I still have and treasure to this day!

I do think though that these trials and tribulations make a marriage stronger — so long as you work hard and survive them! Even so, many years on, I could still shed a tear when I think of the sadness for us all — but particularly for Ken who can never regain those initial precious months. He had been such a wonderful Father to Linda, it seemed hard that he was not to experience the initial baby days of either of his darling daughters.

I was kept in the Elgin Nursing Home longer than is normal — because, as explained, they felt I should wait until Linda was over the worst of her Chicken Pox. Even then I was told not to cuddle Linda until I had put on a gown — and not to let her touch the baby. Very difficult! I wonder if all this was necessary as one is now told that a baby has it's own natural immunity that it acquires from its mother — but this was 1955 not 1995!

The great day came when Ken's Dr. said I could take the baby round to the hospital in the carry cot — and let him see her through the window. Poor compensation when he wanted to cuddle her — but better than not seeing her. Linda was also taken to see her Daddy though again could not understand why she could not climb on his bed — so these visits became rather a trial as she obviously got upset which did no one any good. At least with the baby I could leave her in the carry cot and have a few words with Ken and know she wouldn't object and argue! Sad times...... but they could have been worse.

After 3 months in the Nursing Home Ken was allowed out occasionally, as he was declared free from infection, but not cured. With the diet he received for his T.B., milk drinks every two hours and lots of food but no exercise he had put on about 4 stones in weight and had grown a beard which he assured me he would shave off once he left for the U.K.! So one of the jobs we had to do on these occasional reprieves from the Nursing Home was to buy larger clothes !

Plans were made for our return to the U.K., it was suggested we sailed on the m.v. Chinkoa which was a cargo passenger ship, leaving in about three weeks. It had its own Dr. which was another condition that the medicos insisted upon as Ken had to have daily injections as well as numerous tablets which had to be supervised. He had to have his own cabin (with no fraternising) which was very hard, and I can remember feeling like a naughty school girl when found creeping out of Ken's cabin one evening!

So in April of 1955 we left Calcutta on m.v. Chinkoa, for this long sea trip — which the Dr's felt would be beneficial for Ken.

It was a slow boat. It actually took 8 weeks and called at numerous ports to discharge and load cargo. We managed to get two cabins — Ken was on the top deck in a cabin which was next to the Captain's. Fiona, Linda and I were three decks down, but a very nice cabin, larger than we were used to on the Anchor Line.

The other 10 passengers were all delightful with the exception of one lady — who really was a misery. After two weeks on board the Dr. allowed Ken to mix with the rest of the passengers during the day but he had to have a two hour rest during the afternoon, and of course early to bed (on his own)! The time passed very quickly.

As Ken was not allowed ashore in Colombo, a couple off the boat kindly invited the girls and me to join them in driving around the Colombo area, which we all found interesting and wished we could have stayed longer. We had an entertaining taxi driver who insisted on taking us to the Mount Lavinia Hotel which I thought was the most romantic Hotel I had ever seen and wished that Ken was able to be with us.

I was sufficiently impressed with Ceylon (now Sri Lanka) to go back on another leave.

The ship docked to unload or load cargo at various ports in the Gulf, Aden, Suez, Port Said, through the Straits of Messina, Marseilles, Barcelona, Gibraltar to London. Sometimes we arrived in port at night and the loading and unloading would be finished early in the morning so we did not get ashore — but usually we managed a few hours on dry land.

The food on board was excellent and the Company (other than this difficult lady) good. The Captain by the name of "Bun" kept us entertained during dinner with stories about his various marriages — (and he had had 7) and was quite a comedian. At night there was the usual Bingo, Horse Racing, Cinema, and even a wee dance as all the crew members joined in the evening festivities.

On arrival in the U.K. we went to stay with my Mother in Yorkshire, Ken's Mother had very sadly died the previous year.

Ken had a check-up at the T.B. hospital in Ilkley — and we were delighted when they declared him fit. We then went up for a holiday to Pennan on the North coast of Scotland near Fraserburgh. Ken's sister and brother-in-law had bought a small fisherman's cottage actually on the coast there. The only snag to my mind was that the cottage had no inside toilet and we had to go out to the beach where every cottage seemed to have its own little wooden hut. This was fine during the day — other than the fact that everyone in the village knew how many times one visited the loo — and how long you were in there! At night I found these visits a bit of an ordeal with the wind off the North sea whistling through the cracks in the door which was a bit "off putting".

We had a wonderful summer though — Linda used to wander up the cliff to the farm to collect the milk and enjoyed seeing the animals, and we made various day trips to surrounding villages and enjoyed the very beautiful country side.

We met up with Ken's old friend Gordon Petrie — where we went to Balmedi Beach which was freezing — and Ken and Gordon regaled me with tales of how they had gone swimming off this beach on New Year's Eve!

Scotland, as you all know, is a truly beautiful and picturesque part of the U.K.. though I do stipulate that to appreciate it fully you do require good weather — it can also be very bleak! But we were lucky. Ken told me that his Mother used to be the Headmistress at the local Pennan school which was still there — I don't think it had changed — and many of the old villagers remembered Ken's Mother.

While we were up at Pennan, Ken received a letter from his Head Office in London saying they were pleased to hear that the T.B. Hospital in Yorkshire had declared him fit, BUT — they would like him to visit their own Specialist in Harley Street. We drove back to Yorkshire where I stayed with the children, my Mother and my brother who was then living at home.

Ken went down to the London Specialist on his own. Imagine our shock when he came back with the news that whilst they were happy he had made such good progress, the Specialist had suggested that if he wanted to return overseas again and to be SURE all the infection had disappeared, that he return to Hospital for 5 months! This came as a bitter blow — as though we hadn't had enough separation!

To speed up the proceedings it was suggested that he went into the Brompton Hospital for two weeks as a Private patient — which was quite expensive, but this then enabled him to jump the queue for the Sanatorium under the National Health scheme at Frimley. I stayed with my Mother as Ken at this stage was on a very small salary — a gesture from the Company as he had not worked for 10 months — and with the best will in the world only about 4 months could be counted as Leave as he had not finished his last overseas Contract. So the Company agreed to pay him a retainer and it certainly didn't stretch to my living down near the Sanatorium with the children.

Fortunately my Mother was more than happy to have us, though I'm sure she found the noise of the children too much at times. When we first came home, she did say she thought Linda was rather precocious — having asked my brother if he was the Cookie or the Bearer! Not having had an "Uncle" before she didn't realise the significance — and as there had always been a Cook or a Bearer or both in her life, this seemed a natural conclusion for the child to draw. Darling Mum didn't quite appreciate this — though I have to say she and Linda became firm friends in later life!

My Mother was finding it increasingly difficult to continue with the Post Office and the weekly balance was becoming even more of a nightmare resulting in her nearly always having to put money of her own in to balance the weekly books. Fortunately the Post Office Accountants usually found the paper discrepancy and the money would eventually be refunded. This was a great relief and restored her confidence which sometimes wavered. She really was a marvellous woman, how she coped with all the monetary problems after my father left her at the age of 60 I don't know.

She never had much money of her own and didn't get any affection or love from my father in later years — so in my opinion she had a pretty sad life, BUT she was always cheerful, happy and smiling and a source of encouragement to everyone.

As the weather that summer was so good, Fiona was able to spend a great deal of time in her rather large pram in the garden and all the customers would have a few words with her, while I was doing all the chores. I used to take Linda to the local school — Littlemoor — so her days were full and Fiona and I would go and meet her after school.

Ken in the meantime had gone down to Frimley Sanatorium, and had been put on full bed rest for two weeks — he was not allowed out of bed even to answer the call of nature!   After the two weeks he was allowed up and his daily exercise program increased until he was chopping down huge oak trees at the end of the 5 months.   For Occupational Therapy he attended a carpentry class and made a small stool for the children which we still have to this day and also made a delightful Panda — just about life size, for Fiona, which was highly treasured.

At this time, I think the Dr's were far more concerned with Ken's weight than his T.B. and said if he didn't lose weight he would die of a heart attack — never mind T.B.!   But as we all know it is more difficult to lose weight than to put it on — but slowly he returned to normal.

Life at Yeadon was nearly all work — with two children and I felt that I had to do the shopping and cooking for the family and their washing and ironing, as it appeared I had more spare time than either my Mother or Brother.

Linda started school at the Littlemoor Council School now known as Littlemoor Grammar School, this was where I had started my school life,   I have to say that when I was there I hated it — but Linda seemed to enjoy the other children's company though I do remember her saying she found it difficult to understand the Yorkshire dialect!   I wasn't surprised as to this day I often have difficulty understanding some of the expressions they use.   The school was within walking distance of Mother's bungalow, and she loved the independence of walking home with her friends.

I was delighted when one of the neighbours with whom I had been to school, suggested that we took the children for a picnic to Bolton Abbey.   Food was prepared and Linda, Fiona and the pram were loaded into the car along with all the picnic things and items for the baby.   This jaunt was a nice break and we found a picturesque spot near the river. We kept Fiona in her small pram until we had spread the travelling rug and unpacked the food, and then we unstrapped her and let her wander about.

We were about 30 yards from the river bank, but as with all children, it was the river that interested her, and she toddled off hugging the large Panda that her Daddy had made for her.  I dashed off after her, but just as I was within grabbing distance, she fell and rolled like a ball down towards the river still clutching her Panda!  I made two further attempts to grab her and just managed to get hold of her ankle before she went into the river!  Percy Panda continued to roll down the last few yards and fell into the river where he was swept down towards some fishermen.  Thankfully I had managed to grab Fiona but was horribly shaken when I realised that she could have been with Percy Panda!

My friends knew that Percy was a sentimental toy so they decided we should get into the car and drive down to where the fishermen were standing, hoping that the road was more direct and we would get there before Percy!  We explained to the fishermen what had happened — and shortly Percy came into the picture and the fishermen were able to net him and return him, rather wet, to Fiona. I was so shaken and found myself waking up at night imagining what could have happened!

During the five months Ken was at Frimley he was allowed two weekends at home.  He looked so much better having lost nearly all the excess weight — and whilst I know he didn't enjoy this enforced imprisonment, he has always been very philosophical — and he knew it was for his own good — thus he accepted the status quo more readily than I did.   He has always been very grateful for this extra treatment.

Eventually the five months passed and he was discharged from the Sanatorium — with a completely clean bill of health, and they said there was no reason why he should not return to his overseas assignment.  He was advised to take prophylaxis for the next two years.

As we were to go overseas again  the Doctors suggested that he take two years' supply of the various tablets with him in case they

were not obtainable overseas.  At 20 tablets a day for two years —
that was a LOT of tablets!  When Ken handed in the prescription to
the dispenser — he was convinced there had been a mistake in the
quantities prescribed — but on checking with the Doctor he asked
Ken if he could come back to collect the pills in about an hour's
time as it would take some time for him to obtain and pack the
number of tablets required.

When Ken returned to the Hospital to pick up the prescription he
was handed two huge barrels and tucked one under each arm and
off he dashed to King's Cross station to catch the train.  However
when going down the steps at King's Cross, the top of one of the
containers became loose and all the tablets were scattered all over
the steps and floor.  As you can imagine this caused complete
confusion and as there were far too many pills for him to pick up he
went off to get the Station Master as he was afraid that some children
might take them for Smarties!  The Station Master organised
someone to sweep up the Pills — but the funny thing was that the
following day when Ken was again at King's Cross station, he found
two of the pink coloured tablets had found their way down onto the
platform!

The news that we could return overseas again was more than we
had ever dared to hope for, but there was even a bigger surprise.
The Company decided that he should take up an appointment as
Branch Manager in Bombay.

# FOUR
## Bombay
### *October 1956—September 1960*

This transfer to Bombay where Ken was to be Branch Manager, not only meant a promotion, but also we became eligible for a Company flat and a Company car and driver!

The Company flat in Bombay had been let by the previous Manager, when he left for South America a few weeks earlier, to two Americans and therefore would not be vacant for 8 weeks. It was suggested therefore that Ken went out on his own initially. A young bachelor had been sent as stand-in when the previous Manager left until Ken was able to take up his appointment. To save the expense and inconvenience of running a flat on his own the bachelor had moved into P.G.(Paying Guest) accommodation with a Mrs Betty Curry. She was married to a sea Captain who was not often in town, so to help her expenses she was prepared to take in the odd P.G.

When Brian, (the stand-in) was leaving, Ken was asked if he would like to take over this P.G. accommodation rather than move into a Hotel which would be more expensive. It seemed a good idea — so this was agreed. Had I known how glamorous this lady was — I might have been happier had he moved into the Hotel!

Ken sailed on m.v.Strathmore on 26th July 1956 — and I followed in September, 1956 on the m.v.Circassia, the sister ship of the Cilicia that we had travelled on in 1948. We were sad not being able to return to India together, but I was pleased to have a little longer with my Mother.

My brother Eric offered to drive us to Liverpool and this again meant going over the Pennines which had given us so much trouble on our last leave when we were nearly snowed in.   The car was laden with our luggage and it was not an easy drive.   It can be very bleak over the Pennines and easily becomes impassable in bad or snowy weather.   We arrived in good time and met up on the landing stage with some old friends, who were returning to Calcutta and who were pleased to hear that Ken had recovered from the T.B.   As a result I had a really enjoyable trip back to Bombay.

I think there was always a charisma about these sea trips — whichever way you were travelling — people were always in high spirits and happy at the thought of either returning home after a long stint overseas — or equally happy about returning to India to old friends and a life style, which even in those days was magnificent.

It was a good trip — the Bay of Biscay was reasonably calm and no one suffered from sea sickness.   We called at Gibraltar and saw the Apes who really are cheeky — had the usual stop at Port Said and yet another visit to Simon Arzt and coping with more Gully Gully Men and their incredible "sleight of hand" producing chickens from the most amazing places!   They really are very clever — but one is always left uncertain as to what else they might have removed from one's pocket or handbag!

I bought yet another very ornate leather pouffe which again was rather smelly — but this time I sprayed it with perfume and packed it in the Hold!   We then sailed through the Suez canal which I always found interesting — and dropped anchor in the Bitter Lakes to allow the north bound convoy to pass.   Why I enjoyed the Suez Canal I really don't know as it is mile upon mile of the same vista, but each time I took more and more cine films of it — and didn't realise until I had had the films developed how repetitive it was, and certainly didn't warrant the six reels of film I had taken!

The well seasoned travellers assured me that the Red Sea was the hottest they had ever known.   There didn't seem to be a breath of air — and  the swimming pool was emptied whilst we were at anchor so we could not cool off in that!    Eventually we reached the very busy port of Aden.

A crowd of us went ashore and again hired a dilapidated taxi to do a little sight seeing.    Nothing had improved from our last visit and we saw sand and rocks and more sand with the odd camel jogging along with heavily laden carts.

The local female population all wore Burkas and one wondered how on earth they survived the heat in these bell tent arrangements. The children who were not yet considered old enough to have to wear the Veil or Burka,  stared in amazement at the way we dressed, obviously wondering how we could be so brazen as to walk about without our faces, legs or arms covered!

The males on the other hand didn't seem to object too much!

The Duty Free shops had some excellent merchandise for sale so we returned to the Port area where we were persuaded to buy watches and electrical goods — which were remarkably good value, so one didn't need a lot of coercing!   I bought Ken his Xmas present — an Omega gold watch — which he still cherishes and wears daily — so one can't say "I was taken to the cleaners" with this purchase!

We had the usual entertainments on board — Housie Housie (another name for Bingo), Horse Racing, Cinemas, and every few days there was a dance.    The children had their Sports afternoon and a Fancy Dress party which Linda thoroughly enjoyed and again she won the first prize for the best fancy dress costume — and on the Sports afternoon she tried to encourage Fiona to swim a little faster — with no great deal of success — but it was a fun afternoon.

Fiona travelled well and was quite happy at the time she had to spend in the Nursery whilst we were having meals etc., mind you, having Linda popping in to see how she was, and often staying with her, helped a lot.    Certainly our meal times were not as disturbed as mine had been travelling with Linda on her own — as then my name was repeatedly called over the tannoy system — as Linda had not initially adjusted to the Nursery or the Nurse.

One of the families we had become friendly with in Calcutta was also travelling back after leave, with three children and two of the boys were around Linda's age, so need I say she had a Ball. During the day we spent most of the time in or around the pool — and at night the older children were allowed to watch the films and participate in the Horse Racing. Not the betting of course, but they acted as Horses!

Linda did manage to give us all a fright by getting herself locked in the wardrobe in the cabin during a game of hide and seek with the boys. They came to me quite concerned as they had been looking for Linda for what seemed to them ages, and began to think she had fallen overboard as they just could not find her. I panicked and called the Purser — and an announcement was made over the tannoy system asking if anyone had seen Linda, who by this time was well known. I asked the boys if they had looked in their and our cabin when they first reported her missing and they had assured me they had!

At this stage however, Linda hadn't realised that she could not get out of the wardrobe, so when she heard the boys in the cabin calling her name, she just kept quiet and hid behind some of the long dresses, delighted they hadn't been able to find her. However, when I began to panic the first place I looked was the cabin and heard a muffled noise coming from the wardrobe as by now Linda was getting bored and decided the boys had given up their search for her, but then discovered she couldn't open the door!

When I opened the wardrobe and found her anxious face I was delighted to find my lost daughter, as I had imagined all sorts of horrible possibilities. When one has been so worried the first thing you do is explode at what appeared to be a rather stupid game — but I can tell you I was VERY relieved as you do hear such terrible stories about people falling overboard and I wondered if she had tried to hide in a lifeboat and perhaps missed her footing. One of the first places the ship's crew looked was in the lifeboats!

The night before we arrived in Bombay there was the Captain's dinner — when there was an exchange of phone numbers and general excitement at the thought of arriving in Bombay. The next morning everyone got up remarkably early and hung over the side of the ship waiting for Bombay to come into sight. We finally arrived around 6.a.m. and I was reminded of the first time I had arrived there in 1948 — little knowing what lay ahead.

I was thrilled to death when I saw Ken standing on the dockside, it had been a long eight weeks! Everything was familiar to me now and I felt as though I was coming home.

Bombay compared to Calcutta was really a dream. Very cosmopolitan, and much more westernised than Calcutta. It is India's second largest city and the one nearest to western tastes, but also India's richest and busiest industrial centre.

It has the greatest number of Parsees, who fled from Persia in the 7th century to Bombay where they remained in or around the area. The Parsee ladies were quite beautiful and dressed superbly with their ornate saris embroidered in silver and gold thread, and spoke excellent English. Gold chains, bracelets, rings, ear rings — all appeared to be part of their normal dress!

Parsees, as you doubtless know, dispose of their dead by exposing them to the elements as distinct from burying or cremating them. In Bombay this took place on Malabar Hill where the "Towers of Silence" were situated. However, we were not prepared for one of the rather gruesome aspects of this custom, as one could be driving near Malabar Hill and find a finger, hand, or foot, had been dropped by the Vultures (that dispose of the corpses) on the road in front of you. This practice fortunately was stopped whilst we were in Bombay as the Authorities placed a grille over the body which prevented the birds removing any large bones.

The Company flat was in an excellent situation being opposite the Breach Candy Swimming Pool which in those days was for the exclusive use of Europeans. It was a beautiful pool built on the shore — so one could sit and watch the waves and the ships at sea whilst watching the children swim.

Besides this very lovely outside pool which was huge, there was also an indoor pool which was nearly Olympic size where I was to spend many hours with the children when having their swimming lessons. Linda, along with many other children, was taught swimming and diving by Barbara Rabeneck — and it seemed that all children who were taught by Barbara — excelled. So much so that swimming became Linda's career in later life and to-day she has her own Swimming School in Singapore — entirely due to Barbara who was her mentor.

I used to sit and watch her lessons and became so interested in the techniques that Barbara used to encourage the children and in her form of teaching, that at a later date in Karachi when a swimming instructor couldn't be found — I took over for a short time and thoroughly enjoyed it.

Every morning two horses would appear in the compound outside the flat with their Syce in case the children wanted to ride — they would return again in the evening hoping that their enthusiasm would mean more money for the syce!

We had been most fortunate in taking over the domestic Bombay Staff which had been employed by our predecessor — the Bearer was a joy as his English was not only perfect but his comprehension was excellent, so we didn't have the misunderstandings that we had in Calcutta. He seemed to hold the household together. There was never any bad feeling between the staff — and he seemed to anticipate our needs before we actually knew them ourselves! The only thing I found slightly disconcerting was his Christian name of "John Thomas" — and when I initially shortened it to "John" I was corrected that it was "John Thomas". I don't know if he realised the western implications! He was from Ceylon (Sri Lanka now) so had no immediate family problems which was refreshing.

Ken and I were rather amused as it appeared that he decided when he thought our sex life needed reviving and he would carefully lay out my most glamorous black nightie draped over the pillow every Saturday night and occasionally during the week. The rest of the time he would lay out my very ordinary cotton ones!

We engaged a delightful South Indian Ayah called Alice, who was so very gentle and had a lovely face which endeared her to us from the start!

The cook produced excellent meals and was in himself scrupulously clean — they all spoke good English which was a relief and a big improvement to the staff we had in Calcutta.

The household routine was more or less the same as it was in Calcutta, but I had now learnt that I was the Memsahib and laid down my own rules regarding the running of the house.

The Hamal was a full time member of the staff instead of coming in twice daily and the Dhobi collected the washing every morning — and it was returned by 5.00.p.m. beautifully ironed and starched. Most of the dhobies took their washing to the Dhobi Ghats, an entire area given over to the washing of Bombay's clothes as they did in Calcutta, though here, after the clothes had been washed (bashed) on the rocks, they were spread out on other rocks to dry — which looked very attractive with the blaze of colours of the variegated saris.

As the Dhobi would be working for several households it was amazing to me that the washing didn't get mixed up with other people's, as nothing was marked. Occasionally in Calcutta I found items which were not mine — but were always in a poorer condition than the ones I had sent! Initially I tried to sort out the problem of mixed washing — but it became all too complicated — so I gave up and put up with the well worn towel I had acquired instead of the nearly new one I had sent.

Here in Bombay we didn't have that problem and I put this down to the efficiency of the Bearer who seemed to have our interests at heart.

We had quite a few Company visitors whilst we were in Bombay — and entertaining them during their short stay usually meant inviting the heads of various companies with whom Ken did business to a dinner party. This is why it was essential to have a good Cook and an intelligent Bearer. One felt very responsible for one's servants; they gave you the most dedicated service and in return you felt you had to do all you could to help them if in trouble.

Other than "John Thomas" some of the servants could be infuriating — and so often had some very good reason why something hadn't been done, which you knew and they knew you knew — to be an absolute lie.

Yet at the same time there was a great deal of respect between master and servant, but you not only had to look after your own staff member, but all his family. Their problems became your problems — and they looked to you for help and guidance and on the whole they were most grateful for any advice or help you gave. We still get the most touching letters from our various servants in India and Pakistan giving us the news of their families, and also telling us how we are missed!

Our Ayah from Bombay wrote to me enclosing a letter from her daughter thanking Ken and I for paying her school fees, as it was through the education she had at the Convent she had been able to get a good job and had just bought her first house! With so much poverty in the country, this was very gratifying to know that we had at least been able to help one individual to achieve a better standard of living.

The Hamals seemed to give me the biggest headaches — and they would tend to ask for more time off than any other servant, always having a very justified excuse — IF it was true. For instance the most popular excuse was that someone had died and they had to attend the funeral. I kept a check on these excuses and found that the Hamal's father had died three times!

It was surprising how quickly we had adjusted to having servants — not that by taking a sea trip we suddenly became incapable of coping with the chores but it was unheard of for Europeans not to have servants — after all it gave jobs to many people — who in turn were supporting large families — so we tried — very successfully not to feel a degree of guilt! Also of course it took some time for one's body to adjust to the heat and humidity — so I suppose, we did have an excuse!

Even as chokras (young people on their first tour) we had been expected to employ at least 5 servants — even though we were so often hard up, we could not cut down on the household help.

Each servant had his or her own particular job — and with the caste system there was no way that the Bearer would wash a floor, or for that matter the Hamal serve at table. The cook would not leave the kitchen, other than to go to the Bazaar, and none of them would do any washing! You couldn't therefore "buck the system" as all the salaries were so small that the six servants cost only what one daily help would have cost in the U.K. So one got used to having this large staff, and all that went with them.

We were able to have long weekends at the two Hill Stations, Poona (now called Puni) and Mahbleshwar. It was wonderful to spend a couple of days in a cool climate and the old homes we stayed in were delightful. The children were able to ride horses and as we usually went up with other families with children — they thoroughly enjoyed these visits.

In Bombay a friend who worked for Burmah Shell was going on leave and asked if we would look after their two dogs. We had always said that with the high incidence of Rabies in India, that much as we would love a pet, with the children we would not have one. However, these particularly good friends told us they would have their dogs put to sleep rather than leave them in the kennels, which really were deplorable. The children were obviously upset at this turn of events, and as our friends also had children and obviously the dogs were free from worms and had had regular check ups, we decided that we would take ONE dog for the six months!

Her name was Sherry, a sweet little Cairn and we all grew very fond of her, so after 6 months we weren't too distressed when we heard from our friends that Burmah Shell had posted them elsewhere — and they were not prepared to have the dog put into 6 month's quarantine, so, would we please have her put to sleep!

Obviously, we couldn't do this — so Sherry became part of our permanent family.   Unfortunately Sherry was obviously rather promiscuous and we soon realised that she was expecting puppies! We never knew who her husband was as she was never allowed out on her own and the Hamal who would occasionally take her a walk — denied all knowledge of any romance on Sherry's part.   When we saw the puppies we began to think she must have mated with a goat!   The funny thing was that she gave birth to only three puppies — the last to arrive was obviously a runt — but even so we were all horrified when we found she had eaten it!   I suppose that is nature's way of coping with a puppy that obviously would not survive — but we did rather "go off" Sherry at the time.   We kept one of the puppies and gave the other to a friend.

Bombay was what they term "a Dry State" — the consumption of alcohol was not permitted unless you held an Alcoholic's Permit. This entailed a special application declaring that you were an alcoholic which, if I recall correctly, had to be countersigned by a Dr. before being submitted to the local authorities.

Depending on age, and to an extent sex, the individual would be granted one to four units — each unit entitling you to one bottle of spirit or 9 bottles of Beer.

Unfortunately this led to the most incredible consumption of illicit liquor amongst the poorer Indians, to the extent that industrial alcohol, methylated spirits and finally furniture polish had to be put on permit;  many poor souls killed themselves by consuming this type of alcohol.

For those expatriates who could not survive on their Permit allocation, black market whisky and gin were quite readily available at both Juhu and Marve beaches, at, strangely enough, prices which were a rupee or two cheaper than the legitimate outlets.   This liquor came from Goa or more frequently over the side of vessels awaiting to get into Bombay harbour, rowed ashore during the hours of darkness and buried in the sands at one of the many beaches.

Many times you would be sitting on the beach and a rather

disreputable little man would approach you holding a long thin stick and offering you gin or whisky — but with no sign whatsoever of any bottles. If you could not resist the cheap prices offered and agreed to purchase a bottle — then he would dig his stick into the sand innumerable times, possibly quite near where you were sitting until he obviously hit the crate or bottle — and would then dig in the sand and hand you the bottle. All this was highly illegal — so not a wise thing to do, but very tempting as the cost was way below that of the similar item in the shops, and you didn't have to surrender any of your precious coupons!

They had even more surreptitious means of trading their wares, and would request appointments with Expats in their offices — only to offer them a crate of whisky or gin. This would be delivered late at night to the Expat's home. There was quite a booming business conducted this way. They knew for instance that ALL Expats would have an Alcoholics Permit, so once the liquor was IN their home, it would be hard to prove that it was not part of their legitimate supply.

If you went to a Hotel and wanted a drink you had to show your Alcoholics permit and then go into a room that was completely blackened out so you could not corrupt anyone by your outrageous habit. Each drink you consumed was marked on your permit — and 8 drinks in a Hotel would count for one point!

Frankly I was horrified when I was taken by one of Ken's staff to the office where you obtained your licence, to find it said I was an alcoholic — but if I wasn't — then I would not get a permit!

The Prohibition Police were very active and had the authority to search your home if they thought you had excess liquor or for that matter guests who did not hold a permit. There were quite heavy fines if you were found to be contravening either of these regulations. They usually raided houses where there was a large party going on — or they had seen Indians entering the premises. No Indians were permitted these liquor licences — though I think there was probably a little corruption at the issuing office on occasion, as wealthy Indians did sometimes produce a certificate as they claimed they were from overseas or had some other lame excuse. There was no doubt about it that money could influence decisions!

Because of Ken's promotion we had to entertain quite a lot — and to invite people round without being able to offer them a drink wouldn't go down very well with the guests. Most Expats therefore had started to brew their own liquor and so we joined the band wagon. We bought the necessary kit and started to brew potato wine, tea wine (which tasted rather like Sherry) raisin wine and other brews which were not so successful.

We kept the large gallon bottles in the bathroom bubbling away — as I felt that if the Prohibition Police did raid the house, I would lock myself in the bathroom — strip off — pour the liquor down the loo and appear slightly annoyed in a towel! This fortunately didn't happen and we became quite blasé having no less than three large bottles bubbling away at one time.

As you can imagine, there was quite a rivalry amongst us to see who could produce the most palatable wine or spirit.

Prohibition produced more alcoholics than I have ever seen. We were invited to a party given by one of Ken's clients and as Ken was on a trip to Madras at the time — as he was also responsible for that area, he thought it would be diplomatic if I was to call in at the party for an hour or two — as it was an account he did not want to lose! I didn't really like going to parties on my own, nor did I think my presence would make the slightest difference to any account, but I decided I better attend but instead of going at 7 p.m. for drinks I would arrive at 8 p.m. in the hope that the party would start breaking up around 9 p.m.

They were serving Home Brew at this party and I have never seen so many people completely incapable within such a short time! Obviously the spirit level in this particular brew was way above normal. I had an orange juice and left as I was sure that no one would be aware whether I was there or not!

This party was talked about for many months — as most of the guests collapsed on the floor and had to leave the next morning. Quite a lesson for the "Home Brew" enthusiasts.

On one epic occasion we were leaving for a dinner around 8.p.m. and when we got downstairs the driver pointed to the Prohibition Police who were searching in the bushes around our flat — probing with their long sticks — and waving their torches in every direction. I immediately thought that someone had tipped them off about the bottles in the bathroom — which had reached a stage that they were about ready for bottling.    We kept our legitimate liquor bottles for this — so that once the liquid was in the authorised bottle, we felt safe.    I felt we should return upstairs and pour the lot down the loo — but our wonderful Bearer suggested that the Ayah sleep on the floor outside the loo and if the Prohibition Police did enter the flat — she took on my role of pretending to be having a bath — and disposing of the liquor.    The one snag was that the home brew did smell alcoholic — and I had an air freshener in the bathroom to help with the disposal of any fumes.

We went to our dinner party — rang up to enquire what was happening and were delighted when we heard that the Police had left having found 3 bottles in the bottom of the garden in the adjoining block of flats!

The Prohibition Police had the authority to enter your home and inspect the Permits of the guests who were drinking — but not only was it a crime to be found drinking without a permit, merely to be in the room with people drinking if you had not a permit, was not only a crime for that individual, but for the host of the party for permitting this to happen!    Whilst I only heard of two occasions when homes were raided on these grounds, but it did make one anxious.

One of my friends had had her house burgled and a lot of sentimental items had disappeared.    When she called the police and was so obviously distressed — they suggested she went to Chor Bazaar or Thieves Market where she probably would be able to buy back her own treasures!    She asked me to go with her and we were quite shattered at the extent of the items for sale — all of which one assumed had been stolen or acquired illegally. Mind you, there were also Gucci and Dior fakes being passed off as the real thing! My friend had no success on this occasion in seeing any of her stolen articles, but during a visit four months' later she was able to purchase two items which had been taken from her home!

In another part of the Bazaar you would see hundreds of wealthy Indians choosing jewellery from trays — rather like selecting an hors d'oeuvre — but they were all solid gold.

The British Navy used to come into Bombay for "Rest and Recreation", and as Ken was now the No.1. in the Company we were included on the invitation list and invited on board for cocktails. As the navy vessels were usually anchored off shore we had to go out on small boats which tossed and turned in the waves. Going out was easy, but returning after a couple of drinks was often a different matter and I am sure the Navy boys manning these boats were always relieved when they got everyone back to dry land.

The Navy drinks were strong — and I felt very much the worse for wear after three drinks — but it was thirsty weather — the conversation was scintillating — and I realised that I had to visit the ladies room! I asked one of the Officer's I was talking to where the ladies went to wash their hands, and he looked a little baffled but suggested that he took me to his cabin — where I would have complete privacy! I was sufficiently compos mentis to realise that perhaps this was a little "irregular" — but even so I followed him down the companionway — down the steps — and he unlocked his cabin door — and very gallantly gave me the key in order to lock up when I left! How wrong I had been as to his intentions!

The odd thing about this story was that we left shortly afterwards — went home and went to bed, BUT the next morning I awoke clutching the key to Cabin 29! The embarrassment was in getting it back to the ship without causing too many comments!

Once the children were attending the local school — I decided to apply to the British High Commission to help with finances — as whilst our standard of living was high, actual spare cash was not! I think the excellent references I had received from the High Commissioner in Calcutta must have been a help and I started working again in the Visa Section and had similar amusing contacts with the public as I had had in Calcutta. I certainly had my education broadened whilst there.

There was a member of the staff — who I now think must have been a nymphomaniac — but — initially I did not appreciate this. One morning she arrived in the office looking particularly distressed and was obviously near tears. Trying to help I asked her if there was anything I could do? She then burst into tears and said she thought she was pregnant. As she was married with three children — I really couldn't think this was such a disaster, and tried to point out that it would be nice for her third child to have a companion, and children did keep one young.

She then completely flawed me by asking what she should tell her husband as they hadn't slept together for over 2 years! This really put my gas to a peep — as I didn't know what advice to give.

She was a Catholic so she said that an abortion could not be considered, but neither could she have the child — so perhaps she would have the abortion, but naturally would not be able to tell her husband.

In the end she decided she would tell her husband that she had to go into a Nursing Home to have a Cyst removed. He was naturally very concerned — sent her red roses even though she was only in the Nursing Home for 24 hours. The following week he said he wanted to buy her a couple of new dresses as he thought she was very brave! This in itself she thought amusing and was delighted to have the money to buy new dresses!

The saga didn't end there. About a month later the Bank for whom her husband worked, remarked that they still had not received the Nursing Home bill for the surgery his wife had had and asked if he would let them have it as soon as possible. Well the bill had already been settled by Mr. X, who felt responsible! When questioned by her husband, my friend decided to ring the Secretary at the Nursing Home to ask them to send the bill to the Bank. They then told her that the Bill had already been settled by Mr. X! To try to untangle this mess — my friend went to the Nursing Home and asked them to send the bill to the Bank in the ordinary way and when they had received the money would they refund the initial payment. When this was received by Mr. X he gave it to my friend saying he felt she had earned it!

This was not the end! Another of her paramours, who had been on a business trip overseas, returned to Bombay and when he heard of this incident — HE insisted on also paying the bill as he said he felt he was responsible!

Who says crime doesn't pay? Besides roses, two new dresses, the refund of two Nursing Home and Surgeon's Bills she even received a very nice gold necklace from boy friend number 3!

I subsequently met her at a business Cocktail party — and much as this particular lady loved her alcohol and parties — I saw her leaving early. The next day at the office I commented on her early departure and she told me she had to get her husband home as she had put two sleeping tablets in his last drink — and she wanted to get him home before he fell asleep. When he was asleep she intended to creep out and join boyfriend number 2!

Another occasion she told me she was coming home from a party alone, and when she got into the house she heard her husband getting up to go jogging. She stripped off, wrapped herself in a towel and said she decided she would join him on his jog! I think it nearly killed her — as she was NOT a sporty type- but it saved her being found in her evening dress!

Meeting this lady (?) was certainly an eye opener as far as I was concerned! Mind you, this was 1957 — people reading this to-day won't think it so very out of the ordinary but to me it was mind boggling! The sequel to this story is that a few years later when looking for a secretarial school for Fiona I rang up a certain school to make an appointment to see the Headmistress. A very efficient young lady answered the phone and she told me she was a student secretary for the day — and that when the girls had reached a certain stage in their secretarial course they were given a job in the school office.   I was so impressed with this young girl's efficiency I decided I would mention it to the Headmistress when I saw her, so asked the young girl for her name.   I nearly fell over when she told me — as it transpired she was the first child of the promiscuous lady at the High Commission in Bombay!   I decided to give this school a miss!

One of the joys of Bombay after Calcutta was that we were close to the beach — and several Companies provided permanent Beach Houses for their staff to be used at the weekend.   Whilst our Company did not provide any such luxury, we found we were invited most weekends to either Juhu or Marve.   We enjoyed these breaks immensely — the beach houses were well equipped and each had its own servant so whilst we took food out with us, the servant would cook it!   The sands were great (but then I hadn't seen the beaches in Australia) — the children equally loved these weekends — the beaches were quite safe and not crowded — and when they weren't swimming they would play beach games with the parents.   We had B.B.Q's on the beach and friends from other Beach Houses would join us and it was quite usual to end up with 20 people for either lunch or dinner — sometimes for both!   We thoroughly enjoyed the few hours away from the hustle bustle of Bombay.

I should mention that during this tour in Bombay, Ken had to visit Delhi on business and he decided to drive up there and so I was able to accompany him.

We set off from Bombay early in the morning — drove through the Ghats to Deolaly where the old British Army Station used to be and which gave rise to the "doubt to one's sanity" and referred to as the "Doolally tap" — fever!   Then on to Delhi, via Agra and Fatehpur Sikhri.   I had been in India 10 years by this time and never travelled very far, so this opportunity was too good to miss BUT I was very concerned about leaving the girls — even though we had the Ayah, Bearer and Driver and my new found friend Margaret, who lived in the same block of flats, who had happily agreed to keep an eye on them — and would have had them to stay, but I felt they would be happier in their own environment. Being a worried Mum I rang up every evening to check that all was well. The first night I phoned, Linda — never one to miss a trick — told me that a little girl at school was giving away cute little white mice with pink eyes and could she and Fiona have one? I thought it would be a small compensation for our being away — so obviously agreed — and they were to be kept in bird cages on the Veranda! Apparently the sun on the Veranda was too strong for them — so they were moved into the third bedroom which had patio windows and their cage was placed near the window! This proved disastrous as I mention later!

I found this trip fascinating — Jaipur, 55 minutes from Delhi, is built of pink stone, referred to as the Pink City and actually did have a pink glow around it, and the effect particularly at sunset is very beautiful. A Walled city, it was the home of the Rajputs — a fierce race of warriors who apparently fought with one hand and painted with the other (not at the same time)! This is the most renowned of Rajasthan's cities. Rajasthan often gets in the news in India because of its comparative poverty, aggravated by the occasional droughts that come as unwelcome reminders of how much of the state is desert. But in many ways it is also one of the most attractive states with numerous distinctive assets. The stone for the Taj Mahal came from one of the Marble mines, the forests abound with wild animals, and the artificial lakes provided water that made lovely cities appear to bloom with the cascade of flowers.

The women stride gracefully in long colourful swirling bright skirts, tight blouses, stoles and a vast profusion of silver bangles. We often saw them balancing huge brass jugs on their heads as they went to and from the local well and they continued to look serene and very happy. The men all seemed to wear rose red or pink turbans, though no two alike.

We stayed at the Rambagh Palace Hotel — it was a Maharajah's Palace and was made of marble, surrounded by lawns, flowerbeds and trees.   The old town is charming, and although very busy it was quite picturesque, with scores of side streets filled with stalls and shops.   In the heart of the old town is the present Maharajahs Palace where the Maharajah now lives.   One can see a crumbling red stone wall on the other side of the river, that is believed to have been the site that Shah Jahan intended as his final resting place.

Part of the city's charm is its feudal character.   It's easy to imagine the mighty Maharajah and his horde of devoted (they had no choice — they had to be devoted!) slaves.   We were told at the Rambagh Palace Hotel, that crocodiles used to swim in the Palace pool whilst elephants nibbled the local foliage.   I was surprised at the 110 feet wide roads but I was told that it was to accommodate the old-time elephant processions.

Friends we had made in Calcutta, Olive and Syd Reece who were now living in Delhi, had invited us to stay with them whilst in Delhi and very kindly took us sightseeing around Delhi, which as India's capital city is really a double delight as it is two cities in one.

The first presents itself when you drive in through — a forest of green, trees and foliage, interspersed with the homes of industrialists; the enclaves of Embassies and several very modern Hotels.   But the second Delhi is quite different, and consists of a sea of people pushing and being jostled and harried but never appearing to lose their inherent cheerfulness.

New Delhi remains distinctly British and the old imperiousness remains.   Old Delhi could only be in India and the 5,000 years of turbulent history can be seen everywhere in the narrow overcrowded streets and alleyways.

I was told that in 1911 the British laid the foundations of New Delhi to glorify the Empire and it is now the capital of the new Republic of India.

Parliament House is a vast circular building rimmed by an open colonnade, the massive secretarial blocks and the Viceregal Lodge crown the impressive Rajpath Avenue which can be compared in its majesty to the Champs-Elysee in Paris or Pall Mall in London.

One end of the Rajpath Avenue is the Indian Gate, a memorial to the Indian soldiers who died in World War I and I gather modelled on the Menim Gate in Belgium. At the other end is the home of the head of the world's largest democracy.

The best shopping is around Connaught Place but a far cry from Bond Street! The shops were not department stores, but small family owned businesses selling everything. Nearby is the Jama Masjid, India's largest Mosque, also built by Emperor Shah Jahan which can hold 20,000 for Friday prayers.

We visited and climbed the Qutb Minar — (pronounced Qutab Minar) which is a 13th Century minaret 234 feet high. The sides are covered with intricately carved quotations from the Koran which get larger as the tower grows higher so that it can be read with ease from the bottom of the minaret. There seems to be confusion as to why it was built — some say it was built to call the faithful to prayer by the Muezzin whilst others say it was simply a victory tower.

Close to this minaret we were taken to the famous Iron Pillar which stands in what was once the courtyard of a Mosque. This we were told had been there since the 5th Century and throughout the 1,500 years in spite of being made of iron, it remains rust free! We also paid a visit to Gandhi's Black Marble Tomb.

It took us nearly two hours to go round the Red Fort in Delhi, known as the most magnificent Palace in the East — or perhaps in the world and built by Emperor Shah Jahan. It really is huge. The Moguls built it out of red sandstone, and it covers a large area, All the Mogul Emperors lived there, except for their glorious interlude in Agra. It is from here that the famous Peacock Throne, then valued at twelve million pounds, was carried off by an Afghan invader — they said it was the biggest haul in history! We felt we should have had more time there, but there was so much to see in a very limited time.

One of the four Observatories built by Jai Singh, the Rajput Astronomer, is the Jantar Mantar, which our hosts took us to visit.

The heat in Delhi at this time was quite reasonable — though warm — but I would hate to have done this sight seeing when the temperature was around 105 degrees!

We then went on to Humayuin's tomb which was built in the 16th century to mark the beginning of a great period in Mogul architecture which apparently culminated in the Taj Mahal. Both are memorials to love. The Taj Mahal at Agra was built by Shah Jahan as an everlasting tribute to his wife, Mumtaz Mahal. She in turn built Humayuin's tomb for her Emperor husband, Shah Jahan.

The Reeces' house, like so many of the homes in the East, was quite magnificent, with the full complement of servants — which were at least 4 more than we had. They had a garden and had two Mali's (gardeners) and two Chowkidars (watchmen). The Chowkidars seemed to spend most of their time sleeping — and when we returned home one night about 1.a.m. it took us quite a time to waken "the watchman"! We were told that it was essential to have Chowkidars — even if they slept through the night as they acted as an Insurance Policy — no-one would burgle a household who employed Chowkidars — otherwise they might lose their jobs!

Ken and I then left for Agra to see the Taj Mahal and booked into Clarke's Hotel.

How does one attempt to describe the Taj Mahal? So much has been written about it — that it would be presumptuous of me to try to elaborate further. It certainly lived up to all my expectations.

I think the way it is presented by walking through a large gate into a sizeable courtyard with a high wall blocking the view temporarily. In this wall there is a very small door and as you walk through it you are at the end of a lovely lake type lagoon — and there is the Taj.

It really is mind boggling! When we saw it, one of the minarets was covered by bamboo scaffolding and I have since gathered that there is always one of the minarets in this state, I suppose it is a full time job keeping it in its pristine condition.

On top of the entrance gates are 22 small domes which record the number of years the Mausoleum took to build. Around the 90-

foot-high entrance portico are quotations from the Koran in Arabic script. This must have been a popular form of decoration as we had seen it on the Qutb Minar.

Besides the exterior which looks so different when viewed from a distance and appears to change as you get nearer and seems to foster countless optical allusions, I don't think anyone had told me how richly carved and decorated the whole building is. Nor had I any idea that the interior would be so perfect. An intricately carved marble screen shields the tombs of Mumtaz and her husband Shahjahan The marble walls are exquisitely decorated with pietra dura inlay ( the method of setting semi-precious and precious stones which we were told were brought from all over Asia, Russia, Egypt, Baghdad and other places) into the marble tiles. Some of the decorative flowers are composed of as many as 64 separate inlays.

We employed a local guide in Agra as we were badgered for the first 15 minutes by literally hundreds of bodies wanting to show us around and we decided the only way to get rid of the seething mass of humanity was to actually employ one of them! He quickly disposed of the others. He obviously had a vast knowledge of the Taj and Agra — even though his English was somewhat limited but one got the general gist of things. He pointed out some very small mirrors implanted in the marble in one of the rooms so placed, it is said, so that Mumtaz Mahal would be able to see the memorial built for her husband.

Shahjahan who never thought small, decided he wanted a twin structure to be built in black marble directly across the river from his wife's tomb, to serve as his final resting place. Unfortunately Shahjahan's son and heir, Aurangzeb, who did think small, arrested his father, deposed and imprisoned him in the Fort and ultimately buried him beside his mother in the Taj Mahal.

We were indeed fortunate in that our visit coincided with a full moon and so we also were able to see the Taj by moonlight — an unforgettable sight.

As we were spending two nights at Agra — we also had time to drive to Fatehpur Sikri — which in its own way was equally as breathtaking. This is really a ghost town in the desert and was occupied for only 14 years. It grew out of nothing, but it is said that Akbar came to Fatehpur Sikri to seek out the blessings of a Mystic as he wanted a child. His wife became pregnant and Akbar was so delighted he decided to build a fabulous city overlooking the village.

However it is a trifle confusing to find that at Fatehpur there are three magnificent tombs, one for Akbar's Muslim wife, one for his Hindu wife and one for his Christian wife!

Fourteen years after it was built the whole Court moved to Lahore because political troubles had broken out, but it is thought more likely to have been because the water supply at Sikri had dried up! The City remains in many aspects exactly as it was when Akbar left — slightly dilapidated — but the main structures remain and one can imagine what Court life must have been like in days of its grandeur. I remember there was something resembling a large Draught Board and it is said that Akbar used dancing girls as pawns in this game.

Another interesting building is the Panch Mahal, called because of its five storied structure, each floor with half the pillars of the preceding one and an enormous central pillar from where it is said Akbar sat on his throne and Hindu, Muslim, Buddhist and Christian advisers would toss ideas at him.

I strongly recommend that anyone visiting Agra also finds time to visit this interesting deserted city.

I will never forget my embarrassment at the Red Fort in Delhi when after a morning of sight seeing I really felt I had to visit the ladies room. I fortunately knew the word for bathroom was gussal-khana so I tentatively asked our guide "Kidda Gussal-Khana" meaning "where is the bathroom". He then beckoned me to follow him — which I did and we wandered into the desert — but no sign of any Toilets. Imagine my surprise when he suddenly pointed to the ground and said "you make piss here"! Whereupon he squatted down on his haunches — obviously ready to wait for this event! He couldn't understand why I no longer needed the "Gussal-Khana!

I don't think anyone can possibly do justice when trying to describe all these interesting Palaces and Monuments, that abound in and around Delhi, but as they made such an impression on me I felt I had to mention them.

We returned to Bombay after this fabulous trip and were so excited at the thought of seeing the girls.   A little of my enthusiasm was dulled when I discovered that these "cute white mice with pink eyes" were in fact large white RATS.   I confess they seemed to be reasonably tame and would stand on their back legs pawing the air with their front legs!   They were also obviously pregnant!   So instead of two dear little creatures of about 2" we first of all had 2 LARGE creatures about 8" — and within two days they both produced within hours of each other, litters of 5 and 4 babies!   Linda confessed ignorance that she had particularly chosen "pregnant" mice/rats!   Any mention of drowning the babies brought tears — so — we had 11 rats growing larger daily.   We had to go out and buy more bird cages to keep them in — and when I suggested that perhaps we should give some of these "pets" away — that also met with cries of how unkind I was even thinking of such a thing.

However, things came to a head — when I came home one day to find my beautiful imported curtains were in holes as the rats had been placed too near the window and had managed to pull the curtain into the cage and had chewed horizontal holes for the height of the bird cage!   I was far from amused and Linda's explanation that "they didn't mean it" didn't help in the slightest!

In bed that night I was going over the day's happenings as I often did, when I suddenly realised that if I cut a 9" strip off the side of the curtain — no one would be the wiser — and the curtains could still be used.   The next morning I took the curtain down to the Tailor and carefully explained the situation asking him to cut off 9" from the side of the curtain.   He shook his head — which I now knew meant YES (and not NO) and said "Aitcha" which also meant "yes".

He told me to come back at 5.p.m.! Can you imagine how I felt when I found that he had cut 9" off the bottom — carefully leaving the holes down the side of the curtain! Now, they were really ruined!

I felt these animals had to go, but as Linda would be leaving for Boarding School shortly, decided we would wait until we left on leave — and arrange with the Bearer to take them to have them put to sleep! I subsequently learnt to my horror, that when we finally left, the Bearer had become so attached to these animals that he could not bear to take them to the vet to have them put to sleep, so he and the Hamal had taken them in their bird cages to the largest rubbish dump which was attached to one of the first class Hotels and, I admit, the dump was crawling with brown rats as all rubbish dumps were, and he released them and brought the bird cages back!

Fiona had started Nursery School when she was 3, and went to the Breach Kandy Kindergarten school which was at the bottom of our road. Alice the Ayah used to take her down in the morning with her little school bag containing a drink and some biscuits — but, even at that age, she had an amazing aplomb, and one got the impression that her little suitcase contained nothing less than the Budget Papers!

Linda went to Walsingham House School in Bombay; it was near the sea front and the driver dropped her at school and picked her up after school. In her last year it became very obvious that plans would have to be made for Boarding School. Most of her contemporaries had already left for schooling in England and she wasn't making the progress she had done previously. We had been most anxious that Linda would not have her nose put out with the arrival of the new baby — and so kept her with us in Bombay for the extra year. We hoped having another year with the family would give her time to get to know her sister, and that she wouldn't feel she was being sent away to school because we had Fiona!

Neither of us had been very keen on the idea of boarding school — but there was no alternative in Bombay at that time, also we felt that for children brought up overseas, it was essential that they experienced what life was like in the U.K., and there was no doubt that the students from the U.K. schools were noticeably more self assured, worldly wise and appreciative than children brought up in the East.

We wrote to Gabbitas Thring and other school Consultants asking for their advice, and then spent hours pouring over the Prospectuses they sent. As we were shortly due for leave, we decided to make the final decision when we had the opportunity of viewing the schools for ourselves.

Various friends of ours had children at Ashford School in Kent and they appeared to love it and we felt assured when we met the Headmistress who seemed kind and understanding. Unfortunately Linda never really settled at Boarding school which we found very distressing.

In July, 1958, we were due for leave and sailed home together on the Chusan, and as with all our sea trips we thoroughly enjoyed the camaraderie which existed amongst all the passengers, and the excitement that prevailed — knowing that the Leave they had waited 2 — 3 years for, finally had arrived. There always seemed to be a "party" mood on board.

Not being quite as large a ship as some, — the crew had the time to be most attentive and Linda I know thoroughly enjoyed this trip — she was even allowed to go on the Bridge — and horror of horrors held the wheel for a time (under strict supervision I might add). She was allowed to participate in the evening entertainments up to 10.p.m. — when the cinema shows usually finished. There seemed to be so many facilities for children that we felt we hardly saw her so I think I can say, without fear of contradiction, that Linda enjoyed the trip as much as we did. We stopped off in Aden — Port Said and Marseilles and arrived at Dover early in the morning.

The last night on board a crowd of us were sitting in the Bar chatting after the evening entertainment, when the Bar Steward asked if any of us would buy 20 Balkan Sobrani cigarettes — as he only had 80 and it wasn't worth having to record these on the list he had to prepare for Customs.. Although I have never smoked — I agreed with the other three passengers that we would take 20 each — to help him out. As you all probably know they are multi coloured cocktail cigarettes and LOOK very attractive.

I thought I could use them on our dining table for dinner parties where it was custom to provide cigarettes and matches for one's guests. A custom I did not agree with, but one wanted one's guests to feel free to smoke with their coffee.

When we came to Customs and were asked the usual question about what we had to declare — Ken declared his usual cigarettes and whisky and when asked, I happily declared my 20 Balkan Sobrani — which Ken knew nothing about! The customs officer then asked if this was part of our allowance — and I foolishly said yes. He then asked Ken to unpack the valise containing the other 380 cigarettes, but of course — there were 400 cigarettes and these 20 Sobrani's were over and above our ration! So.....once again I was in trouble with customs and they made us unpack EVERY suitcase whilst the boat train was waiting! They didn't summon me on this occasion but I did get a severe reprimand from the Customs Officer and an even bigger one from Ken who never did anything questionable!

We went up to Yorkshire to stay with my Mother who had stopped working once she was eligible for a pension and so was delighted to have our company. I felt she was beginning to show signs of her age and had been neglecting herself and the bungalow, which was badly in need of re-decorating which we did over a period of weeks.

It turned out to be a busy leave as one morning, when making Mother's bed, I noticed that one of the legs on her bed had penetrated the carpet — and on investigation discovered that the floor board under the carpet appeared to be wearing away. I was frightened that the whole leg would at some stage disappear, so we called in the friendly carpenter — showed him the problem and asked him to replace the plank of wood that was affected. As my mother hated having the inconvenience of workmen in we arranged to have this done one day when we had made plans to take her off to Scarborough for the day. We left the key with the carpenter and departed about 8.a.m. fully expecting on our return that the offending floor board would have been replaced — the carpet put back in place and my Mother would be none the wiser. She would have been embarrassed at our paying for this work, so decided that there really was no reason for her to know anything about it!

Imagine the shock we had when we returned about 6.p.m. to find about 5 workmen working feverishly UNDER the floor area and all the floorboards from the Kitchen, Hall, Lounge and Bedroom had been removed! Little hope of keeping this a secret and my Mother was quite horrified (as we were)!

Mr. Kirk the Carpenter explained most apologetically, that when he removed the offending plank, he discovered the problem was the dreaded Dry Rot and he found he had to keep removing more and more of the floor boards, which eventually extended down the Hall, into the Kitchen. Then he discovered that not only the floor boards but the heavy joists that supported the floor boards appeared to be affected. What a blow — but obviously there was no going back, and if not dealt with the problem would only have got worse. So the workmen left and promised to return the next morning.

Before they left they erected planks from the Kitchen to the Lounge — the one worry was that Mother might slip or over balance so we had to accompany her whenever she wandered down the Hall to the bathroom!

This whole venture was a disaster as one thing led to another.

In removing the joists, the electric wiring had to be removed and this was found to be worn and dangerous and needed replacing. An electrician was therefore called in to replace the worn wiring before the carpenters could finish their work. However, worse was to come, whilst the carpenters were working in the kitchen and were trying to replace the gas cooker that had to be removed, they discovered that there was a leak in the gas pipes which was not safe

— so they too had to be replaced!

The chaos for the next few days can hardly be imagined — the temporary planks that had been installed to enable us to get from the Dining Room to the Bedrooms and Bathroom, were far from secure and had to be lifted each morning to enable the workmen to get under the floor boards. It was a tricky business living under such conditions — but Mother did not want to leave — so we camped out in the turmoil.

I must say that everyone worked very quickly — the gas pipes were replaced where necessary as was the offending electric wiring allowing the carpenters to continue and in three weeks the work was finished — new floorboards throughout and all that appeared to be needed was a complete redecoration. Obviously this was the time to do this as most of the furniture had been removed to the garage — so — when the carpenter moved out — Ken and I started papering and painting and in a couple of weeks the bungalow looked just the way it did the morning we had left for Scarborough — though much fresher!

Financially this was a bitter blow and mother certainly hadn't the money to pay for these repairs, and as we were living in the bungalow obviously we were the ones to do it. The carpenter who had known our family for years was very understanding and we paid his bill off in the remaining three months we were home having acquired an overdraft from the "friendly bank"! Not the sort of leave we had hoped for. I remember there was a popular tune played on the radio at that time called "The Gasman Cometh" — and whenever I heard it I was reminded of the saga of "St. Ivel" (the name of the bungalow).

When we arrived home this time, we finally made a decision about a Boarding School for Linda and booked her into Ashford School in Kent in September 1958. She was 12 — and although most children started boarding school at age 11 we had selfishly kept her with us for another year — which with hindsight we realise was wrong. By the time she entered Ashford — most of her class were already in their second year and had formed friendships and were well settled.

In those days we had 6 months' leave and because we wanted to be near Linda for her Exeats etc., we had answered an advertisement in the well known magazine, "The Lady" offering a cottage near Heathfield for rent. This would be a lot nearer Ashford than if we had remained in Yorkshire.

The owner replied and said the cottage was available and quoted a figure of £78 which we assumed was either per month or perhaps per week and we thought for a winter let it was on the high side, but it sounded delightful and was in the right area. So having spent the first part of our leave at Yeadon we moved down south.

We arranged with the owner, who was a titled Lady, that we would pick her up from the station at Heathfield, and she would take us to the cottage. We both anticipated that this Lady would be elderly and possibly rather dowdy — (don't ask me why we thought this but one forms impressions from conversations I suppose!). Imagine our surprise when a most attractive and very smart lady came through the turnstile — and immediately approached us. This was our titled Lady the owner of the cottage! She was delightful, I really think Ken thought it a pity that his wife and children were with him!

She took us down to the cottage which was "cute" — and we decided to take it for the remainder of our leave and asked if we could settle with her then to save worrying about forgetting the date etc. She agreed and repeated Pounds 78 — which we again had assumed was for the WEEK — but she meant for 12 weeks! How could we resist? My only complaint was that there were mice in the kitchen and I hated going in when it was dark as these little creatures always seemed to run across my feet!

We were kept busy, buying Linda's school uniform, sewing on name tabs and packing her school trunk. The uniform had to be bought from the school shop — which was in Guildford. The clothing list seemed formidable — I still can't understand why she had to have 12 pairs of navy blue knickers and 12 knicker liners! The knicker liners were never worn and were returned in her trunk at the end of the school year in pristine condition!

Will we ever forget the day we had to take her to school — or perhaps I would be more correct in saying the week before she had to go to school? I still can feel the anguish and concern as to whether we were doing the right thing — but of course had to appear confident and happy in front of Linda no matter what we felt in our hearts, as she had her own private worries, which we didn't want to add to.

The headmistress welcomed us as did her House Mistress, and I was a little sad when they asked us not to contact her for a month other than by letter. We had taken our leave so that we could see her fairly regularly whilst she was settling into school and have her out for as many exeats as possible — but I suppose the Headmistress had far more experience about girls settling into school than I had, so hard as it was, we didn't go back to the school for a month.

I don't know who was the more delighted at the reunion when the month finally passed — Linda or us — she brought a friend with her for this weekend who was also from Bombay which helped when it was time to return to school.

Half term was two weeks after this exeat — so it made parting on this occasion a little easier. The same friend came for half-term as of course her parents were in Bombay and she and Linda seemed to get on well together.

The end of term came and we were very excited when we went to pick Linda up from school. Fiona was thrilled to have her sister back in the family albeit for only a few weeks.

We had our first fall of snow shortly after picking her up from school so we had a White Xmas and as neither Linda or Fiona had ever seen snow they were delighted. The cottage was at the bottom of a hill, so we all had a wonderful time tobogganing. They were very excited and didn't seem to feel the cold, though I confess I was frozen after a very short time!

We had friends from Bombay who stayed for about a week as this "small" cottage could actually sleep 9! It was a lovely leave only spoilt by the thought of Linda having to return to boarding school, when the Xmas holiday was over.

From the day we picked Linda up from school she used to count how many days were left before she had to return! I tried to console myself with the thought that there were over 800 other girls at the school and all whom we had met seemed to be happy and enjoyed it. So I felt it was only a matter of time and that the second term would be much better than the first! As usual — I was wrong!

I never cease to be amazed at the attitude of my grandchildren — who literally count the days before they can return to school for entirely different reasons! They just can't wait to get back to school — and whilst assuring their parents (and grandparents) — that they love seeing them — they say it is MUCH more fun at school!

This Xmas holiday passed far too quickly — and the new term started about the 4th January, so once again we set off for school — this time to leave her until the Easter holiday when she would join us in Bombay. I admit that Linda managed to keep cheerful — and we genuinely thought she was reasonably happy at school.

After this leave, the three of us returned to Bombay on the m.v. Himalaya, feeling rather lost without Linda.

Her weekly letters at this time varied from being happy to being blatantly miserable. The girls had sent her to Coventry and she complained she had no friends. She wrote a very sad mixed up letter saying that she had told a terrible lie! She had told some of the girls that the reason she was miserable was that her Mother had banged her head on a Port hole going back to Bombay and had been hospitalised ever since. I think there was an inference to my being "unstable" or "mentally deranged"!

One of the girls, however, had accused her of lying and threatened to write to me to find out if this was true. Linda naturally wanted me to substantiate her statement — which I was prepared to do — but merely to say I had had an accident. I most certainly didn't want them to think the accident had resulted in my being "a Kangaroo short in the top paddock" (a lovely Australian expression I have since learnt!). However, this was not necessary as the girl in question merely wrote to thank me for some "tuck" I had given her — and said she hoped I had got over my accident! I didn't consider a reply was necessary in the circumstances!

I re-joined the High Commission shortly after returning and there was a great deal of excitement in the Office over the preparations for the visit of HRH The Duke of Edinburgh planned for Friday the 30th January, 1959.

The British High Commission staff were all invited to a special enclosure at the Santa Cruz Airport to meet the Royal visitor. He was standing in an open jeep, so we had an excellent view of his arrival being in the front row. He gave the group I was with a special wave which we all thought was directed purely at us!

We had already received an invitation from the Deputy High Commissioner and Mrs. Norris, to attend a Reception at their residence on Malabar Hill on the occasion of the Visit of HRH the Duke of Edinburgh. You can imagine the excitement — as we felt being in the outposts of the Empire we were definitely forgotten.

The dressmakers were bombarded with orders, We were told on an accompanying note with the invitation what to wear i.e. Dinner Jackets for the men and Evening Dress, worn with Gloves for the ladies. I fortunately had a suitable evening dress and had bought gloves whilst on leave for the St. Andrews Ball — so that was not a problem. Prince Philip as always, mingled happily with the guests accompanied by the Deputy High Commissioner and Mrs. Norris. I was thrilled when he asked me how long I'd been in India and what my husband did — he seems to have an ability to really sound interested which must be difficult, and this endeared him to all the Guests.

In those days anything to do with Royalty was, to say the least, a great thrill — and for my part still is! We were all strong Royalists and everyone was overjoyed at the informality of these chats.

Although the Company were not over generous with air fares for either wives or children in those days, by working at the High Commission I was able to bring Linda out for most of the holidays — not of course half terms which did present a problem. So, Linda flew out for the Easter holiday which was wonderful. It was the first time she had travelled alone — and naturally we were very relieved when we saw her step off the plane.

She rejoined her swimming teacher for the lessons which took place twice a week. She told us that they hadn't had any swimming at school in the winter term — but it was starting in the Spring term and I think she was looking forward to this as obviously she would excel.

I continued to enjoy Bombay — it was warm, though we lived very near the sea and so had the benefit of a sea breeze most of the time.

As in Calcutta, I was always appalled at the number of children our servants had. On the salaries we paid them we knew there was no way they could afford that number. I therefore tried to educate them on various birth control methods — but — this at times became a little embarrassing as they often did not appear to understand what I was saying. So on one occasion I rang up the Family Planning Clinic and made an appointment. This in itself was very amusing as they assumed the visit was for me! I did manage to get two of the Ayahs on to the Pill — but once we were posted and they had no income they could not afford to buy any form of contraceptive — so — the breeding program started yet again.

Prostitution in Bombay was restricted (so we were told) to an area which was referred to as "The Cages". One evening a crowd of us returning from a dinner party passed through this area on the way home. It was quite depressing as this particular area appeared to be a series of small cage like rooms with the girls behind the bars. All very sad — and one wonders to-day with AIDS what has happened to them all. Visitors from overseas would always want to see this area, as the squalor and depravity could not be believed.

We were told that the prostitutes would accept an apple in payment for services rendered — which gives one an idea of the depths to which these people were driven.

During the summer holiday we spent a lot of time at the Breach Candy Swimming Pool — I took some leave from the High Commission — and thoroughly enjoyed being with the girls full time again. Linda was not only a terrific little swimmer, but a delightful diver — an unusual combination to excel at both activities. Her bedroom was stacked with all the cups and trophies she had won for diving and swimming at the various Galas she had entered. This must all be attributed to her Swimming teacher, Barbara Rabeneck who encouraged all her pupils to achieve that little "extra". All the girls admired her and she was Mentor to so many.

The fact that in later life Linda made a career for herself through her swimming is proof enough that her lessons were very important. She started her own Swimming School in Singapore, called "Simply Swimming". Young Fiona appeared "inspired" with the successes of her sister and in her own way tried hard to imitate her. She did win the smallest cup imaginable in one of the Galas for one length of back stroke at the age of 5 which thrilled us all. Linda was very proud of her sister!

There was another family of "Campbells" in Bombay at the time with three daughters — all gifted swimmers and frequently the newspaper headlines after a Swimming gala would read "The Campbell sisters did it again". The press were convinced that as they had the same surname, they must be of the same family!

Whilst in Bombay there was one incident that caused everyone a lot of anguish.

Apparently a pariah dog (an unlicensed stray — often quite wild) had got into the surrounds of the Breach Candy Swimming Pool and one of the Chowkidars, along with his friends, had chased the animal round the pool trying to scare it into leaving the premises. He had a long stick and kept hitting the poor animal when he could reach it. The few Europeans who were present at the time tried to interfere and stop this brutal behaviour, but the Chowkidars were like men possessed and they were determined to eliminate the dog one way or another.

Eventually the dog, which did look deranged, fell into the pool and was swimming around for some time before a gang of helpers were able to catch it and it was sent to the local Government Vetinerary Department, whose practice it was to keep the animal for 10 days to see if it developed Rabies. Everyone's mind was obviously on Rabies, and we were all waiting for the ten days to pass when hopefully the dog would not have died.

That particular day, we had not attended the Pool in the morning, when this incident had taken place, so it was after we had been swimming in the afternoon that the story of the Pariah dog was related. Everyone felt that whilst the dog had looked distressed, in similar circumstances anyone of us would have been equally distressed!

One of the British Naval ships was in port at the time and as the sailors were given temporary membership of Breach Candy — it transpired that over 200 sailors and overseas visitors had actually been swimming in the Pool that particular day.

The following day Linda returned to school — we had a very tearful goodbye at the Airport — but we felt relieved that her friend Karen who had stayed with us in England and was from the same school, was on the same plane. Once they were air borne — and were given a meal and the usual hand-out of games, they would soon recover. I can't say that applied to me — I wept all the way back from the airport and thought what a stupid life we were living. I never accepted these separations very happily and yet had to put on a brave face for the sake of the children.

I realised the alternative would be to return home and Ken would have to take a job that he hated — as having acquired such seniority so early on, which entailed making Company decisions involving literally hundreds if not thousands of pounds — it would be difficult to return to a system where one had to fill in a requisition form for a new pencil!   In later life both daughters admitted that they were glad that Daddy had not returned home — as they had a more exciting and interesting life than they would have if we had returned to the U.K.

Two days after Linda and Karen had left for the U.K. — we heard that the dog had died!   You can imagine everyone's anguish as it would be a couple of days before the Pathological Department, to whom the dog's brain had been sent for examination, would have any result — but — it didn't look good.

Then the blow came — the dog did have Rabies and chaos reigned.

The Health authorities advised that everyone that had been swimming in the pool that day — or subsequent days, should report to their Dr.'s who in turn would recommend having the course of rather painful injections in one's stomach, which could not guarantee immunity — but — would certainly help.

A few months earlier, a European in Bombay, had contracted Rabies from a rabid monkey — and had died the most horrific death — for which there had been no treatment and no relief from the symptoms.   This was in everyone's mind and the Dr.'s surgeries were full of patients requesting the preventative injections — which consisted of 28 jabs in the stomach.

We realised that we had to get in touch with the school — so I put a phone call through to the Headmistress.   It was a terrible line — the old fashioned type where if one party is speaking the other appears to be cut off — and then you both speak together so nobody hears!

I started the conversation by saying that Linda and Karen could have contracted Rabies — and at this juncture I was interrupted by the Headmistress screaming down the phone "Linda and Karen are going to have babies!?".   "No" I screamed back — "they have been in contact with Rabies" — and again I was interrupted by "they have been in contact and are going to have a baby"!

Eventually, she kept quiet long enough for me to explain the situation and I said that it was essential that the girls started a course of treatment which would be given at the Tropical School of Medicine in London. This was a 2 hour journey from the school, but she said they would make arrangements with the Hospital and the girls would start their treatment the following day.

Linda, who had, and still has, a phobia about injections, was completely shattered at the thought of having all these injections in her tummy. We decided that I had better fly home, if I could get a flight as this was obviously going to be a traumatic experience. Before I could make any plans however, the World Health Organisation announced that these injections were only necessary if a person had been in contact with the dog or it's saliva. The virus diluted in Chlorine, could not affect anyone, and therefore it was unnecessary to have the injections. There was much rejoicing as you can imagine!

In the meantime contact had been made with all people who had been in the pool that day — this included the British Navy whose ship had already sailed — and arrangements were to be made to have the vaccine flown out to them — and all the business visitors who had been in Bombay for a couple of days and had used the pool, along with the numerous school children from schools all over the place who had returned after their holidays, all had been contacted and told to approach the W.H.O. A marathon task in which everyone became involved one way or another.

I don't think there were any real tragedies as a result of this incident, but it certainly gave everyone hours of anxiety.

We were joined at the High Commission in Bombay where I was working — by a very sweet 17 year old — a good worker and a delight to have around. One day she was looking rather glum and on enquiry she told me that her Father who was a Sea Captain on a Cargo Ship, had sailed with her Mother. The Company permitted a wife to accompany her husband on one trip per year. Obviously they always chose the longest sea trips to compensate for all the months they spent apart.

Sue, had expected her Mother back within 8 weeks, but the ship was delayed and the Bombay landlord had given them notice about a month previously. Sue was not overly worried about this as she expected her parents back — but it appeared the Landlord had been to see her and told her she had to vacate the flat on schedule. Obviously she was worried. I tried to console her and told her that if the worst came to the worst she could come and stay with us.

The following morning she told me that "the worst had come to the worst" and the Landlord insisted she vacate the premises — so she arranged to have their personal items stored by B.I. (British Indian Navigation Company) for whom her father was employed and so I told her she was most welcome to come and stay with us until their return which she really thought would be in a few days. As it transpired, her parents were delayed yet again as the ship had to pick up more cargo and so this "weekend" finally extended to three months!

I have to say that Sue was the most delightful guest one could ever have and we thoroughly enjoyed having her to stay. It was like having another daughter, and to this day I look upon her as such! I don't know if our enthusiasm was reciprocated as I distinctly remember her anguish at coming home at night to find Fiona's pet Hamster running around the bathroom!

The pet shop had told Fiona that Hamsters needed a lot of exercise, and although we had bought it an exercise wheel, it squeaked so much that it kept everyone awake, so we decided when the girls had finished in the bathroom at night that the Hamster could have its run. Sue, who often came home late after a dinner date, found this a bit off putting, as when she went into the bath room, the Hamster would run over her feet — and although on contemplation she realised what it was — initially she thought it could have been a rat!

I continued to work in the High Commission which I enjoyed. I was promoted from the Passport and Nationality Division to the Visa Section. This brought me into contact with a completely different type of person — all foreigners who were wanting to travel to the U.K. or to one of our then Colonies or Protectorates.

Previously I had only dealt with British Nationals — or Nationals trying to prove they were British through one of the many clauses in the British Nationality Act. In some of these cases one had to show a lot of tact and understanding as people can get very upset when one has to probe into their background. So many of us have skeletons in the cupboard and I suppose it is natural to resent having them resurrected. So in many ways it was a relief when I found I would no longer have to ask these impertinent questions.

However, this new appointment was not free of embarrassing moments. Registration of Births, Deaths and Marriages had not been compulsory in India and therefore it was difficult for anyone who had been born in India or whose parents had been born in India, to produce the necessary documents required for the issue of a British Subject Passport, quite different to the "British Subject, Citizen of the U.K. and Colonies" endorsement that appeared on the Passports of people born in the U.K., or who had derived their Citizenship by Descent or Naturalisation.

Therefore many of the Indians who were working in The Gulf travelled on "Certificates of Identity". These were quarto sized sheets of paper with the applicant's photo, thumb print and name and the name of their father. They also had the High Commission Seal. These were issued for a return journey.

When these workers from The Gulf came back to India on leave they were anxious to obtain a bride to travel back with them. As a result we would get applications for the new wife to be included on the Certificate of Identity for travel to the Gulf. Before we could do this we had to see some evidence of marriage — and this usually took the form of a Certificate from the local Imam or Mullah, saying that a marriage ceremony had taken place and it contained the names of the two people concerned.

The Dowry system was still quite prevalent among the less educated, and these Certificates would indicate what form the Dowry had taken. It was quite usual to see that the groom had received a Dowry of two or three thousand rupees, but more often than not, the

Dowry would show that the groom or groom's family had received 5 cows, 6 goats and 36 hens or he may have received so many hectares of paddy field. The less acceptable the bride was, the larger the Dowry had to be. In some instances you would see that the bride's parents had paid the Dowry in gold ornaments, chains, ear rings, bangles, nose ornaments etc. If the bride was lucky some of these items of jewellery would be given back to her by the husband, as it was also customary for the groom or his family to give some form of gold to the bride.

There were daily queues of these people waiting to get into the High Commission and I found them all very interesting and amusing, but also at times exhausting!

Each application had to be accompanied by a photograph of the bride, but then so many of the ladies were in strict Purdah and they would produce a photo which for all the world looked like a bell tent! It was often very difficult to establish that a marriage had actually taken place to the particular lady mentioned on the certificate. As the Muslim religion permitted each male to have four wives, we had to be particularly careful that the person applying to have his wife included on the document, hadn't already taken a wife.

If they were travelling on a Travel Document issued by the British authorities, they had to abide by the same regulations that appertained to British Nationals and therefore they were only permitted ONE wife and not four as the Muslim Religion allowed. You can imagine this took a lot of explaining as few of them had a good command of English and the documents had to be carefully checked.

I remember one particular instance when an applicant produced a marriage document and a Purdah photograph to have Nur Bint Frizal Aziz included on his travel document. I noticed that the previous year I had already added a wife, Fatima Bint Ahmad Jalawi. I questioned him about this and pointed out that whilst the Muslim religion may permit four wives, while he was travelling on a British Certificate of Identity — he was only permitted one. He got very excited about this and started shouting and explaining in great detail to my utter embarrassment that the wife he had included last year was a complete failure and he had only received 2 goats, 2 buffaloes and 1 cow as a Dowry but when he got this lady into bed he found she only had one tit!

Trying to explain that this was hardly cause for him to be allowed another wife on his travel document — he again got very heated and told me that this present wife, for whom he had received 20 chickens, 30 goats and 7 bags of rice — had BOTH tits as he had checked before marrying her!

The more I explained that we could not permit this wife to be included on his travel document the more excited he got and I swear the whole office and all the people in the queue were well aware that this lady had a full complement! The Visa officer finally came to my rescue before more intimate details were disclosed.

The reasons for wanting to take a second, third, or fourth wife were very varied — either they could not produce children — or produce male children — or they were frigid and no good in bed — or he just didn't like her any more! But we were equally insistent that we would only include ONE wife on their Certificate of Identity and if they already had had one included, there was no way we would waive our regulations.

Doubtless, knowing the mentality of the people — they would manage to get the new wife to the Gulf by some other means — but they usually tried the legitimate method first — which was much cheaper than having to bribe officials.

After we had been in Bombay four years Ken was asked to go to Karachi for a short visit as the Manager there was ill. Ken was quite shocked when he saw Dermot who had come out to Calcutta with another Irish boy and joined the staff there, but had subsequently been transferred to Karachi.

It was customary, and a courtesy, that newcomers on arrival at their new post would go to the British High Commission or Embassy, and register. This kept the High Commission advised of the U.K.

residents for whom they would be responsible in a time of emergency, which was very essential. Ken was amused when Dermot first arrived in Calcutta as he had travelled on an Irish Passport. It was felt however that he should apply for U.K. Citizenship and register at the British High Commission in case there was an emergency during his time in India. He therefore had to sign the necessary papers disclaiming Irish Citizenship, before being issued with a U.K. Passport with the status of "British Subject". After collecting his new Passport he looked very concerned and said to Ken in a broad Irish accent "and to think my father fought in the Rebellion — if he ever finds out I will be in trouble!"

It appeared that poor Dermot found working conditions in Karachi too demanding — and so Ken went up there to try to sort things out. He returned after the month but Dermot unfortunately did not improve and so he was repatriated and Ken was then asked if he would go to Karachi permanently as Manager for Pakistan.

So, it wasn't long before we were on the move again — Bombay had been one of our shortest tours. Ken flew up to Karachi in August, 1959, taking Sherry the cross Cairn/Dachshund we had "acquired" with him. Fortunately there was no quarantine in Pakistan, and it was cheaper and easier from the paper work point of view for the dog to fly than for it to come with us by boat.

I had the packers in — and they did an excellent job — our household possessions were collected by Cox and Kings and despatched as freight on m.v. Cilicia. Fiona and I had bookings on the Cilicia and we sailed for Karachi on the 14th August, 1959. We stayed in The Palace Hotel for the first few days before moving into the Company flat.

We were quite sad to leave Bombay and to say goodbye to India, as we had enjoyed our time there and acquired a lot of new friends. I confess though when we returned to Bombay many years later by boat and during a two day stop over went to visit our old flat we did wonder why we had enjoyed it so much! The flat had deteriorated over the years and from being a very pleasant home it was now a chawl (a slum) which was all very sad.

# FIVE
## *Generalisation on India*

There are so many languages and dialects in India that even Indians speak English among themselves.

It is of course important to learn to count in lakhs (100,000) and crores (10 million) as these are used instead of the English counterpart. English has developed some peculiarities in India, and you will hear some unusual grammar and pronunciations. It is often difficult to tell the difference between thirteen and thirty or fourteen and forty as Indians often say one but mean the other! To avoid confusion therefore they often say one-four or four zero — which is much safer!

In the eyes of the simple Indians all western tourists are rich, have sex with numerous partners and drink enormous amounts of alcohol, except for the hippies who often come down from Nepal and are always "stoned". They have a great respect though for the British in business — and the lack of corruption in any business dealings. I think it is correct to say that after Partition in 1947 many of them were very sad at losing their mentors.

The Indians we met in the streets were all very polite and eager to help — but they don't like to admit that they don't know something and therefore will tell you anything rather than admit ignorance. Asking directions when travelling can therefore be hazardous — and one should always ask at least three people in the hope that at least two of their replies will agree — even then — you can't depend on their being right — and their additional assurance that "it's only five or ten minutes away" or "very near" should not always be taken seriously!    But always their reply would be accompanied by a delightful smile!

One needs a lot of patience when dealing with Indian Government Offices as they will send you from window to window to window — or even building to building and you can wait for hours — so we had to give ourselves a lot of time.    I suppose that is why we used the office staff to undertake things that would appear to be our responsibility, and after we retired and had to do these things for ourselves, it was a terrible shock!

This applies to all of the sub-continent by the way — not just India!

The beggar situation in India is very sad but one must not get carried away as the reason there are so many beggars is that it obviously provides a reasonably well paid income.    Some are more aggressive that others, they can be crippled, lepers, often blind and some appear to have nothing physically wrong with them, but they are all well organised and know their job.    A woman who approaches you with a baby in her arms saying she needs money to feed the baby will pass the baby on to another woman in her clique when she feels she has earned sufficient for her daily needs.

In India, alms replace in part, the social security systems in other countries.

However, don't be misled by these few examples — the poverty in India is real.

When I first arrived there seemed to be so much to learn;  one had to be careful about your choice of clothes, men can possibly get away with wearing shorts, but women shouldn't wear them.    Ladies are advised not to wear sleeveless or see-through shirts — which to us seems very hard in the temperatures you have to cope with.    I was told that as a lady I should remember I was way down the caste list, so shouldn't enter any Hindu kitchens and never offer food with your left hand because it is considered unclean.    That is the hand they use to wash themselves after visiting the toilet!    Shoes are considered particularly unclean both to Muslims and Hindus and should be taken off when entering their homes or when visiting Temples and Mosques.

In short — when living in a foreign country respect their religions and traditions even if you find them hard to accept or you can't understand or appreciate them.

# SIX
## Karachi
### *September 1960—November 1969*

As explained earlier, a few months after returning to Bombay from our 1959 leave, Ken was asked to go to Karachi where the present Manager had suffered a nervous breakdown, and subsequently had to return to the U.K.

Ken was to take over the Karachi office as Manager for Pakistan, and whilst he flew up with Sherry the dog, I was left in Bombay to supervise the packing and arrange the shipment of our household goods in about 3 weeks time.

Fiona and I sailed to Karachi, on the Cilicia with all our goods and chattels.

I was sad to leave Bombay — but then I was always sad to leave any posting no matter how many doubts I may have had about it initially.

Prior to moving to Pakistan we had been given a pamphlet called "Guide to Living in Pakistan" which we took as a joke though in hindsight I think it was perhaps serious!

The advice on our driving was — DON'T. However if we found it necessary we were told to remember that:—

1. The larger vehicle has the right of way.
2. A Police vehicle also has right of way.
3. Any vehicle with a Flag has right of way.
4. A speeding vehicle with horn screaming and lights flashing has right of way.
5. Cows have right of way!

Parking.
1. Parking on most main roads is prohibited except for:—
   Government vehicles.
   Vehicles too large to be towed away by the lifter.
   Mercedes cars of a recent model were exempt from parking prohibitions.

Pedestrian Rules.
   Look BOTH ways when crossing a one way street!
   Cross a street wherever you like!
   Zebra crossings denote an area reserved for beggars who will make the area "homely".
   A footpath is meant for setting up shops, sitting, sleeping, taking drugs, urinating and similar pursuits.
   For walking — use the road!

Getting things done.
   This is impossible.  Forget it.

I hope when we were given this pamphlet — it was supposed to be funny — BUT quite a lot of it was correct!

We moved into the Company flat at Husain De Silva Park in Clifton — near the beach — one of a pleasant block of flats chiefly occupied by Europeans.    Again we had to go through the whole business of acquiring and adjusting to new servants.    Having seen the condition of the flat we were to occupy we felt that the previous Bearer had not really cared for it as one would expect.    Perhaps he had taken advantage of the Manager's illness — but — all things considered we decided to employ our own.

We took on a Christian Bearer called Anthony — and a Muslim Cook called Ahmed — amongst the other normal contingent.    It took a long time to decide on an Ayah (a Nanny) — she was the most important member of the family as far as I was concerned — and besides providing references — which we knew could be faked or borrowed — we had to convince ourselves that her reasons for leaving her last employment were legitimate.

This all took time — phone calls to the people who had provided references to see if they were genuine and applied to the person we were contemplating employing.  Then there were police check-ups and after our previous experience in Calcutta — a full medical to ensure that she was free from infectious disease — VD or skin troubles.  Theresa was the third Ayah we had investigated and all her references were genuine and she passed her medical.

It was essential that the Cook also had a stringent medical and was not a "carrier" of any of the Dysenteries — or the Hepatitis virus.

Theresa had three children living with her Mother — her husband was working up The Gulf and only got leave every three years — and so her children were aged 1,4 and 7!  I mentally made a note to ensure that I persuaded her to go on the pill before her husband's next leave!  She was very small — very wiry and an excellent worker, and she very soon became part of our family and to this day we still keep in touch.

The Cook was another problem — he just could not cook and the excellent references he had produced from American families were explained when he asked for a supply of tinned goods!  When I explained that we rarely bought tinned goods and lived on fresh vegetables, fruit and meat, fish and chicken — he became quite surly.  The meal he produced after this was quite inedible.  The vegetables had been cooked for about an hour — the meat was so tough — and his idea of a sweet was pineapple and custard!

When I interviewed him he gave me a resume of the meals he could "cook".  They all sounded good — but I didn't realise they were all out of tins or cartons from the U.S. Commissary. So he had to go.

I then took on a Madrassi who was a good cook — but his cook's book (accounts), were quite ridiculous and I was being charged about 4 times the cost of the items in the bazaar.  Even when I tackled him about this — he insisted that he was charging me the correct prices.  At the end of the month when I did my own accounting —

and I realised just how much he had made that month out of the cook's money.   He was also given the order of the boot.

Then — I heard that the Burra Sahib (Manager) of Shell had been transferred and that his Cook would be available.   I knew that Shell did a lot of official entertaining — and had in fact been for dinner at their very lovely home — and had the most magnificent meal.   So....... when they left Karachi — her Cook came to work for us.

At last I was able to catch up on all our entertaining — and without doubt, the meals this cook produced would leave a Cordon Bleu cook gasping with admiration.   Not only did the meals taste delightful — but they were presented with every original connotation you can think of.   His desserts were often produced on a thick bed of ice into which he had embedded small bulbs and batteries — so that when the bearer turned off the lighting and walked in with this "masterpiece" the red, blue or green lights certainly enhanced the sweet, although in point of fact — it was so delicious it required no enhancing.   Many of his sweets were smothered in spun sugar which was finer than hair and the lights seemed to bring out a golden hue on the spun sugar.

Enough of this — you will gather he was an excellent cook and we were all delighted as Ken had to do quite a lot of official entertaining — and this relieved me of many headaches.

However, he must have been with us about 3 months when I went into the kitchen one morning, rather earlier than usual — and to my utter horror found this wonderful cook squatting on the draining board and urinating into the sink!   I was mortified when I realised that this was the same sink he washed all the vegetables and fruit in — AND — that he probably had been doing this for some time! Obviously I walked out very smartly but asked him to come and see me in the dining room.

When I questioned him about this rather "odd" behaviour — he seemed quite indignant that I should mention it.   He pointed out that as we lived in a 5th floor flat and the servants' communal toilet was on the ground floor with no lift — he couldn't spare the time to keep going up and down stairs. He said he was an old man and therefore his bladder required frequent emptying. I should add that he was aged 50 — though he did look 60!

So — really felt I could not cope with his rather odd habits and in spite of his being such an excellent cook — he had to go.

Perhaps I was too fussy — as we never got anyone in the same class cooking wise — but — I would never be able to trust him to change his habits.

Linda came out for her summer holiday and was friendly with the two girls who lived above us in the same block of flats. Besides the two daughters they had a son and they were all at boarding schools in the U.K. Like ourselves, they could not afford to bring the children out for every holiday, therefore their son had gone to spend one of the holidays with a school friend.

On the day he was returning to school his young friend wanted to show off his father's gun and in fooling about pointed the gun at his friend and apparently pulled the trigger and our friend's son dropped down dead! You can imagine the feelings of both sets of parents who were distraught — but it brought home to everyone the stupidity of (a) having guns in a home and (b) leaving them loaded. The family left Karachi shortly after this incident.

About this time there had been a merger in the Company and Ken was now the Manager of these two merged companies and we had to move to a new flat. This was a large flat in a block of 4 — with a pleasant communal garden and all the residents were employed in one of the Insurance companies in Karachi.

The flat was in Clifton very close to where Zulfiqar Ali Bhutto, the future President of Pakistan lived, when in Karachi. There were occasional demonstrations outside his house and on one occasion we found a bullet hole in our bathroom window which we assumed had been mis-directed! After this I felt that visiting the bathroom was not without its hazards.

Fiona had started at the British Overseas School known as the

B.O.S. and the premises were practically next door to us.   She seemed to do quite well — as they had European teachers — though the actual school building was really just a 5 bedroomed house.

There was a very large flat roof on this block of flats and when we had electrical problems in our bathroom it meant that workmen had to come onto the roof and dig up part of it in order to get to the electric cable.   We suggested when they re-cemented this large hole they had made, that they smoothe it off making a square which looked less unsightly!   When this was finished — it looked just like a miniature dance floor.   We found some sealer which gave it a very smooth finish and as a result were able to use this for dancing. We had many parties on the roof with music relayed from our Lounge below.   There were a couple of occasions we hired a three piece band and had a most enjoyable evening.   The inconvenience we had suffered through the electric fault we decided was well worth it!

We spent most of our evenings on the roof where the evening breezes made it so much cooler than in the flat, and most of our entertaining was done there.   I made the discovery whilst sitting on the roof one evening with my portable radio that if I extended the antenna and let it rest on the wire washing line we could actually receive overseas news.   This came in very useful when India and Pakistan went to war in 1966 as we heard very little local news but were now able to hear from the overseas news what was actually happening in Pakistan!

The odd bomb had been dropped and on one occasion we had some friends up for a B.B.Q. and then turned on the radio to listen to the news and were shattered to hear "Parachutists had just landed at Bath Island".   This was not an Island but part of the mainland and was less than 2 miles away.   We were actually looking over that area and couldn't understand why we hadn't noticed any aircraft. Our guests, some of whom lived in Bath Island thought they had better leave and Ken went down to the car park to see them off.

I stayed on the roof tidying up, collecting the glasses and put the washing line away!   I suddenly heard a clomp, clomp, clomp of heavy footsteps climbing the stairs!   I immediately thought it was the Indian Parachutists and so hid under the table cloth which had held the Buffet.   I felt quite scared — but had to laugh when I saw the old Chowkidar (watchman) doing his nightly inspection.   He was a formidable apparition — a very muscular Patan with a large flamboyant turban and heavily embroidered waistcoat, over his rather "off white" Dhoti — and when he saw me under the table — think he too was slightly alarmed.   I tried to explain what I had heard on the radio — but had to be careful what I said or I might be regarded as a Spy listening to what appeared to be forbidden radio stations.

I returned to work at the British High Commission — as this helped with the air fares to bring Linda out for her holidays.

This latest promotion for Ken was not without its traumas. Unions were very active in Pakistan — and one heard all sorts of stories when the Unions had more or less held the Managers to ransom in order to get their demands met.   On the whole, Ken was lucky — but there was a time when he always left for the office with a bottle of water, a box of sandwiches and an empty container!   This was because the Unions would for no apparent reason decide to "ghurow" the Managers in an attempt to get them to meet their demands.   This meant that the whole staff would troop into the Manager's office and squatting on the floor would surround his desk and not permit him to move.   If he decided to call their bluff and did stand up and attempt to move out of the office, they would say that he had attacked them as it was impossible to move without touching them!   Most Managers therefore went along to the office well prepared with food and drink and a container in case they were "caught short" as they would not be permitted to even go to the toilet!

Another infuriating habit during the "ghurow" was that five times a day there would be a call to prayers when the whole staff would stop work — kneel down and pray!   The prayers could take as long as 20 minutes — so not much work was done.

On the whole Ken's Union was quite amenable and, other than having this stoppage of work by the "call to prayers", they did not take any personal action and on one occasion, when Ken was coming into the office after lunch, the whole staff had decided to stop work and were walking down the stairs as he was walking up!    Even though they were breaking all the office rules, the heads of the Union each shook Ken's hand as they passed on the stairs.

Finally an Agreement was reached by a compromise on both sides and things returned to normal.    Other offices were not so lucky.

After the departure of the excellent Cook — we must have tried at least 6 other cooks — but each in turn proved very unsatisfactory — or perhaps we had been spoilt — but none lasted very long.

However with the move, resulting from the merger, we were able to take on the resident Cook who was good so again I felt relieved. We were warned however that there was one problem — he enjoyed a drink! — but usually this was after his hours of duty when he could be heard singing in the servants' quarters.

After one particular dinner party — I decided that we would never serve any sweets (desserts) that contained liquor!

On this occasion we had 12 guests for dinner — drinks were served and I went into the kitchen about 9.p.m. to tell the Cook that we would have dinner in 10 minutes.    Imagine my horror when I found him lying on the floor with the empty bottle of Rum at his side — with not a potato peeled, a vegetable prepared and the sirloin of beef still in the fridge with no sign of anything to eat!    We were to have had rum baba's which he did so well and foolishly when he asked for the rum I did not measure it out as I should have done but gave him the bottle!

Apparently the Bearer had been trying to tell me that all was not well in the kitchen — but I had misread his gestures and thought he was telling me that dinner was ready!

The cooking facilities were primitive in the extreme and with the best will in the world there was nothing I could produce at this hour

— so Ken ended up taking everyone to the Club for dinner!

I was loath to get rid of the cook as I had already been through about 14 — and realised that good cooks were hard to find. Also once it became known that you were changing your servants at frequent intervals — you would be "black balled" and could end up with no one. But obviously in future I would have to pay more visits to the kitchen during the evening to see that all was well and the dinner was on the way — and — if liquor had to be added — I would stand and watch it go into the dish and not into the Cook.

We had been told that the "Burra Khana" (an important dinner) brought out the best in both Pakistani and Indian servants, and that unexpected guests were always catered for, even though the soup may have been a little thinner! Assuming that the Cook remained sober of course!

However we had a rather hilarious occasion when the Cook really excelled.

We had become quite friendly with the No.1. of one of Ken's important business clients and I had invited them in for a casual dinner to look at snaps of Bombay where they thought they were to be posted. I stressed that it was a "casual" invitation over the phone — no printed invitation as was usual, and they were to come in after attending a Cocktail party.

Because it was such a casual invitation I had not entered it in my diary.

This particular evening Ken and I ordered dinner early completely forgetting that we were to have visitors. We had the usual three course meal and whilst sitting at the dining table the door bell went and the Bearer appeared announcing the arrival of these friends! They were in Cocktail attire and I hadn't even changed for dinner! He showed them into the Lounge and immediately I realised what had happened, but did not want to be "caught out".

Having greeted them, I excused myself and disappeared into the kitchen and asked the Cook if he could produce dinner for 4 in half an hour. We had one of these typical confused conversations when he said "But Sahib and Memsahib have HAD dinner" — I told him I knew but that we required another dinner as two guests had arrived. He then said "I just make dinner for two then" NO said I — dinner for 4. He disappeared into the store room rubbing his head.

As you can imagine I was very nervous about what would be produced, but this is where the servants really excelled. After just over half an hour, the Bearer announced that "Dinner is ready Memsahib" and we all trooped into the Dining Room to find the table beautifully laid with a new flower arrangement in the middle. (Flowers "borrowed" from some neighbours garden no doubt) — and the meal commenced.

How he did it I don't know — but he produced soup with croutons, a fish entree (which I recognised as the previous day's lunch) covered with a rich sauce and decorated with capers. Then a wonderful mishmash of a main course which I didn't recognise, but had apparently come from next door and had been adapted to party status by the addition of some Brandy and cream; it was quite delightful, though obviously we could not eat very much! Then he produced Brandy Snaps which I could smell cooking whilst we had the main course! There was cheese and biscuits and cookies with the coffee — and I swear that the guests had no idea that we had already had dinner though both Ken and I had to make excuses about the amount we ate saying we had been out for lunch that day and were not very hungry. It's surprising how you can chase peas and vegetables around your plate without actually eating them!

In Karachi I was again very worried about the number of children our servants had — and when the Hamal asked for an afternoon off — which was quite unusual, but he told me that his wife was in hospital having gone into labour. As this would be their 6th child — I expressed concern and asked him if he would like me to write to the Dr. and ask him to perform a small operation that would prevent any further pregnancies. The Hamal seemed delighted when he had had this explained to him by the Bearer — so I started to write to the Dr. as I knew if I promised to pay for the sterilisation, and the Hamal signed a release form, it would be done.

However, I then heard the Bearer and the Hamal in deep conversation and obviously there was a problem! I enquired what was the matter — and nearly fell over when the Hamal apparently told the Bearer that "they" had already had an operation the year before but his wife was still pregnant! He went on to explain that HE had had the operation and had received a radio from the Government for having this done!

I decided in the circumstances not to explain anything further as obviously his wife had been a little promiscuous.

We had a delightful Christian driver — but three times during the first 3 years he worked for us he asked for time off because his wife had gone into labour! I found that at the age of 24 his wife had also had six children. Therefore I felt I had to get onto my favourite theme — that of encouraging birth control — or — in a case like this where they already had more children than they could support — that sterilisation for the wife was the only answer. We had seen the snags of the male sterilisation with our poor Hamal!

However, the Pakistani or Indian male — along with I suppose his European counterpart — felt that male sterilisation would result in their losing their masculinity and would be bound to affect their sexual drive. Even the Governments incentive to give small radios to every male agreeing to be sterilised — had had very little effect on the increase in the birth rate.

I therefore suggested to the driver, when he told me he wanted to take his wife into hospital as she had gone into labour, that I wrote to the Dr. and asked him to perform this simple sterilisation whilst his wife was in the hospital. This way there was no reason for anyone to suspect that she was in hospital for anything other than having a baby. I told him it was a simple operation — two little "snips" and she would know nothing about it and there would be no more children.

His eyes lit up — and he said this was a "bahut attcha bunderbust" meaning a very good arrangement! I rang the Dr. and explained that I would be writing to him and would pay for the sterilisation but I didn't want his wife to be discharged until this had been done. The following day though the Driver appeared for duty looking very glum and told us his wife had given birth to another girl — and that the wife's Mummy was horrified when the driver was given the consent form to sign, for the sterilisation in the hospital and forbade her daughter to have it done! It really was impossible getting the message of birth control through to the older generation — who themselves had had numerous children and could see no reason for interfering with God or Allah's wish. The very sad thing about this story is that the wife went on to have another 8 children and after we had left Karachi died having her 16th!

I felt quite discouraged that in spite of all the money the Government and numerous European organisations had spent in promoting Birth Control — that the older generation refused to accept it and had such a hold on their offspring.

When we lived in India in the early 50's the population was 365 Million and now it is 1,000 Million. The population of Pakistan is now 110 Million. Unfortunately the standard of living does not improve.

We had brought Sherry, one of our dogs, from Bombay. She flew up with Ken and the Captain allowed her to be in the cabin — as in those days we travelled First Class and one did receive more favourable treatment as there was more room.

As we lived in an upstairs flat she was taken out by the Hamal at least 6 times per day. The servants had one day off per week but we tried to give them public holidays as well and as explained, when the Hamal was off duty there was no one to exercise the dog so I obviously took this on.

One afternoon I was changing to go to the Yacht Club when Sherry started whining and rushing to the front door obviously requiring a toilet walk. I was in my bra and pants so decided I would open the door and let the dog rush down to the garden on its own.   As it was not used to going out on its own — there was a certain reluctance for it to go into the garden so I stepped out of the front door to direct it down the stairs and let it know I approved of this jaunt.   To my horror the door slammed behind me — and there I was on the open landing of this block of flats, which would be bad enough in the U.K. but in a Muslim country — a disaster.   There was nothing for it but to ring the door bell in the adjoining flat and hope that the Memsahib would answer the door.   She didn't.   I was faced with her Muslim Bearer who looked horrified — but he did allow me in the flat to use the phone.   I rang Ken and explained what had happened and he came back home with the key.

There was a very active Yacht Club in Karachi — probably because it must be one of the few Yacht Clubs in the world where one can Race throughout the year and the conditions are so varied. Ken and I had never sailed before but once we went out to the Golf Club and saw the condition of the "browns" as they were called because there really was no grass, and we'd ruined a couple of Clubs — we decided Golf was not for us.   So we joined the Karachi Yacht Club — where several of our friends spent their weekends. They assured us that if we crewed we would very quickly learn how to sail!

Karachi harbour was an ideal spot for this as one could sail all year round and the Courses set by the Duty Officer were always different and made Racing as such, far more exciting than using the same course week after week.   The Yacht Club was on Bunker Island, a short launch trip from Karachi dock area, which the men appreciated as there was no telephone and they could not be contacted once on the Island.

Starting to crew for a qualified helmsman was without doubt the best way of learning to sail.   There was very little social sailing as the Club's main interest was Racing and races took place on Tuesdays Fridays, Saturday and Sundays.   These were taken very seriously and there was keen competition between contestants.   Obviously if you wanted to continue to crew — you had to learn quickly and raised voices could be heard round every Mark as helmsmen shouted instructions to their crew!

When we felt reasonably confident and had learnt the rules — we decided to buy a 14' Dinghy numbered 36 and we had hours of enjoyment sailing her.    Both Ken and I were so enthusiastic that we split the Racing — I raced on Tuesdays and Fridays, and Ken raced on Saturdays and Sundays.    Rather like learning to drive a car, we found it easier to crew for some other helmsman, also we felt we could learn more about tides and winds from someone more qualified.    It was great fun and we both thoroughly enjoyed the Club.

One of our great friends, Bill Hamilton, was a 3 handicap golfer, but having seen the golf course in Karachi decided to join the Sailing Club just after we had joined.    He was anxious to start helming and decided that he could learn to sail by reading a book far quicker than sailing as a crew member for weeks on end!    After a couple of weeks he felt sufficiently confident to take a boat out — and to everyone's amazement he went out single handed and sailed up the harbour.    Ten Minutes later we were all amused as he sailed past the Clubhouse shouting that he hadn't read the chapter on stopping! He solved the problem by capsizing in front of the Clubhouse.

There were one or two memorable incidents — for instance, the day I borrowed my boss's 14' Dinghy — with his permission of course — and doing a gybe I managed to capsize in the middle of the harbour!    This was bad enough, but as we turned over I remembered that the previous day I had written to the insurance company asking them to extend the insurance which had expired. the previous day!    What I didn't realise was that my boss had removed the buoyancy bags to have them checked.    So this boat was not insured and without buoyancy and I watched it disappear!

Each boat had a Tindal (boat boy) who was responsible for rigging the boat and for taking it out of the water — and putting it in the water at the beginning of each race.    Each Tindal took a personal interest in their particular boat, so this Tindal was quite horrified when he saw his beloved boat sink. He immediately gathered up a crowd of his friends and they rowed out to rescue me and about 4 of the Tindals jumped in the water, one of whom swam down and secured a rope to one end of the boat. Shortly — another Tindal went down and managed to pull the rope under the boat. All that was left was to try to raise it hopefully without damaging the hull. After about an hour they managed to pull the boat to the front of the Clubhouse where more Tindals helped right it and baled it out! The only damage was a broken mast — so reckon I was very fortunate.

Usually we raced with one crew member, but twice a year there was a single handed race which I decided to enter. For this particular race we had to go round the various buoys and then sail up a Creek which had very shallow areas. I managed to beach the boat on a particularly shallow area and although I jumped overboard and tried to push it off but had no success. I watched as the rest of the fleet passed me — they managed to continue round the mark and then ran back on the tide. I had visions of spending the night on this sandbank I had found — but again these wonderful Tindals came to my rescue and I was delighted when I saw the Rescue Launch appearing in the distance!

In spite of these disasters, I did manage to win the Western Command Trophy — which was a 7 race event, and whilst I had won one or two Beer Tankards for single races — I felt this was really an achievement. Ken was unable to enter for this series as it took place on Tuesdays, Fridays, Saturdays and Sundays and many of the business men could not get away for the Tuesday races which started at 5.30.p.m.

On occasions like this the Cup was filled with Champagne and passed round the Club members — I remember it took 4 bottles of Champagne to fill it — and the price of Champers in Karachi was exorbitant — so I was glad I didn't excel too often!

Another tradition at the Club was that if anyone rang the Club Bell — this meant they bought drinks for all the members in the Club at that time. I became Prizes Secretary and at one Prize

Giving event I was trying to attract the attention of the Members and foolishly rang "the Bell" — another costly evening!

Linda and Fiona both learnt to sail in Karachi and became good sailors. I confess they usually sailed with one of the Club Tindals. On one occasion when Linda was out on holiday, she went out with the son of one of our friends on his Father's large "Tom Tit". Up to now Linda had only helmed a 14' Dinghy — so I was a little concerned when I saw that these two had taken our friend's 22' boat out without a Tindal!

They set off in great style — but there was a strong current in the middle of the Harbour and when I saw them crossing what we knew as the Shipping Lane, my heart sank, particularly when I saw a large ocean liner approaching. They did take evasive action — but with the strong current when they had "gone about" the tide seemed to be pushing them back into the shipping lane. I heaved a sigh of relief therefore when I saw the liner pass them — but — they then appeared to get caught up in the back wash and lo and behold they actually hit the back of the Liner!

Fortunately they did not capsize and the impact seemed to push them off the Liner and all they had to do was get back to the Clubhouse and see what damage had been done.

As you can imagine all the Club members were watching this incident and when they got back to the Club house were reprimanded by the Head Tindal — not to mention what the parents said! All in all they handled the situation very well — but they should never have got into the situation in the first place! A small re-paint job on the bow of the "Tom Tit" was the only visible damage — so think they got off lightly. We never heard if the Liner was scratched thank heavens! Having been given permission for the Yacht Club to operate in the Harbour on the condition that we kept out of the main Shipping Lane — we were very concerned that no incidents by the Yacht Club would jeopardise this.

Whenever there was a British Naval Ship in the harbour — the Yacht Club invited the ships crew to participate in the Mauritius

Cup Race.   The Cup had been donated by H.M.S. Mauritius and was sailed for by all visiting Naval Ships.   Because they realised the sailors would be at a disadvantage not being familiar with all the Marks in the Harbour round which they would have to sail — the Yacht Club provided the Crews for the Navy and the Navy boys crewed for the Yacht Club.

On one of these occasions I was crewing for a very young naval officer.   The race was in two parts and we had finished the morning session and had gone ashore for drinks and lunch.   The Navy love their beer and there were no restrictions on the Club's hospitality — so they all did rather well!

In the afternoon session we got a very good start and after sailing for about an hour found we were leading the fleet.   I was very excited — but horrified when this young officer said he would have to return to the Club House as he "had drunk too much beer and what went in — had to come out".   I suggested that he used the bailing bucket, and as I was sitting in front of him promised that I would not turn round!   At this stage we were about 300 yards from the Clubhouse so you can imagine my amusement when he said that he was more worried about the spectators at the Club!   I am afraid I retorted that I didn't know what he had that was so spectacular but I could not believe that it could possibly be seen from that distance!

On another Mauritius Cup race, I was again crewing for the Navy and in hanging out on a particularly strong beat — lost my toe strap and fell overboard!   The helmsman took it all in good part and Went About and picked me up.   Unfortunately the Navy lost this particular race in which 12 boats were participating, by about 2 points.

At the end of the proceedings we had the official presentation when the Captain of H.M.S. Appleton, who had not participated in the race, thanked the Club for their hospitality and expressed the Navy's regret at not having won the Cup.   His eyes twinkled as he said he felt there had been a sabotage attempt by a certain Yacht Club crew member who had decided to bail out in the middle of the race!     He said, however, the Navy had a way of dealing with situations like this whereupon he made a bee line for me — took me in his arms and literally dumped me off the Jetty!

I was more than a little surprised and as I sank to the bottom decided he would not get away with this entirely — so as I surfaced, covered in green slime from a somewhat dirty harbour, I staggered up the steps and onto the stage where the Captain was still speaking — and I threw my arms and legs around him — covering his spotless white uniform also in green slime!     Fortunately the navy boys thought this was great — though looking back from my senior years — I don't really feel proud of this!

New Year's Eve at the Karachi Yacht Club was really quite something — and the best I have ever known either before or since. Being on this small Island it was impossible to cater for large numbers on a grand scale with the facilities available, which were very adequate for Curry lunches and Gula Malacca but not a Xmas feast. The ladies therefore formed a Committee and we each provided part of the meal.

The Pakistani Turkey was a glorified chicken — and so we had to cook about 40 of these to compensate for their size, and we made mince pies, Xmas Pudding, Brandy Butter, Fruit Salad, and although Pork, Ham and Bacon were unobtainable in Pakistan — the Diplomatic Members of the Yacht Club who were permitted Diplomatic Privileges gave legs of Ham and Pork.     These were cooked in our homes as there is no way you would get a Muslim Cook to touch anything to do with a Pig which they considered unclean.

Some of the talented ladies would make Xmas crackers containing all sorts of amusing items, and the Club was beautifully decorated — though one year, when we were unable to get any balloons, condoms were decorated and hung from the beams which in those days was VERY daring!

We made a small charge for the evening and sometimes were

able to organise a band — but when funds were short we had to rely on Records or Tapes.

The Party was always organised around a theme and the members would dress accordingly, and the Club decorated around the theme. Each year a Members' Cabaret was presented which was the highlight of the evening, and one was usually surprised as to how much hidden talent the members had. I wonder why it is that a show can be so much more amusing when you know the participants?

One particular evening which stands out in my mind was a presentation of "The Bridge on the River Kwai" when four rather rotund male members were introduced by the playing of this tune. They had their arms folded on top of their heads and huge black top hats made of cardboard which came right down to just above their nipples. Their nipples were made up very artistically as eyes, and they had a nose painted on their chest below the eyes and their tummy buttons were made up as cupid lips. An evening shirt with a black tie was pinned to the top of their black trousers and the arms had been stuffed with paper. They really looked very realistic and people just could not understand how the impression of little men had been made out of chest and tummies!

As the music played these Top Hatted men moved their tummies in and out in time with the music and they had practised a little dance step — but as none of them could see, other than through a small hole in the top hat — they all seemed to go in separate directions — and the tummies were of varying sizes from large to gross and when they moved their tummies in and out, their lips appeared to move! Their top hats covered not only their heads but the top of their shoulders, with only this very small spy hole in the hat, and when they moved they often lost the spy hole! Then the little dance routine they had practised became a little disjointed with one of them turning left when the other three turned right. They'd realised there was something wrong and made valiant attempts to catch up — but to no avail — which only added more humour to an already hilarious presentation.. Very amusing but very difficult to describe.

Some of the lady members organised a Cabaret and did a dance routine — which after a couple of weeks' rehearsal was really professional and then there was a sing song by some of the male members who had written words which fitted in with popular tunes and included topical anecdotes about various members of the Club and their antics during the year. No-one was spared but it all led to a truly amusing and most entertaining evening which was a huge success.

Dancing continued until dawn and whatever the form of music — everyone had an excellent evening and it usually ended up with Scottish Reels, always an Eightsome and then, as many of the members had been to the Caledonian Ball — there would be repeats of the dances they had learnt for that particular evening.

As the Club was on the water — when the New Year was ushered in we had the benefit of seeing all the ships and harbour craft showing their enthusiasm by hooting and blowing whistles. The highlight of the evening however was always the Members' Cabaret.

New Year's Day was always a holiday so the launches worked until morning and often we would go on for breakfast to either the Sind Club or one of the members' homes. These evenings were indeed memorable — and I think this bears out the fact that the worse the posting, the closer people became and the more genuine were the friendships made. To this day we still have a nucleus of friends from our time in Karachi and people are shocked when we say we enjoyed our time there.

A very charming couple, Robin and Jean Reid, who lived in a magnificent home always had Open House on New Year's Eve — they were not members of the Yacht Club but knowing that all the enthusiastic members would be going over to the Club — they invited us all to their home for a drink before catching the launch across to the Club.

They had a teenage daughter and so very kindly invited all the young and they had their own particular party with games, Scottish Dancing and the like — and the old fashioned numbers like The Lambeth Walk. They saw the New Year in together. A very weak punch was provided for the older members — and lots of fruit punch for the younger ones and a very good meal. The Club members who had children at this party — would leave the Yacht Club after the midnight celebrations and pick up their young — but — when they were older, they too joined in the festivities at the Club.

Another highlight of Karachi's social scene — was, as I mentioned, the St. Andrew's Ball or the Caledonian Ball as it was sometimes referred to. This was held in one of the large Hotels — most of the ladies wore long white evening dresses with their own particular tartans hung over their shoulders — and all the men were either in evening dress or wore kilts. Each member of The Caledonian Society was allowed to invite six guests, and it was surprising how many new friends members acquired just before the Ball! When inviting your guests you usually ascertained that they would be able to attend the dance practices that took place about eight weeks before the Ball. By this time your particular "eight" were expected to be step perfect. Even so there was often confusion when one guest upset the rhythm by being in the wrong place or turning the wrong way!

A first class meal was always served with all the usual Scottish rituals. The Chieftain for that year would start off the proceedings with a Speech and then the Haggis would be produced on a silver salver accompanied by 6 or 8 serious looking Scots, one of whom carried a bottle of Scotch, with the skean dhu down his stocking used for stabbing the Haggis, which was "addressed" and duly stabbed.

An amusing toast was made to the "Lassies" by the most eligible bachelor which had obviously taken him some time to prepare, and one of the single "Lassies" would respond with an equally amusing toast to the "Lads". I was always surprised at the hidden wit which surfaced on these evenings.

The Chieftain gave a very long amusing speech and proposed a toast to the guest of honour, who in turn reciprocated similar sentiments.

The Guest Speaker was chosen carefully — often the British High Commissioner or some other equally important dignitary and again we were entertained with amusing anecdotes and usually a brilliant speech. The final toast of course was to The Queen when there was often a sigh of relief from some of the members, as this was the signal which allowed people to smoke or leave the table temporarily.

Then the dancing started — Scottish Reels that you'd learnt interspersed with modern dance numbers. The first Ball I went to I confused the M.C., who was wandering around looking resplendent in his Black Tie and white gloves, for a guest that no one appeared to want. As we were in the middle of an Eightsome I grabbed this gentleman's arm and pushed him into the centre of our eight as I really felt very sorry for him. I was quickly informed of his status and his duties and so had to apologise. Being a Sassenach I was not at all familiar with the Scottish ceremonies or how seriously they were taken.

When we were in Calcutta we were told that, a few years before, an elderly gentleman who just could not wait for the toast to The Queen had relieved himself under the table. On this occasion the dinner was in a Marquee and being on grass he hoped it would not be noticed — but unfortunately his "aim" was not very correct and a lady sitting opposite found the hem of her dress very wet when she got up to dance!

If one of your guests at the dinner was unaware of this Protocol, then you as the member of the Caledonian Society were held responsible for their misdemeanours, and in the middle of the dinner would be reminded that your guest had not adhered to the Protocol. All very embarrassing!

We often said that the dance practices that preceded the Ball were often more enjoyable than the Ball — certainly they were much more hilarious as the dancing at the actual Ball was taken quite seriously.

Ken occasionally called his Managers from up country to Karachi for a meeting and booked them into the Beach Luxury Hotel. (Foreigners would frequently say that there was no beach and very little luxury by Western standards, but for Karachi it was without doubt the best Hotel and run by a delightful Parsee family). Ken was amused to find that the Lahore Manager always had his breakfast about 3/4 of an hour before the other Muslim Manager. He always ordered bacon and eggs and by the time the other Muslim arrived for breakfast he was eating toast with no sign of the bacon and eggs.

He was caught out on one occasion as when the other Manager joined him and was asked what he would like for breakfast he said he would have the same as his companion! When the bacon and eggs arrived there was a lot of embarrassment and the poor Bearer was accused of making a mistake.

At home when entertaining mixed guests (Muslim and Christians), we were often quite amused when we had carefully arranged for any Pork dishes to be placed on a separate table, to find the Muslims helping themselves to the food from this table but they assured each other they were eating "pink chicken".

Most of us entertained at home as our houses were larger than in Europe — and having staff to do all the hard work certainly made it very easy. It was quite usual to have 30 or 40 people to a Buffet dinner which meant one could reciprocate the invitations you had accepted more quickly. Back in Europe I much prefer the small dinner party where one can talk to one's guests and not spend the evening flitting around trying to be the good hostess. Mind you, the weather helped, as we quite often held parties in the garden — or on the roof — with dancing until the early hours in spite of the heat!

We were invited to a rather large Pakistani party where there were quite a number of European guests. After a sumptuous Buffet dinner the dancing started and this elderly Pakistani gentleman asked me for a dance. We knew him quite well — though it was his son who was our particular chum as he was a member of the Yacht Club. The music was fast — and my partner was a good dancer in spite of his age, but when a slow fox-trot took the place of the quick step he held my right hand down by his crutch whilst continuing to hold me with his right hand. I was suddenly aware that he appeared to be distressed and was "fiddling" with his zip.

I thought the poor man had suddenly realised his zip was undone and he was surreptitiously trying to zip it up. How wrong I was — as the next thing I knew was that his "male member" was brushing my hand! I was so horrified that I just walked away and left him in the middle of the dance floor with his "masculinity" on view to everyone whilst he hastily tried to re-zip his fly! We didn't want to embarrass our host or hostess so stayed for a further 10 minutes during which time three other ladies said the same thing had happened to them! One is left wondering why Muslim men keep their women in purdah — and yet take advantage of Western women.

When Linda came out for her summer holiday one year, we went shopping in Elphinstone Street — I was horrified when I found some of the young Pakistani men actually lying on the pavement in order to look up Linda's skirt! This was a side of Muslim countries I found hard to accept. But then we have unacceptable people and habits everywhere it seems.

A young Assistant came out to Karachi to join Ken — he was a charming boy — perhaps rather introverted — and we were slightly concerned when he came round for dinner and we would ask him how he spent his weekend — and he told us he had gone out to the beach on his own! As a result we were inclined to invite him to the flat more than we normally would.

He was extremely good to both the girls — very polite — and I gather very good in the office. He lived in another block of flats at Clifton and there were one or two Insurance boys in the same block.

Can you imagine the shock we had when we heard whilst on leave that this young man had been murdered! He had been rolled up in an Indian rug and his flat ransacked.    It later transpired that he had been attacked by a pair of homosexuals who either had a grudge against him or hoped to convert him.    It did appear that his sexual preference was the cause of the murder.

As indicated above — Karachi had been dry for over 3 years with not a drop of rain — and yet Bougainvillaea and Frangipani bushes always seemed to be in flower.

In 1963 many of the British community were invited to a Reception for The Queen and Prince Philip where certain members of the hierarchy were to be presented.

When receiving our very official invitation telling us what to wear — (Hats and Gloves for ladies — suits or evening jackets for men) we were also told where our drivers should drop us AND where we should stand.    If you were to be presented to The Queen, then you were allocated an area in the Marquee which had been erected for the occasion.    The rest of us who were not such special guests were allocated an area inside the Guest House where we were to stand to watch the Royal couple walk through to the Marquee.

About fifteen minutes before the Royal Party were to arrive — the heavens opened and all the rain that we hadn't had for the last 3 years seemed to fall!    As usual the rain caused terrific traffic jams and therefore a few people had not actually taken up their positions when the rains started and they were caught in the downpour and arrived looking very dejected.

The next thing we knew was the Marquee collapsed- the rain had been collecting on the roof of the tent and was unable to run away — hence there was a horrible ballooning effect and within seconds the whole Marquee fell down.    The electricity was quickly switched off otherwise there would have been some nasty shocks and, perhaps deaths, but all the ladies who had been looking so resplendent in their new Ball Gowns with fantastic hair styles and the gentlemen in their Black ties were lying sprawled in the mud.

Every effort was made to disentangle these people but there was no way they could be presented dripping in mud — and many of them went home in a state of shock. Those of us that were not to have been presented and were therefore inside Government House were not aware of the excitement outside — and therefore when The Queen and HRH Prince Philip arrived — and were shown around the rooms we were standing in — we were quite surprised. As a result — several of us were in a position to actually talk to the Royal couple — though we had all been told that we didn't speak until we were spoken to — but obviously there was a lot of time for the Royal Couple to wander around inside the Guest House. They were told of the accident outside and of course expressed their regret.

Prince Philip came up to the group I was standing with and started talking to various individuals. He asked me what my husband was doing in Karachi — and fortunately he had heard of Ken's employers. A very well known surgeon was also in our group having been one of the lucky ones that had been in the Marquee but had been able to get out seconds before it collapsed, and Prince Philip noticed he was dripping wet and so asked him how long he had been in Pakistan? The surgeon told him 20 years or so — whereupon Prince Philip said he thought he would have known better therefore not to stand in a tropical rain storm!

During my time in the East I had been invited to Receptions for The Queen and Prince Philip in Calcutta, Bombay and now Karachi and every time Prince Philip had spoken to me. I have never been addressed by the Queen — who always seemed to go in the opposite direction, except in Calcutta when she did come to the table I was sitting at, but only spoke to one of the gentlemen at the table, asking him which Company he worked for and how long he had been in Calcutta.

As I am a most enthusiastic Royalist — these little incidents meant a lot to me — and I never cease to wonder how "The Royals" can cope with their lives in a Goldfish bowl.

Linda had been at Ashford since 1958 but when she came out for her Easter holiday in April 1962, she was so distressed and obviously miserable at boarding school and pleaded with us to allow her to leave.   This was very disappointing to us but she had been running slight temperatures which we found worrying, bearing in mind our experience with TB in Calcutta, also we realised, according to her letters, that she had never really settled at school — though once IN school we were told she was reasonably happy.

I could not bear to see the misery she was in when it was time to go back to school — which after nearly 3 years I felt was unusual. We therefore wrote to the school — paid a term's fees in lieu of notice and planned that as we were nearly due for leave we would all return together and look for a Secretarial College or a school that had a Secretarial curriculum.

The Company only paid one return air passage per Contract and one term's school fees, which I still think was very hard, so it was necessary that I kept on working, meaning I could not spend my days with Linda.   Nowadays employees get their children brought out EVERY holiday, and all their school fees paid!   I wonder what the term "the good old days" refers to?   Possibly discipline and respect!

We tried to fill Linda's time with extra French and English lessons and she spent a lot of time at the Sind Club Swimming Pool where I would pick her up after leaving the office.   Even so she clearly had a lot of spare time!

Obviously she got bored and occasionally strayed from her routine and would go to the cinema when she should have been at French or English lessons.   The poor soul was very unlucky as it seemed someone would see her and for one reason or another they'd pass some comment to me such as   "Did Linda like the film?" "Who was the boy Linda was with?".

I therefore discovered that she had formed a friendship with an American Marine who was a Security Officer at the U.S. Embassy. I thought it would be as well if we met this boy but when we were free it appeared he was always on duty!   When he rang asking to speak to Linda, conversation was very stilted, in fact monosyllabic and I did question what sort of education he had received!

Naturally, I was delighted when the time came for us to go on leave and she said "goodbye" to this newly found friend.

In August, 1962 we were due for leave and flew home via Beirut where we stayed at the famous St. George Hotel where in the bar they had a tank with a lady swimming through it periodically.

Then on to Athens where we spent three days — which really was a disaster; Ken and I wanted to sightsee, as we were only there for 3 days and there was so much of historical interest to be seen, however the girls wanted to go to the beach! I wanted to please everyone and felt like "piggy in the middle" but Linda was already in the depths of despair having left Bill — so I felt it would be easier all round to go to the beach. So — the girls won and off to the beach we went.

In Rome, not having previously booked a Hotel, we had difficulty finding somewhere to stay.

We certainly were not looking for 5 Star accommodation, but everything reasonable appeared to be fully booked. Eventually we had to accept a room with four beds in it, in a rather grotty Hotel — so grotty in fact that we actually found a pair of sox at the bottom of the bed so insisted on clean linen. This in itself took for ever as we spoke no Italian and the Room boy was far more interested in looking and admiring Linda, than in discussing anything as mundane as "dirty linen"!

After dinner the girls retired to bed and as we were all sleeping in one room Ken and I decided to go and have a look round town and have a drink. When we got back we found that the girls had had a visitor — none other than the room boy who apparently knocked on the door asking if Linda would like to go out! Fiona was apparently sent to the door to tell him she was already out!

I think they were pleased to see us back and the following evening we took them with us and all retired early!

We did manage to do some sight seeing in Rome — we took a bus tour and, although I don't think the girls were very enthusiastic about seeing The Vatican, Coliseum or the Pantheon, they obviously

241

enjoyed throwing coins into the Trevi Fountain which is supposed to ensure one's return to the Eternal City. Sitting in Street Cafes on the fashionable Via Venito and watching the world go by impressed Linda — though Fiona was anxious to move on after her ice cream!

Having wandered up to St. Peter's Piazza, Ken and I were, I suppose, in somewhat of a daze with all we had seen and therefore when we went into the Vatican it was some minutes before we suddenly realised that in walking round — we had lost Fiona! Having looked in the immediate area we all three went off looking for this wee girl. I suppose it was only a matter of five minutes or so, though it seemed like an eternity, before we finally spotted her kneeling in one of the areas where prayers were being offered by the Priest. She was quite oblivious to the fact that she had lost us and obviously very impressed with the Priest and seemed to be following his words of wisdom most intently!

We loved Rome — though I hated having my bottom nipped (and other areas) — and as this happened whilst walking alongside Ken, I wondered how single girls coped with the Italian sensuality.

We had another stop in Barcelona where we were met by someone from the Company — who seemed very happy to show us around. We had one request as the Hotel we had booked through the Travel Agent was, we felt, rather expensive, and wondered if he knew of anything more reasonable as we really did not have any extra cash. (Mind you I think all Hotels are expensive when you are in them for an overnight stay of perhaps 10 hours — and spend 8 of those sleeping!) He very kindly made a few phone calls and then told us we were booked into a very central Hotel. This turned out to be twice as expensive as the first one! I should add that our friend was a bachelor.

Anyway — we toured Barcelona — and were shown the Stadium where the Olympics of 1992 would take place. The city really abounds in historical sights which have been there for centuries such as the ancient Cathedral with its magnificent choir stalls — the most famous street, the Ramblas — and then we had lunch in the very famous Grande Hotel.    Here I managed to find the Caballeros when I went to wash my hands and whilst in the toilet was horrified to hear men's voices and it suddenly dawned on me that I should have gone in the door marked Senoras!

I was terrified of leaving the toilet as I couldn't even explain in Spanish why I was there.    So I stayed in the toilet for about ten minutes before I thought it was reasonably safe to appear — but even then there was one poor little man standing against the stall — who looked slightly alarmed — but not as alarmed as I was!    Ken and our host wondered where I had been and were very amused when I told them!

We then flew into Palma and took a taxi to Puerto Andraix — a delightful part of Mallorca which we had had recommended by friends whose parents had actually retired to the Island and were running The British Club in Palma.  Through them, we had booked rooms in a small Hotel near the beach.

We felt this was a wonderful opportunity for us to have a family holiday, as when Linda was at school we always went straight back to the U.K. in order to spend as much time as possible with her. Now we were all together — and realised that as the girls grew up and had outside interests, this would not happen very frequently.

Puerto Andraix was a wonderful spot and for three days we had a lovely holiday together, Linda and Fiona had a room on the ground floor and Ken and I had a room upstairs.    The owners were delightful, the food excellent and the weather was kind.  Our friends in Palma took us out on their boat for the day — and then introduced us to The British Club where we had a meal before returning to Puerto Andraix.

One morning at breakfast the Manager came over to our table to say there was a phone call.  Ken stood up ready to take the call when the Manager said it wasn't for us but was for Linda!

She returned to the table beaming — with the news that this dreaded Marine would be arriving in an hour!    The story was that he was flying back to the States and when they got to Barcelona the

Airways asked for a volunteer to stand down as they had a hospital case that had to get back to the States urgently. Bill — the Marine — thought this a wonderful opportunity — so had volunteered and had flown to Palma where he rang Linda to ask for directions to our Hotel!

This seemed more than a coincidence — as why would he be flying via Barcelona from Karachi to get to New York? Anyway — there was nothing we could do about it — other than try to continue to enjoy the "family" holiday!

Bill arrived — and the Manager of the Hotel who had already been approached by Linda, found a room for him. He was asked if he would be paying by cash — and apparently the Manager seemed quite happy with his reply. That was the end of the "family" holiday — but Linda and Bill obviously enjoyed their time together and spent hours on the beach — and as we rarely ate at the Hotel for lunch — it wasn't until the evening that we'd see them.

My initial impressions formed on the phone — were correct — and I really think this boy was one step from being illiterate, though being from the deep South we only understood half the things he said anyway, and he never said very much. Trying to be kind — we thought perhaps it was shyness — but — there was certainly no shyness in arranging the trip!

No mention had been made of his departure date — and as he had been with us 5 days we asked him when he would be leaving. He vaguely said that he might be leaving in three or four days! I pointed out that he would have to have a confirmed booking and suggested that we took him into Palma in the hire car — to make a reservation. Reluctantly they agreed to go the following day.

I felt this departure date couldn't be early enough after Fiona grumbled at breakfast one day to say she didn't like being on her own and that Bill was always coming through the bedroom window and then they both went out! The next day I had the girls moved upstairs next to us as this room was now vacant! This went down like a lead balloon as far as Linda was concerned — and don't think

Fiona was her favourite sister for a couple of days!

We booked the hire car and drove them into Palma to the Travel Agent where Bill was offered a seat in two days time or four days later. Before he could make any decision I quickly accepted the booking for the next day, although not as soon as I would have liked!

I then asked Linda to ensure that Bill paid his Hotel bill the night before he left as he would have to catch the 6.30.a.m. bus and the Manager would not be on duty at that time.

The next trauma was that Bill had no money — and the Hotel Manager would not cash his cheque (reckon he must have shared our views on his suitability for our daughter). There was nothing for it — but a visit to Palma yet again to enable him to go to the Bank where I hoped they would cash his cheque.

Finally his Account was paid — and he said goodbye to us the night before he left. Linda then asked if she could go into Palma on the bus with Bill — we pointed out that she would have to return on her own and there was only one bus back in the late afternoon and we felt that as time was now so short that we should spend the remaining few days together. She then asked if she could walk to the bus stop with him! This seemed quite reasonable — but — when we went down to breakfast at 8.30.a.m. there was no sign of Linda!

The Manager said she and Bill had left at 6.a.m. After breakfast we walked all over this little Port — but no sign of Linda. Could she have gone to Palma — but there was no return bus until 4.p.m.? We were very worried — teenagers are unpredictable — and our day was spent worrying where she was and whether she was alright.

We met the 4.p.m. bus and sure enough — there was Linda IN HER BIKINI! Perhaps nowadays you don't think that was unusual — but to us — for her to dress like this in a foreign country was not only an insult to the country but displayed a complete lack of personal pride.

When questioned about this — she said she went to the bus stop to say goodbye — and when the bus came Bill got on and then she rushed on to give him another kiss!    The bus started and it didn't stop again until it got to Palma!    Some kiss!

Linda was moody for the rest of the holiday — and whatever we did to try to improve things was to no avail.

On leaving Puerto Andraix we had a couple of days in Paris where we stayed at the Hotel Rue de Richelieu (near The Louvre).    Ken was anxious to visit The Louvre, so the next morning off we went. I don't think anyone has got through the Louvre as quickly as we did!    It did not appeal to either of the girls who really could not understand why Daddy wanted to spend so long looking at a portrait of a lady; it happened to be the Mona  Lisa which didn't mean a thing to them!    I was very conscious that they were both bored stiff and Linda morose and wanted to move on — so I moved with them. I really felt once again like "piggy in the middle".

Poor Ken — I think he could happily have spent the day browsing and examining each painting in detail!    He said next time he went to Paris, he would go on his own!    One could hardly blame him!

We flew back to the U.K. in early September, 1962 and started to look for a school that would accept a 15 year old.    It wasn't easy as we were then in the era when children were registered at  schools virtually at birth — and — no one was anxious to take on a pupil who would possibly fail to pass her exams and thus  reduce the schools pass ratio — which — to any school is so important.

I think we saw about 12 schools — but either they were not able to offer us a place — or if they had a vacancy — Linda hated the look of the school or took exception to the staff.    There seemed little point in putting her into a school which would make her as unhappy as she had been at Ashford.

Finally, we were told of a small Private School where swimming was high on their list of subjects catered for, and this of course was a great attraction to Linda.

Frankly, the school reminded us of something out of Charles Dickens — rather dark — in a large private house and the Headmistress definitely elderly.

Ken and I were not at all happy about the school, It was not on the list of recommended schools and it seemed no one had heard of it. We found it was dark and very dismal and one was left wondering what their scholastic record was like. When we expressed our doubts to Linda she became very indignant and said she would be very happy there and she had experienced the sort of school we thought suitable and hated it!

So....... Linda entered Miss Wolf's Academy in September, 1962 and I have to confess she settled well — and told us that the staff all knew her name within the first 24 hours whereas after 2 years at Ashford hardly any of the staff members would call her by name. Mind you, Ashford did have 900+ pupils and this Academy only had 80!

She was allowed to join the Beckenham Ladies Swimming Club where she apparently excelled and made a name for herself with her swimming and diving and broke a lot of the local records.

Fiona and I returned to Karachi early in 1963 on the Cilicia; Ken had left earlier by air as our leave was over, but I wanted to reassure myself that Linda was happily settled before leaving for Karachi.

Fiona and I sailed on the Cilicia once again and were able to spend four hours in Gibraltar, where the Apes as usual were very obliging and Fiona was fascinated that they were so friendly — all I could think of was, did they have Rabies?

We met up with a lot of old friends on board — who were also finishing their leave — and it was a relaxing and pleasant holiday after the trauma of getting Linda into a College that she liked.

Linda's first year at Miss Wolfe's Academy was apparently a success — she had good results — was taking a course in Secretarial duties which she found more interesting than studying History. She was doing very well with her swimming and during her second year there was talk of her going to Blackpool for the Trials for the Olympics. So — all seemed well.

Just before Easter that year, she wrote to ask if she could spend her Easter holiday with a school friend, rather than spend it with my brother and his wife in Yorkshire. As we didn't know the family we were a little concerned and would have been much happier if she had gone to Yorkshire.

I felt that the friend's mother, Mrs. Robinson, should have written to us and invited Linda to stay — so we rang her and she said she was very happy to have Linda. I insisted that we would pay her for the visit as I wanted to ensure that Linda would not be a liability. Linda was not the best of correspondents and the next thing we heard was a telegram from Miss Wolfe, the Headmistress, asking us to give details of Linda's whereabouts as she had not returned to school after the holiday!

In a panic, we rang Mrs Robinson again, but she assumed when Linda left them — she had returned to school! Her daughter, Norma, who was a little older than Linda was apparently not returning to school, but was to start work.

What a dilemma! Nowadays one would immediately inform the police imagining your daughter had been abducted, raped or even murdered; as a Mother I couldn't help having these thoughts, but in those days this seemed a little drastic.

I rang my elder brother George, who lived in London — and we discussed my returning to the U.K. to try to find Linda and persuade her to return to the Academy. Flights were not easy to get at such short notice and finances were even harder to obtain. My brother persuaded me to wait for a while as he didn't see what I could achieve by returning home — and that he would make enquiries through the two addresses I was able to give him.

In my heart I felt that we would hear from her shortly and couldn't see what I could achieve if I flew home — it would be like looking for a needle in a haystack. I would have to resign from my job which would add to the financial burden — and I had nowhere to stay in the U.K. other than bunking with friends or with George who was living in a one bedroomed apartment. As you can imagine I was distraught — and as all mothers do — imagined all sorts of things.

We did eventually hear from Linda who she said that she was fed up with school and felt she was capable of keeping herself and so had got a job as a Typist/Model in Poland Street, London, and was sharing a flat with three other girls.  What to do??

By now I realised that Linda had a will of her own and a strong desire to be independent and free from parental control.  Even if we could persuade her to return to Miss Wolfe's Academy it would be short lived and she would not be happy so.... we decided to try to accept the status quo!  She wrote fairly regularly and said she was enjoying the job and her independence!

In September, 1963, Ken had to go over to East Chittagong on a business visit — and I was having a medical that morning.  I don't think Ken had arrived in Chittagong when the Dr. told me he had found a lump in my breast which he thought was "suspicious" and he wanted to operate the following day!

Poor Ken — I phoned the office he was visiting in East Chittagong and, as he hadn't arrived, I left a message.  He rang me back and when I told him the news he caught the next plane back!  I was so pleased to see him as I imagined I was going to have my breast removed.

Actually when I came round from the anaesthetic and looked down, I was convinced that it HAD been removed as there appeared to be a 6" difference between the two sides!  The Dr. assured me he hadn't done any radical surgery, merely removed a tumour about the size of an apple!  I felt he lied!  However, two days later they removed all the dressings and low and behold the missing breast appeared!  I was extremely relieved as you can imagine, but to this day don't know how they disposed of the breast as my right side was flat after the surgery!  I had to wait for the biopsy before I could get too confident — but this came back as a benign tumour. Relief!

Linda's letters indicated she was enjoying her job and I have to admit that she appeared to be doing extremely well in supporting herself.    Because we didn't approve of this move we were not prepared to subsidise it — but she had, and still has a wonderful spirit of survival.

We subsequently learnt, however, that she was not too happy in the job she had taken, which was the one Christine Keeler of all people had vacated when she started her infamous career, and became involved with Profumo and Ward!   I don't think Linda knew who Christine Keeler was at that time but it certainly did nothing for my peace of mind!

She had found she would have to get a new wardrobe suitable for business, and I have to say she never asked for financial help, and we didn't offer any as we both felt this was a foolish venture, and we hoped she would return to Miss Wolfe's Academy and finish her Secretarial course.

Not to be daunted she opened charge accounts in various stores to get the clothing she needed.   Why these stores encourage young girls to open accounts and then sue them when they can't meet their bills I don't know.

Apparently that winter Linda was smitten with the very nasty Asian Flu and was quite ill, so had to take time off work — for which she found she would not be paid!   Her landlady naturally wanted the rent and these Stores that had encouraged her to open charge accounts were also demanding payment.

Eventually she went to my brother asking for help to settle her outstanding accounts — he rang us and said he would pay all her bills on our account on condition that Linda returned to Karachi.

As you can imagine this was not a happy meeting!   She arrived tearful and very upset as she had been doing so well.   We felt she had a huge chip on her shoulder, and life as you can imagine, was not easy for any of us.

I felt that it was bad for her to sit around all day doing nothing and so when a business friend of Ken's, who had watched her swim in the Sind Club Galas, offered to try to get her into the Inter-Continental Hotel as a Swimming Supervisor, we were delighted.

Linda jumped at the idea and we felt this was a providential move as at least she would have a disciplined life as she had to report as 9.a.m. and she would have a little pocket money, hopefully enabling her to save.

Basically she had to act as a Life Guard and supervise the young children and give the odd lesson.    As I said, she was a brilliant swimmer and Diver and as the Manager's wife was a gymnast she would encourage Linda to perfect some very difficult dives.    At times there were no children or classes and so she would sit round the Pool and read a book.

It was here she met Frank — an Australian — who like many young men seemed to do quite a lot of their business sitting round the swimming pool!    Apparently he used to buy her the odd coffee or Gin and Tonic — though we knew nothing of this — we were just grateful she was obviously happy and enjoying the job AND getting paid for it!    Frank was rarely mentioned — and I never for a moment thought there was anything of a serious nature in their friendship.    To me he was an acquaintance!

In November, 1963 Ken was invited to attend the Attock Oil Reception in Rawalpindi — and although this was a business connection, Ken and I had been friendly with the host and hostess when they were in Karachi.    So, I was included in the invitation and they invited us to stay in their very lovely home.

Although a largish house there was only one toilet — and so in the middle of the night when Ken was creeping out to attend to the call of nature, he found the light was on in the toilet — so he returned to the bedroom.    I was fast asleep — but apparently he waited for about half an hour for the light to go out — and as it didn't, he wondered if someone was ill.    Obviously things became very uncomfortable for him, so he decided the only thing to do was to utilise the window!    Unfortunately the window was over the bed on my side!    I awoke to find this apparition, leaning over my head!

The ironical thing was that the bathroom light was still on in the morning — the children had forgotten to switch it off!    To add insult to injury — immediately below the bedroom window — our car was parked — and the Mali (gardener) couldn't understand why it was wet when it hadn't been raining!

We had various visits from HM Ships on Rest and Recreation — and various social events were arranged for their entertainment. In turn we were invited on board — and this meant lovely eats — Ham, Cheese, Caviar and items that were not readily available in Karachi. HMCS St. Laurent arrived in April that year, also for Rest and Recreation, so more entertaining and being entertained.

Whenever the Navy was in town — people would make a point of including them in any social occasion that we felt they would enjoy. They would be invited to lunches, dinners and on jaunts to the beach.

On the whole I think they enjoyed these occasions although we did have two Sailors who were so bored with a drive out to the Beach, which took about an hour, that they read comics the whole way! When I enquired if they were not interested in the local scenery — they retorted that every Port to them was the same — when you'd seen one — you'd seen them all! I did wonder why they had accepted the invitation and wondered if in fact they had been reluctantly detailed to come as there had not been sufficient response to the invitations, which the Navy might have found embarrassing.

One particularly sad weekend, we had gone out with two navy boys to join other friends who were also entertaining the navy. The four hosts and hostesses were busy in the beach hut, unpacking the food and preparing the lunch, whilst one of the wives had gone down to the sea for a swim. Three of the navy boys went with her but before long we heard screams from below the cliff and on dashing down to the beach found that Bridget was being swept out to sea by a rip.

Two of the Navy boys swam after her — one had to give up through sheer exhaustion, and the other actually managed to grab her hand — but he couldn't hold it against the strength of the waves and current — another attempt was made — and by this time all the men had joined in and taken over from the sailor who was obviously exhausted. The tide finally brought Bridget back within grabbing distance and she was brought ashore barely breathing. Someone had dashed up to the local Naval station and an ambulance was called — but alas it was all too late and Bridget died on the way to hospital.

She was a strong swimmer — but obviously the rips were unpredictable and she got into difficulties, but thought she could swim back — and only when she found she couldn't did she scream for help. This of course shattered everyone — as normally the sea around that coast was very calm.

This experience did rather put us all off swimming for a long time — and I don't think we ever swam from that particular part of the beach again.

Life has to go on — but it was a very sad and shattering experience for all.

I continued to have bouts of the Dysentery I'd suffered in Calcutta and Bombay — sometimes the obvious Bacillary — occasionally Amoebic, which was only diagnosed through stool tests, and Gardia.

I seemed to be continually going to the Dr. with "my little tin" but the amazing thing is that one can have eight stool tests which are negative but the ninth one will show the Amoebae. In Calcutta I had to be hospitalised and given Emmetine Injections accompanied by bowel wash-outs! Nowadays they have drugs which are equally efficacious and far less demoralising.

I had a rather frightening experience medically in Karachi. On the roof at Clifton we used to grow various floral bushes — usually Bougainvillaea which really thrived in Karachi. I did however have a very lovely Moon Flower — and although it only flowered once a year — usually for one day — I was very proud of it — and we would try to arrange a party on the roof on the night we thought it would bloom, as not many people had these unusual plants. I discovered however, that this plant had acquired small green flies which were eating the leaves — so decided I would go along to the local Horticultural shop and ask for advice as to how to kill these flies.

I should perhaps say that this man spoke very little English and my Urdu was very limited, however he gave me a small bottle of "Dwie" (medicine) which he told me to put in a flit gun, fill the gun with water and spray the whole plant.    He gave me no other instructions — so at lunch time I dashed home and started to spray the plant with this concoction.

After I'd finished I suddenly felt very tired and decided I would lie on the bed for half an hour.   Within seconds I felt most peculiar and tried to get off the bed — but started vomiting violently and I realised something was very wrong.    Between these bouts of sickness I managed to get to the phone and rang Ken and asked him to come home — but before I'd finished my conversation I must have passed out.

Ken came home immediately and found me on the floor with the phone in my hand rolling in vomit!  He rang this wonderful Pakistani Doctor we had and explained what he had found — and the Doctor came within 10 minutes.   He stayed with me for 2½ hours giving me an injection every 15 minutes.   Ken had found the flit gun and eventually I was able to indicate what had happened.

It transpired that the shop had bought a quantity of this insecticide which should have been used for agricultural purposes only — heavily diluted — and that full protective clothing should be worn, with gloves and a gas mask.

This little man thought if he bought the supply in bulk he could bottle it and sell it at a vast profit not realising how lethal it was. After my experience my Doctor arranged to have the whole consignment confiscated and the British High Commission put out a warning so that other people would not suffer a similar fate.   This poisoning was yet another cause of my liver problems.

Another of Ken's assistants told him he wanted to get married and when we were on leave we were asked if we would go and visit his fiancée to assure her that life in Karachi wasn't all that bad. The lady came out for the wedding but as neither the groom or Bride had any family, we felt we should take over as locum parentis. We had organised a wedding for a friend in Bombay, so we had an idea as to how many bottles of bubbly one needed for each 10 guests and how many pounds of wedding cake and short eats would be required. Most European weddings in Karachi were Buffet style or Finger Food, a complete contrast to the Banquets put on by the Pakistanis.

The bride's bouquet did prove a problem as Karachi was basically desert and we had had no rain for about three years. However, the wonderful flowering tree, the Frangipani, which grew in our garden, came to the rescue. Each flower was wired and used in the bouquet and the flower arrangements.

Soon after the wedding, though, they requested a posting back to the U.K. — the Bride had not settled well in Karachi — and I think she found the number of previous girl friends her groom had been friendly with rather inhibiting. Be that as it may — they went home and another Assistant came out to take his place.

Ken went out to the airport to meet him and on the journey back to the flat, he told Ken he wanted to get married!

By this time, we were becoming quite adept at arranging weddings in the East — so naturally offered to have the Reception in the flat. His fiancee came out to Karachi about a week before the wedding and she was joined by her bridesmaid who came from Kenya. All the arrangements went well until we came to the Bride's Bouquet and here the Bridesmaid, who knew nothing about living in Karachi, insisted that the Bouquet should be made up of Bronze Roses!

I tried to point out that we'd be lucky to get any flowers at all in Pakistan, other than the usual Frangipani — and as for roses, which in the best of circumstances would die within 24 hours — not to mention BRONZE roses — there was no way we could oblige. This seemed to irritate the Bridesmaid who told us that the Bride had always planned to have a bridal bouquet of Bronze Roses!

I found this very discouraging as naturally we wanted to do all that the Bride's parents would have done — and for her to feel that it was a memorable day which could not have been bettered. Eventually we got the message across and a great friend of ours, Peggy Porter, who was an expert at floral arrangements had a talk to them — and said she was very willing to help — but Bronze Roses she could NOT provide!

Peggy stepped in and did the flowers beautifully in the church and at home for the three weddings we'd already had in Karachi. This was a great relief — and left me time to organise other things. The tunes for the church service had been chosen and the hymn sheets printed — the cake was ordered — (they wanted three tiers) and the Church looked beautiful. I had arranged a Bridal Shower for her a few days earlier at the flat.

We thoroughly enjoyed having Ann to stay — she was a sweetie — but it goes to show just how old fashioned I was when, on the first morning she stayed with us, she put her packet of Contraceptive Pills on the breakfast table and I fondly thought they were vitamins! Shortly after this I too was converted to the Pill — but it was still in the days when rumour had it that the use of the Pill over a long period would surely produce cancer!

The Groom had his Stag party the night before the wedding and we just hoped he wasn't too much under the weather after having his final fling. I always think Stag Evenings should be a week before the Wedding to give the Groom plenty of time to recover!

The wedding was to be at noon with short eats at home — before the cake cutting and the speeches. I decided that we would move all the furniture in the Lounge the night before and decorate the bridal table on which the cake was placed. Peggy came round and arranged the flowers in the flat and I have to say it all looked very attractive and we went off to bed just after midnight.

About 5.a.m. we were woken by a very excited Fiona who told us to get up immediately — as the Cake was on the floor and the dog was eating it! Panic .... how would we get another cake in time — so we dashed into the Lounge to find that one of the pillars on the cake had sunk and as a result the top tier had toppled onto the floor and the dog was tackling the angels! I felt that the only solution would be for a two tier wedding cake instead of the three — but when I called the Cook — he had other ideas.

First of all he repaired all the broken angels on the first two tiers which the dog had ignored, with sugar and egg white — and then I found him cutting out a cardboard circle onto which he built in cardboard the top layer — this was duly covered in white icing and decorated and then placed carefully on top of the four pillars. I wouldn't have believed that he could have done such a fantastic job and it really was quite impossible to tell by looking at the cake that the top tier was anything but genuine!

After the cake cutting — we moved the top two tiers and merely cut up the bottom layer — and were able to present the second layer intact to the bride and groom on their return from their honeymoon! No mention was made of the top tier — and we assumed they thought it had been eaten! What would we do without these fantastic "Boachhies?" even if sometimes they drank too much??

Two months after this, two other friends of ours, Paddy and Phil Williams were getting married and again we offered to have the reception in the Company flat. This time we had no disasters — perhaps we were becoming adept at arranging these occasions, and being in the East with servants — it really was quite easy.

In November, 1965, whilst working for the British High Commission, I was asked if I would like to transfer to the India, Pakistan and Burma Association. This was headed by Charles Gorst in Karachi and Sir Percival Griffiths in London.

On one of Sir Percival's visits he asked me out of the blue if my husband was a member of the Oriental Club in London. If not he would be very happy to propose him and arrange for a Seconder. I really didn't think that Ken would be interested as we were living in Karachi and when we were on leave we couldn't take the children into the Club, and we didn't entertain when in the U.K. other than at home. However, Sir Percival told us that the entrance fee would be going up and he felt that we would get a lot of pleasure out of the Club.    We joined and Ken had to meet the Committee when we were next on leave.

The irony of this is that we always took our leave in August to coincide with Linda's or Fiona's school holidays, and the Club was always closed in August!    I am sure there are few people who were members of such a Club and never set foot inside it for over 8 years! However, it has proved very useful when we are on leave as whenever we go in for a meal we always meet some old friend from the past.

My mother at this time had gone into a Residential Home as she really could not be left on her own.    She was found by the police one evening wandering into the village in her night-gown, but wearing a hat.    Then another day she had turned on the gas stove intending to cook herself a meal — but forgot to light it — fortunately a friend arrived to see her and thus prevented a very nasty accident.

On another occasion, which if it wasn't so serious was rather amusing.    She had turned on her electric blanket which had obviously fused and started a fire in her bed which very quickly spread to the mattress  and thence to the pillow — and then the curtains caught fire.    Neighbours who lived opposite saw the flames leaping around the windows and immediately called the Fire Brigade — they then tried to get into the bungalow but they themselves were elderly and so waited until the Fire Brigade arrived.

These gallant gentlemen broke into the bungalow and rushed into the bedroom, threw the curtains, mattress, pillows into the garden and put the fire out.    The neighbours came over to see how Mother was — only to find her STILL sitting in the Lounge with the T.V. on quite oblivious of the noise and the fire!

My brother was now married and had moved out of the bungalow but he quite rightly agreed with the Authorities that she really could not be left on her own — so he arranged for her to go into this Nursing Home.    She looked upon this with mixed feelings and sulked for the first few weeks which made it very difficult  for the staff.    She did not want to mix with the other inmates — and stayed in her room and finally they found she had fallen out of her chair and had fractured her leg!

She was then taken to the local hospital and when we went home — we were very distressed at the deterioration in this wonderful lady.    Added to which she was very confused — and at times thought she was in a First Class Hotel and used to ask us how on earth we could afford to keep her there — but on another occasion she said she never thought she would live to see the day when her daughter would put her in the Workhouse!

As you can imagine I found this very distressing — but fortunately this view didn't last long and there was an amusing side to her "reincarnation".    She thought she was staying in a Hotel and insisted on tipping all the staff whenever they did anything for her.    Every cup of tea warranted a two shilling tip — and when a meal was put in front of her — then she left half a crown on the tray!    Matron was very understanding and would return all these tips to me the next day when I visited the Home and then Mother would in turn ask me if I had any change as she had to have money for tips!

She was a very proud lady and so when she became incontinent she used to blame the faulty ceiling and would ask for her bed to be moved so it didn't get wet through the leak in the ceiling!    When we weren't there then she would ask the staff so very nicely if they would be kind enough to move her bed away from the drip from the ceiling.    To humour Mother and avoid her being thoroughly demoralised if she learnt the truth — the staff would go along with this continual moving of the bed!

Another occasion I went into the Hospital whilst Ken was parking the car and when Ken walked in a few moments later Mother said in quite a strong voice "Oh — so they have let you out of jail then?" I have to say that this did have a somewhat electric effect on the other residents who eyed Ken with great suspicion.

We had to return to Karachi after our leave which I found very distressing as I really could not see her recovering.    The Dr's said she could go on like this for months and obviously she was in the best place and as she thought most of the time she was in a Hotel — and not the dreaded workhouse, it was a reasonably good arrangement.

Eric was living quite near the Hospital and was very attentive, though his wife's mother was far from fit but he and his wife visited Mother as often as they could.

In spite of being sad to leave the U.K., chiefly because of Linda and my Mother, it was good to get back to what to us at the time was "home". I returned to work and Fiona continued at the British Overseas School.

We were invited by some friends — also from the Yacht Club to their lovely home for dinner one evening. They did live rather a long way out and most of the roads away from the centre of Karachi, had no street lighting. This added to the ever present hazard of the camel carts, that trundled up and down Drigh Road also with no lights, made driving quite exacting.

We knew we had to take a left turn to get to their house, onto a secondary road, but did not realise it was a sandy track — and as we were late we were travelling about 40 m.p.h. when suddenly Ken jammed on his brakes — the car skidded to a stop on the unmade road about 10 yards from a deep gully — which had we hit it, would certainly have killed us. Thank goodness Ken saw it in time! Obviously we had taken the wrong turn off but why this road had been left with no indication at all that the road was not only unfinished but dangerous, I don't know. But this was Pakistan!

We were told that after Partition, in an effort to throw off the British Empire influence, it was decreed that traffic would in future travel on the right hand side of the road, and not the left. This may have worked very well with motorists; however the camels had a different attitude! Camels were used to bring in fresh food early in the morning and so often the camel cart driver was fast asleep leaving the camel to negotiate the road alone. They were creatures of habit and so although they set off on the right hand side of the road —

they ended up on the left. It became obvious that the camel had no intention of changing his habits — so the road change was dropped!

The mail in Pakistan was often very unreliable — and therefore people with really important documents or letters that were urgent would keep them until someone was returning to the U.K. or for that matter anywhere out of Pakistan, and ask them if they would be good enough to post them!

One particular couple were always approaching us and asking when our next overseas visitor was arriving — and then asking if we would be so kind as to ask them if they would post some letters for them. It seemed quite a normal request — and usually people were more than happy to help. We did feel however, that this particular couple had a remarkable amount of mail which they considered urgent. Even so, we continued to ask our visitors for their help — though on occasions we felt they were stretching the bonds of friendship above and beyond.

Most of our guests were only too willing to help — but one particular VIP said he had no objection to taking the mail so long as he could open it. Obviously, as we had been told it was urgent, we said we were sure it would be alright.

Imagine our embarrassment when the letters were opened to find pornographic material of the most intimate and obscene nature. We didn't know what to say to our visitor and just hoped he realised that we had no idea what the letters contained.

We were both so embarrassed that we didn't even want to disclose to these so-called friends what had happened, but merely said that in future our guests did not want to hand carry mail for third parties. I feel sure they must have realised why — and perhaps it stopped their obscene and depraved behaviour. They were members of the Yacht Club and therefore it made it very difficult to avoid them — and most certainly one would never dream they could both be involved in such way-out sexual practices.

We became quite friendly with a Pakistani couple — who had

their own Oriental Rug business, and through them — we became very interested in these truly lovely rugs. Besides their factory, they ran a very effective Cottage Industry and we were invited to go out to the villages to examine the rugs that were being made in the bustee areas by the villagers.

Usually one adult craftsman sat in the middle of the loom with two young boys on either side of him. He had a very intricate pattern of an original, Persian, Bokhara or Caucasian rug in front of him and he proceeded to copy this very accurately, by yelling out the colours they had to use next. So you got "char lal" (four red) teen kala (3 black) and I can tell you these instructions were yelled out very quickly and the children worked with remarkable speed.

At one of the bustees we visited I was very taken with the design of a Caucasian rug they were working on — it was half finished, so I enquired if it was for sale — and the price — and we agreed to buy this when it was finished which they said would be in about 9 months. Ken and I during this period went out occasionally to see how the rug was progressing. Finally we were told it was finished and that if we liked to come out the next day we could see the next process.

The rug was quite thick — and rather fluffy by Oriental standards and didn't really resemble the very beautiful rug it was supposed to be a copy of, but I was assured this would change when the excess wool was removed. The rug was placed on a cement square in the yard, and buckets of water were thrown all over it until it was saturated. It was then scraped by a metal broom like arrangement — and all the various colours then started to flow out of the rug. It looked a mess and I began to wonder why on earth we had said we would buy something that had not been finished.

Immediately after this the rug was saturated with Sulphuric Acid and the same process of scraping began for a further 15 mins. Then more water was poured over the rug and this was followed by Hydrochloric Acid. By this time I did not believe that any rug could survive all this acid and so stuck my finger in the rug — and received a blister for my cynicism! More water, more scraping and eventually the rug was left out to dry having had as much of the water as possible pushed out.

We were told that the next stage would take place the following weekend when the rug had had a chance to dry. Quite frankly at this stage I really was wondering how on earth I could get out of this purchase without offending our friends.

The next weekend we arrived to find them rolling the rug over a metal cylinder and then a blow lamp, of all things, was produced and slowly pointed to the reverse of the rug burning up all the stray wool and the fluff. This was truly terrifying to watch — over 12 months work seemed to be about to be ruined. Then the rug was rolled in reverse and a huge pair of sheers snipped the fluffy side of the rug — cutting it down to about quarter of an inch. This made me feel a little happier about our purchase, but obviously we didn't have the time to watch the whole process.

The next week we were allowed to pick up the rug and it was quite beautiful — and had the most wonderful change of colour when viewed from different ends. This is our most prized possession as I don't think there are many people who have an Oriental Rug in their Lounge which they had watched being made.

In April, 1965, we were due for leave again and we all sailed on the Lloyd Triestino's "Asia" for Naples. Linda's current boy friend Peter, — or so I thought — came to see us off and introduced us to his Burra Sahib (boss) and his wife — Stew and Alicia Stewart. They were a charming couple and we spent a lot of time with them and the friendship continues to this day.

As we were altogether once more we had planned, what we felt was a very nice holiday, but this didn't interest Linda so she approached a friend of ours who had lived in the same block of flats and asked if she could accompany her on the train to London. Linda was to have done a refresher course at a Secretarial College in London as we didn't feel the range of Secretarial skills she had acquired at Miss Wolfe's Academy which had been cut short, was sufficient to secure reasonable employment.

Before we docked at Naples, Linda had asked if she could go straight home with this Karachi friend who was going direct to the U.K.   She did not want to holiday with us and we knew this would mean none of us would enjoy the holiday  and she said she would far rather go back to London and stay with her friend Sue.   Linda also talked about getting a job  —  but I pointed out that no one would employ her at a salary she could live on unless she  had obtained Passes in Secretarial skills.

What did I think she would need to keep herself in London she asked?  — and I said at that time that a minimum of 8 pounds a week, which would be an existence but she could survive on it,  if she shared a flat.

So Linda returned directly to the U.K.   We were sad to say goodbye to her at Naples, as we really felt this would probably be the last family holiday we could have, as Fiona would shortly be starting boarding school.   We had an interesting trip planned, which we felt she would have enjoyed.   But it was not to be.

Having disembarked, we hired a car and drove down the coast to Sorrento which has a most picturesque harbour with its numerous small yachts, boats and other craft anchored or pulled onto the beach with the hills in the background and white washed houses overlooking the Bay of Naples.   A lovely spot where we spent the night,

We drove along this magnificent coastline to Positano and Amalfi and the next day we took a boat over to the magical Isle of Capri a lovely island surrounded by a rocky coastline garlanded with vineyards and shrubs and exotic gardens where the rough seas had formed many interesting caves.   The main towns are Capri and Anacapri.

A funicular railway took us to the picturesque town of Capri. We drove round the Island seeing the various spots of interest including  Gracie Fields' home whose villa is now a shrine to her memory.   We could well understand why she chose Capri!

A bus took us up to Anacapri — where we had lunch and spent a delightful day.

Fiona had just been having orthodontal treatment and been given a plastic tooth guard which she was supposed to wear all the time, except when eating. Whilst having lunch that day she had removed this guard and put it in her pocket. On the way up the funicular railway she pulled her hankie out of her pocket — and out came the tooth guard and fell down thousands of feet. I think we had just paid $1,000 for this — so were not amused as she had used it for about 2 weeks!

The town of Capri has a charming piazza with a maze of streets with fashionable boutiques and restaurants, and we thoroughly enjoyed wandering around and having lunch on the piazza.

After lunch we took a small boat to the Blue Grotto, and on the boat trip again saw Gracie Field's island of dreams from a different angle.

We were amused at the driver who excitedly pointed out a "snake on the road side" which was obviously an old fan belt — but he didn't realise we were fairly familiar with snakes and this was obviously part of his tourist spiel!

We then returned to Amalfi which is about 38 miles south of Naples, reached by a coast road that is considered to be the most beautiful in Italy. We returned to Naples via Salerno and the following day we drove south and saw the awe inspiring sight of Vesuvius — Europe's greatest live volcano. We visited Pompeii where time stopped in 79AD when the Vesuvius eruption totally destroyed the city. We saw the human and animal bodies petrified by the lava — and wandered around the streets imagining what it must have been like to have been living there when there was this horrific eruption. Even Fiona found this interesting, though hard to believe!

After all this excitement we flew to Rome the eternal city, which is the hub of the ancient civilised world and is also a sightseer's dream. This time we were able to see some more of the tourist spots that we had missed on our first visit. We saw the Roman

Forum and Coliseum, went up Gianiculum Hill and saw the seven hills of Rome, and threw coins into the Trevi Fountain yet again. (it had obviously worked the first time we did this as here we were back again!)

From Rome we went to Paris and stayed at the Hotel San Remo and explored the left Bank. There is no doubt about it, Paris is a wonderful city but I wished I had paid more attention at school to my French lessons. The class spent their time teasing the French Mistress by putting live mice in her desk and watching the results, and went so far as to put aperients into her coffee, which certainly kept her out of the classroom!

Before arriving in London we spent a few days with Paddy and Phil Williams whose wedding we had organised and who were now living in Jersey. Phil had been posted to Jersey after leaving Karachi — and we were very impressed with the Island, but shattered when we found that for a non resident to buy a house there in those days was around £600,000 — and the regulations regarding taking up permanent residence required one to also have a large bank account! As Phil was employed on the Island they were able to avoid these regulations and have since been able to retire on the Island.

When we got back to the U.K. we were met by Linda who seemed genuinely pleased to see us and very excited as she said we could go and stay with her in the flat she was sharing with her friend Sue who had gone away for the weekend.

Linda was living at Redcliffe Gardens and we moved into this rather pleasant flat. Ken insisted on unpacking his suits and shirts and as there was no wardrobe space, he hung these on the picture rail around the bedroom. We then went out for dinner and returned to the flat around 11.p.m. when Linda noticed a light in Sue's bedroom! General panic as Sue had obviously come home early, — and Linda felt guilty at not having asked Sue if we could stay the night. We crept into the flat and hastily packed and carried our luggage down the stairs into the car.

Whilst Ken was loading the car, along came a policeman who was obviously very suspicious about the way we were behaving — i.e. trying to keep quiet and stealthily tip toeing down the stairs so as not to wake Sue. We then noticed that, in packing so quickly, one of Ken's shirt tails was hanging out of the suitcase! We could understand why the policeman was looking suspiciously at us!

He approached us and asked what we were doing at that time of night. Linda explained that she lived in the flat and that her flat mate had returned earlier than usual so her parents and sister who were to have shared her room felt they had to leave. I think he believed us — and Ken and I drove off to find some accommodation for the night in London.

By this time it was after midnight — and we thought we would go to the Overseas Club and see if they had a room. As the parking was difficult I was sent in to enquire from the Night Receptionist, who looked equally as suspicious as the policeman, as to why I should be wanting a room so late at night! He hesitated and looked through his booking list and I think would have said "No" if I hadn't added at that moment that we would also require an extra bed for our 10 year old daughter. This I felt assured him that we were not having a dirty night out!

He helped us into the Club with our luggage and think when he saw Ken's shirt tail hanging out of the case — he too was a little suspicious.

We met Linda for lunch the next day, and had a good laugh at our antics of the previous night. Apparently her flat mate Sue was in a foul mood the next morning and told Linda exactly what she thought of her entertaining men whilst she thought Sue was away. She had seen the suits hanging around the bedroom and Ken's shaving kit in the bathroom and had obviously assumed the worst. This had been cleared up and all was well once more.

During lunch Linda reminded me of the conversation we had had about what I considered a sufficient income to live in London.

She then said she had got a job at a pound a week more than I had stipulated as a basic income, working at the BBC as a copy typist — and she did NOT want to go to a Secretarial College. Rightly or wrongly she eventually convinced us that if she went to Night School the end result would be the same! I wonder!

Whilst she had been at Miss Wolfe's Academy she had learnt to type and the basic skills needed in an office, but had received no official qualification. As we had not had a very happy time with her previous schooling — we felt perhaps that we should permit her to continue at the BBC where we felt promotion would eventually be good so long as she went to Nightschool.

So Linda started her working life — which only lasted about 6 weeks!

This friend Frank, she had met in Karachi at the Intercontinental Hotel Pool, was obviously keener on continuing the friendship than we had been led to believe and he turned up in London and wanted to take Linda to Ireland to meet his Mother! She took unpaid leave — and he paid her fare to Ireland — all this without our knowledge.

We had left the U.K. — happy that she was settled in a job which we felt could lead to promotion; her living arrangements with her friend Sue were more than acceptable as it was a very pleasant flat and Sue, being that much older, we thought would be a good influence. However, three weeks after we returned to Karachi she had left the job and gone to Ireland with this Frank she had met at the Hotel in Karachi. He was anxious for her to meet his Mother!

We had only been back in Karachi a short time when to our horror we received a Telegram from Linda in London saying "Passing through Karachi en route to Singapore — please do not have me taken off the flight — will explain when I see you"!

Her flight arrived on a Friday which is a Muslim Holiday and Karachi was basically Muslim, so rather like our Sundays, when everything closes, so we were unable to get an official airport pass to go into the Transit Lounge to see Linda who we discovered was booked straight through to Singapore.

I was so distraught that I made enquiries about having her made a Ward of Court — but as she was nearly 18 it was explained that by the time this was authorised she would be 18 and it would not apply!

Through some friends who worked at the airport, we were able to arrange that she came out of the Transit Lounge accompanied by one of the BOAC staff and we had about ten minutes with her. What a story she told us!

It appeared that Frank had indicated that he was in trouble in Pakistan and was wanted by the Police as he was a member of the CIA Apparently he told Linda that he had been sent to kill someone in Rawalpindi and as he could not get back to Karachi without being arrested — he said he wanted her to go to Singapore as he NEEDED her!

I am afraid I said his only "need" was to take her to bed! I was accused of relating everything to sex. However, he had arranged for her to stay with some friends of his — and — until this problem was solved he needed her by his side!

What could we do — her flight was called — we'd only had about 8 mins together which if anything had made me more unhappy than I was before I saw her!

Our only advice was that when she wanted to return to the U.K. or back to Karachi with us, she only had to approach Ken's office in Singapore who would provide her with a ticket. This we had been able to arrange with the Manager and that he would debit us with any expenses incurred on her behalf. She told us she already had a return ticket!

We were as you can imagine very unhappy — I think "distraught" would be a better word, and the next morning — devastated, as the morning papers contained the news that War between India and Pakistan had been declared and there was no communication of any sort, in or out of Pakistan!

The only thing I could think of was to try to discover the truth about this so called "murder" and so I made an appointment at the

Australian High Commission. I told them my problems and asked if they could tell me if what I had been told was true? They immediately said they could not divulge anything about an Australian citizen, but their advice to me was that I got my daughter back immediately! From their attitude I was sure they knew more about this but obviously were not going to disclose it to me. I then approached the British High Commission who said they would try to help. Two days later I was told that not only was this man wanted by the police, but was wanted by Interpol! They could tell me no more — but we knew that Interpol was basically only interested in drugs and gun running!

One would read about things like this — but never did I think it could possibly happen to me and felt I had had my share of traumas in my life.

I did manage to get a letter to Linda telling her what we had been told — and suggested she return to Karachi but her reply was to the effect that she never thought her parents would believe such nonsense, and that we were letting her down! I pointed out that we were not alone in our views and that we had been told he was not only wanted by the Police but Interpol and this had been substantiated by those in authority. We suggested that if Frank was innocent of these charges — why did he not return to Pakistan and dispute them?

To cut a long and involved story short we eventually received a telegram from Linda saying "Pakistan business now cleared will you agree to wedding on 10th January?". This caused a lot of soul searching — if we said "No" — then we would probably lose our daughter — and she may just go and live with this man — which to our mind in those days was not really acceptable. If on the other hand we said "yes" and they came to Pakistan for the wedding — then IF he was guilty — he would be arrested and we would get our daughter back and would be there to help her.

So...we sent our telegram off saying "Yes — we agreed to the Wedding". This was early December. Linda arrived within 2 days — obviously elated that we had agreed to the wedding and told us this rather dramatic story.

I still find it all rather hard to believe, but have to say we do feel that Frank was a victim of circumstances — and very sad that things turned out as they did at that time.

It appeared that Frank had lost his Passport some time ago — and it had obviously been picked up by someone — who had about 5 other Passports and he then used this latest one as yet another alias.   There were so many coincidences; they both worked for Pharmaceutical Companies — they had both been staying at the Intercontinental Hotel in Karachi around the same time and they both travelled fairly frequently.   On one particular trip from Bangkok to Dacca — this man was arrested and had Frank's passport with him.   Naturally — his name was put on the Black List — hence his being wanted by Interpol.

Where the story originated about his having killed someone and being a member of the CIA — I don't know as it was never substantiated.

We were naturally delighted to have our daughter back with us and as promised plans were made for their wedding on the 10th January, which incidentally was our wedding date.   Invitations were sent out — the Church booked and we decided to have the Reception in our Clifton flat.

Frank arrived a few days before the wedding — and we all went out to meet him — and I confess that we were wondering if he would be arrested when he came through Immigration — but no — there were no problems.   He did apologise for all the worry he had caused the family.   Whilst we felt very sorry for what he had been through — and the anxiety he too must have suffered, we still felt he was wrong in having taken our daughter, first of all to Ireland and then inducing her to go to Singapore, without first asking our permission.   She was after all 17 — but as he was considerably older I suppose he was not used to asking permission for anything. Nowadays this will all sound puritanical — but in 1966 it was unusual to say the least.

The Wedding was a great success — Linda looked quite beautiful — but then she always did. Fiona made a very pretty bridesmaid and Linda's great friend Caroline Willans was her Maid of Honour.

The Reception was again in our flat at 73 Clifton, and we had about 60 guests — many Yacht Club members and very close friends — though unfortunately no family members. However, there were many telegrams from overseas, some very touching and others very humorous. There was no shortage of Staff as our own servants brought in their friends — who were only too anxious to earn a little extra money, so no one was without a drink for very long!

Linda and Frank left for the Airport around 6.p.m. — obviously sorry to leave the party which continued for some time. They were to spend their Honeymoon in Penang — the so called "Pearl of the Orient" and then on to Singapore where Frank was now working.

I had to hold back the tears as all Mothers do — after all she was the first chicken to leave the nest — and she was the same age I had been when I entered into that disastrous marriage. Naturally we hoped she would have a happy, healthy life with Frank — who obviously was devoted to her — we just wished we had had the opportunity to get to know him a little better.

The War between India and Pakistan still continued and it was difficult to know how it was progressing. Our one source of information was from a friend who worked for BOAC and he was able to keep us reasonably up to date with information gained from the various Crew members that arrived from overseas. So a few of us would meet at the Sind Club early each evening and hope that Bob would arrive and let us know how the war was going!

Occasional bombs would be dropped which caused a lot of consternation amongst the locals, but to any of us who had experienced the 1939 to 1945 War — they really were insignificant.

I have to say that one of my happiest moments was in Karachi on the 29th May, 1967.

Ken and I had been to a business dinner but had been invited to join a party at the home of Peggy and Hamish Porter after the dinner — so about 11.p.m. we arrived at the second party and as we entered the house — everyone present started singing to the tune of "Hello Dolly" the words "Hello Granny" and this was my first intimation that Linda had given birth to a darling little girl.   Her husband had rung us at home and Fiona had taken the call — and she knew how excited we would be AND she also knew that we were attending this party at the Porter's — so she rang them and asked them to tell us so we could phone Linda!   To this day I can't hear "Hello Dolly" without thinking of this very happy evening.

As Karachi was a couple of hours behind Singapore time wise — so we were able to ring her immediately — and we really were over the moon — after all — this was our first grandchild.

I suppose I shouldn't have been so shocked when on the 20th June, 1967 we got a telegram saying that Mum had died.   She had apparently contracted pneumonia and I think all things considered she would not have wanted to continue with her life in the Hospital. It was impossible to have her at home — as she needed constant supervision — and my brother felt there was no point in asking me to return when she acquired pneumonia, as they felt she would recover.

I still have regrets at not having gone home for the funeral — but felt I should have gone when she was alive not when she had died — though as was pointed out to me she wouldn't have known whether I was there or not.   She was cremated in the Crematorium at Horsforth.   I just hope her "after life" is happier than the one she had on earth, as although always cheerful — she did not have very much to be happy about.

We went home on leave in 1967 and had arranged to stop off in Singapore for a few days to see Linda and her husband and of course our new grand-daughter.   We had planned to stay for about ten days not wishing to overstay our welcome — after all — house guests are rather like fish and tend to "go off" after three days!   However, they both made us feel so welcome and persuaded us to stay longer!

We were enchanted with our new grand-daughter and this gave us an opportunity to spend more time with her.

Ken's sister Dot and brother-in-law, John, were living in Kuala Lumpur at this time where John headed up Malayan Cement and so we all drove up from Singapore to see them.

We drove to Kuala Lumpur from Singapore and had to cross the Johore Causeway and go through Immigration. Johore is a sprawling ramshackle place, thick with street stalls — and as we drove through it going North we passed the Sultan of Johore's Palace.

Having just left Singapore which is a well disciplined, efficient and spik and span city, where the majority of people appeared to understand, if not speak, English, it was a cultural shock to cross this short causeway and find oneself in a completely different environment.

A few years later when Ken was working in Singapore and I took a friend from the U.K. up to Kuala Lumpur, we were even more shattered.

The bus we boarded in Singapore was scrupulously clean — newspapers were put on the floor as we boarded to ensure the floor remained clean. The driver and co-driver were in spotless uniforms, very courteous and anxious to help and there was an English Video for our entertainment and praise be, the Toilet facilities on board were spotlessly clean. All this for about S$30 compared to the air fare of around S$150.

When we got to the Causeway at Johore, again the crew helped us with our luggage as it had to be hand carried through Customs and we were told to join the bus on the Malay side of the Immigration booths.

We couldn't believe the change in attitude once we boarded the bus again on the Malay side. Already the bus looked dirtier — the driver and co-driver had been partaking of their breakfast and had left the empty cartons on the floor — gone were their smart uniforms and they wore slightly "off white" shorts and Tee shirts — no hats — the Video that had been playing in English was now in the Bahasa and far too loud — but there was nothing we could do about this as the crew no longer spoke English!

When we were driving up with Linda, though, the first shock was that all the road signs were in the Bahasa with no English equivalent. (Subsequently years later, when Ken and I were driving in Malaysia, we spent hours looking for "Utara" on the map with no success. We then discovered it meant "North"!|)

Few of the locals spoke English and they obviously expected you to speak Malay — therefore — trying to map read or follow the road signs was impossible. But we got to Kuala Lumpur and found the very luxurious home that Ken's sister was living in with a well trained team of servants.

As a surprise we found they had booked their Company house at Fraser's Hill for the weekend, so after a couple of days in K.L. we drove up to this very popular Hill Station.

To get into Fraser's Hill from the main road, one had to negotiate the last 10 miles on a brilliantly engineered road, which is single track, up through the jungle. To make this possible they had introduced a timetable so that cars going up to Frasers Hill had to synchronise their arrival at "The Gap" to coincide with the convoy going up. This gave them one hour before the down convoy left the top.

The cars were counted at the departure and arrival gates and the road would not be opened for the oncoming traffic until all the cars that had entered were accounted for — and if one did not appear in the scheduled time — the people in the corresponding convoy had to wait until the road had been checked, and if the car had broken down — it was moved.

It was on this stretch of road that the Governor was murdered during the trouble with Merdeka.

Fraser's Hill is the nearest Hill Station to K.L. — it can be misty and chilly and therefore very popular with people anxious to escape the heat and humidity of Kuala Lumpur.

The house we were staying in had been used by the Japanese as a Hospital after the fall of Malaysia. The servants were the same ones that had worked for the Japanese (not very active!) and one had a feeling that they were rather anti British. The food they prepared was excellent — and we had a very enjoyable holiday.

There was a lovely little 9 hole golf course and lots of delightful walks — and — a very small "Club" where the resident Expats who had retired up there seemed to congregate every evening for their sun-downer and made visitors feel most welcome.

We returned to K.L. and after this super holiday we flew to Bangkok and then on to Zurich where we spent a few days and visited Sue and Alex Hegi.

Sue was the young girl who came to stay with us in Bombay for a weekend and ended up spending about 3 months — by which time she was part of our family and we still feel very close to her. She married Alex whilst we were in Bombay and they shortly moved to Zurich.

They lived in a flat in Nurensdorf on the outskirts of Zurich and we were quite tickled with some of the regulations that applied to flat life in Switzerland.

We were not allowed to have a bath after 9.p.m. but more importantly, we could not flush the toilet after 9.p.m. and of course no music! We had lived in flats for some years now and found these restrictions rather intimidating — but — at least very considerate to your neighbours!

When we arrived at Zurich airport we found we had lost all our luggage, but as Alex worked for Swissair he was able to instigate a search and the cases were finally delivered to us in Amsterdam AND we received about £30 per head in order to buy toilet and other necessities whilst in Switzerland.

This incident reminded me of a story about a gentleman flying to Washington and New York via London from Bombay and he had three pieces of luggage. He asked if one of the cases could go direct to New York and one to Washington and the third to London. The booking clerk told him this was not possible. "Why not?" said the passenger — "the last time I flew my three cases ended up in three different destinations and I didn't even request this!

Alex very kindly took a few days' leave and drove us to all the local beauty spots. The weather was wonderful — and so I wore summer clothes and open toed sandals which I find so comfy if a lot of walking is entailed. However, I had not bargained for the heights we would reach, and the higher we climbed the lower the temperature dropped. Alex and Sue were obviously prepared for these changes in temperature and so had come equipped with anoraks for us all, but I was still stuck with my sandals! We went up a chair lift to the top of a mountain — and when we reached the top and disembarked — we were standing in at least 6 inches of snow! The other people on the chair lift were all well equipped with climbing boots and thick sox — so I really did look like a country cousin — and I might add — felt like one.

Beautiful as the scenery was — I was delighted when they decided to take the chair lift down to the valley where the car was parked and the sun was shining!

We had a day in Zurich and drove round the Lake and had lunch in a super Swiss Restaurant overlooking the Lake. The restaurant was renowned for its fantastic chocolate cake — and other delicious desserts were served, which played hell with one's diet.

Switzerland really is most picturesque — and I would thoroughly recommend it for a holiday — though do take two lots of clothing — one in your hand luggage!

When we arrived in Amsterdam we were delighted to be able to retrieve the missing cases. We were met by the Oord family — also from Karachi Yacht Club, who were Dutch and had two daughters Retake and Hilde who had been at school with Fiona in Karachi and they were great friends. Hank had hired a mini bus so that we could all get around without having to use two cars.

As hosts they really excelled themselves and drove us to s'Hertogenbosch because Ken's regiment had relieved this town during the war and they had been the first troops to enter. Hank pulled his leg and every time we saw a fat lady he would ask Ken if that was his girl friend?   The children thought this was very funny! They took us to Maduradam, a large miniature village with everything mechanical;   we had seen nothing like it before — quite amazing.   Then on to Delft where the pottery is made, and we bought a little souvenir, which we have to this day.

In Amsterdam Hank seemed quite happy driving us around the city and showed us the Wallaghes (the Red Light District) which I thought was very tasteful when you compared it with similar areas in the East.   The rather beautiful ladies were sitting in windows, filing their nails or looking at magazines and when someone knocked at the door they got up answered the door and then drew the curtains! Some curtains seemed to be perpetually drawn!

In front of some of the windows there were queues and I asked Hank what these "girls" would charge.   Being the perfect host he parked the mini bus, left us and joined one of the smaller queues! When he came back he quoted a figure which translated into five English shillings!   I should add, that having asked the price he left the queue!

Ans Oord is a delightful person and had a most interesting life. We had known her many years before we learnt that she had been responsible for saving the lives of at least 36 airmen during the war. Their house was particularly suitable for hiding people — as it had a roof with communicating doors, which meant that when the house was being searched by the Germans, the airmen could move into the next house through a door in the adjoining roof and fortunately they avoided detection until their escape was arranged.

Mind you this was the least of her problems; she then took it upon herself to get them to one of the inland seas where she would take them in her sailing boat to join another group being taken out, and hopefully not be detected.   I should add that Ans was a brilliant sailor and won many of the trophies at the Yacht Club — though at the time none of us had any idea where she had gained all the experience!

Ans was, and still is, a very private person and never spoke of her escapades during the war — in fact it was like drawing teeth to get her to tell you about it — and she always seemed surprised that we would find it interesting.

Eventually a film was made incorporating her work for the British and Allied airmen — unfortunately I still do not know the name of the film as Ans was very loath to talk about her experiences.

We eventually got back to the U.K. and it was time for Fiona to go to Boarding School — most of her friends at the B.O.S. (British Overseas School) had either already gone or were going that year.

Bearing in mind our experience with Linda and Boarding School we really felt that the most important aspect must be that the staff were kind and caring. We had had good reports about a Catholic School at Effingham and after vetting several schools we finally decided on St. Theresa's Convent at Effingham. Neither Ken or I were Catholic but Linda had been so unhappy at school we felt that the Nuns would be kind and understanding and she would settle better in this atmosphere.

In later life we discovered we were wrong — that the Nuns did not excel in distributing affection or understanding — but then they had 700 pupils to cope with — and it would be impossible to give all the students specialised attention.

We had the usual rush of getting uniform and labelling every item and then went through the agonising business of taking her to school and saying goodbye.

We stayed in the U.K. for another month so we were able to have her out for her first Exeat and she also brought a friend with her.

The weekend went all too quickly — but having the friend did help a little when it came to returning to school and I hoped that the friend's parents might reciprocate this weekend as they were living in England.

Need I add it was not a very cheerful weekend as both Fiona and I kept counting the hours left before she had to return. Having been through the sadness of parting with Linda, it seemed we had to go through it all again.    Even to this day I have cried watching parents at airports saying goodbye to their children — so you can imagine the state I was in when it was our own children!

Ken and I flew back to Karachi after this weekend, feeling we were deserting Fiona — and there was a lot of heart searching as to whether I should have stayed at home.    My mother had always said that a wife should put her husband before her children — as they would grow up and leave home — but if you neglected your husband there would be many ladies who would step into the breach to ensure he wasn't bored!    I think in hindsight this was good advice, but I was far from convinced at this stage!

Fiona's regular letters from school led us to believe she was reasonably happy — there was another friend from Karachi at the school — and so we felt assured that she was settling.

We then heard that she had been admitted to the school Sanatorium with what they thought was Flu — and although she recovered reasonably quickly — this dreaded so called Flu kept re-appearing.    I think she was in the School San at least six times during the term — with a fairly high temperature — and feeling lethargic.

When she came out for her first holiday in December 1968, we therefore took her to our Doctor and explained the problem.    He did a series of tests and discovered what she was suffering from what was an unusual type of Malaria — obviously acquired in Karachi prior to going to the U.K.    Apparently this type of Malaria does not affect anyone with pigmentation in their skin — hence the Pakistanis, Indians and Malays did not acquire it.    Therefore the drug which was required to treat this type of Malaria was not sold in Karachi.

It took quite a lot of organising but eventually we had the drug flown in from the U.K. and Fiona started her treatment at the Seventh Day Adventist Hospital.    She needed an injection every day, which she had in the morning and after an hour, if there had been no adverse re-action, she was allowed home for the rest of the day, but had to be back in Hospital by 6.p.m. This went on for 10 days — but it had meant she was late returning to school as the treatment had to be finished.

Fiona came out for her Xmas holiday on the 11th December, and I took some leave in order to spend as much time with her as possible.

For someone who never had any of the childhood illnesses I certainly made up for it when I started living in the East, starting in Calcutta after I had to have the 8 pint blood transfusion after the Ectopic Pregnancy — which was followed by Typhoid Fever ten days later and subsequently Hepatitis. I then seemed to have medical traumas of one kind or another, in every country we lived in.

For instance in Karachi in 1968, I was driving home from the office one afternoon and I suddenly found I could not see. I panicked and stopped at the side of the road — and then suddenly I felt I could see a little so started to drive home again. This must have happened about 6 times within a distance of about 3 miles and when I got home I was terrified and lay on my bed weeping — which it turned out was the worst thing I could have done! As I told you I had lost the sight of my left eye when I was in my 20's — and considered I had been very lucky in retaining the sight in my right eye.

However, a phone call to Ken and a visit to the Eye Specialist confirmed that I had a Detached Retina in my right eye — the only one I could see through. They suggested I went into hospital immediately and surgery was arranged as soon as the fluid had dispersed. The tear in the Retina was large — and with crying I had formed a lot of fluid which had to be disposed of before they could consider surgery, as they were afraid it might detach completely.

Ken got in touch with his Head Office who really were terrific — as they contacted Moorfields Eye Hospital giving them the diagnosis and extent of the detachment from the Karachi Eye Surgeon. Their reply was that as the tear was so large it would be very dangerous to fly home as with the pressure they felt the whole Retina would detach and that in the circumstances I should have surgery in Karachi.

I have to confess that the Eye Surgeon — a darling little man no taller than 5', was even more nervous than I.   He told me that he had only done two similar operations and out of these only one had been successful!   Just what one wanted to hear before such serious surgery on your one remaining eye!

The next problem was that to do this operation he needed a very dark and sterile Theatre — and there was only one he could think of that was not in constant use and this belonged to a Surgeon in private practice.   He was approached and gave his consent — and I gather the Theatre was adapted for eye surgery early that evening and I was taken into the Operating Theatre — presumably having had pre-med but, I assure you, being well aware of all that was going on.

I will always remember prior to starting the surgery the Muslim Surgeon called on Allah to help him, which did nothing for my morale!

The next trauma was that Karachi suffered one of its worst "black outs" which lasted about 2 hours — so the surgery had to be delayed — but eventually — the lights re-appeared and Allah was called upon once more!

To start the surgery he had to inject an anaesthetic into the eye — this I did not like — and consequently dread ever having further eye surgery.   Lasers were not available at that time — certainly not in Karachi and therefore I had about 5 rather thick stitches which had to be removed after a few days — they were not the dissolving type.   The surgery seemed to take an inordinate time and after it was over both eyes were heavily bandaged and my head was resting between sandbags and it was stressed that under no circumstances must I move!   I thought this would be for an hour or so and had no idea it was going to extend for a few days.   When you are told not to move — you feel a compulsion to do so and it quickly becomes an obsession.

Fiona was out for her Xmas holiday at the time, and we deferred her return to school as I really felt that perhaps I would never be able to see her again and of course she was concerned about "Mum" so her return to school was delayed by about a week.    It was our Wedding Anniversary whilst I was in the Nursing Home and when Fiona came into my room in the morning she presented me with a very large parcel.    She told me I had to guess what it was — and there was no way I could cheat with all the bandages on.    I really was intrigued as the paper came off the parcel and then I found something that Detached from the main package — followed by another odd shaped piece — and I really could not guess.    She told me to take care as it was breakable — and yet it didn't feel smooth like China and it was too rough for glass.    My fingers roamed all around it and in the end I had to give in and ask her what it was.

It was a large red clay Kandara Horse — and the pieces that were loose were the ears and tail.    This has been our cherished possession all these years and although the tail and the ears have snapped on occasion — it has been repaired with super glue and still takes pride of place.

I got very distressed and frustrated as the Asian nurses would come into my room and ask stupid questions like "Mrs. Campbell did you have a pink pill or a blue pill at 10.a.m." as I couldn't see a thing, I really felt this was highly inefficient on the part of the staff. At night there was a nurse on duty who spoke very little English and certainly did not understand a word I said.    I was not supposed to cry — but I felt so up tight that I would plead not to be left on my own — as at night I could see forms in my bandages which terrified me — and when I rang for the nurses naturally they were always busy.    I think they were giving me so many tranquillisers to stop me moving that I became slightly deranged and was really scared.

Obviously Ken could not spend all the time with me — though he came every morning at the crack of dawn and fed me breakfast, he would try to pop in at lunch time and was back in the evening.

Once again in my life my friends were fantastic.    One of whom arranged a roster so that someone would come to the Nursing Home as Ken left around 8.a.m. and every hour throughout the day someone was visiting me, certainly at meal times as the normal staff would just place a tray in front of me and move onto the next patient. So many glasses of water and cups of tea were spilt, until I had these regular visitors.

At first I didn't realise that it was an arranged roster, I just thought it was luck that as one visitor was leaving another would arrive. At night Ken engaged a night nurse who spoke English — but I continued to have these horrible nightmares and clung onto the night nurses' hand for most of the night. I think it must have been the medication that had this affect — as looking back I feel quite ashamed that I was so frightened.

The eye was dressed daily — but I could not see anything — which I naturally found distressing. I kept asking about the stitches which were very uncomfortable and which I was terrified of having removed and the nurses kept telling me not to worry.

The day came when I was to be discharged and early in the morning the Surgeon arrived for his final check up, and the removal of the stitches. Fiona was in the hospital at the time and was told she could remain in the room. When I tell you it took nearly 2 hours to get these 5 stitches out — I am not exaggerating.

First my eye was clamped and then "an attack" was made on my eye with what looked like scissors. I defy anyone not to blink under these circumstances — whether they had a clamp on or not. The clamp kept slipping and another attempt was made — finally the first stitch was cut — but — this didn't remove it and I then had to endure a pair of tweezers which seemed to attack the eye once or twice with no apparent success but finally the offending stitch was grabbed and literally thrown away. Fiona went round the room later retrieving all these stitches.

When the bandages were removed and the stitches were out I could see outlines and the first thing I saw was Fiona's face gazing with concern.

I returned home and was taken round the flat feeling for any obstruction and the servants were told not to move any piece of furniture. Naturally they didn't remember and I found myself getting very bad tempered when I tripped up or bruised myself through their forgetfulness. After a couple of weeks I was getting very depressed — and so it was arranged for an occupational therapist to call every morning for a couple of hours. She started my therapy by teaching me to weave baskets.

She brought the frame with the metal warps and so it should have been simple — but I found it a bit of a challenge to weave this alternating pale blue and white plastic strips in and out. Initially this seemed simple — but for some reason after I had done a couple of rounds I seemed to get confused as to which colour I should have been working with and would spend hours trying to achieve that extra inch of weaving — so that I could proudly present a finished basket to my tutor.

However, my confidence and humour were sadly depleted when the following day the Therapist would arrive and examine the basket and always said "well done — you have worked hard — BUT" and then I heard her undoing all my carefully worked weaving as apparently I had made a mistake on the first or second row!

After a week of this I became thoroughly demoralised and on one occasion when she again said I'd made a weaving error early in the basket — I threw the darned basket across the room and said "Who wants to make b....y baskets anyway?" I was however persuaded to finish this and I still have the basket to this day which I confess is well made and looks very attractive — as well it should after all the heart break it caused!

After I had been home about 10 days I was given a pair of dark glasses with black sides and a top which fitted closely to my forehead. In the middle of these black glasses was a small pin hole and I could then see shapes and became more optimistic. This period seemed to last forever — and I really did begin to wonder if I would ever see again properly. I had repeated visits to this wonderful surgeon —

who seemed delighted with his surgery, and kept assuring me that, all things considered, I had been very lucky.

I confess I wasn't easily convinced at that time! My dark glasses were replaced by normal glasses and I could at least see — though not as well as I would have liked — but was told my sight would keep changing. I had 16 pairs of glasses in the next four months, eight for reading and eight for distance use as every week when I saw the Ophthalmologist he found my sight had changed sufficiently to warrant a change of glasses. To this day I am still using some of the frames from these glasses!

The Surgeon told me after the surgery — that he had placed a silicone ring around the Retina as a precaution to prevent it from detaching again.

After about three months I visited the eye surgeon for a check-up and I could tell he was not entirely happy. He broke the news to me that he felt there was a possibility that the Retina was detaching yet again, but that, with the silicone ring in the eye, he thought it would be safe for me to fly home to Moorfields Eye Hospital, and as they had more up to date equipment than he had it would be safer.

Arrangements were made for me to be admitted to Moorfields and the eye was duly examined. They praised the Surgeon in Karachi for what he had done in the most difficult circumstances, and were quite shattered that his equipment was still so antiquated — but — with his skills he had done a remarkable job. They did say that nowadays in London they would not have had me bound up for so long, and the operation would have been less traumatic. The problem seemed to be that the eye was rejecting the silicone ring which would have to be removed.

Surgery was arranged for the next day and I must have had a General Anaesthetic as I knew nothing about this — but when I became conscious the first thing I asked the nurse was "how many stitches did I have". I nearly had a coronary when they told me 18! They couldn't understand my distress and assured me I wouldn't know a thing when they were removed. After my experience of having only 5 stitches removed which seemed to take for ever — I certainly was not convinced about these 18 stitches.

I got myself into such a state over this and when I kept asking when the stitches were to be removed they kept saying — "not for some time yet". Need I say — they lied — as the next day a very suspicious tray was wheeled in followed by the Doctor and his nurse! I really didn't have time to worry as within seconds the Dr. seemed to rest his hand on my cheek and I felt a slight tickle — whereupon he said "that wasn't so bad was it?" and to my utter amazement found he had removed 9 stitches. They were obviously fine and had been inserted in a sort of running stitch so that when one was pulled the whole 9 were removed. This was repeated on the other cheek and within minutes all 18 stitches had been removed — and I felt nothing — I just couldn't believe it!

I am not trying to run down in any way the treatment I received in Karachi — the Surgeon was brilliant but I realise how deprived the country was in having no up-to-date equipment which made the surgery so difficult. He only had the old fashioned needles that had to be sterilised and were used over and over again and consequently became quite blunt — all because of lack of funds.

When we returned to Karachi after this visit to Moorfields we felt so very grateful to this brilliant surgeon that we took a supply of needles and sutures with us in appreciation for all he had done for me.

Our next leave was in July, 1969, when we flew to Nicosia; picked up a car and started our drive around the Island. We had a delightful day in Kyrenia in the north of the Island, staying at the Dome Hotel, then took the coast road to Famagusta (which we weren't over impressed with), then on to Larnaka and to Limassol where we spent a couple of nights and picked up bottles of the very cheap Brandy which is produced there. We then drove to Paphos and Troodos up in the mountains then back to Nicosia. A very interesting trip, and we found the Island cheap — with pleasant happy people — though it was not as green and lush as we had expected.

We decided to spend a day in Athens chiefly to re-take some of the films we had taken on our previous visit which had been lost in the post.

Then Sue and Alex Hegi had invited us to stay with them again and so we had another glorious few days. Alex seemed to arrange that we went up every cable car and chair lift in the vicinity, but this time I had suitable shoes!

We got back to the U.K. in time to pick Fiona up from school on the 17th July, 1969. We then had a few days in Epsom with Olive and Syd Reece — then on to Norfolk to stay with Vera and Claude Tyler — in their 18th century house at Reepham. Vera was Linda's Godmother, and we have been friends since 1947 when I lived in Greenford.

About this time the Company had agreed to include overseas staff in their House Purchase Scheme which meant they lent you an amount of money at preferential rates, which could perhaps cover the deposit on a property.

For some time we had thought that overseas staff were definitely being left behind in the property market and that by the time we returned home — usually for retirement — we would not be able to afford the prices that would be appertaining then. So we were determined that we would not wait any longer to get on the band wagon and would buy a property, even if it wasn't something we would necessarily want to live in on return to the U.K. for good.

Although this was a generous offer on the part of the Company, we still were restricted as to the price we could afford to pay, so we ended up buying a small flat in Putney which we felt was in a good letting area. I had had a few doubts about this — thinking Putney was rather congested for a leave — but it was first class — small and easy to run — and so accessible for the West End and Kings Road, which never ceased to be of interest.

On a previous leave we had rented a flat in Putney — so felt comfortable about living there. The commuting was good with an excellent train and bus service, and a good range of shops.

Finding this flat, decorating it and finding a tenant seemed to take most of our leave and our good friends Olive and Syd Reece with whom we had stayed in Delhi, had again kindly invited us to stay with them whilst we were flat hunting.

After we moved in to Burton Lodge in Putney we had quite a few friends to stay and were able to visit the Theatre on four occasions — something we hadn't been able to do in any of our Eastern postings. The weather had been good and we were quite sorry to leave. Before we left we had found a tenant and we hoped that the rent we received would help pay off our mortgage!

After all the decorating and the upheaval we decided we would take Fiona for a short holiday, by converting part of our air ticket London-Aberdeen-London to London-Paris-London.

We had been invited by the Oords to join them at Crans Montana in a chalet they had rented, so we flew into Paris where we hired a car and drove to Dijon Icogue near Crans, where the Oords were staying. The Chalet was out of this world — it had its own heated swimming pool — every modern convenience — beautiful surroundings — snow topped mountains, and glorious sunshine every day. We had a wonderful 8 days with them and when not touring the surrounding countryside, we spent our time relaxing round the pool or in the pool — it was a lovely holiday which we all enjoyed.

Again I must stress what a lovely country Switzerland is — no pollution — warm and bright and the people so pleasant.

After leaving Crans we drove from Montana along the Rhine — over the Gotthard Pass to Sentis and then back to Zurich. Time was passing and Fiona was due back at school so we drove back to Paris in one day.

Unfortunately it was late when we arrived in Paris having got completely lost en route, as we had no idea where we were going and had difficulty reading the road signs! There was a Metro strike on, which had caused more than the usual chaos on the crowded roads and the Hotels were all fully booked with commuters who couldn't get home.    Not a good time to arrive!

Not having driven in Paris before it was hair raising — and to make matters worse, we had no accommodation.

As it was impossible for Ken to park the car I was despatched into the Pensions or Inns to enquire if at that late hour they had any accommodation.

No one spoke English and so I had to rely on my school girl French which didn't do a lot for me!    Every Inn or Pension I went into — they shook their heads and I was told they had no rooms available.    Ken was getting a little worried and asked me what I was asking for?    He said he quite understood why we were getting negative responses to my "Pardonnez Moi? Avez vous un chambre de lit pour moi et mon homme!"    He suggested that the next time I substituted "homme" for "mari" — and mentioned the word "enfant" — as it happened this seemed to work and the next pension I went into — we got a room!

This was in the 60's when people, even in Paris, were not as broad minded as they are now.    It seems quite ridiculous in this day and age — but that is how things were!

We were very fortunate in finding this very reasonable Hotel in the Rue de Richelieu (near The Louvre) which Ken said reminded him of a five star brothel!    Whilst not luxurious, at least it was clean and very reasonable which was amazing in Paris at that time.

After two happy days in Paris we drove to the airport to catch our plane, picked up our U.K. car and drove Fiona back to school the next day.

# SEVEN
## *Nairobi Interlude—September, 1969.*

We had a further week in the U.K. packing up before flying to Nairobi, and Fiona was allowed an Exeat for this last weekend — and again she brought a friend with her, which helped on the Sunday evening when she had to return to school.    Can't say it helped me very much — and I felt quite distraught having to say goodbye.

This last week in the U.K. was hectic — packing up for our trip to Nairobi.   Bob and Muriel Geddes, who were great friends from Karachi and who were now living in Kenya, had invited us to visit them on our way back from leave.

We had to take into account when packing, not only the Boat trip from Mombasa to Karachi, but also the very different clothing which we would require when visiting the Game Parks.   Then we also had to do a great deal of shopping for the next two years getting items unobtainable in Karachi.   A complete waste of time and money as it turned out!

On the 27th September, 1969 we flew to Nairobi and were met by Bob and Muriel.    They lived at Karen in a superb bungalow in 6 acres.   This was without doubt the holiday of a lifetime and the most memorable we have ever had.   Muriel and Bob were the most terrific hosts who had planned a simply wonderful itinerary for us. I can't begin to tell you how much we enjoyed Kenya.

We spent a few days in their lovely home in Karen, on the outskirts of Nairobi, where many Europeans lived.

The strict security in the house rather amazed us at first, but then we realised it was a relic from the days of the Mau Mau troubles.

Not only did they have a watchman, but ALL the external AND internal doors and windows were locked in the house each evening, — which meant when we wanted to visit the cloakroom in the middle of the night we had to unlock our own bedroom door and then unlock the corridor door and finally the toilet door, by which time I felt the whole house would be awake!

The first evening Bob and Muriel gave a dinner party for us and had included about six of our ex Karachi friends who were now resident in Nairobi — I must say we envied them this posting where the climate was superb — no pollution and of course so much wild life which was a continual source of interest.

Talking to some of these friends I decided that whilst I thought we had problems in communicating with our servants who occasionally gave us headaches — this was nothing compared to the stories I was told about the African servants!

I gather that most of these anecdotes have received fairly extensive coverage, but we certainly had not heard them before.

One of their old friends, who lived in a rather antiquated old house, found that by the time the Boy (Bearer) had walked from the kitchen to the Dining Room — the food was usually cold — so they decided to get a builder to put in a serving hatch from the kitchen to the Dining Room which cut out the rather long walk down the corridor. It took about two weeks to do this, but finally it was finished. The Memsahib explained to the Cook and the Cook Boy that they would now serve through the hatch, as she wanted no more cold dinners.

Imagine everyone's surprise at the first dinner party after this was completed, when there was a grunting and shuffling and, lo and behold, there was the Bearer squeezing himself through the hatch balancing a serving dish in each hand!

Not to be outdone by this story another couple at the dinner party told us that they were hosting a Buffet party in their garden which was beautifully lit by large flares all the way up the drive. One of the dishes was to be Suckling Pig and so the cook boy was told not to forget the apple in the mouth.     You can guess — yes — he appeared carrying this poor little pig on a beautiful silver salver — but the apple was in the Cook Boy's mouth!

I thought the funniest story of all was told to me by one of our friends who had also been in Africa.

These people were thoroughly fed up as their cook boy was always looking dirty.    The Cooks were not expected to wear uniform but they were expected to change their clothes daily and LOOK clean. But he was a good Cook and they didn't really want to part with him.

As they left to go to the airport to meet a visitor from Head Office, the Bwana apparently shouted at the Cook to take off his filthy shirt and trousers and put on a clean apron.    That was exactly what he did!

These friends went into the kitchen later to tell the Cook boy they would have dinner in ten minutes only to find the Cook with nothing on but his clean white apron!    The front view was not too bad but you can imagine no doubt the shock they had when he turned round!

Unless you have lived in Africa or India and employed servants — you will doubtless find this hard to believe — but it happens — and I guess we have to put it down to a "communication problem", for which we must be to blame in not acquiring a better command of Swahili or Urdu!

The following day we were taken to the Nairobi National Park — which was a great surprise.    Because it seemed so close to Nairobi, we imagined that it would not have very many animals — again we were wrong!    It is quite fantastic and shouldn't be missed by any visitors to Kenya.    We saw a variety of animals — actually saw a Cheetah chase, catch and eat a small Waterbuck, with vultures flying overhead waiting for the remains of the carcass.    I thought this very sad, but I suppose this is nature's way of controlling the animal population.

A little further into the park a Lion attacked a Buffalo and brought it down — whereupon it was surrounded by the rest of the Lion family, but the Jackals and Hyenas were standing by watching and waiting until the Lions had had their fill.   They would not dare venture nearer until the Lions had left the carcass and then of course they had to ward off the vultures.

Before leaving the Park they took us to the Animal Orphanage, which is a refuge for any animal found abandoned or hurt in the Game Reserves.   There were a number of animals in the Orphanage at the time, and we were very impressed with the care and attention that was given to them.

Whilst we were staying at Karen, Ken received a request to ring his Head office in London!

How they contacted him remains a mystery, but I suppose he had told someone that he was stopping off in Nairobi for a holiday on his return to Karachi.   Head office had therefore rung the office in Nairobi to ask if Ken has been in touch or if they knew where he was staying?    Apparently our host had told someone at the Club that he was having U.K. visitors for a couple of weeks — and — presumably this resulted in a little sleuth work — and Ken was found. I gather that the Manager in Nairobi was slightly alarmed at this turn of events as he thought perhaps he was being posted elsewhere and that Ken was being offered Nairobi!

Anyway — the outcome of this phone call was that Ken was asked if he would like a transfer to Malaysia and, as we had been in Karachi nearly 10 years by then, we thought perhaps it was time we moved on and had a change.

In the meantime we continued with our holiday.   Bob had some business to do which involved visiting many of the Safari Lodges — so we were invited to accompany him and Muriel on this simply wonderful tour, where we not only saw the animals but experienced a wide variety of the superb accommodation available at these Lodges.   The highlight of this whole wonderful holiday was still to come.   Our friends drove us to the Outspan Hotel in Nyeri where we had lunch and had to check in before joining the jeep parties driving to Treetops Lodge in the Aberdare National Park where we were all going to spend the night.

You have to make advance reservations and you are not allowed to drive your own car to Tree Tops, and it has to be left at the Outspan Hotel. The trip from Outspan to Tree Tops was ten miles along a bumpy sandy road. The White Hunter, complete with Rifle, met us at a pre-arranged spot where we were off-loaded — our overnight bags taken by runners — and we were given a pep talk by The White Hunter, a Colonel Doig, who stressed that we must keep together on the 200 yard walk to Tree Tops. He pointed out the dangers of charging animals and we noticed Hides had been erected along the path behind which we were told we could run "if necessary!" which in itself gave a degree of excitement.

I noticed that the White Hunter kept looking around stealthily as though he expected an elephant to appear! Quite disturbing particularly when one was told about the parties that didn't "make" Tree Tops without being charged and there were photographs to substantiate this in the lobby.

Once inside we were shown to our rooms and we were told that tea would be served on the Veranda at 4.p.m. By to-day's standards I suppose one couldn't say the accommodation was luxurious, with the creaking floorboards, trestle tables, the small rooms and shared bathroom facilities. Frankly, we didn't notice any of these deficiencies — and in any case, we had been allocated, through the kindness of our friends, one of the rooms with its own bathroom! To us — we were far more intrigued with what Tree Tops had to offer.

A plaque reminded us that various crowned Heads of State and Presidents had stayed here and that it was during Princess Elizabeth's visit that she heard of the death of her father King George VI. She returned to London and at the age of 25 she acquired all the responsibilities of the Sovereign and this was the last holiday she would ever have with a degree of privacy and freedom.

Afternoon tea was served on the veranda and one would have

thought that the Baboons had also been invited as they rolled up in their hundreds once the tea was poured, and clambered all over the Veranda and joined us. We were asked not to feed them, but there always has to be some "clever dick" who ignores any official instruction — and there was a rather nasty incident when the Baboons who had been fed by one of the tourists attacked him — wanting more to eat! Why are people so stupid, I ask myself?

Some of the monkeys were well behaved and very tame — whilst the others had to be watched — and they had no social graces — in fact were downright thieves!

During tea, when we were able to take our eyes off the Baboons, we noticed that the water hole was dry which is most unusual and was surrounded by Buffalo, Impala, Water Buck, Bush Buck, Giant Hog, Sykes Monkeys. They seemed to take it in turn and when one species left — another species arrived — they too apparently have a "batting order".

At sunset the Baboons all clambered down from the Veranda and wandered off into the forest and at the same time one saw more and more animals appearing out of the dusk.

At dinner for some reason I was sitting next to the White Hunter and he kept me supplied with copious glasses of wine.

My adrenaline was at an all time high whenever we were informed that either Elephants or Lions had appeared at the water hole — and I think everyone spent more time dashing to and from the viewing windows than sitting and eating. One idiosyncrasy of the Lodge was that food was sent down the middle of the table on a kind of trolley, which cut down the time spent serving meals considerably. The dishes were prepared in the kitchen and the plates put onto the moving rail so the people at the bottom of the table were served first.

More and more animals kept appearing out of the dusk meandering towards the water hole. In spite of there being no water, they came to eat the salt which is put out daily to attract the animals — and ensure that every visitor did see their fair quota of animal life.

That night was unbelievable — we saw Elephants galore, a Lion, 4 Zebra, quite a few Gazelle, 2 Giraffes, 8 Wildebeest, hundreds of Waterbuck and the odd Hyena, and lots of shadows which the White Hunter identified for us. When one herd of Elephants left, another would arrive — some with babies — and it was difficult to get to sleep as the waterhole was flood lit and all through the night there was action of some kind or other. We were given a chart to mark up the number of animals we had sighted during the night — but it was hard to keep an accurate account.

Unfortunately I suffered from the over generosity of the White Hunter who apparently kept filling my wine glass every time I dashed to the viewing window — and with all the excitement I became very thirsty and obviously, as there was no water, kept emptying my glass. When I finally lay down of course I realised that all was not well — and spent the remainder of the night when not dashing to see the animals — ensconced in the loo feeling very sorry for myself and wondering what I had eaten that had upset me so much!

The next morning I really felt dreadful and actually took a plastic bag with me on the transport to the Outspan Hotel — (just in case!).

However, I felt slightly exonerated when about a month later, when back in Karachi, we were having some Dutch friends to stay who also used to work in Karachi and therefore I had arranged a Buffet dinner for them in order to meet all their old friends. When we met Ans and Hank at the airport we noticed that Ans looked decidedly "under the weather" and she was mortified when I told her what we had planned for the evening. They had also had a stop over in Kenya and done the Treetops visit. She had also sat next to the White Hunter at dinner and she really felt he had spiked her drinks as she was so very ill that night and still felt dreadful. I told her of my experience and we wondered if this was really a coincidence or if for some reason we had antagonised this gentleman!

Beyond the Outspan Hotel, I think at Nyeri, we stopped to view the grave of Baden Powell.  At this stage I felt so grim that I actually lay down beside the grave and said "if it's good enough for Baden Powell — it's good enough for me"!  We were then on our way to the Mount Kenya Safari Club — where we were to have lunch before returning to Nairobi.    However, I think the consensus of opinion was that "I'd never make it" — so regrettably we returned to Nairobi and I have felt guilty about this all my life.

We stopped at Hunter's Lodge and had a delightful lunch sitting on the side of a Lake which abounded with beautiful coloured birds most of which we had never seen before.

We drove through Naivasha where, up to 1950, BOAC used the lake as Nairobi's airport, using flying boats on their four day journey from Southampton.  It is one of the Rift Valley's fresh water lakes which is home to an incredible variety of bird species and has ebbed and flowed over the years, at times half empty and then rising an amazing fifteen metres.    Because it can be used for irrigation purposes the surrounding countryside abounds with fresh fruit and vegetables and beef cattle.

The lake also featured strongly with the decadent Happy Valley crowd and is mentioned in the book and the dreadful movie "White Mischief"  We were told that it was near here that Joy Adamson of Born Free fame lived.

Our next stop was at Lake Nakuru National Park where at the lake we saw literally several thousand Pink Flamingoes — feeding, preening, grunting and honking — and most certainly when a flock decide you are a little too close for comfort they take off and there is a pink mass moving across the sky — in fact the whole Lake seemed to be fringed with pink masses.    I do remember there was an odd odour around the lake which we put down to the excessive excreta of the birds.

Since the park has large areas of grassland and bush there are many animals to be seen.  When we were able to tear our eyes away from the Flamingoes we noticed the amusing little Warthogs running with their tails erect.   There were also Water Buck and Buffalo and in the bush we saw the odd Thomson's Gazelle and even a Leopard. On the northern shore of the Lake there was a small herd of Hippos. All very exciting!

We of course would never have recognised most of the wild life but our hosts obviously were well acquainted with the animals and kept telling us the names of the animals we saw, for which we were very grateful.

Bob and Muriel then insisted that they would drive us to Mombasa to catch the m.v.Asia. This seemed to us to be above and beyond, but apparently a number of the Lodges Bob had to visit were en route to Mombasa, so how could we protest?

We drove 165 km south to Amboseli National Park on an excellent road, and stayed at Amboseli Lodge from where there was a spectacular backdrop of Mount Kilimanjaro — Africa's highest peak. I was over the moon when I saw a huge herd of Elephant making their way sedately across the grassy plains with Kilimanjaro in the background. This was all that I expected Africa to be. But it got even better!

Whilst this is not one of the larger Parks, nor, we were told, does it have the profusion of game that we saw in some of the other Parks, it does have the White Rhino and of course herds of Elephants. Bob spotted a White Rhino in the distance which is very rare, (he told us he had organised this the last time he was there!).

Whilst staying at the Amboseli Lodge or driving through the Park the following day, we saw Buffalo, Lion, Gazelle, Wildebeest, Hyena, Jackals, Giraffe, Zebra, Baboon, Warthog — we tried to keep a record of what we had seen — as one of the Lodges had provided a Record Book for visitors, but it became difficult at times as one became so excited you forgot to note them at the time and couldn't remember later!

We were amused to see two giraffes who appeared to be "crossing necks" which from where we were watching gave the impression of one Giraffe with two heads. Some of the sightings, of course, were so brief that had it not been for our hosts I would not have recognised the animals but the Gazelles, Jackals, Baboons, Warthogs and Zebra actually came close to the Lodge and this enabled me to study them closely. They seemed quite oblivious of the fact that they were being watched!

Although small, this is a well established Lodge where you see plenty of animals ALL THE TIME! The brightly coloured birds are so tame that they come along and literally join you at the table waiting for crumbs — and if these are slow in appearing they will jump on your plate and help themselves!

The next excitement was to visit Tsavo National Park which is the largest national park in Kenya. It has been split into Tsavo East and Tsavo West — and it is Tsavo West that is the most popular. Here we stayed at Kilaguni Lodge which really is beautifully situated, looking out over the rolling hills. The large water hole which is flood lit at night, is right in front of the Lodge; in fact every room, including the restaurant, the bar, the veranda and all the bedrooms, overlooked a water hole and one could watch the wild life which continually came down to drink.

During lunch we saw a couple of Impala engaged in a fight and nearer to the Lodge there were Waterbuck, Marabou Storks, Ostrich, who all seemed quite oblivious of the curious tourists who peered through the windows! Gradually the animals wandered off, but shortly we saw two Zebra appear and we noticed a squad of Mongeese frolicking immediately under the veranda window.

The next stop was at the Tsavo Inn for tea, this is 186 miles south of the equator and quite delightful. The previous week two lions had been swimming in the children's swimming pool which had caused quite a deal of excitement and the residents had virtually been imprisoned in their rooms which are all separated from the main dining block. I gather there were a lot of hungry people until food could be arranged to be sent to their rooms!

The night was spent at a new Lodge at Ngulia in Tsavo West National Park — and en route we saw herds of Elephants, far more than we could count, and literally hundreds of Giraffe dotted about hiding in the trees. They really do have a terrific camouflage — and in their attempts to hide they remain close to each other and again so many of them appeared to have two heads! Then of course we saw Antelope, Impala, Thomson's Gazelle, Wildebeest or Gnu, Coke's Hartebeest (another form of Antelope), lots of timid but very fast Zebra and of course Warthogs.

As this Game Lodge was relatively new, we saw very few animals at night — they would have to be encouraged to make scheduled appearances as they do at other Lodges. However, we were so tired I don't think we could have stayed up to see them had they appeared.

The next day we went to Mzima Springs in the morning, and here the main attraction, besides the Springs, is that there is an underwater tank in the river bed which you can walk into and watch the fish, snakes, crocodiles and other creatures swimming about. Quite fascinating as the water is clear and of course it is very bright. We were very lucky and actually saw an old Hippo prancing along — which gave us quite a fright to see him at such close quarters! We had intended to have a picnic lunch here as there were not many places that were considered safe to get out of the car. However the monkeys made it impossible to unpack our picnic, so we decided to move on to Kilaguni Lodge for lunch.

After lunch we set off to cross to the East side of Tsavo National Park and chose to take the river route (only to be used in the dry season). This was an experience we won't forget in a hurry!

To begin with we saw so much Game that there wasn't a minute when one of us wasn't proclaiming how many Elephants, Giraffe, Zebra, Buffalo, Rhino or Hippos there were on the left or right — in fact we became quite blasé and finally stopped passing any comment. But the main excitement was that on this 33 mile journey, we had to cross about five rivulets — on each occasion as the car was loaded with all our luggage — we "wondered" whether we would make it. Anyway we got through four of these crossings and had done 27 miles, which had taken us much longer than we thought it would.

We'd just watched with awe a Hippo that insisted on running along the side of the river bank keeping up with the car — when suddenly we came to another small river crossing.   This time however it seemed to be deeper than usual — and at first we thought it would be quite unsafe to try to get across.   Anyway, time was against us, it was getting dark and we had to be in the Tsavo East Game Park before 7.p.m. — and if we turned round and went back we most certainly would not get in.   Also — no one knew where we were and if we got stuck we'd be there for the night AND of course unable to get out of the car!

Anyway, Bob and Ken got out of the car and tested the depth of the river with a stick they tore off a bush whilst Muriel and I kept an eye open for "wild life".   (Considering I missed half the animals that everyone else saw en route — felt they were rather pushing their luck with me as a spotter!).   It was decided that the river bed had a good strong foundation so having weighed up the pro's and con's of proceeding or returning — we decided to proceed!

It was quite hair raising — but we made it — but imagine our feelings when we hadn't travelled more than 200 yards, and were still exclaiming how lucky we were — when we found TWO large Lions on the side of the road — within spitting distance.   Just imagine if we had been stuck for the night!

To cut a long story and many more animal sightings short, we got into Tsavo East Game Lodge.  They had locked the gates on schedule — but Bob's persuasive manner seemed to work wonders, — and the Warden duly unlocked the gates and we spent a very pleasant night at Voi Safari Lodge.

This Lodge is built into the natural rock and commands a breathtaking view over Tsavo National Park — a glorious position, but funnily enough we saw few animals round the water hole — other than Antelope.   It was here that we were told that m.v. Asia was leaving a day early, so we had to leave early in the  morning for Mombasa instead of spending another day in the Park.

As it happened — when we got to the Nyali Beach Hotel in

Mombasa, we were told the Asia's departure had again been delayed — so at least this gave us a good opportunity of having a look around Mombasa — we had a beer at the Mombasa Club — Lunch at the Oceanic Hotel — then we bought lots of cold stores for Karachi, and took Muriel and Bob on board for dinner. We woke the next morning expecting to be at sea, only to find we were still tied up! So we had a few more hours ashore and finally sailed at 2.p.m. What a holiday and what wonderful friends!

The trip on the Asia was glorious — lovely lazy days — rather nice not being awakened at 6.a.m. to see "big game" — the food and service were excellent and there was a superb Italian Band playing every evening, and of course the usual alternative entertainment, Housey Housey, Horse Racing, Cinema — and games on the Sports Deck during the day, a wonderful end to a holiday.

The boat docked for 24 hours in Bombay and as it was nearly 10 years since we left, we were delighted to have this opportunity to have a nostalgic look around. In spite of the obvious improvements such as fly-overs and hundreds of new sky scrapers — Bombay was a big disappointment. It seemed so squalid, dirty and generally run down; perhaps there is a lot to be said for the old adage that old battle fields and old girl friends should not be revisited! For some reason even taking into account devaluation, we felt things were VERY expensive.

We had loved Bombay when we lived there, but it had deteriorated and we were delighted to get back to Karachi.

We had been in Karachi nearly 10 years by this time and, as you will have gathered, whilst in Nairobi Ken was approached about moving to Kuala Lumpur in Malaysia. Anyone proceeding to work in Malaysia had to obtain a Work Permit before arriving and this meant he had to remain in Karachi for a week or two — these things took time we were told and they weren't kidding!

Prior to leaving Karachi, Ken had to take Peter Duerden, who was taking over from him, on a tour of the area for which he would be responsible and to introduce him to the Company staff and their major clients.   To my amazement, I was permitted to go with them and had a most enjoyable trip.   Peter has a very dry sense of humour which appealed to us both and made the trip, which in itself was interesting, also amusing.

We flew to Lahore where we were met by the Lahore Manager, Agha Jamal Haider.   Here having taken us round Lahore and seeing the Fort and Temples there, plus the Canon referred to by Rudyard Kipling.   He drove us North across the Indus river and on to Rawalpindi and Islamabad, — the new capital of Pakistan which to me seemed odd.   Usually Capitals are well established and have been in existence for many years but in this case Islamabad had been "built" to be a Capital and there was little tradition or history attached to it.   It seemed sterile whereas the other Pakistani towns we visited were full of historical interest.

We then drove North past the confluence of the Indus on to Peshawar where we spent a few days.   One day we drove to the Khyber Pass and along its 50 kms, past all the old British Army Regimental signs, until we reached the Afghan frontier, and looked over the bridge to Afghanistan.   We were a little disturbed by the number of fierce looking tribesmen with various coloured Pugri's walking around, all heavily armed, with one if not two rifles slung over their shoulders.   I may say I thought they looked as though they would go off at any moment!   In the distance up in the hills we did hear the occasional gun shot — whether it was practising — or the real thing we will never know!

In Lahore we were lavishly entertained by Jamal Haider.   I remember we ended up at a so called night club where belly dancers performed and danced amongst the audience.

I suppose it was natural that as the only foreigners in the place we should be the centre of attraction and they made direct tracks to where we were sitting and cavorted and wriggled in front of the men — but then I was shattered when a particularly masculine looking dancer, though dressed as a lady, came over and put her arms round me and became very affectionate.   At this gesture all

304

my hair seemed to stand up on end and I felt most uncomfortable. Later on I was told she was a Hijra — a person born with both sex organs! I was very relieved when we left.

When we got back to Karachi, the packers arrived and took a couple of days to crate all our belongings and then we flew to Singapore to await the issue of Ken's Work Permit.

We had thoroughly enjoyed our time in Pakistan, and came to the conclusion that the worse the posting, the more we seemed to enjoy it. One had to make one's own entertainment and friendships became so important.

On our last night we had a rather hectic farewell party in the flat, which had been "home" to us for nearly 10 years, and held so many memories for us both. All the servants were in tears — and I confess to shedding quite a few myself! They all seemed so very grateful for the gratuities we had given them — which we assessed at one month's pay for each year of service plus, of course, one month's pay in lieu of notice and their leave pay. Not everyone felt this was necessary, but after ten years we felt they most certainly deserved this — and as we had managed to get jobs for them all — one hoped that the gratuities would be put away for a rainy day!

We left the flat after midnight and our last night in Karachi was spent at the BOAC Resthouse at the airport. I was quite tickled to see when we were shown to our rooms a plaque over one of the beds saying "HRH Prince Philip slept here...." I felt very tempted to add "and so did Dottie".

We were sad to leave Karachi — we'd made some wonderful friends — and are still in touch with them nearly 25 years later — which must prove something!

# EIGHT
## *Malaysia*
### *November 1969-February 1973*

The Malay Peninsula, 125 years ago, was sparsely populated, and politically disunited, and as a result, economically undeveloped.

It was basically dense tropical jungle, and the inhabitants, who were chiefly Malays, lived along the coast and rivers in small settlements.

Initially, the small amount of tin ore that was produced was mined by Malays, and sold to the Dutch. It was the further development of tin that led to the influx of Chinese. As more tin was being mined, immigration increased, but the Chinese communities which developed, were self-governing, and often antagonistic to one another. There were also conflicts among the Malays and between the Malays and the Chinese — chiefly over their interests in tin. It was because of these conflicts that the British were called in to provide relative calm and stability.

This in turn enabled new areas for tin mining to be opened up — and a further influx of Chinese. They played the most instrumental role in the Malayan economy at that time.

When the world price of coffee fell — rubber was substituted and planted extensively, and chiefly because of the development of the automobile industry, the world demand for rubber rose rapidly and of course the demand for estate labour. Tamils from southern India were therefore recruited and brought in to work on the estates and the Government also recruited them to work on the roads and for construction work.

So, like the Chinese, the Indians came to Malaya to perform specific roles in the developing economy, and gained a foothold and shortly a monopoly of these roles.

Whilst the majority of Indians in Malaya are Tamils, there are also significant numbers of Moslem Pakistanis and a prominent number of Sikhs.

It was through the British that the three groups to a degree integrated, though contact between them was "formal". The Malays lived in villages, the Chinese in towns and the Indians on Estates. All three groups adopted British cultures and official communications were in English. Even so the majority had little accurate first-hand knowledge of each other and a lot was derived from dubious sources.

Anticolonial movements had grown in the Malay Peninsula during the 1920's and 1930's, influenced, no doubt, by pressures for Independence in India. The Japanese occupation of Malaya between 1942-1945 taught the Chinese Communist guerrillas, that Westerners were not invincible, which gave a new impetus to the Independence movement.

After the war the guerrillas waged a terrorist campaign against the British. The Emergency, as it was called, lasted from 1948-1960 until the rebels were suppressed.

Malaya came peacefully into existence in 1957, prior to which it was British, but it changed its name to Malaysia in 1963.

In 1957 the Malay Peninsula became the Malayan Federation and in 1963 it was expanded to include Singapore, Sarawak and Sabah in the Federation of Malaysia. Tension however soon led to Singapore's departure and the consequent loss of the Federation's principal port and industrial centre.

For our part, arriving in Malaysia in 1969, we found it a country of beautiful scenery and of course the blend of cultures mentioned above — Malays, Chinese, Indian, indigenous Orang Asli "original people", and a few Thais, Japanese, Sri Lankans, Filipinos and Indonesians — not forgetting expatriate Westerners like ourselves!

The Malays are in the majority in the region although they were preceded by aboriginal people, small pockets of whom still survive.

The Chinese are the second largest ethnic group, the largest group of which are Hokkien, followed by Teochews, Cantonese, Hakkas and Hainanese. The dialects of these groups are all different and they often have to resort to English to communicate! The Malays felt that the Chinese were engaged in a population explosion and were likely to outnumber them in a few years and thus would control the vote!

Whatever country we have been living in, I have attempted to learn sufficient of the language to make myself understood — with not much real success I might add! Though perhaps I did manage a little of the "kitchen" language! However, I did find picking up the Bahasa was remarkably easy and also good fun. Basic Bahasa is very simple. There are no tense changes; you indicate the tense by using words such as yesterday or tomorrow or just add suda (already) to make anything past tense. Many nouns are pluralised simply by repeating them; for instance "anak" is child and "anak anak" means children, "buku" is book but "buku buku" is books. The every day street language is referred to as pasar or market language. Other language simplifications include the omission of the articles "the", "a" or "an". Thus you just say "buku baik" (book good) rather than a good book. The verb "to be" is also omitted so again it would be "buku baik" rather than the book is good.

Just as many Hindi words have found their way into Indian English many Malay terms are used in everyday English in Malaysia. You'll often read in the papers or see advertisements with the words "bumiputra", which literally means "sons of the soil" but means Malay-Malays not Indian-Malays or Chinese-Malays!

Ken and I were always amused by the "Jaga Keretas" the little guy you paid to look after your car when you parked it — in point of fact if you don't engage a "Jaga" — you'll find when you return to your car that you should have done!

Malaysia consists of a confederation of 13 states and a capital district of Kuala Lumpur. Nine of the Peninsula states have Sultans and every five years an election is held to determine which one will become the Yang di-Persuan Agong or "King" of Malaysia. The States of Sabah and Sarawak in East Malaysia are rather different from the Peninsula Malaysian states since they were separate colonies, not parts of Malaya prior to independence. They still retain a greater degree of local administration than the Peninsula states.

The East and West coasts of Peninsular Malaysia are surprisingly different both in population and in geography. The west coast is lower lying and has a larger coastal plain. is more heavily populated and connected by more roads and railways. It was on the west coast that tin was initially discovered and where the rubber plantations were first developed — the two mainstays of the economy.

Kuala Lumpur — or K.L. as it is almost always called, was Malaysia's capital city and is a curious blend of the old and the new. A band of prospectors looking for tin landed at the meeting point of the Kelang and Gombek Rivers and they gave K.L. it's name which means "Muddy River" On one hand it's a modern and fast moving city with high-rise office blocks and multi-lane highways, but the old colonial architecture still manages to stand out proudly.

With so many cultures and religions there are quite an amazing number of occasions to celebrate. Some of them have a fixed date each year, the Hindus, Muslims and Chinese all follow a lunar calendar which results in the dates for many celebrations varying each year.

The major Muslim event each year is Ramadan. the 30 days during which Muslims cannot eat or drink from sunrise to sunset. Fifteen days before Ramadan the souls of the dead are supposed to visit their homes. Hari Raya Puasa marks the end of the month-long fast with three days of joyful celebration. For about two weeks beforehand all the ladies in the family are busy baking Hari Raya biscuits, cakes various curries — and everyone that visits during this three day period is given a meal.

The principle Chinese festival must be the Chinese New Year where Dragon dances and parades mark the start of the New Year. Families hold open house, and unmarried relatives, especially children, receive Ang Pows (money in red packets). When you are in business you try to clear all your debts — there is a desire to get all renovations and replacements to your home finished before the celebrations and people go around wishing each other a Kung Hei Fat Choy (a happy and prosperous new year). We have been invited to many of these festivals — chiefly in K.L. and Singapore. We learnt that it is usual to put an odd number of notes in the Red Packet — either 11, 21, 51, 101 etc. The celebrations for Chinese New Year last 15 days, and end in yet another celebration.

The Chinese servants would receive double pay for this month — which if they were all Chinese could be quite expensive. However we always seemed to have a mixture of religions on the staff which not only helped with days off but also relieved our financial commitments.

One of the most dramatic Hindu festivals is Thaipusam in which devotees honour Lord Subramaniam with acts of amazing masochism, by carrying kavadis, heavy metal frames decorated with peacock feathers, fruit and flowers. The kavadis are hung from their bodies with metal hooks and spikes driven into the flesh. Other devotees can be seen with their cheeks and tongues pierced with metal skewers. The Batu Caves were very close to The Cheshire Home — and on one occasion when visiting the Home I saw part of this festival — but one was left wondering how the participants would survive the ordeal.

Ken's "hand over" to his new position must have been the shortest on record! The previous Manager had been posted to South America and as the delay in the issue of Ken's Work Permit had not permitted a handover in Kuala Lumpur, he arranged a stop over whilst we were in Karachi, en route to his new posting. The actual hand-over therefore took place at Karachi Airport and lasted a couple of hours!

One of the last things Ken's predecessor said to him before he boarded his plane after the "hand over" at Karachi airport, was that he had left in the Company house — a dog, two cats, a bowl of fish and a bird! He did say he would quite understand if we had them all put to sleep, but he couldn't bring himself to do this as he had assured his children the animals would be well looked after.

As we were bringing two Bitches with us from Karachi I wasn't over enthusiastic about taking on the dog. Darling little Sherry somehow had managed to get herself pregnant in Karachi and when we saw her offspring we did wonder if it had been with a goat! Sherry was blonde and petite — her puppies were black and judging by the size of their paws we knew they were going to be large! Anyway we called the puppies Piddles and Puddles for obvious reasons — and decided to keep Puddles who was called Poo from then on — not I might add for any obvious reason as she was well house trained!

Anyway on arrival our two dogs had to go into quarantine — so there was no immediate hurry about disposing of Scamper — the dog we had inherited! We were able to despatch the dogs from Karachi before we left — they each had to have dog boxes and I really think the Carriers who had the boxes specially made, must have thought they were to carry elephants (and they would have been able to turn round easily!).

We'd been told to let the dogs sleep in the boxes at home, so they would be used to them before the flight and not be too distressed. There was no way these boxes would fit in the flat and frankly I doubt if they would have been acceptable on the flight. We suggested they replaced them with something more suitable for the size of dog, particularly as we were charged according to the size of the container, on top of the air fare.

They were picked up in the evening when it was quite cool in Karachi and were to spend the night at the airport so they were

311

ready to board the early morning flight. It was quite cool — if not cold — at night, so I had put their coats on with a little notice on each box saying "My name is Sherry — please remove my coat when it becomes warm" — and Poo had a similar notice. They were met at Subang (Kuala Lumpur Airport) and handed over to the Vet by the couple who had come up from Singapore to take over until Ken was able to get his Work Permit. The temperature and humidity in Kuala Lumpur of course were high and there was no way these dogs needed their little coats on — so our friends decided before the dogs were settled in their large kennel at the Quarantine Kennels, that they would remove them. I should say that both these dogs normally were very docile — but obviously they were upset after the flight and there was no way they were going to part with their coats! So the coats had to stay on until the Vet appeared later and, believe it or not, muzzled them both until the coats were removed!

Kuala Lumpur was, and I suppose is, an excellent family posting, unfortunately our family by now were rather scattered — Linda living in Hong Kong and Fiona at Boarding School in England.

We hadn't been in Kuala Lumpur very long when we were presented with our first grandson, Shane — born in Hong Kong on the 8th April, 1970, a most attractive baby and now grown into an even more attractive adult. We were naturally most anxious to see him and as I'd only produced girls — we were all very thrilled about this new addition to our family.

The time came for Sherry and Poo to come out of quarantine — and of course the inevitable happened! We had become very fond of "Scamper" by this time, though he was NOT a thing of beauty — he had a long drooping wart near his genital area which for all the world looked as though he had been doubly blessed! But, he was a very good watch dog and yet very affectionate with the family. He had been used to sleeping outside — which made us feel very secure as we had quite a large drive and the actual gate could not be seen from the house. However, whenever anyone stepped through the gate — Scamper would bark and rush up the drive. He seemed to know our friends very shortly and never made any attempt to bite them — but — funnily enough he was very suspect of the locals — who in turn were afraid of him — so we felt he was our insurance policy.

As he was an outside dog and Poo and Sherry were inside dogs — we felt we should keep them all! Of course the inevitable happened and Poo and Scamper were discovered making love under the dining table! We really didn't want any more dogs! I had heard that if you poured cold water on them that they might separate before any consummation had taken place, so I dragged them both into the downstairs cloakroom and put them under the shower.

I got soaked, but don't think it had any effect on the dogs and sure enough we were presented with no less than NINE gorgeous puppies! We should have put some to sleep immediately — but Fiona who was in K.L. at the time pleaded with us to keep them all saying she was sure she could find homes for them! I was happy to agree to this as they were so very cute.

After six weeks with them we did manage to give most of them away to friends, but decided we would keep one. None of the puppies looked alike — but there was one that looked like Sherry (it's grandmother) blonde and long haired and really looked like a ball of fluff. So we named this particular pup "Mrs Brown" as it was so like my boss's dog in Karachi that I sometimes looked after — who was called "Mr. Brown". Original as it was, I do think we should have thought of a more suitable name!

To hear the servants shouting "come here Mrs. Brown" did cause a few raised eyebrows and I had a particularly embarrassing moment when waiting at the check-out in the super market when a friend of mine in the next check-out asked me how Mrs. Brown was. My reply of "afraid she is failing fast and think we must shortly have her put to sleep" caused sufficient consternation in the queue for a lady to approach me later asking me what I meant by that remark!

She found it hard to believe that anyone would have a dog called

"Mrs Brown" and thought I was talking about a neighbour or an Aunt! Fortunately my friend came to the rescue and confirmed that indeed "Mrs Brown" was a canine!

Whilst we had the pups, Linda and her husband came to stay with us along with her mother in law who was visiting from Ireland. Elissa, our grand-daughter was now walking and seemed delighted with her wee brother.

This was the first time we had lived in a house — having always lived in flats, apartments or Units — and I confess it was a really lovely modern house — a large garden a quarter of which seemed to be covered by the most beautiful Orchids of about eight varieties. There were also two very prolific Rambutan trees which kept us, the servants and our neighbours in Rambutans for many weeks. An Avocado Tree which actually was in our neighbour's garden, but had all its branches on our side of the hedge and so we were never short of Avocados. Fortunately the Chinese family whose garden the tree was in — did not like Avocados so were quite happy about this arrangement. Unfortunately after about four years they decided to chop their tree down — so we lost our plentiful supply of Avocados!

We inherited our predecessor's two Chinese servants — a little old man called Lim and his wife who was called Mui. It transpired they had been with the Company many years — so I realised it would be difficult to change them even though they never seemed to get into "top gear"! The servant arrangement was far superior to anything we had seen in India or Pakistan. They had their own little house consisting of two bedrooms, a Lounge/Dining Room, a large well equipped kitchen and a bathroom and two toilets! Their house was attached to ours and there was a bell connected so that we could ring them in their house at any time. They also had two children — a daughter Kim aged about 12 and a very charming son called Heng aged about 14. We did wonder if the children were adopted as Lim and Mui, who were husband and wife, seemed to us to be far too old to have children of this age.

Then we had a Muslim Kabung (gardener) — who seemed to spend all his waking hours sweeping up the leaves from the numerous trees dotted around the garden. I have to admit though that we had the most beautiful flowering shrubs not to mention the Orchids, so think he must have done something else other than sweep leaves! He always had a headache — and although we sent him to the Dr. on numerous occasions he came back with little packets of powder which he then applied as a paste around his forehead These looked most peculiar and as the headaches never got better and I did wonder if it was a means of ensuring we didn't expect him to work too hard! His hours were long — but I did feel he could have done his amount of work in about 2 hours. Then we had Samad the Muslim driver — a slick individual — but a very efficient driver.

The Company now supplied items like curtains and bed covers which were replaced every five years. Prior to this we had to buy our own and of course every time we moved the curtains never fitted the windows in the new accommodation so, we ended up with piles of curtains which wouldn't fit anywhere! This was a much better arrangement though it was obvious that the curtains in the house were worn out and needed replacement and this venture took up quite a lot of my time — as nothing was simple. When we chose a material and ordered it — we could wait weeks before we were told it was no longer being produced and would we please choose another!

I knew that I could not take up any paid employment as I would have to obtain a Work Permit — which we knew the "powers that be" would not issue. I decided therefore to join the British Women's Association who met once a week — and I discovered they ran all sorts of interesting courses. Now I had more free time I enrolled in a Chinese Brush Painting Course — and produced some very interesting Scrolls which even surprised me. Guess what everyone got for Xmas that year?? Other than one recipient, who I found had hung my lovely Scroll in the Toilet behind the door — I was flattered that most of my friends gave the present pride of place in their homes.

I also joined a class to learn how to do Copper Tooling — and again produced quite a few masterpieces of Kitchen Gods, Kandara Bulls and even progressed to scenes.

As we needed new lampshades it seemed a good idea to join the Lampshade making course and I was thrilled with my results, as all the lampshades needed replacing and I felt I had saved a lot of money.

I started to learn Kitchen Malay — only to be completely disillusioned when the Government changed from Malay and insisted on people speaking Bahasa which made it very confusing!

Bridge lessons were another interesting pastime — these took place once a week in a class of 12 and initially I felt it was quite beyond me, but I always enjoy a challenge and was determined to at least be able to play social bridge — even if not at competition standards. A few of us wishing to improve our standard arranged extra Bridge games in each others homes.

One evening we went to a Cocktail Party and I was introduced to an amazing lady who I was told had had 7 husbands and obviously would not see 60 again, but she was vibrant and her enthusiasm for her various charities was infectious. She smoked and drank heavily, dressed beautifully and was quite a character — but — her pet Charity was The Cheshire Homes.

When I was initially introduced to her and she discovered I had come to live in Kuala Lumpur permanently — she literally pounced on me and asked me to join the Committee of the Cheshire Homes before any other charity approached me. I was a bit taken aback as I didn't feel I was Committee material and women en masse tended to overwhelm me. However, she was not to be daunted and said she would pick me up the following day and take me out to the Cheshire Home which really was in the Woop Woop. I was introduced to the two Anglo Indian ladies who seemed to run the Home and then taken round and introduced to all the residents and patients. I was very impressed with their wonderfully cheerful attitude to life and, no matter what their disabilities, they were determined to do their little bit to help the Home, and in so doing, help each other.

They were all industrious, and busy making various gift items which I discovered were later sold by the Home at various charity lunches but mainly at the Zoo Shop run by the Home at the Kuala Lumpur Zoo.

I was then asked if I would attend a Committee Meeting the following week and frankly having seen these wonderful people who were all disabled in some way or other, who were making such a determined effort to help the Home — how could I refuse?

Not only did I have to appear at all the Meetings but was asked if I would take charge of the Zoo shop which was run and stocked by the patients from the Cheshire Home.

As an inducement the residents were given something like 5 or 10 cents for every item they finished for the shop.    The balance went towards the running of the Home — which was all self financing.

I thoroughly enjoyed my numerous visits to the Home and found myself, along with the rest of the Committee members, giving Coffee mornings when we would try to sell all these wonderful items the residents and patients had made.    The Zoo shop brought a small income, but also gave the staff and patients who accompanied the staff member, the opportunity to get out of the Home and see another side of life.

I found this work very humbling, and became quite attached to some of the residents whose determination to conquer their particular disability was an example to us all, and made me realise more than ever, that we do take things for granted

The Committee members would invite a group of the residents to their homes for a meal and to play some games — and I admit to feeling very guilty when they were wide eyed at the size of our homes and our life style.    I sometimes wondered if it was a good idea.    We also took them occasionally to any Shows that were in town — and this was an expedition in itself when we had to enlist the help of our husbands to help lift and carry the patients and their wheel chairs into the bus we had hired for the occasion.

At the same time I was asked by The Blind Society if I could spare the time to go to their centre and read to some of the blind students. Sometimes we would read a book and put it on tape for them to study at a later date. Since I had been threatened with blindness twice in my life — I felt this was something very close to my heart. They had a very good Braille library which was well used — so you can imagine how distraught we were when torrential rain lasting about a week flooded the Library and ruined many of the books. Those that we could salvage we took home and spread them out all over the garden hoping the sun would dry them without damaging the Braille. The wind of course was a problem — and one particular gust caused complete chaos as of course none of the helpers could read Braille so it was necessary to enlist the aid of the patients before we could get them back into some sort of order.

Fiona came out for her holiday and seemed to have a problem at school. As we had allowed Linda to leave two schools and spend some time with us — it seemed only reasonable that we should do the same for Fiona, particularly as there was a British School in K.L.. So she was enrolled in the B.O.S. School (British Overseas School) in Kuala Lumpur.

I think through the latest removal and all the inevitable packing, I had developed a bad back and found it difficult to move, so went to the Dr. hoping for an injection to relieve the problem.

He started by asking me if I had been under any undue stress or did I have any marital problems, was my sex life satisfactory and when I assured him these were fine — he then asked if I had any other worries. I laughingly retorted that I had no worries other than any mother of a teenage daughter had, and this he seized on. Did I have any children in K.L. — which school did they go to etc. He then said that if he was to be the family doctor he was honour bound to warn me that there was a drug problem in some of the schools. He asked me if I knew anything about drugs and when I said I'd had no experience — he said he would tell me the warning signs to look for!

He told me if Fiona went out on her own in the evening I should never go to bed until she was home. I should then make a point of kissing her goodnight, whilst smelling her breath for alcohol (as often drugs and alcohol went together). I should examine the pupils in her eyes to see if they were enlarged and engage her in conversation to see if there was any slurring of speech. Another thing to keep my eyes open for was any locked cupboards or drawers!

I went with a bad back and left a nervous wreck! However, he was doing his job and I suppose he meant well.

I have to admit that I always waited up for the children — sometimes in bed reading a book, but they would always come in and say goodnight. After this doctor's visit I did find myself checking her pupils and smelling her breath — but there was nothing unusual. We discussed the drug scene — and she said she knew that there were drugs being experimented with by teenagers — but no one had approached her. I felt she was very sensible and really stopped worrying about the dreaded drug problem!

Fiona used to come home from school, do her home work and was usually in bed by 10.p.m. They say history repeats itself — and once again I was told that Fiona had been seen at the local night club about 11.30.p.m. As she'd said goodnight to us around 10 p.m. I couldn't believe this — but — once bitten — I decided I had better check this out. I knew she could not have gone via the front door as we would have seen her as the Staircase was off the Lounge where we sat in the evening. So if she was going out then it must be through some other way.

I examined her bedroom and decided the only place she could get out of the house would be through one of her bedroom windows which looked out onto the roof of the servants quarters. I sprinkled talcum powder outside the window — and sure enough — the next morning there were footsteps in the talcum powder. I knew she was friendly with an American Chinese boy from the American School — and wasn't very happy about this — so this had to be sorted out.   Fiona was apologetic — and I think there were no further midnight rendezvous.

She was also friendly with Terry — a rather nice American boy — though his hair style left a lot to be desired — just a mass of long curls which reminded me of a flue brush.   We were going down to Singapore for a long weekend by car and Fiona asked if Terry could come with us as he wanted to visit his aunt!   We agreed to give him a lift and told him to be ready at 8.a.m. when we would pick him up.   We had gone about 10 miles when suddenly I was aware of whispering in the back of the car and so asked if there was anything wrong?   Fiona then said that Terry had forgotten to bring his passport!   So we had to return and this added 20 miles to our journey and meant we didn't get to The Causeway before the rush hour.

When we were going through Immigration at The Causeway — the Immigration Officer told us that they would not allow Terry in because of his long hair!   As we were already late — this was all we needed.   Nothing would have given me greater pleasure than to cut it — but he asked if he could tie it back and wear clips to keep it off his face — and the Immigration Officer agreed.   I instilled in him the need to keep his hair like this all the time he was in Singapore or he would be deported.

I have to say that Lee Kwan Yue really should be held up as an example as to how to govern a country.   Singapore is without doubt a most disciplined city.   I suppose fines of $500 for dropping litter, and S$150 for not flushing a public toilet — not to mention the cane for defacing the city with graffiti, helped a lot.   Whatever it is, it certainly works, and rarely do you hear of any crime — or fraud — in the City.   I think the West could learn a very good lesson from him — most certainly we have proved time and again that the velvet glove does not pay.

Back in Kuala Lumpur I had just about forgotten the Dr's

warnings until one day I was passing Fiona's room and found all her underwear that had been ironed by Mui was piled up on the bed. Normally these were put away in the drawers, so decided Mui had forgotten and went to put them away — only to find the drawer was locked! I immediately thought of the doctor's warning! I couldn't find the key so decided I would ask Lim to get me the "key wallah" — but as I did not want the servants to know of my fears I said I wanted a duplicate key for my suitcase. As soon as the "key wallah" arrived and was shown into the bedroom where I had carefully put the suitcase, I asked him to make me a key for the suitcase and then told Lim there was no need for him to remain in the room as I was not leaving. The servants would never leave a workman in the house without supervision — so I had to make this point and as soon as Lim left, I told the "key wallah" I had another problem — and pointed to the drawer in Fiona's wardrobe. He very quickly made keys for both the case and the drawer — and I paid him and showed him downstairs.

Immediately I went to the drawer and will never forget the sheer horror when I opened it and found numerous small bottles of various coloured pills AND some tobacco looking stuff. I was mortified and immediately thought of the Death Sentence which had recently been introduced.

I tried to tell myself it was medicine — but in my heart I felt it wasn't so I immediately went down to the Dr. with a sample from each bottle and told him what had happened. He asked me if I had noticed anything suspicious in Fiona's behaviour and I was able to say no — (I didn't mention her nocturnal wanderings which suddenly loomed in my mind as possibly important). He examined the tablets casually, and the tobacco looking material, and said that the only way he could be sure if they were in fact drugs, would be if he sent them to the Narcotics Bureau. If they discovered they were in fact what we feared — he pointed out that Ken would be deported within 24 hours — all Fiona's friends would be questioned and their homes searched, and he also reminded me of the death penalty in Malaysia associated with drugs! He asked me if I really wanted this? Naturally I said no — but — asked his advice.

He pointed out that finding these tablets did not necessarily mean Fiona was taking them. He suggested I counted them, then put them back and each morning I should check if any had gone. If they had — then we would have to re-think.

I had a busy time making a record of the contents of each bottle and decided I would wait and see what happened. As you can imagine this was one of the worst periods in my life — I couldn't sleep and couldn't stop worrying about what could happen! Then I thought how foolish I was putting the tablets and pills back — as if she was taking them even one tablet could become addictive. So — I ground up numerous Cascara Tablets to a fine powder, emptied the contents of the capsules down the toilet and filled each capsule with the Cascara. At least I would know if she had taken any without having to count them!

Nothing happened; each morning I checked the number and obviously none had been taken.

After three weeks — I opened the drawer to find the lot had gone! I immediately rang Ken and told him what I had found and as we knew that the tablets had been there the night before, realised that Fiona must have taken them to school! Ken returned home — dismissed the driver and we drove to school at lunch time to pick her up and try to prevent any of these pills being passed on in any way. Fiona was rather a long time leaving school and just when we began to think she was not at school or we had missed her — she came running out looking slightly concerned. Why had we come to pick her up and not the driver? We took her a short ride as we did not want to discuss this in the house — and told her what we had found and pointed out the possible consequences.

She burst into tears of course and then told us that she had been keeping them for Chris, the Chinese boy. He had been in hospital for 3 weeks having fallen off his motorbike — and did not want to leave the pills in his home as his father was very strict.

Actually it was rather a sad story — Chris's parents had fallen on hard times, but having entered their son into the American School, the father, who was not young, was struggling to meet the fees, wanting his son to have the benefit of a good education. Chris realised the sacrifices his parents were making on his behalf and didn't want to ask them for any extra cash for extra curricular activities — so — when he was approached by some boy saying he would pay him well if he could get him some Marijuana and Amphetamines, he decided he would do this on this one occasion to obtain some extra cash. When he fell off his motor bike and was hospitalised he took the drugs with him rather than leave them in the house — and when Fiona went round to visit him in hospital (which we knew nothing about) — he asked her to keep them for him! Obviously we could not let this go so went round to see Chris and his father — both of whom ended up in tears and Chris assured us that he would not participate in anything like this again. His father was a delightful old Chinese gentleman and we couldn't help feeling sorry for him.

Fiona had flushed the pills and Marijuana down the toilet when she saw us waiting for her outside school — so — there were no drugs — and so we decided to let the matter rest. It had been an extremely worrying time as you can imagine and could have had disastrous results, but it had had a salutary effect.

The Malaysian Government were very strict and had numerous religious taboos. They considered dogs and pigs unclean — and expect ladies to adhere to a certain rather strict dress code, whilst their own ladies are covered from head to foot by an Abaya and sometimes wear a Yashmak. Therefore they strongly disapprove of the Western form of dress. If a Westerner offended a member of the Royal family, they were deported within 24 hours, sometimes they didn't even realise what they had done.

Whilst we were in Kuala Lumpur some young Westerner had been following the Royal cars and was getting impatient and wanting to overtake. Eventually he tooted and overtook the then Agong and gesticulated, having followed the entourage for about 10 minutes. He was out of Malaysia the next day.

I am a great believer that when a guest in a foreign country one should abide by their regulations as far as possible. Bearing this in mind, you can imagine my concern when a couple of New Zealand friends came to stay with us who love animals and actually say they prefer them to humans! We had taken them to the beach where the dogs had been swimming — and my friend then insisted that we wash the salt out of their coats in clear water. We had come off the beach to show these friends the Yacht Club which we had recently applied to join. I explained to them there was no clear water — so this friend picked up the dogs and took them into the ladies' showers and changing rooms!

I was terrified that someone would see her and the dogs — as well I may have been! To avoid one of the dogs running around and attracting attention I too went into the shower to hold the second dog and try to persuade my friend to leave. She turned on the shower — whilst I was still trying to persuade her to get the dogs out of the ladies room before anyone saw them. Whereupon a ghastly little European boy came into the shower room and shouted to his Mother that there were two funny ladies and two dogs in the shower! The next thing we knew was that the Commodore of the Yacht Club, the Secretary and two Committee members — all male — barged into the ladies' shower room and asked us what the hell we were doing! My friend, instead of apologising, said she was giving the dogs a shower — whereupon one of the lady members who had come to enjoy the spectacle said she would not use the shower after a dog. My friend said she couldn't understand why as in her experience most dogs were cleaner than their human counterparts! Can you imagine my embarrassment?

I should perhaps tell you that Ken had only just met the Committee and we were still awaiting their written acceptance of our membership of this Club — which we now felt would not be forthcoming.

When we told Ken about this incident, he was not amused and wrote a letter of apology to the Committee explaining that our friends were not familiar with the Muslim customs.

Our application was actually accepted — and we did become members of the Club. We couldn't help noticing that there were now new notices outside the showers saying "Dogs not allowed in the showers"!

As if this was not enough — we were anxious to get them away from the Club so walked along the beach, to where we had left the car, with the dogs on a lead. There was a small Island off this beach connected to the mainland by a very narrow strip. The Island belonged to the then King. My friend wandered onto the Island, let the dogs off the lead taking no notice of my remonstrations that she should not be there, and thinking that perhaps she could not hear me, I walked onto the Island to get her and the dogs off it. Imagine my horror when I saw the Royal cars draw up and what was obviously the Yang di Pertuan Agong get out and walk towards his Island.

I managed to get off the Island in time and watched with horror as my friend called the dog back onto the Island and I saw it brush against the Agong.

I really felt after this ghastly weekend that we would be asked to leave Malaysia — and each day waited for the official letter. We were lucky — either they didn't know who we were — or they didn't think it worth pursuing!

We hadn't been in K.L. long when we experienced one of the worst storms which caused widespread flooding. Even Ken, who never took days off for any reason, was unable to get to the office as, with the flooding, the water round the office entrance was over 9' high.

The Royal Selangor Club — always referred to as "The Dog" apparently acquired this name because it is said a European lady used to exercise her numerous Dalmatian dogs around the Maiden, in front of the Club, the area which normally was devoted to sports.

During the floods people could be seen rowing across this area which was the only way one could get across.

Malaysia, which was once an active tin mining area, had few if any mines operating.   Even so, the tin seemed to act as a magnet whenever there was lightning around — and one could watch the forked lightning hit the ground.   Usually this was accompanied by torrential rain or storms.   On one occasion I had some ladies in for tea and we were sitting on the very large Patio when suddenly we saw lightning hit the bottom of the garden.   I had been told that lightning never hits the same place twice — I can tell you they lie!

Within seconds there was another flash of lightning which was half way up the garden — and by this time I suggested we all rush inside.   We didn't even have time to get to the French Windows leading into the Lounge when there was yet another flash which hit the metal pillar actually on the Patio and sparks flew all around! This certainly made us move!   I have never known such terrifying storms as we had in Malaysia.

Downstairs we had an inside cloakroom which had no windows in and, after this, whenever there was a storm I would make for this cloakroom, quickly followed by the dogs, who were even more frightened than I — if that was possible.   They seemed to have an intuition when a storm was coming and became very agitated, running in and out of the house, as if to warn me that it was time we took refuge in the cloakroom   Even to-day I will do all I can to avoid being outside when there is lightning.

We had been warned never to use the phone when there was an electric storm as the lightning had been known to travel along the telephone line to the actual hand piece!   I didn't need a second warning!

There was also an accident on the golf course when one of the players disregarded the rule that when there is lightning around one returns to the Club House immediately.  He discovered that holding a metal Club was asking for trouble!   He was lucky in that  he survived but had to go to hospital.

Another player had rather a surprise whilst holding his Club, when a spark between his Club and the keys in his pocket, gave him a very nasty burn! Again he was lucky in that he survived — though whether this spark had any permanent effect on his "private parts" we never knew!

Unfortunately some people were not so lucky.

These storms of course had disastrous results on the plants, bushes and trees. As a result the guttering on our house became blocked and had to be cleared regularly to avoid flooding.

One of the duties of the Kabung was to keep the guttering free; and one day he told us that the guttering was loose in places and there appeared to be signs of rotting. We called in a roof specialist who said he felt the whole guttering must be replaced — and he would start the work the next week.

About a week after this work was finished, Lim asked me if he could take his son to the doctor. I asked what the trouble was and he said he had a fever — so I went in to see him and took his temperature which was 103! I then said that I would get our doctor to call and see him — but this obviously upset the family who insisted that they had their own doctor. So, not wanting to rock the boat, I asked Samad the driver to take him in the car.

When they got back I went into their quarters and asked what the doctor had said. I was slightly irritated when I heard that the only comment from the doctor was that "he had a fever" and he had given him some tablets.

Trying to find out what exactly was the problem, I asked for their doctor's phone number and rang him to enquire what exactly was wrong with Heng. This doctor asked me how long I had been in the East — and when I told him — he then said I would perhaps understand therefore what he was going to tell me. Lim, Mui and Heng were convinced, because their priest had told them, that Heng's illness was caused by our having the guttering replaced! Every nail that went into the roof over Heng's bedroom had actually penetrated his heart and that he would not get better until we had the guttering removed!

The doctor was obviously as amused as I was — and when I asked him what we could do — he suggested that we told them that we were arranging to have the nails removed and in the meantime he had given Heng some antibiotics and he just hoped they would take effect before we had to have the guttering done!

We could just imagine what Ken's Head Office would say, when they had just paid a bill for having this guttering replaced, when they found out we had had to remove it "as the nails had gone into Heng's heart".    It really was hard to believe — but the elderly parents were convinced this was the cause of his problem.

By the grace of God and Guanamycin, Heng started to improve — though of course we had told them that we were arranging for the removal of the nails!

Lim and Mui were delightful — but they did have some "unusual" traditions.    Repeatedly we would find small Altars set up in the garden, surrounded by candles, and offerings of food for the Gods. Every Chinese festival was celebrated in our garden.  The Festival of the Hungry Ghosts was a particular one we were invited to attend. This is when the souls of the dead are released for one day of feasting and entertainment on earth. Food was put out by Lim and Mui — on this same Altar and they told us the ghosts eat only the spirit of the food but thoughtfully leave the substance for mortal celebrants! Nothing is wasted.

Down in Chinatown on another occasion we saw Chinese operas — which take place in a marquee type of tent with rows of chairs to accommodate the public.  As westerners we found the high pitched singing — accompanied by the beating of drums, just a bit too much and we never stayed very long although these festivities would last until late in the evening.

We loved the Moon Cake Festival which takes place in September when Moon Cakes are on sale for two or three days.  They are made with bean paste, lotus seeds and sometimes a duck egg.  I preferred them without the egg!   At the actual Festival, colourful paper lanterns are carried in the evening in the form of animals, or some other decoration — and you can imagine how pretty this festival is. Lim and Mui's children would invite friends round and we enjoyed seeing them walking up the drive with these lanterns on sticks — all different colours and shapes.

This in many ways is similar to Deepavali which takes place the following month and is a Hindu festival to celebrate Rama's victory over the demon King Ravana.   Tiny oil lamps are lit outside all Hindu homes — around the gardens and spreading onto the pavements.   We would take the children for a drive in the evenings to see all the lights — which we enjoyed as much as they did.

My niece who had visited us in Calcutta en route to Malaysia was now living in Klang, a fishing port about 19 miles from Kuala Lumpur, so we were able to see her quite frequently.   She had four children, three girls and a boy — though she had lost two children — one the twin of her son.

The youngest daughter was diagnosed as having Leukaemia — and she was in and out of remission, but latterly seemed to spend all her time in hospital.   My poor niece — who had her own medical problems,  spent every day at the Hospital with her daughter — so I would try to get in to see her as often as possible and try to convince her that there still was hope.   Occasionally Julie would go into remission and be allowed home for a few days, but it was pretty obvious that she was a very sick little girl.

Her husband's family, whilst supportive, apparently were inclined to blame the mixed marriage.   Sadly she died at the age of six having been taken ill when she was four.

We enjoyed our weekends and often would drive down to Port Dickson about 94 km south of K.L. where there was a fine stretch of beach extending for about 17 km to Cape Rachado.   We usually stayed at the SiRusa Inn or the Pantai Motel and spent our time swimming and would play the odd game of cards in the evening. We also spent occasional weekends at Fraser's Hill, the nearest Hill

Station where it was so much cooler.  The Cameron Highlands were a little further away, but another delightful Hill Station.

There is no doubt about it, there is a lot to see in Malaysia and some of their beaches are excellent — this was the second time I had seen Turtles struggling up the beach to lay their eggs.  It seemed such an effort for them, as they had tears pouring out of their eyes, that you felt you should help by lifting them to the top of the beach which they were struggling to reach.

We were also at the beach on one occasion when some of the baby turtles hatched, which was mind boggling.  They struggled to get out of their shells — sometimes bringing part of their shell with them — and then started to trek to the sea.  They always seemed to know in which direction this was — but — the sad thing is that whilst they are waddling down to the sea — many of them are devoured by Pariah dogs or vultures which swoop down and carry them off.  No wonder the turtle lays so many eggs — as so few survive.  The Pariah dogs would often dig the eggs up from the sand — and you'd see the tell tale remainder of all the shells left behind.

We spent a very happy holiday in Penang on one of the long holiday weekends.  We stayed at the Golden Sands Hotel on the Beach, but I cannot reconcile Penang being called "the Pearl of the Orient" as to my mind the beaches do not compare with the East Coast with its translucent waters.

Penang is also known, however, as the "Isle of Temples" — a title well deserved.  The most interesting Temple being the Clan House which is a sort of Imperial Palace and then the Goddess of Mercy Temple — not forgetting the Snake Temple at Sungei Kluang, where you will end up with a couple of snakes around your neck. This after just having been told that all the snakes but ten are poisonous!

Those that have had their venom removed all have a small red dot on their head — so we were told — so small I found it difficult to see them — so was not at all happy until they were removed from my shoulders.

If you are interested in jungles then a trip to Taman Negara is well worth while — though a meagre possibility of seeing any large wild life, and one has to be prepared to suffer a bite from the odd Mosquito!

The best Satay in the whole of Malaysia is to be found in Kajang about 20 km south of K.L. and we occasionally drove down there for lunch on a Sunday.

As with all our postings we seemed to have numerous overseas visitors, all anxious to see something of the country — and therefore I felt I became quite a good tour guide, which I enjoyed

I would take most visitors for a drive out to the Batik factory and here they would see the process of printing Batik. The factories were all very primitive, but interesting, and quite amazing how they produce such delightful prints out of the confusion which surrounds the manufacture.

One could watch the whole process at different stages, starting with the completely white muslin type cotton — they would then choose one of their many ornamental metal presses which would be dipped into boiling wax and then pressed on to the white material. The whole bolt of material would receive this treatment and then it would be placed into a dye — which obviously dyed all the material, other than that underneath the wax.

When the material was dry, the whole process would be repeated with the press in a different place and then the material would again be dyed yet another colour. This would be repeated depending on the number of colours they wanted in the finished material. Finally the material would be placed in a vat of boiling water which would remove all the wax leaving the various colours intact. The material would be dried, ironed, folded and despatched to the shops.

In another part of the factory the actual metal presses were being created in copper — it was extremely intricate work and each press had a handle fitted to enable it to be dipped into the boiling wax without burning your hands.  Occasionally they would permit you to purchase the old presses which, when framed in a velvet or colourful backing, made interesting wall decorations.

Nearby are the Batu Caves which are unusual in that they are contained in a towering limestone formation and apparently were little known until about 100 years ago.  Later a small Hindu shrine was built in the major cave and it became a pilgrim centre during the annual Thaipusam festival.  The major cave, a vast open space known as the Cathedral Cave, is reached by a straight flight of 272 steps, which I sometimes found quite daunting.

They constructed a primitive lift to get nearly to the top of the steps, but when we lived there initially — there was no way up — other than to climb.  One particular week when we had rather more than our usual influx of visiting dignitaries, I actually climbed up the 272 steps no less than four times!

Also reached by the same flight of steps was the long and winding Dark Cave, but this was closed latterly as the quarrying in the limestone outcrop has made the caves unsafe.  There was also a small cave at the base which was converted into a Museum.

On returning from the caves I would include a visit to a jewellery factory where one could see the very fine silver filigree jewellery being made.  Then across the road to where Copper was being beaten into fabulous plaques, jugs, bowls.

When I refer to a "factory" don't be misled — they often started out as small sheds — but over the years they expanded.  In the case of Batik — the initial shed developed into several sheds and then progressed to a village and show room in which they housed the finished Batik, jewellery, copper and Pewter.  Before we left Malaysia, this village was included by the Tourist office in their itineraries and consequently bus loads of tourists visited daily and brought a lot of business.

All the visitors seemed to enjoy the National Museum which is extremely interesting, and even the children seemed to enjoy these visits.

The Company had bought a debenture at the Lake Club, which permitted the current Manager to use the Club. We were very fortunate in having this, as, besides the usual amenities, swimming tennis etc., the Club had an unusual restaurant, named very aptly as the "Orchid Room".

Here the most beautiful orchid arrangements were set in a velvet background to complement the colour of the various flowers in the frame. These were inset into the walls of the restaurant with a spot light playing on them. A delightful setting for a meal and a lovely Club.

Attempts were being made to establish a new capital of Selangor State at Shah Alam. It was undergoing a major construction and development plan which was due for completion in 1986 — but the recession in 1985-87 slowed things down.

Now, however, it is thriving with a new Museum, Cultural Centre, Theatre and Library and the new State Mosque. The sparkling silver and blue mosque is quite spectacular and resembles a lunar station. Non-Muslims can visit parts of the Mosque so long as they remove their shoes and cover themselves completely with a Black Abaya which has a hood attached. Not the coolest of garments to wear when the humidity is so high.

Fiona was nearly 16 and it was time she moved from the B.O.S. (British Overseas School). As she was not very academic and had no particular leanings towards any specific career, it was decided after a family discussion that she would take a Secretarial course.

Again we had to make a decision as to where she would do this and after a lot of research she was enrolled for a year's course at Riverston International College, at Beckenham in Kent. I think she enjoyed the course as it gave her the freedom school didn't permit.

Whilst she was not over enthusiastic about doing Secretarial work — it has most certainly given her the entree to various vacancies, which she would not have been eligible for without her Secretarial studies. I think the same thing applied to myself and Linda, without a Secretarial qualification many appointments would have not been open to us.  Often the qualifications were not actually used, but without them, one would not have been considered for the appointment.

As things turned out, both girls went on to own their own businesses — and have found the skills they learnt of great assistance.

Linda, who was the least enthusiastic about taking a Secretarial course, has found it invaluable in running her own very successful business in Singapore where she started a Company called "Simply Swimming".  Mind you, whilst this was only possible because of her swimming skills and her qualifications in that direction, without her secretarial background it would have been difficult to do the administration.

Fiona had various secretarial jobs before she too started her own very successful Property and Relocation business in Hong Kong where she employed 16 people.  Whilst she now has staff to do most of her secretarial work, when she first started the business she found her secretarial background of great help.  She has also had a very useful book published called "Setting up in Hong Kong" which was on the "best seller list" for quite a few months and a hive of information for anyone who is being posted to H.K.

Early in 1972, The Queen, HRH Prince Philip and Princess Ann paid an official visit to Kuala Lumpur, where there was a Reception for them.

It was arranged that all the High Commission staff could go out to the airport to meet the Royal party, along with our spouses, which was a great thrill.

I was particularly fortunate as again, because Ken was the No.1. of a British Company, we were invited by the High Commissioner and his wife to attend the Reception.

Included in our invitations was the Pass for the car and details of the time we had to attend, what we should wear, and how to address the Royals IF spoken to.  For ladies we were told that "Hats and Gloves would be worn".  Well this put the British Community into a slight quandary as there was nowhere in Kuala Lumpur where you could buy a hat! There were two ladies who immediately started making hats, but obviously they could not cope with the quantities required and so the headlines in the local newspapers were to the effect that the "British Community, in Quandary" and went on to explain that ladies were having difficulty in obtaining hats for the Reception.

I was not unduly worried as I already had a hat which I had purchased for the Royal visit in Karachi. Prince Philip came up to the group I was standing with and started chatting — he turned to me and said "I understood you ladies were having problems buying hats — where did you get yours from?" I told him I had bought it for his visit to Karachi some years ago — whereupon he said "you mean I don't even warrant a new hat now?"

I am full of admiration for the way the "Royals" really seem interested in what one is doing in the these far flung areas.

At the end of 1972, Linda and Frank, who were now living in H.K., were divorced, and as with all divorces it was a traumatic time for everyone but the people that suffer the most are the children.

Fiona finished her Secretarial course at Riverston International whilst we were in Malaysia and started working for Fisons in London as a Secretary and apparently thoroughly enjoyed the job. She was coming out to K.L. for a month's holiday as it was her last free passage from the Company.

After a couple of weeks with us, she announced she would like to stay with us in K.L. and as she felt that her shorthand speeds were not really up to her holding down a No.1. job, she wanted to take a speed class. It was much cheaper for her to do this in K.L. where she could live at home — rather than return to London. We were naturally delighted that she made the choice to take the course in K.L.

She did this for about 6 weeks when she was approached by a Chinese girl who asked her if she would help her out by standing in for her in an afternoon job. College was from 9.a.m. to 1 p.m. and the Chinese girl had secured this employment, but they wanted someone to start immediately, which she couldn't do.    So Fiona agreed to do the job for her for two weeks.

At the end of this time the American Director came out from the States and asked Fiona if she would join the staff permanently.  She told him that she wasn't looking for employment at this stage, but was really taking a speed class and would be returning to the U.K. when she had acquired the necessary speeds.  She also indicated the salary wasn't sufficient for her to be interested!

He then asked her what salary she would expect, and when Fiona told him, he not only agreed to pay her this amount but he would also permit her to finish her speed classes in the morning which took about two hours!

She felt that was an offer she couldn't refuse and quite enjoyed the work — the company imported Computers and she accordingly thought she would stay a few months if only to build up a bank balance, so that she had funds when she returned to the U.K. which she seemed determined to do.

Our years in Malaysia were happy and I suppose I should say "hot" as the humidity was high — but we got used to it and air conditioned cars and bedrooms helped a lot.

We were only in Malaysia 4 years when Ken's Work Permit had to be renewed.    Whilst the Government were anxious to Malayanise it was accepted that Heads of Overseas firms would be granted Work Permits automatically.

Ken was not concerned therefore when he did not hear from the authorities about his renewal but with only two weeks to go before his present permit expired, he phoned the authorities concerned only to be advised that there was some problem with his Work Permit and it was not being renewed!

Despite numerous visits to the Immigration Office and even with the help of the British High Commission, we have never been able to discover any reason for this.    His file appeared to have "mysteriously disappeared" from the archives when questions were asked! We had heard of people being deported within 24 hours for expressing a derogatory opinion about a local Malay or the Government — but at least they had the satisfaction of knowing why.

In this case — we were given two months to pack up — or we were told we could have longer if we needed it — but no explanation as to why we had to leave, which to this day perplexes us. We had both been involved in various voluntary organisations — which we enjoyed — and I can only say — they are the losers. BUT there is still a big question mark as to WHY, which frankly annoys me.

There were other heads of firms who received the same treatment — so one can only deduce the reasons for these actions.

However when we received our next posting to Hong Kong we were delighted at this chain of events, though still annoyed at the intrigue which the "powers that be" refused to explain.

As the Company initially had not indicated what our next posting would be — we decided to take our leave by flying to the Seychelles and then on to Mombassa, and decided to call in Cyprus. Our flat in the U.K. was let at the time, so we felt we might just as well spend longer getting home.

So in March, 1973 we visited the Seychelles for the first time. According to some Islanders, the garden of Eden lay in the Seychelles; it is in many ways an Island paradise with a superb climate and idyllic palm fringed beaches.

Politically and socially however, the Seychelles were a long way from Paradise, but there was little sign of this when we visited it in 1973 and again in 1975.

The Islands became a Republic in 1976 after 162 years of British Rule, the first President was playboy James Mancham, who was replaced after a Coup in 1977 and there have been several Coups since then.

We had friends who had retired to the Island two years earlier. She and her husband had started a small cottage industry, selling pretty little items made with Shells. Our friend was very gifted and at the same time very anxious to help the local population, so she not only trained them in making all these delightful artefacts but guided them in business acumen and of course paid them well.

Many of them worked at home and produced the finished items for sale in the shop they had opened. There is no doubt that she was thought of very affectionately by all the locals. When they finally left the Seychelles the "Shell Shop" continued to flourish — which was very rewarding.

We booked into the Beau Vallon Hotel which we made our headquarters, but travelled all around the Island and also went over to Praslin Island. These are the two main Islands but 90% of the population live on Mahe of which Victoria is the capital.

Altogether, the Seychelles consist of about 98 Islands and we were told they were all as lush and delightful as Mahe where we stayed. There are so many beaches which you have entirely to yourself and it was possible to take tours to many of the other islands. We hired a Mini Moke on both Mahe and Praslin Islands where the coco-de-mer, the world's largest coconut grows.

The standard of driving is horrendous; they seem to completely ignore white lines, double yellow lines, they double park on narrow roads, cars will stop without warning and two drivers each travelling in opposite directions will stop and talk and block the road. Of the 6,000 vehicles on the road we were told that 1,000 were involved in accidents! This makes days at any of the wonderful beaches even more attractive! Even so — the Islands are beautiful, the beaches fantastic and well worth a visit.

After these few days in the Seychelles we arrived in Mombasa and spent a day exploring the area in more detail, then we flew to Nairobi where we were met by Audrey and Mike Thompson and Jane and Frank Gosling.

This was very embarrassing as it appeared both couples were expecting us to stay with them! I don't quite know how this happened, but I think both "assumed" we would stay with them when we wrote and told them we would be arriving in Mombasa on the m.v. Asia and would be flying out of Nairobi a few days later, and would ring them on arrival in Nairobi to arrange a get together.

Anyway, this tricky situation was solved by our spending half our time with each couple! The Thompsons, who were also in Insurance, we had known in Karachi and this was their next posting — and we thought them so very lucky!

The Goslings had been our neighbours in K.L. for the first three years until they were transferred by their Company to Nairobi. When their Contract finished they decided to stay on and established their own business and were obviously doing very well — the two children enjoyed their schooling and all the family had their own horses which were obviously family pets and a great joy to them all.

Shortly after our visit, the political situation became such that they felt they had to leave — and under the law at that time they were unable to take any capital with them and the cherished horses were given away to friends. When we subsequently met them in the U.K. they were feeling the pinch. However, they shortly emigrated to Canada and started a new business from scratch, which I am glad to say has been very successful.

Whilst staying with them they took us to the Rift Valley and one or two of the Game Parks we had missed on our last visit, and yet another visit to the Nairobi National Park which we enjoyed so much.

We then flew over to Cyprus where we had been invited to stay by David and Ann Archibald, who had been transferred there after Karachi.

We had a wonderful week with them — again touring parts of the Island that we hadn't seen on our last visit. We went over to Limassol where we bought some sheepskin rugs and then flew over to Athens for a couple of days. Obviously we were not very anxious to return to the U.K. in March!

One of Ken's business associates who had heard of the treatment Ken had received from the Malay authorities, and knew that our own flat in London was let for a few more months, kindly offered us his flat in London for a week.    Not only this but he entertained us lavishly.

Here I had my first introduction to Greyhound Racing at White City.    I may not have been madly enthusiastic about the betting but we both thoroughly enjoyed the evening, and had a fantastic meal overlooking the track.  The enthusiasm of the other spectators was infectious and we became excited at the prospect of the dog we had put our money on coming in first.    Actually I think our chosen dog is still running!

After this, when I thought we would be taken back to the flat — we were taken to "Churchills", the famous Night Club.   There were two other male visitors in our party and so when we arrived at Churchills and were shown to our table, where two ladies were already sitting, I initially thought they were either the wives or girl friends of the two visitors!   How naive can one be? Trying to make conversation with these girls was difficult — and obviously they had not been chosen for their scintillating conversation!

I said that it was the first time we had been to Churchills and asked if they had been there before.    I admit they looked rather bemused at my remark, and said they had been many times!    It must have been well after 3.a.m. when it began to dawn on me that they were actually Hostesses who had been engaged by our host for the evening to ensure that the two men without wives would have an enjoyable evening!    I was very glad that I was with Ken and that there hadn't been THREE ladies engaged for the evening entertainment!

After a week in the  London flat, which was super — we were able to do a couple of Theatres and acted like tourists during the day, visiting Westminster Abbey, The Tower of London, The Vaults, and the Museums.    It is surprising how little we knew of our own country — but then we had both left in 1948 and when on leave were intent on seeing as much as we could of the girls or our close relatives.

Some very good friends of ours from K.L. offered us a house

they had recently bought in Sutton which they had not lived in and they did warn us that they felt the house would be in a pretty terrible condition. We were very happy to move in, but it was in a shocking state and I understood why our friends said there was a lot to do before they could live in it! They weren't kidding — but as they refused to accept any rent — we felt we should at least make an attempt to clean it and see that the electric appliances were working, before they arrived for their leave. The garden was completely grown over with weeds — so we had a very busy three weeks before going North to visit family members and friends. Along with many people they were quite shocked at our sudden departure from Malaysia.

It was about this time that Ken was officially offered the H.K. appointment — and we were very excited at the thought of going East again — particularly to H.K.

# NINE
## *Hong Kong*
### *July 1973-May 1981*

I am always grateful that we started our overseas life in Calcutta and not Hong Kong. Had it been in reverse — we certainly wouldn't have settled so well!

Hong Kong was a British Crown Colony until 30th June 1997 and was regularly referred to as "The Colony", it was one of the few remaining places in the world where the word "colony" did not have an insulting connotation.

To give a little background, the first tea was produced in China, before India, Ceylon and Java started growing it. The Portuguese were the first to establish a settlement on the South China coast and used Macau as their base. They traded Tea and Silk between Canton and Europe. Traditionally, payment to China for the tea had been made in Silver, but as the British were already trading with India, they began to barter with the Chinese with Opium from Bengal.

In 1839, the Dragon Emperor ordered that trafficking of the destructive "foreign mud" was wiped out. As a result the merchants were imprisoned in their own warehouses until they promised to surrender their opium. They were eventually promised reimbursement by the Crown — but it was not long before Opium was once again used as currency for tea which resulted in open warfare between the British and Chinese.

This Opium War lasted two years during which time a Captain Charles Elliot was given the task of finding a safe deepwater base where the British ships could be refitted.

It is amusing to read that in 1841 he found this pile of small rocky Islands, which were then the base of operations for pirates, smugglers of opium etc., and that anyone setting foot on these small Islands was in imminent danger of almost certain death, but it has now become this booming metropolis — Hong Kong.

Captain Elliot took possession of these Islands from China as a prize of war!   Everyone in England said Elliot must be out of his mind and that he should be run out of the navy.   The British newspapers were full of cartoons of this simple minded naval officer who had accepted a pile of rocks as a prize of war!   What a pity he is not alive today to see just how his "pile of rocks" has prospered!

The Opium War dragged on until the Chinese were defeated in 1842. and the Treaty of Nankeen was signed, which gave the British the Island of Hong Kong in perpetuity as compensation for their lost opium.

The British Admiralty realised that Hong Kong Island was almost indefensible, and could easily be conquered and so they fought the second opium war and the British received the Kowloon Peninsula, to the north of Hong Kong Island.

Later, as the population began to grow, it was obvious that the adjacent farmlands would be required for the production of foodstuffs.   Instead of having a further war, the British entered into a lease with the Chinese for what is called the New Territories (north of Kowloon), an area of about 365 square miles, and it is this lease that ran out in 1997.

In 1898, Britain leased Kowloon, the New Territories and outlying islands from the Chinese for a 99 year term.   This expired in June 1997 and the Chinese reclaimed the territory.

Hong Kong is unbelievable — it really is a ridiculous piece of Real Estate only 29 square miles and the population, when we were there, was around 4.7 million and in 1996, it was 6 million and growing.

It is my considered opinion that Hong Kong is probably the most fascinating and exciting spot in the world. Here one gets magnificent scenery, good climate, marvellous shopping, superb food, excellent accommodation, sight seeing galore and a colourful population so that walking along the streets is a full-scale tourist treat. H.K. has always got the maximum out of all the people who live there — and they in turn give more than in any other city in the world.

It is a remarkable and stimulating collision of the East and the West — and one can't land at Kai Tak Airport without feeling a surge of Adrenaline which keeps you in top gear for your whole visit. Long may this continue under the new regime.

Living there for 8 years, as we did, was without doubt the most exciting period of our lives.

We found so much humour in the day to day living — from simple things like the "Chinglish" that the Chinese spoke, which one had difficulty understanding, to their choice in naming their Companies. We saw adverts such as:—

"Lee Kee Shoes"
"Hop on Bicycle Company"
"Tak Kee Furniture Company"
"Age Ng Beauty House"
"Hang On Pawn Shop"
"Kin Kee Florist"
"Fit Mee Tailor"
"Cornie Medicine Company"

Whether these Company names help or hinder business — I don't know — but they added a little humour when driving in the congested streets or when you were stuck in a traffic jam.

It is said that Hong Kong harbour is easily the most beautiful and fascinating in the world and supersedes Naples, Rio de Janeiro and Sydney, a sentiment with which I have to agree. The harbour alone, filled with ferries criss crossing between H.K. Island, Kowloon, the outer Islands, Causeway Bay and Discovery Bay, and the Hydrofoils, Jetfoils, Hover Ferries which ply between H.K. Island and Macau, not forgetting the luxury liners, are in complete contrast to the junks and sampans. A Kaleidoscope of colour and a continuing source of interest.

There are 235 Outlying Islands and therefore I can never understand the few Expatriates who say they feel "hemmed in" and complain "there is nowhere to go" at the weekends. Many Companies have their own launches which the staff can use on a roster system, and then there are the various Ferries — with regular services to Kowloon on the Star Ferry and Ferries to the main Islands, Lantau, Lamma and Cheung Chau, Peng Chau, and the Sampans which you can hire for visits to the outlying Islands that have no regular Ferry Service like Po Toi Island.

The Star Ferry still remains the most popular method of crossing the harbour, though business people will often use the Mass Transit Railway (MTR).

You'll gather — we loved Hong Kong and still do!

When we arrived initially we were staying at the famous Mandarin Hotel, which in those days was without doubt the foremost Hotel on H.K. Island. Now there are so many first class Hotels that the Mandarin takes a back seat.

Our first flat was a "leave flat", the owners letting it whilst they went on leave, and had been rented for us prior to our arrival. It was on Lugard Road at the top of the Peak with the most magnificent views over the south of the Island — WHEN — there was no mist! We'd obviously arrived at the wrong time as every day we woke to this thick fog.

An additional hazard was that the flat was approached by a road which was the width of one car with no more than about 6 inches to spare on each side. As if this wasn't enough to get one's adrenaline pumping, there was a waterfall on the right of the road in one part which flowed over the road, which didn't help. When there had been a lot of rain one felt the force of this waterfall would push you over the edge!

It was necessary to get a Police Permit from the local police station to use the road — and a fine of HK$2,000 was payable if you didn't have this.  Obviously all residents (and there were 6 families in this block of flats who used the road) automatically were issued with permits — but when we had a dinner party we had to include the police permit along with the invitation.  I think a lot of people found they had previous engagements rather than take their life in their hands manoeuvring their car on this desperately narrow road.

We had a driver called Steven — who was the living spit of Bruce Lee the Chinese actor who had recently died.

On one occasion when driving along this ghastly road in the mist — we came across three Chinese ladies, and to enable them to get past, Steven stopped the car to allow them to walk round it.  When one of the ladies saw the driver, she let out a scream and appeared to collapse.  It is a Chinese custom that if you stop to help someone like this — you immediately become responsible for them — so the driver, having ascertained that he hadn't actually hit the lady — drove on.  I asked him what had happened — and he told me that the lady on seeing him thought she was seeing the ghost of Bruce Lee!

After living on Lugard Road for about 2 months, Ken's predecessor left and so we moved into the Company flat at Kellett Grove.  Whilst the flat was very adequate it was still on The Peak and I still found living in perpetual mist depressing.  I used to ring Ken in the office to find out what the weather was like in town — and even though the weather was usually excellent down there — we continued to have mist.  I therefore took the Peak Tram down to the shops and sometimes took the Ferry over to one of the Islands — anything to get away from the mist!

In 1974, a year after our arrival, the Company joined forces with one of the largest conglomerates and formed a new Joint Company. This seemed a good opportunity to see if we could move.  Neither of us liked living in the clouds — where you often woke thinking you must be in heaven — so we hoped to move to something lower down.

When Mrs. Brown (the dog!) arrived she had to go into quarantine

— and this was on the Kowloon side and the actual kennels were on the outskirts of the aerodrome — so it was very noisy with planes taking off and landing every three minutes.    I wasn't impressed with the Kennels — but fortunately the quarantine in H.K. was only for four weeks, but I used to go over to see "Mrs Brown" every day. This was quite an expensive and time consuming venture as to go through the tunnel between H.K. Island and Kowloon cost HK$10 per trip.    The traffic was terrible so the trip often took me 4 hours, as I would spend about an hour with "Mrs. Brown", brushing her and taking her out of the run as she enjoyed the small patch of grass that was in the exercise area.

We had only brought one dog with us from Malaysia as we felt that as we were returning to flat life it was better to leave Poo in Kuala Lumpur with our successor who was most anxious to have her.    Sherry we had to have put to sleep at the age of 17 as we really didn't think she would survive the journey.

Mrs. Brown had quite a problem in adjusting to life in H.K. — for one thing she refused to go to the toilet on the concrete in the kennels — and so had to be taken out to the one square of grass that was available in the quarantine kennels.    The first time I went out to the kennels, the vet told me that she had not urinated since arrival and when I took her to this square of grass — I could well believe this as she must have spent 4 minutes attending to the call of nature.

It took some time for her to adjust to this concrete jungle — and the "doggie toilets" that were so prevalent around H.K. — she refused to use.    With a HK$500 fine if she didn't use them — I became quite panic stricken and used to go around with a small shovel and a plastic bag — just in case!    She eventually adjusted — but it took time.

I made the acquaintance of an American lady who was obviously as concerned about her pet as I was, and she also visited the kennels every day to see her Poodle.    When Ken didn't need the car I used it to visit the kennels and naturally I offered this new found friend, Audrey, a lift and we became great chums.    Even to-day we are in fairly regular communication even though she is now back living in Dallas.

She invited Ken and me to her lovely flat at Woodland Heights for dinner one evening, and we were both so impressed with this apartment and would love to have lived there — it was well out of the mist AND it had the most fantastic views of Hong Kong Harbour.

One day I took Audrey to the market to buy vegetables and fish as Americans normally used the Super Markets and never went to the local markets — so I felt it was time she was introduced to the way "the other half lived".   I don't think she was very impressed when she saw the way they killed the chickens — dipping them in boiling water, which made it easier to remove the feathers.   The poor wee pigeons were literally skinned alive — so — Audrey decided it was the Supermarket for her from then on!

When we returned to the car after buying vegetables etc., we found the driver surrounded by Chinese and he was actually signing autographs!   They too thought he was at least related to the famous "Bruce".

But I think the funniest story of all was after he had asked for a day's leave to go to the Hospital.   Naturally, we gave him the day off though I remember it was madly inconvenient as we had three overseas visitors and I had planned to drive them over to the New Territories.

The following day we were driving past the T.B. Hospital and the driver pointed this out and said "that was the hospital I went to yesterday".   "Good heavens" I said — "you haven't got T.B. have you?"   Whereupon he told me he had to have an operation but seemed reluctant to elaborate on this.   However, when we got to the Hotel where I was to pick up these guests to take them on the Ferry — just before I got out of the car he said "Mrs. Campbell — you see it was too long so I had to have it chopped off"!

The mind boggled, but I felt I should not pursue this any further at this stage, but I thought I better ring Ken and tell him what had been said.   Ken said he would look at the medical chit he had brought in to explain his absence. Imagine his surprise when he saw that the driver had had a self requested circumcision!

It appeared that an American film producer had advertised in the press, that they were looking for someone to play the part of Bruce Lee, the actor, in a film on his life. Bruce Lee, the actor had apparently been circumcised! I really didn't think that in a film this would have been an important omission!

Some of the driver's friends felt that he stood a good chance of getting the part and so had sent an application along with his photograph and along with about 200 others he was requested to attend for an interview. After a further two interviews he was eventually put on the short list for an audition!

The funny thing is that when he was asked to go for the audition, he came back with the script — and was asked to learn a short scene from the film by heart. His spoken English was quite good, but his written English was poor. He asked me if I would help him to pronounce the words — so we had the ridiculous situation of my reading the part to him and then, if you please, taking the part of Bruce Lee's wife so that he could respond at the correct juncture! Although he was on the short list I didn't think his English was of a sufficiently high standard for him to get the part.

But I was wrong — so we lost Steven as our driver and acquired a very quiet youthful looking Chinese driver called David. The complete opposite in every way to Steven.

I later heard that he lost this opportunity after further screen tests — maybe it was his lack of English — or the fact he didn't have a coach in the subsequent tests!

Fiona came out to join us at the end of her Secretarial course and very quickly obtained a job working at the Holiday Inn.

When Audrey and Lowell had to return to the States, they offered us their flat — and amazingly enough the Company agreed to our moving, even though the rental was high and of course the Kellett Grove flat was owned by the Company. However the time seemed to be right for selling property and the Company were anxious not to have any long term investments in H.K.   So in February 1974 we moved into 5D Woodland Heights.

After a few months in this new flat I heard that a larger flat was available and as Fiona was now living with us, having finished her Secretarial course, we felt we needed the extra room.   So again we moved — and I have to say the new apartment was very impressive. It was three storied with a miniature waterfall and fish pond under the first staircase — and the Dining Room had a marble floor and next to it was a Breakfast room.   Then the usual three bedrooms and three bathrooms, a study and large Lounge, AND again, most importantly — it was not in the mist!

Our life style in Hong Kong was quite different to that of the past — most families managed with one servant — who would cook, clean and even baby sit and look after the children.   If one had more than 2 children, then an extra servant would be employed. So in many ways this was a good stepping stone to returning to life in the U.K.

However, as we had so many visitors — who usually came out with their wives, I found it impossible to act as a tour guide, do the household chores and provide a first class dinner — so — we decided we would have to engage a servant.

The next door neighbour suggested that perhaps her Chinese Amah would have a friend that would want employment.   We arranged an interview — but — never having employed a  Black and White Amah — I had a lot to learn.   I found that I was the one being interviewed and I listened to a tirade of all the jobs that the Amah would NOT do.   It sounded rather like this:— "I no wash floors; I no clean silver; I no do washing; I no clean windows; I no work after 7.p.m.; I no do shopping"!   I was left wondering what she was prepared to do — so told her I didn't think she was suitable.

Three more Chinese came for interview — and I received the same monologue.   After this it appeared that we had been "black balled" as we were considered bad employers!

This was the first time we had encountered such antagonism —

and I wished I could have any of my Indian, Pakistan or Malay servants — who might be slow, and sometimes ignorant, but always willing.

I decided that I would place an advert in the local paper and by doing this hoped I could cover a more extensive area and would not be influenced by the apparent boycott.

I received a number of replies — some quite hopeless but I was very impressed with a letter I received from a young Indian girl who told me that she was dissatisfied and unhappy as she had not been paid by her present employers for over six weeks and was working until 2.a.m. most days.

I asked her to come for an interview and she explained that she hoped she could get off duty for a few hours but if she didn't turn up it was because her present boss had prevented her from taking this time off.

She arrived — and told me the most amazing story.    She had been brought to Hong Kong by her very wealthy Indian employer who initially got her in to H.K. as a tourist, and she was paid under the minimum wage.    When her tourist Visa expired he had applied for a Work Permit for her — and because of his position, she was allowed to stay.    Her Contract had to be made out to indicate she was receiving more money than she actually was — BUT — her employer explained to her that he would only pay her a certain amount each week, but that he would keep the balance of her pay until she went on leave.    When she asked for extra money — which she was due — to send home to help her family — he refused to pay her.    Her contract also indicated that she had to have 1½ days leave per week and all public holidays.    In the last 5 weeks she had only been off duty for 1 day and this was to go to Immigration to have her Passport stamped with the Work Permit! As her employer entertained a great deal she was expected to stay on duty until the last guests left.

I should add that it was an extended Indian family and so there was no end to the duties she had to perform, if not for one member of the family — then for another.

It seemed to me that there was no way he would sign her release certificate which would enable us to employ her. He was on a good wicket and I couldn't see him giving this up easily until her two year contract was up. However, nothing ventured, nothing gained.

I rang this gentleman — whose family and he were well known throughout the whole Colony, but I pretended I had no idea who he was and so decided to attack the problem from a rather unusual angle.

I said that I gathered he was having financial problems as he had not been able to pay his servant for the last 4 weeks — and that during this period he had been unable to give the maid the statutory time off as agreed on her Contract. Not only that, she had had to work over and above the permitted hours.

I sympathised with his circumstances and said I was happy to relieve him of this responsibility and thus avoid any investigation if she were to approach the Immigration Department! I wish I had been a mousy in the wall when he took my phone call — he must have been mortified that there was some European in the Colony who (a) had not heard of him or his family (b) thought he was having financial difficulties (he was more than a millionaire!) and (c) knew that he had been contravening the conditions of the Work Permit.

I could hear him muttering for some time — but think the seriousness of his actions made him soften and the thought that he might be black listed by Immigration for contravening the conditions of the Work Permit — he obviously decided that this "ignorant European lady" might just report him and therefore to everyone's amazement — he agreed to release her.

He couldn't resist asking me if I knew who he was — and I replied that I had no idea but I did know he must be having financial problems otherwise he would never have resorted to contravening the terms of the Contract!

How I enjoyed this conversation, and when I met him socially after this, which I often did — I longed to remind him of our conversation.

So — Mena arrived with her few possessions — as he had even taken her uniforms off her before allowing her to leave — and had searched her bags before she departed his large luxurious home.

As he had signed her release papers I was able to employ her more or less immediately and we found her a most grateful, hard working maid, if perhaps a little naive.

She couldn't believe that she could have 1½ days off every week — and I realised that she didn't really know how to spend this time. However, she soon settled — and seemed happy to spend her free time sewing and crocheting.

She must have been with us nearly two years when she came to me one day holding five photographs of Indian men.  She said "which one would you choose Memsahib?".  She then went on to explain that her father had sent her these photographs and she had to chose one of them so that he could arrange her marriage during her next leave.  In India I was well aware that the Arranged Marriage system still existed — but here in Hong Kong it seemed incongruous.

Anyway — I said I really didn't think you could judge anyone from a picture, as good looking people often did not have good hearts — but on the other hand less attractive people often had big hearts — so I felt it was entirely up to her.

A few days later we got around to the dates of her departure on leave as she said she had to tell her father who was arranging her marriage.  I asked her if she had made up her mind as to which of the five men whose photos she showed us — she had decided to marry.  She dashed off and brought the photo of the man she had chosen.

When I asked her how she had come to this very important decision — she explained that photo A wanted as a Dowry, 1 paddy field of rice and 3 cows;  photo B asked for 4 goats, 2 cows and a bull;  photo C wanted three dozen hens and 2 cocks, but Photo D wanted solid gold!

She felt that as she was living in H.K. it was easier for her to buy gold cheaply and it would be very difficult to organise all the animals the other suitors wanted AND most important, as it was usual for the Indian groom's family to give the bride for the wedding at least two items of gold — she would probably get two pieces of the gold back, which she would certainly know to be genuine!

Naive she might have been — but stupid she wasn't!

When we went to book her air passage she queried why I was buying a single ticket and not a return.   I said that as she was getting married I really felt she should stay in Bombay as I most certainly could not cope with a baby in the apartment.   She was most indignant and said she didn't understand — she wasn't going to have a baby she was only going to get married!   I pointed out that getting married usually produced a baby (she was Catholic) — to which she queried — "how come?"

She got very upset at the thought of not coming back to us and after two days of crying she finally pleaded with me to allow her to return.

I said that if she was prepared to go on the Birth Control Pill — then I would feel happier about renewing her contract.   I reminded her that this would be against her religion — but this appeared to be of little consequence!   When I pointed out however, that the Pill must be taken every day and she must not forget to take it she said — "oh dear, how will I remember?"   I suggested that she put the pills in a vitamin jar and kept them in the kitchen.   "Oh dear, I couldn't do that as my father and my brothers would also want a vitamin pill"!

Anyway — I bought her 2 month's supply of the Pill and for the next 3 weeks she took one regularly, so I felt quite happy that she had got into the routine and would not forget to take it for the next month whilst on leave.

We saw her off at the airport — she was in tears at leaving us even for so short a time — as I don't think anyone had ever been really kind to her — and we looked upon her as another addition in our family — and she had most afternoons off duty and got plenty of time off.

The month passed — and we went out to the airport to meet Mena — who got off the aircraft looking sad and far from well. She said little on the journey back home — but when we were alone and I asked her how the wedding had gone — she burst into tears and said "you didn't tell me what terrible things would happen" — and slowly I heard her story.

She had arrived in Bombay and the family met her — but she had no time with her future husband other than at the official engagement party and, because of the shortage of time, the wedding was arranged for the following week.

The usual preliminaries that are associated with any Indian Wedding took up the whole of the week. She had to go to the Church and the priest gave her the pre-marriage talk and he stressed that the church did not agree with birth control! She asked him what was wrong with using birth control and he suggested she talk to her Mother. She explained that her Mother had died when she was 9 and so the Priest gave her a book to read.

I said I thought this was very nice of the Priest — whereupon she exploded that it was a VERY DIRTY book with dirty pictures and so she threw it away!

Anyway — she got married and they left for Bangalore by train for their honeymoon. En route she was taken very ill and started haemorrhaging — so was taken off the train at the next stop and put into hospital!

She then told me that the hospital questioned her as to whether she had been taking any medicine. She daren't tell them that she was on the pill or that she had forgotten to take it for 9 days! Remembering what I had said to her about taking the Pill regularly, she had taken 2 weeks supply the night before the wedding!

She spent most of the honeymoon in hospital, but was discharged three nights before they were due to return. She spent the last three nights with her husband. The first night she told me she slept with his sister whom they were visiting — the next night her husband insisted that she at least came in the bedroom as his family were

356

wondering what kind of man he was permitting his wife to spend the night with his sister.  She said that he felt his family thought he was half woman and half man and Mena then asked me if I understood?

She agreed to allow him to spend the night in the room with her but not in the bed!   But... the following night he got into bed with her and she thought it was all beastly and she felt I should have warned her what would happen and then she would not have got married!

To me it was incredible that anyone could be so ignorant — and I felt very sorry for her — but was delighted that she had only spent one night with her husband and hoped therefore the chances of her becoming pregnant would be diminished.

The following day she seemed as happy as Larry and went round the flat singing, and said "Aren't I wicked — I am so happy that I am away from my husband"

Her husband was working in the Gulf and as to be expected he kept asking her to join him — but she refused to go, saying she could not break her Contract — and she was not leaving H.K.

Her next leave came along and by this time I think she realised that she would have to join her husband — her father had written to tell her that if she didn't join him then he would be able to divorce her and then no one would want to marry her.  After he died, who would look after her?   He pleaded with her to arrange to go to the Gulf when she got her next leave.

I had to agree with her father and to help make her decision easier, I explained that we would shortly be leaving H.K. and she would then have to get a new appointment.   So — reluctantly she agreed to travel to Bahrain on her next leave.

We were very sad to say goodbye to Mena- she had been part of our family for four years and was always helpful — and other than the period immediately prior to, and for a week after, her wedding a happy cheerful individual.

We started looking for another helper — and so again I advertised in the local paper as I didn't want to go through the nonsense of the Chinese Black and White Amahs interviewing me and telling me what they wouldn't do!

This time a Filipino called Suzie answered our advert, and her references were excellent — so Suzie joined the family for the next two years. She was a first class cook though I don't think we could ever say she was particularly cheerful — but she was efficient.

With the merger of our Company with a large conglomerate, we were allowed to use their weekend houses at Lantau, Fan Ling and to use the Company Junk. These were allocated on a roster system — and — we particularly enjoyed a weekend in Lantau. There was a resident Chinese Amah there, who besides keeping the bungalow clean would prepare meals for a very nominal figure.

Lantau is the largest of the 236 islands and twice as large as Hong Kong Island. It is the mountainous home of the Trappist and Buddhist Monks, fishermen and farmers and the weekend resort of many Hong Kong residents. The Ferry from H.K. comes in to Silvermine Bay and from there you can take a bus to the top of the mountain to visit the Temple of the Precious Lotus or Po Lin Tse.

We were fortunate in that not only did the company provide the accommodation on the Island, but also a car. Because of the restrictions on travelling on the Island, each car was licensed only for use on certain roads, but not all of them — so it was sometimes easier to take the bus — but not on public holidays!

I think our turn for the Company Junk came up about every 4 — 6 weeks — sometimes more frequently as believe it or not, some families were not particularly keen on spending hours on a boat. A crew was provided with the boat though we would take our own food — but all washing up and tidying up was undertaken by the crew — so it was truly a pleasant holiday. Sometimes we took the Junk to one of the outlying Islands where we dropped anchor and disembarked and found some fish restaurant for a meal. Travelling back at night through Hong Kong harbour with an evening drink — was the ultimate!

No visit to Hong Kong would be complete without a visit to Cheung Chao Island which is south east of Lantau, and shaped like a dumbbell. One got the impression that it must be rather like Hong Kong was 100 years ago. No cars are permitted on the Island — but it is crowded — chiefly with local residents, though as the Ferries that ply between Lantau and H.K. often call at Cheung Chao there are always a few tourists.

If we were not able to get the Junk or a bungalow at the weekend, we would often take the Ferry over to Cheung Chau. As the island has no vehicles and it is so small, one can wander from one end of the island to the other and along the roads that lead to the hills at either end of the island and you really feel you are in old China.

A third of the population lives on the water and fishing is the major industry. One bay is usually crowded with sampans, junks and ferries from Hong Kong. The other bay has bathing beaches, but the whole island gives one the feeling of being quiet and very rural; dogs, pigs, ducks and chickens wander around the streets in a state of organised confusion.

Most of the pigs and poultry end their days in the crowded market where housewives come to fill the twin baskets hung on bamboo poles and balanced horizontally over their shoulders — a complete contrast to the frenetic life style in Hong Kong!

We thoroughly enjoyed our visits to the Island — where we wandered along the sea front, bought lobsters, crabs and prawns from the various vendors whose tanks of fish lined the road side and took these along with some vegetables, also bought off the sidewalks, to a restaurant on the sea front where we sat outside and waited for them to be cooked.

One would often see the odd old lady who still had bound feet and you realised what agony these poor souls must have gone through — and, for that matter, were still suffering from this ghastly habit.

In the village centre we found old shops that were selling Chinese Medicine and potions and we were amused to see on the Menu in one of the Restaurants "Penis Soup" "Testicle Chow Fan"" Snake Soup" and other savoury items!

One can't walk very far without hearing the click clack of the mah-jong tiles — it is amazing what noise a game can generate, particularly when money is involved, and the Chinese will bet on anything! You could always tell when a game was nearing the end, as the excitement grew, the voices got louder and the tiles rattled even more!

Quite often when we had visitors we would be inspired to organise a trip over to Macau — the oldest European settlement in Asia. It is also known as the "City of God" or "the Monte Carlo of the Far East" and has a reputation for more vice per capita than any other spot in the world!

Macau is renowned for its casinos though, as I have said, the Chinese will bet on anything, and the Jal Alai (a ball game peculiar to Macau) will see crowds of Chinese trying their luck and the dog and horse racing attract large crowds.

One had to remember to purchase a return ticket on either the Hydrofoil which takes approx. 1¼ hours, the Jetfoil which makes the trip in 45 minutes or the normal slower ferry taking 2½ to 3 hours. We learnt the hard way that if you only purchase a single ticket — you find the cost of the return trip has suddenly escalated — as the employees at the terminal are well aware that you HAVE to get back — and so — take advantage of this by saying there are no seats. If you are prepared to pay four times the normal price, suddenly they find there are a couple of vacant seats!

The first time Ken and I went over to Macau — without visitors, we went over the Bridge to the Island of Taipa and said we would come back and spend the weekend there — but we never did. We saw the burnt out church of Sao Paulo, the cathedral on top of the hill, The Temple of Kun Iam and many monuments.

One can often pick up an interesting antique — though — you could also pick up a fake and pay an antique price!

On a couple of occasions we spent the night in Macau and the following day took a tour into China where we visited Sun Yat Sen's house — had a fabulous Chinese meal — visited a commune and a school — and received a lot of interested attention from the locals who all seemed to be on bikes — and in those days not so many foreigners had been into China.

So often one heard Westerners complain that they felt hemmed in in Hong Kong and there was nothing to do! I couldn't believe it as to my mind, so long as you are prepared to take the rough with the smooth — there was no end to what one could do.

There were two other islands we enjoyed visiting — Peng Chau a small island off Lantau with its 200 year old temple, and Po Toi Island which one can only reach by a motorised Sampan.

When driving round the New Territories we would pay a visit to one of the Bronze factories or the Candle factory. The most popular at that time were the Lung Kee and the Sum Ngai. Both very much off the beaten track.

The first time we went to the Sum Ngai Bronze factory to buy "instant antiques" which were excellent replicas of the originals, we found a shed with a couple of smaller sheds attached — and a small furnace where welding was taking place. The two men that were working there did not speak a word of English and even their Chinese appeared to be a dialect we didn't recognise. We were relieved when a young girl came out of one of the sheds, and greeted us in English.

She was delightful — and we told her we wanted to purchase a Tang Dynasty Flying Horse which we had seen in town costing around HK$700, and a Sheung vase, which we planned to make into a lamp. We still have this lamp to-day and it is greatly admired.

Would you believe it, after taking down our order, she then took us out into the adjoining field where it appeared various farm workers were turning the soil. She spoke to them in this peculiar dialect which we discovered later was Hokien and two of the workers were then galvanised into action and started digging. This young girl, who told us her name in Chinese sounded liked "Big One" — (though in fact she was minute), told us that they would bring us the horses and the vase we wanted once they had dug them up!

Apparently, after the Bronze items had been cast, they buried them in this field where cows were grazing for about six weeks. It appeared that the chemical re-action of the urine on the item gave them this "authentic" antique look.

Over the years they discovered that Potassium Sulphide and other chemicals would produce the same "antique" effect.   This was a much quicker method than having to bury the articles for six weeks with no guaranteed result — as if the cows didn't "oblige" in the right area — they'd have to wait a further six weeks!

In spite of the rather unusual and tedious method, the items that were produced were excellent replicas,— Vases from the Shang Dynasty, inscribed with the identical characters that appeared engraved on the original.  Rice Cups from the Western Chou period — and as if to confuse you even further, they had a very impressive Stiff Backed catalogue showing the originals which were in the National Palace Museum!

By the time we left Hong Kong some 8½ years later "Big One" was married and had three children  — the shed had been replaced by a large brick structure — a show room had been added — AND the family had built a house in the adjoining field.   Business was obviously good and she had every reason to feel proud.

We returned — 20 years after our first visit, to be greeted most affectionately by "Big One" and two of her children, who had obviously had a good education, and "Big One" and one of the daughters took great delight in showing us round and pointing out the changes — which were to my mind very obvious.

It was a first class business, the present Show Rooms had trebled in size — the tourist buses were calling twice a day and the American clientele were obviously enthralled with the variety of "antiques" and the fact that export facilities were offered.

On the domestic scene, a swimming pool had been added to the already beautiful home — and there were two Mercedes in the garage, the latest T.V. and music centre were in the Lounge!

She told me they were now manufacturing in China where labour was so much cheaper and they had a large export trade.    I was duly impressed as you can imagine.

Such is progress in Hong Kong!

The candle factory was in the same area — and this also was very primitive when we first went out there in 1973 — and it too has progressed.    They specialise in the large ornamental and perfumed candles, and when I see the price of these in the U.K. (when you can get them) I am shattered.

For anyone feeling bored or "hemmed in" there was still the Zoological and Botanical Gardens, the Science Museum, the Space Museum, Flagstaff House Museum, H.K. Museum of Art, a very up to date Art Centre and various exhibitions, Ocean Park, Water World, Sung Dynasty Village, the Jade Market in Kowloon, the Night Markets, and numerous walks with fantastic views.

How could you be bored?

Added to which there are various Chinese Festivals like Ching Ming — the Chinese Festival of the dead which is marked with prayers, offerings and the sound of firecrackers.    You will see relatives flocking to the cemeteries with their bundles of fruit, food and flowers and they will sit by the side of the grave and actually talk to the dear departed, telling them what has happened during the last year!

Another of H.K.'s most unusual and colourful April festivals is the Cheung Chau Bun Festival which is intended to placate the restless spirits of the victims of Pak Pai, a notorious pirate.

Vegetarian meals and prayers precede the main celebrations, and after mid-night when the victims souls have had their fill, there is a rush to climb to the top of a 50 foot tower of buns which had been assembled earlier.    The more buns they are able to grab — the better the good fortune they will have.

Just before we left H.K., this climbing the bun tower was declared much too dangerous.    On the final day of the festivities a noisy and colourful procession through the narrow streets of Cheung Chau takes place with gaudy floats and loud gongs are sounded to frighten away demons, thereby ensuring the safety of the residents for the coming year.

The above sounds rather like an extract from a tourist pamphlet but you'll gather I loved Hong Kong — and felt irritated when people said there was nothing to do — life after all is what you make it.

One of my friends was going on a business trip with her husband and would be away for about a month. She apparently had been teaching English to Japanese and asked me if I would take over her pupils whilst she was away! I said that I was not a teacher and really didn't think I would be suitable particularly as I had no Japanese whatsoever. Not to be daunted she asked if I would accompany her one afternoon when she was giving her lessons. She used to visit the pupils in their homes, though sometimes they would come to her home.

I realised that these lessons were very basic and one did not need to have a command of Japanese. Most Japanese understood English and had a very good command of the language, BUT they were very shy when it came to speaking. My friend explained that her job was to ask them questions so that they had to reply.

She also gave them lessons in social etiquette as many of the Japanese ladies were married to business tycoons and had to entertain Europeans — so they wanted to know how to lay a table for dinner — which glasses they should use — and one of their most important requests was how they asked the European ladies if they wanted to go to the toilet before dinner!

After this interesting insight I decided I would do this for my friend.

I had some interesting conversations with the students — for instance on the subject of asking one's guests if they wanted to be excused, I explained that we would use expressions like "would you like to wash your hands?" or "would you like to powder your nose". Notes were duly made on this subject.

The following lesson was based on a visit to the Theatre where they had been to see a very popular show. They told me how much they had enjoyed it and after the performance there was a lot of "crapping"! I corrected them and explained where they should put their tongues to obtain the correct pronunciation of "clapping". The Japanese generally had a lot of trouble with their "r's" and "l's" — and as they persisted in saying "crapping" and not "clapping" — I said they really should try to correct this as "crapping" was rather rude and associated with going to the bathroom. "Ah soo" — they said — just like "powder your nose" or "wash your hands" — and I then had to try to explain the difference without offending.

Another occasion I was trying to get my student to use her English so we had a question and answer session. To begin with I was very basic and asked what time her daughter went to school, and which school she was attending, and how did she get there. My next question asked about her husband and what time he left for the office — I was told 8.a.m. "What time does he come home?" I asked. She replied "He comes home about four o'clock". I said "that is very early, my husband doesn't get home until six o'clock and sometimes seven o'clock." Ah soo she said — "he must be very tired as my husband goes to bed for two hours when he comes home"! It suddenly dawned on me she was talking about a.m. and not p.m. whereupon I told her that European ladies would not accept husbands staying out all night and would want to know where they had been.

Her words of wisdom were that "if he has been to a naughty place, he will not tell me the truth, so why should I ask?" I suppose that made sound sense — but can't see any Western wife accepting such a situation!

In the month I was teaching the Japanese for my friend, her class just about doubled as I kept being asked if they could make an appointment for their friend — and I felt I should say yes. Anyway, I was enjoying the work and found the Japanese ladies quite delightful — though I was not very keen on teaching the men who seemed to have some peculiar habit of scratching themselves as though their underpants were too tight or they had forgotten to put them on!

I thought the children were brilliant. They seemed very anxious to learn, always did their home work, and often would do more than I had set.

The month passed and I heard from my friend that she and her husband would not be returning as they were being posted to Indonesia.   What to do with the students?   I told them the news and they all without exception asked me to continue with the lessons. I suppose I was flattered and I also enjoyed the challenge, not forgetting the extra pocket money, and I felt I was learning as much from them as they did from me — so I agreed.

When I finally left Hong Kong in 1981 after Ken retired I passed these students to my friend Moira who continued the good work for a further few years.

In the 8 years we were in H.K. we had at least 6 Typhoons — each given a girl's name — and the worst we experienced was Typhoon Rose in 1978.   This made a direct hit on H.K. and a block of flats were demolished with people trapped inside.   We actually saw airconditioners hurtling through the air and many of the ornate advertising boards were demolished — electric signs crashed to the ground and it was chaos for a few days.

H.K. had an excellent warning system — and over the radio and T.V. one got an up to date report and signals were placed near the Ferries.   When the No.1. signal went up — this was merely a warning requesting you to keep your radio on for more news as there was a storm approaching.   When warning No.3. went up all the schools were closed and one was requested to secure any loose objects, bringing in plant pots etc.   But by the time the No.8. warning went up workers were told to return home immediately to avoid queues on public transport etc., and to tape their windows if they were not too safe.

Our dining room windows were sucked out during one Typhoon — which surprised us as the wind was blowing directly on the window — but somehow a vacuum must have been formed and the windows went flying out.    At the time both Ken and I had boards under our bed as we both suffered from minor back problems and so we brought this wood down to the dining room and between us we held them in place for the next two hours.  Had we not done this all the ornaments, lamps and shades would have been broken.

As it was we carefully moved everything from the shelves and placed them on the floor hoping that they would not have quite so far to fall!

Typhoons had a nasty habit of passing over and then turning back on themselves — so you were not sure for some time whether the storm had really passed or if it would return.

One of the "Advantages" associated with working overseas as Expatriates at that time, was that we were given First Class return passages to the U.K. each contract.   Now we are retired of course we travel "chicken class".    Funny how distances seem so much longer now!

When our parents were living, or our children were at boarding school in England, our first priority was to get back to the U.K. as quickly as possible in order to spend as much time as we could with the family.  After our parents died and the children had left boarding school, or did not have school holidays that coincided with our leave, we were able to take advantage of these trips and were able to route ourselves through Europe, or via the States.

As a result we were able to have some very enjoyable holidays. Initially, the Company sent us by sea, which was a holiday in itself, but of course restricted our stop-overs to Europe.    Later, when air travel became more competitive, we had to fly to and from the U.K. There was no difference in the air fare whether we went via the States or via Europe.

No longer did we get a six month leave, nor were our tours of duty so long, therefore we had more opportunity to take advantage of the travel arrangements.

We realised of course that living in a foreign country one had a far different perspective about it than when visiting as a tourist!

Some of our postings most certainly did not lend themselves to promoting tourism — hence my attempt to explain how we enjoyed them.

There were disadvantages of course, parting from one's children when the time came for them to go to boarding school — and health was a major issue.

We covered most of our European holidays when we sailed home and disembarked at either Venice, Naples, Marseilles or Genoa, and went by rail or road back to the U.K.

A lot of our trips were made possible, of course, by the fact that whilst Ken was working in Hong Kong, we were occasionally able to get fares at 10% of the normal fare — so for Chinese New Year, when everything seemed to close for about a week, or Xmas, we were able to avail ourselves of this fantastic concession. Occasionally of course we would add a couple of days leave to the Public Holiday which made the trip all the more worth while.

In 1974, we started having yearly leaves of six weeks, as a result the time seemed to pass even more quickly. One of the first trips after air travel became the norm was made in September, 1974, when we returned to the U.K. via Japan and the U.S.A.

We had been invited to spend a few days with Audrey and Lowell Green in Tokyo. Audrey was the "doggie" lady that I met in the quarantine kennels in Hong Kong, and with whom we became good friends, and whose flat we moved into when they left H.K..

The thing that stands out in my mind about this trip was the exorbitant cost of everything and the fact that so few people understood or spoke English. I was very grateful that we were staying with friends who could guide and advise us as to where to go and what to see, and of course we weren't incurring astronomical Hotel bills.

I was rather confused however when they showed us our bedroom! This appeared to be a fully furnished small Lounge room with tables and the odd chairs — but no sign of any beds! We learnt of course that when bedtime came — all the furniture in the room was moved into the small hall and Futons were produced out of the wardrobes. There was no room for our cases — so we placed these on the floor of the wardrobe. This nearly proved a disaster as when Ken got up in the night to find the toilet — he tripped over the case that was protruding and fell into the wardrobe which had paper thin walls and he very nearly ended up in our hosts bedroom!

I in turn committed a frightful faux pas. There was no bath as such — nor a shower, but in the bathroom there was a large tub with steps up the side. I studied this carefully and then decided that I had to climb up the steps and lower myself into the large tub. I had a good wash — using a lot of soap — and although the water was cold, the weather was warm, so it wasn't too much of a shock. When I got out of the tub I then wondered how on earth I emptied this — so had to ask Audrey and Lowell.

They were hysterical when I told them what I had done as this tub of water was for the whole family for 24 hours and I was supposed to use the small ladle to pour water over me, then soap myself and THEN rinse off using this ladle!

I had ruined the water for everyone — and they had no idea how to empty it as they had a Japanese lady who came in each morning to do the washing and fill the tub.

I am sure that at this stage they felt that house guests were like fish — they went off very quickly!

Our next clanger was that we had to cash some travellers cheques as we had invited Audrey and Lowell out for dinner that night. They directed us to a Department Store that was open on Sundays and would do cash transactions. Ken cashed a U.S. dollar travellers cheque and I can't remember for how much, but we received what we thought was a huge amount of yen.

On mooching around the shop we were shattered when we saw a large Fungi, rather like a mushroom — which cost nearly as much as the money we had received for our U.S. dollar travellers cheque and with this we had hoped to take four people out for dinner! So we decided that we better return to cash further dollars.

When we returned to the Money Exchanger — she let out a squeal of — we hoped, delight — but weren't quite sure, and she gesticulated to the cash till and produced nearly as much money as we'd received the first time and wouldn't take any more of our travellers cheques. We were confused! We found someone who spoke a little English and they were able to ascertain what had gone wrong.

It appeared that she had inadvertently short-changed us and had given us an amount with four noughts following it and it should have had six! Weren't we lucky — and wasn't the cash girl honest? I have to say the honesty of the Japanese is quite incredible — and I am sure you could leave your wallet on a park bench and come back the next day and it would still be there.

Audrey and Lowell took us to visit various Shrines — we went on the Bullet Train to Kyoto — saw the Palace and other places of interest before leaving for Hawaii.

Here we were met by Audrey's Aunt who garlanded us with Leis, and made a great fuss of us as she had stayed with Audrey and Lowell in Hong Kong where we had initially met her. The following day we hired a car and she came with us driving around the Island pointing out all the places of interest.

Her husband had been killed at Okinawa — which she insisted we visited. Again, so much better when you have someone to direct you as you know you are not missing anything of interest.

After this visit we flew into Los Angeles which appeared to be covered in a heavy blanket of smog, and so we were quite delighted to get on the bus to Anaheim where we had booked into a Motel owned by people we had also met and entertained in Hong Kong! We spent the next day going round Disney Land. Who said it was only for kids? We had a ball and were so impressed that on another leave we went to Disney World.

No visit to L.A. would be complete without going to Universal Studios. We discovered many of the secrets associated with the film industry — for instance we were in a landslide when huge boulders came tumbling down a hill and hit the side of our train and we were convinced it would be derailed.  But we weren't!  All these horrific boulders were made of rubber — but looked very realistic.

Trees fell across the railway track — JUST as our train had passed. We witnessed a very realistic shoot out between Indians and Cowboys and had an exciting drive through the Red Sea and saw the water divide just as soon as the wheels of our train touched the water!   You've probably been there and done that — so I won't elaborate further — but it was fun.

We returned to L.A. where we took a tour of Hollywood and had the homes of the Stars pointed out in Beverley Hills and visited the Farmer's Market.

Then onto Las Vegas which was an amazing experience — and we stayed at the Desert Rose Motel which yet again was owned by a couple we had met in Hong Kong.   They went out of their way to see that we did all the right things — and had booked a show for us at Caesars Palace.  Then we wandered up the Strip having a drink in various establishments where there were also first class shows — and we were amazed that other than a slight surcharge on the price of drinks — there was no cover charge for any of the shows.   We saw many of these Shows and visited Circus Circus, Starlight, the Golden Nugget — where we were taken for breakfast.

We were shattered to find the place was "jumping" with people still in their evening dress obviously having been gambling all night! It was here I came to the conclusion that gambling, rather like alcoholism, is a sickness when carried to extremes.

After this we went to San Francisco where we had booked into a Hotel only to be woken up at 2.a.m. the first morning by fire engines and discovered that the building opposite was in flames.  Everyone loves San Francisco — we went in the famous tram that seems to appear in every movie that is made, and went down the steep street where all the car chases occur!   We took a tour to Hoover Dam and of course went to Fisherman's Wharf where we had a meal having spent an afternoon on Pier 9 or was it 19? — and returned to the Hotel exhausted. Even so, we loved it.

Our flight took us across America to Washington D.C. and on this occasion we were not impressed. We stayed at the Pick Lee Hotel where there were warnings about leaving any valuables in the room and keeping your case securely locked! As I saw it, this meant it was inadvisable to even unpack. I admit that I lost three very nice Bras that I had washed and left in the bathroom to dry!

We arrived at the Pick Lee Hotel about 8.30.p.m. to find that we were too late for dinner in the Hotel, so decided we would wander down the road to a Coffee bar and get a bite to eat.

We were told by the Concierge we should not walk in the streets at night and if we had to leave the Hotel to eat that he would order us a taxi. When the taxi came we noticed he locked all the doors as soon as we got in and when we gave him the address of the restaurant we had had recommended, he told us that it would be closed at this time of night (it was only 8.45.p.m. I might add) so the Taxi driver took us down to a coffee shop that he knew would be open.

When we got there though he told us not to get out of the taxi until he had been into the coffee shop to see if they had a table and told us that we should not venture onto the streets when we left the restaurant, but should phone for a taxi and that the taxi driver would come into the restaurant to collect us. We must not stand outside on the pavement waiting for him! I found all this rather scary!

This wasn't helped by an incident in the Coffee bar where we noticed, when we entered, there was a young girl sitting on her own with an empty coffee cup in front of her. The proprietor — who was Indian had obviously already given her the check — but she ignored it.

The place was getting quite packed and so again the Proprietor asked her if she would settle her account unless she wanted something else to drink. Well — there was a tirade of abuse from this young innocent looking girl who used language I'd have associated with dock workers. The gist seemed to be that she had had to f...g well wait for her cup of coffee and that the proprietor could f....g well wait for his money!

After a further ten minutes the proprietor again approached her and said if she didn't settle her bill he would call the police. This prompted another spiel from this girl — and within minutes two burly State Police, heavily armed, arrived and sat on each side of the girl.

They then suggested that she should settle her bill and leave, but this prompted more abuse and just when I thought she was to be arrested — she paid her bill and left! Frankly, to avoid any further incident I felt I would have paid the bill myself!

There was also another fight in the coffee bar at the far end — and I really couldn't get out quickly enough but we had to go through the ritual of phoning for a taxi (which the Proprietor did for us) and we were told to wait until the taxi driver came into the restaurant! Even then when he came in he told us to wait until he had checked outside — and when we got the O.K. we were literally rushed into the taxi and the doors were again locked! Had I known what was involved in having a meal — I'd have gone to bed hungry!

Our next visit to Washington was very different and we realised that on this first visit we were staying at the wrong end of the town.

Before leaving we took a coach tour which we decided was the best way to cover as much as possible in the short time available. Naturally we were taken to the White House, the Space Museum, and all the normal tourist attractions which were very impressive.

The following day we flew over to New York to stay with Tony and Phil Bennett, — (ex Karachi) where Tony was doing a tour of duty for his Company. We had a lovely few days with them as they lived just outside New York in a delightful old Home.

They thought our education and appreciation of New York would not be complete without a drive through The Bronx! I should add that this was in their open car, which I certainly wouldn't want to do again.

At every traffic light we seemed to be accosted by Blacks

demanding money — and one wondered what would happen when we didn't give them any. We had been warned to hide our handbags under the seat as if they were seen — they would be grabbed. I sat like a mouse and said nothing and prayed for the lights to change, and that the car wouldn't break down!

On returning to England at the end of September, 1974 we booked in to the Oriental Club.

The following week there was an air strike in the U.K. and it seemed that if this persisted we would not be able to get back to Hong Kong on time. To avoid this we went to Heathrow and asked what planes were leaving that day? There were very few leaving but they said they had a flight scheduled to leave for Marbella within an hour. We got on it!

So — unexpectedly we arrived in Marbella, hired a car and drove to Torremolinos, and then to Javea where friends of our from H.K. had just bought a chalet and had recommended that we look at the area with a view to buying something for our retirement! We certainly hadn't planned to do this — but as things turned out it seemed a good opportunity. It was a pleasant spot — though we didn't think we would want to retire there when the time came.

In October of that year — a Head Office visitor was coming out and Ken was to meet he and his wife in Taipei, the capital of Taiwan. The Company thought in the circumstances that I could accompany Ken and entertain the wife whilst the men were doing their business.

What a bonus that was — we had four very interesting days there and were shown around by one of the local wives.

Taiwan, or Formosa as the Island was once known, is a political anomaly, a major trading country whose very existence few Governments officially recognise. Virtually none to-day supports Taiwan's claim to be the legitimate Republic of China. In the last 20 years it has emerged as one of the world's most dynamic newly industrialised nations. It is a beautiful island with spectacular landscapes.

China has repeatedly invited Taiwan to rejoin the fold, even offering to preserve the island's economy and way of life. So far the Taipei Government's response has been contemptuous and hostile.

Little of old Taipei remains — though the nightly market with its open air food stalls was still flourishing. The 19th Century Walls and Gates were pointed out and we visited the Lungshan Temple. The National Palace Museum — which is about 5 miles from the centre of Taipei, houses a spectacular collection of Chinese Art Treasures, many removed from mainland China on the eve of the Communist revolution in 1949 by Chiang Kai Shek. We were particularly pleased to be able to buy copies of some old Chinese Prints — which were so cheap and made very impressive gifts.

These Company visitors came back to H.K. with us — in fact we seemed to have quite a few members of the Company visiting Hong Kong, either on a stop-over on one of their overseas business trips — or they came on holiday.

Apparently in Australia, after 10 years' service with the Company the Staff were entitled to an overseas trip. So we had a number of visitors from the Australian Organisation or their clients, and we were very happy to entertain them. I confess to having a wee grumble on occasions when eight weekends in succession we were driving visitors around the New Territories, when we had been invited to a picnic on a Junk which we loved, but had to refuse.

On the whole though, I loved showing people around Hong Kong for the very reason that so many of them had fixed ideas that it was a concrete jungle full of shops, and I did all I could to dispel that illusion.

I felt I was a good tour guide in H.K. — but then I love people — and enjoyed sharing my experiences with other friends.

In turn, of course, all these people were most insistent that we went down to Australia where they would like to reciprocate our hospitality. So — we decided to spend our six week leave in Australia.

On the 24th November, 1975 we flew down to Sydney and booked into the Union Club, which had a reciprocal arrangement with the Oriental Club in London.

What a fabulous country — we really wondered why on earth we hadn't done this before! It has a mixture of everything — mile upon mile of wonderful beaches — mountains, flowers and fauna and I have often said I really can't understand why Australians ever want to travel — as they have everything on their own doorstep.

I suppose if you are interested in history, antiques, castles, old buildings, then perhaps Europe would hold more attraction. I was amused when a friend of mine showing some Australians round some of our Castles and Museums, was asked if one of the buildings was REALLY old? She said "No — I think it's only 16th Century"!

She wasn't being facetious — as she is a Member of N.A.F.D.A.S. and regularly takes groups of people to visit old homes, castles and the like — and of course many of these are 13th century or earlier!

On arrival at Sydney we picked up a taxi at the airport but were taken aback when the driver turned out to be a glamorous blonde — and Ken felt there was no way he could let her carry our cases! She dropped us at the Union Club, where we found a welcoming note from Brian and Barbara Ireland whom we had met and become very friendly with in Hong Kong.

They invited us for a meal to their delightful home at Blakehurst on the St. George's River — a truly magnificent residence with a swimming pool, and a speed boat which was not at anchor but had its own boat shed on the banks of the St. George's River at the bottom of their garden, (or as the Australians call it "a yard") which gives quite the wrong impression to a Brit! They also had a Pool room which was very popular with their son and his friends.

We had a lovely evening with them and we had already begun to feel they were rather special.

It was a coincidence as to how we had met them. Fiona was engaged at the time to a dentist who had a brother living in Sydney. When the brother heard that Brian and Barbara were going to Hong Kong, he asked his brother if he would entertain them. Fiona's fiancé had his own Junk and asked if we would join them on the boat, as he felt that Brian and Barbara might be more at home with the "oldies" than the youngsters.

So... we had a pleasant day on the water and we in turn invited them out to the Club for dinner one evening, They also came to our flat for a meal and we really felt they were part of the family, We all got on extremely well together, seeming to have so many things in common.

Barbara just loved shopping which I enjoyed, particularly when I was spending someone else's money, also I considered myself a good tour guide and so introduced her to all the factory outlets where one could buy Designer labelled clothes, bags etc., for a song. I enjoyed her company and we had fun together — she was a most appreciative visitor.

Altogether we had nine delightful days in Sydney, where we found the hospitality quite over-whelming. (I swore there and then that never again would I grumble about going to the New Territories 8 weekends in succession!) Everyone we met went out of their way to make us love Sydney and the people — and I do assure you that wasn't hard!

Sydney is certainly my kind of city — alive — warm (climatically and from the warmth of friendship). There is so much to see — and on this first visit we merely scratched the surface, but it made us determined that we had to come back — and for a longer visit next time.

The then Manager of the Company in Sydney, Keith Morris and his wife Ida, whom we had met when they were visiting Hong Kong, took us to the Royal Yacht Squadron for lunch. What a fantastic Club! It is situated on the banks of lovely Sydney harbour. All the yachts we saw were literally Gin Palaces, which is the best way to describe them! I suppose in many ways similar to those seen at the Aberdeen Yacht Club in Hong Kong

Ida and Keith could not have been kinder and entertained us lavishly They went out of their way to show us as much as possible of Sydney and its surrounds.  They wined us and dined us and thoroughly spoilt us.

Syd Grant and his delightful wife, also from the Company, took us on another tour and covered a lot of ground in the time we were there.  We drove North to Palm Beach and Ku-ring-gai National Park and West along the Great Western Highway for miles, going through places which sounded so very familiar, Windsor, Richmond, Penrith, Liverpool etc., and then South as far as Cronulla where we spent a night before leaving for Canberra.

Our favourite spot in Sydney seemed to be the Rocks area — I believe this had been converted from Warehouses but is now devoted to tourism, with crowds of interesting little shops, articrafts, and numerous little places for a meal.

We were fascinated by the King's Cross area, which I suppose is really a rather "seedy" side of Sydney.  On a future trip to Australia, Ken and I re-visited this area and walked up and down the neon lit street around 7.p.m.  Ken was looking at some of the rather revealing photographs that were displayed outside the Bars — and as we had been walking for hours, I was really anxious to get back to the Club and have a bath and some dinner.

So I suppose I was standing looking a little "worn" waiting for Ken when a taxi drew up — two girls got out, looked me up and down and said "move on — this is our pitch — and if you look like that you'll never get a customer"!

We took a couple of day trips to Katoomba and the Blue Mountains which really do look blue.  They put this down to the Gum trees which abound and appear to give off a blue haze.  We had a cruise down the Hawkesbury River (or was it up?); took the ferry to Manly and the Northern Beaches — and then had a half day tour to the Southern Beaches — and kept returning time and time again to the Rocks area.

Obviously we had to have a conducted tour of the Sydney Opera House which is a masterpiece containing several theatres all under a very distinctive roof which from a distance gives one the impression of a series of yachts with their sails hoisted. At the time the local residents were horrified at the cost of building this — apparently it had cost 6 million more than was estimated but it is very impressive! I think the only place we found slightly disappointing was the famous Bondi Beach!

As though his hospitality wasn't already "above and beyond" Syd picked us up from our Motel in Cranulla early on the 2nd December and drove us to Canberra calling at Goulburn for lunch. We stayed with old friends from Kuala Lumpur for three days — and they too went out of their way to show us around their City.

Canberra is an amazing Capital — 155 miles south west of Sydney and is a series of satellite towns interspersed with Bush type country, so you continually feel you are in a big village and certainly not the capital. The origin of the City's name is uncertain, and it is thought it may come from an Aboriginal word canberry, meaning meeting place.

We again found the houses were very impressive — it appeared that no two were built alike and all over Australia there are few of the stereotype housing complexes that one gets in the U.K. No matter how small the house — it is different to the other houses in the vicinity — and there are very few double storey houses — after all — they have all the room in the world so don't need to build a second storey as we do in the U.K. and in H.K.

Many bungalow type houses though, if built on a gradient, have two or three floors at the back of the house, but at the front it appears to be a one storey bungalow. Expensive perhaps, but good value for money and much cheaper than a similar dwelling in the U.K.

After three days in Canberra, we were picked up by the Manager for Canberra — Max Purnell who funnily enough was the brother of a friend of ours from Karachi. He drove us to Albury where we spent the night. The next day Reg Kidd from the Melbourne office had driven up to Albury in order to take us on to Melbourne. Of course we were able to see so much more as I hadn't to keep peering at a map and Ken could see the countryside — which he misses when driving.

We called at Wagga Wagga for lunch and were a little amused and slightly concerned that at the local petrol station, the Company Logo appeared UNDER the sign "TOILETS" — not above it — but under it!

Our Drive included a visit to the Mitchelton Winery and Vineyard — and we would love to have bought several bottles to take back with us. Although the wine was remarkably cheap, the cost of air freight did not permit such an extravagance. So we contented ourselves with a couple of bottles that could be consumed at BYO restaurants (Bring your own Bottle). These are very popular throughout Australia — and they do cut down on the cost of eating out.

Reg dropped us off at the Royal Automobile Club in Melbourne where again we were staying on a reciprocal basis through the Oriental Club, in London. A truly old world Club where the service was excellent.

Melbourne, on the Yarra River, is Australia's second largest city, and the State Capital of Victoria. It was founded by settlers from Tasmania and grew as a result of the Victoria Gold Rush. It is now one of Australia's main financial and commercial centres.

Rae and Trish Sinclair (Rae was the Manager for Australia), wined and dined us and Trish took us on a couple of very interesting trips, and provided the most elaborate picnics. We were particularly impressed as this is something we can't do very often in the U.K. and most certainly not on the same scale! Chairs and tables were produced, iced drinks, and a delicious meal with wine followed by a dessert and we sat around a lake with black swans coming to demand a morsel.

We decided that picnics in England would never be the same as so often they have to be eaten in the car as it is too cold to venture out, and most certainly our picnic food is never as appetising.

Trish then drove us to Ballarat and Sovereign Hill where a historical park has been established close to where gold was first discovered. They have produced a realistic gold mining town, where you can see working exhibits of the diggings, huts and shanties furnished in the fashion of the times, and a creek where one can actually pan for gold (so long as you pay your money!)

We did a most exciting evening trip through the Dandenongs to Phillip Island to see the Fairy Penguin Parade.

This was quite amazing; we had been told the Penguins would appear out of the sea and toddle up the beach to their nests at 5.30.p.m. They did just this. Just at dusk and not a moment before, these baby penguins wade comically across the sand right in front of you and often pass where you are actually standing, to go to their burrows in the dunes.

There are brilliant spot lights so you can see literally thousands of these little cute creatures waddling home to rest, looking like a lot of little old men in their evening dress — following each other and toddling up to their nests.

Apparently they leave early the next morning and return to the sea — only to return to the exact spot at the same time next evening. We were so glad we had seen this as the next time we visited Port Phillip Bay the numbers of these delightful creatures had diminished and we saw very few.

Rae and Trish continued to entertain us lavishly and took us around Melbourne — where we saw a few of the wonderful Parks and Gardens which grace the city. It was impossible to see them all in the time available — but the blooms — particularly in the Rose Gardens were a delight.

We decided it was another super city — though the climate was a little like the U.K. and the temperature change during one day could be as much as 40 degrees which made dressing a problem. In the morning it was cool, but by lunch time positively hot — and there we were wandering around in quite warm clothing — but by the time the sun set — it would be chilly again.

Whilst in K.L., we had met and entertained a Dr. Garlick from Melbourne who was in K.L. for about two months. We had kept touch and he and his wife insisted that we contact them when we were in Melbourne. The Garlicks then took us to their beach home at Anglesea — where we spent the night and returned to Melbourne the next day. We enjoyed walking on another lovely beach and catching up on all their news since we had last seen them.

We had to leave Melbourne reluctantly as we were booked to fly to Wellington in New Zealand where we were met by our old friends from Karachi, Bill and Lil Hamilton, who drove us around windy Wellington (and it really is "windy"), then drove us to their super house at Masterton, north of Wellington — it's always great to see old friends and this was no exception.

They had very kindly invited other Karachi friends, Mike and Audrey Thompson, Jean and Ian Strachan and Brian Sivell for dinner. We knew them all from our Karachi days, but Mike and Audrey Thomson and Brian Sivell had been transferred to New Zealand about five years earlier. Jean and Ian Strachan were of course New Zealanders. Now they were all happily settled in North Island — and from what they said they would never want to return to the U.K. as after all the years they had been in New Zealand it had become home.

The following day, after our very pleasant get-together with these old friends, we did a tour of the Pohutu Geyser where various small geysers were erupting continuously — very exciting — but the sulphur fumes were quite pungent all around the area.

Before we left for this trip, Ken's Chairman, on hearing where we were to spend our leave and that it included a trip to New Zealand, asked us why on earth we wanted to go there? He related a story, which to him summed up the whole of New Zealand.

He had an early flight to catch and so asked for his morning tea to be brought in at 6.00 a.m. When he heard the knock on the door in the morning he looked at his watch and saw it was 5.a.m. when in came this little old man with a tea tray. Ken's boss was naturally a little cross that he had been woken a whole hour earlier than he intended. He pointed out in no uncertain terms to this little old man that it was only 5.a.m. and he had requested tea at 6.a.m. "Oh I know" said this little old man — "you see we have 6 guests and only one tea pot!"

Mind you, I think it was unjustified to say this summed up New Zealand in his opinion — he was completely forgetting the beauty, the scenery and the happy pleasant disposition of the New Zealanders. In some ways the country is 50 years behind the times — but then perhaps that is what makes it so attractive?

We did find the New Zealanders took their weekend a little seriously and often found it impossible to get any room service from Friday evening until Monday morning. But there were facilities to "do it yourself" and once we got used to this we were always prepared and kept food in the fridge! Anyway we loved the country and the people and would recommend that everyone make New Zealand a MUST in their future holiday plans.

Continuing with our trip, the following morning we all left by car for Taihape, Lake Taupo and Rotorua, where we spent the next three days. We stayed in a super Motel where each room had its own sulphur Jacuzzi on the patio outside the bedroom — so one could partake of the sulphur springs before nipping into bed each night! (We'd never done that before — and swear it made one feel better!)

They then took us to the buried village which has been reclaimed partially after an eruption in 1886 which destroyed the whole village.

At Rainbow Springs, which we visited the next day, we saw native birds and animals including of course The Kiwi. We also saw the giant Brown and Rainbow Trout and then visited the Agrodome where we were entertained by New Zealand's performing sheep — not forgetting the brilliant sheep dogs — without whom the farmers would not be able to cope with the number of sheep on their Properties. There are considerably more sheep than people in New Zealand.

At the Whakarewarewa Thermal Reserve again we wandered among the bubbling mud pools and geysers. While having dinner in the Hotel that evening we experienced the traditional Maori Haka which was demonstrated with much enthusiasm.

We had a hilarious three days — Bill has a very dry sense of humour and we hadn't been on the road more than 10 mins one day when he was telling us that he had put on his lucky shirt that day so everything would be wonderful. He'd no sooner said this than we heard the police siren and we were flagged down. Bill was told he had exceeded the speed limit and was fined NZ$50 — so much for his lucky shirt!

We left the Hamilton's at Wellington where we boarded the very comfortable Inter-Island Ferry. The trip was made enjoyable as it was a gorgeous day and we were able to sit on deck, sunbathe and take in the scenery. The Ferry took us through all the small Islands, the Cook Straight and the unspoilt Marlborough Sounds.

On arrival at Picton on South Island, we hired a car and drove up to Tony and Phil Bennett's home at Nelson — they had returned home from their assignment in New York where we had last seen them. We spent a couple of nights with them and then flew from Nelson to Wellington and then on to Sydney the same day, only to find that our flight was full. We were travelling on discounted tickets which meant we could always be off loaded — but the saving on the air fare was worth the risk. This gave us a further two days in Sydney.

We decided we would take advantage of this extra time to take a Ferry over to Manly and whilst we were waiting at the ticket office — who should be standing behind us but our very good friends Maureen and Den Parry, who lived next door to us in Karachi. So — we had a very happy day together — catching up on all the news and at the same time having a very pleasant trip to Manly.

We eventually got back to H.K. on the 20th December, 1975 and shortly after returning, Linda told us she was getting married to the delightful Cathay Pacific Pilot she had been living with for some time. It was a very quiet ceremony in the registry office in H.K. Ken hosted a lunch for the main guests and they then had a small

Reception in the evening in their apartment at Shousan Hill. This seemed an ideal match, they got on well together, and Ken and I both liked David immensely so were thrilled for Linda at this turn of events.

David was very amusing. He told us that on his first flight to Russia the crew had been told to be careful what they said in their rooms as they would in all probability be bugged. The crew decided this was not "on" and so they thoroughly searched the room for any sign of a "bug". They had no success but when one of the crew walked across the carpet in his bare feet — he felt a slight protrusion so he pointed to the carpet which the crew then lifted. Low and behold they found some metal object! Without saying a word they got out a screwdriver and carefully undid what they were convinced was the "bug". However at this juncture the chandelier in the room below fell down! How they explained this I am not quite sure!

He related many amusing anecdotes connected with his flying career — but — in fairness to the reader, who may well be contemplating an air trip, I think it best if I don't repeat them.

The children, Elissa and Shane, had accepted David and seemed very happy about the wedding, so it appeared to have all the ingredients for a happy family life. Unfortunately, once married, the relationship seemed to deteriorate, and we were very sad when the following year divorce proceedings were started. I am glad to say they remain friends and David has always kept in touch with us — and he has now married again to a very charming girl.

H.K. was always exciting, there were so many visitors, the social life at times seemed never ending — and Ken, along with other business associates, often had three cocktail parties and a dinner party in one night. I was usually included. Most of these parties we enjoyed but, of course some, were an awful drag and you found you had to work exceedingly hard getting some of the local wives to engage in conversation. The men always insisted that a lot of business was done during, or as a result of, these social occasions.

In August, 1976, we were due for leave yet again and left for

Tokyo where we spent five wonderful days with the Greenes — and saw our old friends the Gardeners — ex K.L.   We certainly didn't commit any faux pas on this occasion!

We then went over to Vancouver, the Gem of the Pacific, which has a magnificent harbour with wonderful mountain views, and overlooks Vancouver Island.   We stayed at the Holiday Inn and acted like tourists, hiring a car and driving around what is the third largest city in Canada — so naturally we got lost!   It's a lovely country with excellent weather and quite a few friends of ours have now retired there.

In Victoria, which is at the southern end of Vancouver Island, we took the car and spent the day driving all over the lovely country and again had excellent weather.   We took the Ferry from Victoria to Seattle where we were met by Sally and Robin Hodgson, also members of the Karachi Yacht Club!   They had kindly invited us to stay with them in their lovely home where I am sure the guest suite was larger than the average flat!   They were excellent hosts, made us very welcome and we were entertained royally.

We hadn't seen them for about 12 years but they both looked years younger, obviously living in Seattle suited them!   Both Robin and Sally were English, but Robin was working for Boeing (and still is I believe).   So as you can imagine once again — tongues wagged!   There is no doubt about it there are no friends like old friends.

Very reluctantly we left Seattle and went by Greyhound bus to Portland where we were met by Renee Drew.   Renee had known Ken and I before we were married — so that's a long time.   She and Frank were the couple who were the paying guests in Calcutta who saved me from going into debt at the time I was trying to survive on my own.

Frank very sadly had died and Renee was now running a Real Estate Office in Portland.

We had a "fun" time with her reminiscing about our days in Calcutta and what had happened to us both since then.   You can imagine there was a lot of ground to cover. In between all the chatter she very kindly drove us around Portland — which is a Pacific port about 60 miles inland and a nice city.

From Portland we flew to Toronto where my nephew Graeme, who had stayed with us in Karachi, had invited us to stay with them. I won't comment on the trip with N.W. Orient — but we were late leaving, missed our Chicago connection and ended up with no luggage (yet again) in Toronto!

We had a great time getting to know, what to me was my new found family as I had never met Ann, Graemes wife, let alone his three gorgeous daughters. They are a lovely family and we thoroughly enjoyed our visit and in spite of my views on "visitors being rather like fish and going off after three days", they persuaded us to stay an extra day which meant we could go to Niagara Falls, which was breath taking, and they also did the tour guide bit and showed us around the local beauty spots.

Not many of our relatives are left now — and it was good to meet up with the Canadian contingent.

After Toronto, we flew to Montreal and spent three nights in the Holiday Inn and visited the Olympic Village- where we were taken on a guided tour and learnt all sorts of interesting bits of news. For instance, hot saunas had been constructed so that the swimming competitors were able to get warmed up before competing, which was reputed to be one of the reasons so many records were broken! — and there was also a lift which took the Divers to the high board thus preserving their energy.

We had to get back to London, where Ken had business meetings in Liverpool, Manchester and London.

Whilst on leave in August, 1975 we decided, that we really needed a larger flat and so had put Burton Lodge on the market, hoping that it would be sold when we arrived in London in late 1976. Because of a damp problem no one was interested and we were told to re-decorate quickly and then put it back on the market.

We managed to achieve this in the time remaining and were also able to make a quick trip to Norfolk to see Vera and Claude Tyler and then flew back to H.K. on the 10th October, 1976.

We had a pretty hectic time on our return with innumerable visitors — which was super, but it did mean we had very little spare time. We took visitors into "Bottoms Up", H.K.'s famous topless bar that has appeared in various films like "The Man with the Golden Gun" etc., so many times in the two weeks after our return that the 'girls' thought I was the Mama San!

In February, 1977 we had a bonus in the form of a trip to the Philippines at the time when Jim and Margaret Clarke from Head Office were visiting.

We flew to Manila on the 19th February, 1977 and were staying on Manila Bay. We did a very quick tour of Metro Manila, — the Bay area, which is a superb natural harbour — a major reason why the Spanish colonists chose it as the site for their capital of the islands in 1574. The old walled city of Intramuros beside the Pasig river dates back to this era, but most of the old Spanish buildings were destroyed in the Second World War. Makati is the city's financial district and also has many fashionable homes.

We avoided some of the less salubrious areas on this trip, like the Tondo area which was a squalid densely populated slum where children — and adults — burrowed in a mountain of refuse for anything they felt might be useful. We then drove to Tagatay Lake, and on to Guermical

On returning to H.K. Ken was as busy as ever both from the office point of view, and socially, but he obviously enjoyed it.

I continued to teach English to my Japanese ladies who in turn introduced me to the art of "Raqui" — a form of removing pain and curing illness by the laying on of hands. Actually their hands were a good six inches from the part of the body they were trying to cure and there was no actual "touching". I had a session with them and I don't know whether it was auto suggestion or if I really did feel a warmth under their hands. But I was impressed. However, they didn't ask me to participate again so feel they must have thought I was a sceptic!

Leave came along again and in August 1977 we decided to return to America — we'd thoroughly enjoyed our last visit — but there was so much to see. We found America very cheap — and were amused that many of the Hotels offered to take your children free if you booked a double room. I felt like immediately adopting about six!

Ken wanted to see New Orleans — so we flew direct to Seattle and spent a few days with Sally and Robin Hodgson again, and then left for Denver and on to New Orleans

Having booked into the Holiday Inn in New Orleans without knowing much about it — we found it very central and on our first morning took a paddle steamer down the Mississippi, though it reminded us of the Hooghly in Calcutta — dirty looking water and not a great deal to see.

We had a wonderful time wandering up and down Bourbon Street listening to all the jazz bands — which we found pulsating. Bourbon Street was packed with people wandering up and down with their cans of Beer, going from one bar to the next and enjoying the music. At every bar their appeared to be topless waitresses or a revue staged chiefly by ladies again very scantily dressed. We went to bed about midnight, but the Jazz went on for many hours, if not all night.

We had been told that whatever we did, we must not miss Breakfast at Brennans. So the next morning we set off for Brennans — as it was a warm day, Ken wore an open necked shirt and I wore a very casual cotton dress. What a surprise we got when arriving at Brennans — all the Americans were in suits — all wearing ties and the ladies looked as though they were going to a Cocktail Party or at leasta formal luncheon!

We did wonder if they would allow us in — but — we seemed to pass muster and were shown to a table for two and asked if we'd like Champagne! We were then handed a Menu — and I was more convinced than ever that the "breakfast" was a mistake — and we had actually come for lunch!

However, the waiter pointed out a long Buffet table on which there were Bacon, Eggs, boiled or "easy over" (a new American expression I learnt that meant they were fried on both sides) Mushrooms, Tomatoes, Pancakes, Fried Bread, Steak, Chops, Kippers, Kidneys, Liver, Potato Browns and any other dish you could possibly think of, oodles of Champagne, Wine, Bloody Marys, and Egg Nogg — all of which frankly made me feel quite ill just looking at them!

Being Brits we are quite conservative about breakfast — and merely helped ourselves to Fruit, Bacon and Eggs, Tea and Toast (everyone had coffee — so I had to put in a special request for tea) — and when we had finished the waiter came along to collect the plates and renewed our cutlery, obviously thinking we had merely had a "starter".    When I told him we had finished — he then persuaded us to try "Bananas Foster" which was the speciality of the house!

By this time it was approaching our normal lunch hour — so I agreed to try this famous dish.    It was a dream — Bananas fried in a mixture of Orange, Cinnamon, Orange Liqueur, Brandy, Orange Peel — and a special kind of Rum which was ignited and then the whole mixture covered in cream.    It was delicious — and I raved about it so much that the waiter came along with the printed Recipe which he said was only for special guests!

I tried to copy it once or twice when we returned to H.K. but I couldn't get the correct Orange Liqueur or the special Rum -and in any case all our guests were far too concerned about their cholesterol to really appreciate my efforts!

After this meal we felt like going to bed — but thought we had better try to walk off all the calories — so did a little sight seeing and went back to Bourbon Street and enjoyed the Jazz.

On the 27th August 1977 we flew to Orlando — which is equally as good as Disney Land and we both enjoyed it tremendously and just wished we had had the money to bring the girls when they were young.

We paid a visit to Cape Canaveral went to Sea World and then hired a car and drove up the East coast. We went through Mississippi, Alabama, Georgia, South Carolina, (spending the night at Savannah where we saw the Rocky Falls) then through North Carolina, Virginia and very cleverly found our way to Chincoteague round the Chesapeake Bay.

Here we had been invited to visit Charlotte Reischer — another friend from our Karachi days who had a large beach house on the water's edge. Have to admit the mosquitoes had a good meal that night, but otherwise it was all very relaxing. We went out fishing and enjoyed having really fresh fish for dinner. After a couple of days with her, we then drove back to Washington where she lived and spent the night in her Washington home before flying back to London, where we booked into the Oriental Club.

Our Putney flat in Burton Lodge had been let whilst we were away and so required a "touch up" if we hoped to sell it and this time the decorating paid off, as before the paint was dry a lady had given a deposit and seemed very keen to purchase the flat.

We started looking for properties once again and viewed no less than 38 flats and felt we had to buy something in a good letting area as we would not be retiring for some years and therefore were relying on the rental to pay off the mortgage.

We finally decided on a three bedroomed flat at Bede House, in a block called "Manorfields" in Putney which was well decorated and the owner was anxious to sell carpets, light fittings, kitchen equipment and some basic furniture which suited us admirably as we didn't have time to do much furniture shopping.

We paid our deposit on the flat, and went to Allders in Croydon, where we bought the extra furniture we would need and asked them to keep it until we gave them a date for delivery to Manorfields. The same agent was handling the sale of our old flat and the purchase of the new one. To us it seemed a simple operation.

Ken had his business visits to Liverpool and Manchester and then we visited Ann and David Archibald, the couple we had been proxy Mum and Dad to at their wedding in Karachi, and have remained very close to them ever since, in fact rather like a "Mum and Dad". They were leaving Jamaica much to their delight I might add, where they had been for the last two years, and were on their way to Korea.

We went up to see some old school friends of mine in Yorkshire spending the night at Rawdon — and I couldn't help thinking how much had happened and how my life had changed since I was there at school.

After our six week leave we returned to Hong Kong and found that Fiona had just returned from her holiday she had been to Sri Lanka, Paris, Hamburg, Vienna, and London, and was back at work with the Holiday Inn.

You can imagine how furious we were on getting back to Hong Kong receiving a letter from the Agents saying that the sale of our Burton Lodge flat had gone through BUT that we had been gazumped on the purchase of Bede House in Manorfields! (Gazumped meant someone had offered more money which the Agents accepted without advising us).

So through the Agent's stupidity — coupled with inflation, we had virtually lost £10,000, because when we returned to the U.K. a year later we found the same flats had increased by that amount in the year!

Now we were left with furniture that would have to go into store and also the furniture at Alders — which we could not now have delivered. I have to say that Alders were fantastic and kindly cancelled our order and refunded in full the money we had paid.

On the 22nd December, 1977 we flew to Manila to spend Xmas with Leslie and David Markham, and had a very happy visit. David had been transferred to Manila on leaving H.K. and they had made lots of friends.

We were included in all their invitations and had a very hectic Xmas. The Markhams had organised a wonderful Buffet in their garden.   The weather of course was super, and the evening warm and moonlit.   The caterers moved in and did everything including providing the most fantastic Ice Carvings for the table — these in turn were lit with coloured bulbs and the whole display was breath taking.

We returned to H.K. on the 27th December, 1977 in time for New Year.

In January, 1978, the Ireland family — these very good friends from Sydney, were in Hong Kong and as I said, we thoroughly enjoyed their company and consequently their visit.   I took Barbara over to Kowloon to Kaiser Estates which was another centre of factory outlets selling designer label clothes.   She had a ball and we came back laden — I confess that as I took so many of our visitors over to these Outlets, I also was tempted to purchase — I could never resist a bargain!

One weekend when we had the Company Junk we had invited a few friends to join us, including the Chairman's Niece and her husband.   They in turn asked if they could bring their house guest along — and of course we were delighted.

During our conversation I was relating how we had been "gazumped" on the purchase of our second flat in Putney — whilst the Agents had foolishly permitted the sale of our first flat to go ahead.   This not only left us with nowhere to live when we returned on leave — but presented a problem regarding storage of our furniture and clothing.

This lady then told us that her husband's Company had a Real Estate business and that she was sure he would be able to help.   Of course the lady's name was Wendy Bentall — and the Real Estate Office was part of the Bentall complex in Kingston!   We decided when we were next home we would look at this Estate Office.

Obviously Fiona had lots of boy friends — and it would appear of different nationalities.   I could always tell when she had had a change of heart or should I say nationality — as she used her tape recorder to learn first of all French when Jaques was the favourite, then Italian and latterly German!

At least she became a linguist far more quickly this way than she had done at school!

I had thought for some time that the latest boy friend must be German because every morning when we woke her — she would put on a tape — "How to speak German" — and she then started to repeat the lesson — so we heard "Wass is Das" — and this same tape would be put on every time she was in her room alone. We had already gone through French tapes and Italian — so we quite rightly assumed that her new boy friend was German speaking.

As a result we were not over surprised when this latest friend invited Ken for lunch at the Furama Hotel where he was then the Food and Beverage Manager. Initially I think they discussed everything BUT his relationship with Fiona, but finally he told Ken he and Fiona would like to get married.

Gerd was Austrian and a Catholic, which I confess worried me slightly as I felt marriage was hard enough work when you married your own nationality, religion and had a basic common language. It didn't really warrant any additional problems that I felt would be bound to arise with a mixed marriage. I have to say my fears were unjustified.

The marriage was planned to take place in Austria on the 17th June, 1978.

The fact that it was to be in Austria also upset me as I felt conventionally it should have been at the bride's home in H.K. I realised being so far away, there was no way we could have anything to do with the organising or planning of the wedding and being in a foreign country where we didn't speak the language — there was little we could do for our wee daughter's great day. The arrangements would have to be left to Gerd's family, who I have to admit arranged things beautifully.

They spoke very little English and of course our German was non-existent.

We had been proxy Mum and Dad at so many of the weddings we had organised, it seemed ironical that when our own daughter was getting married we would not be able to even assist in the preliminary arrangements.

I confess at the time I was disappointed — but with hindsight I have to say that it was without doubt the most wonderful wedding, and there was no way we could have achieved anything so memorable.

Ken and I left H.K. on the 13th June and met Linda at Frankfurt. We were all met at Salzburg by Fiona and Gerd and driven to Gmunden where we were booked into a delightful Ski Lodge overlooking the Lake.

The next day we were taken to see the little church at Gmunden, and we were quite spellbound. What a fantastic setting! It was literally in the middle of a Lake, approached only by a long foot bridge — with mountains all around. The Reception was at the Hotel where we were staying along with all the other guests. It also was on the banks of a Lake so it really was ideal and I think Muti and Vati Koidl have to be congratulated.

There was an amusing hiccup in that Gerd had his bachelor party the night before the wedding.

Foolishly, I think, they had used the rather splendid car they had been lent for the Wedding, and it received a largish dent on the bonnet. Gerd in trying to disguise what had happened arranged for a large floral arrangement to be placed over the dent! However, the dent was not in the middle of the bonnet but to one side — so when we saw the bridal car with this one sided flower arrangement — we did "wonder" — it definitely looked as though it had also been to a party! (Which I suppose it had!)

After the Reception, which as I said was in this same Hotel, we had a delicious meal after which everyone got on to the dance floor after the bride and groom had started the dancing.

Whilst I was dancing with one of Gerd's uncles I complimented him on his command of English — and was a little nonplussed when he told me he had learnt English whilst he was a prisoner of War in England!

We really loved Gerd's family who were so warm and welcoming and in spite of the language differences, we all seemed to get on so well and were able to share jokes. How — I don't quite know — as we spoke no German and their English was limited but we had so many laughs together and got on famously.

After the happy couple had left for their honeymoon, Gerd's brother in law invited several of the guests out on his boat, and we stopped off at some Taverna on the Lake, where more singing and umpa umpa took place.

There was a little high drama when we were returning on the boat, as no one could find Ken — and Gerd's sister got very alarmed and thought he must have fallen in the Lake and possibly drowned! We were all waiting on the boat wondering what we should do when Ken caught up with us and he couldn't understand why we were all so concerned!

With all my misgivings about their wedding being in Austria, I have to say, it really was the most picturesque happy wedding in a wonderful setting — and I haven't found anything to beat it to date.

After the wedding we continued on to the U.K., leaving Salzburg on the 18th June 1978. Having had this suggestion from Wendy Bentall about property, we drove over to Kingston one day. Naturally we didn't contact her husband, but as a result of this visit we were able to purchase a flat in Ulster Court at The Albany, in Kingston, in July 1978. We moved into this flat which was small, but had the most wonderful view on the banks of the River Thames.

When we moved in our freight from H.K. was delivered and we had to store it in the second bedroom which was packed to the ceiling with boxes, some of which spilled over into the Lounge. We realised then that we would need a larger flat but this would have to wait. In the meantime we sent a lot of items to the Auction and so were able to let this flat until we returned home for good.

We left the U.K. on the 28th August, 1978 and spent 4 days in the Seychelles en-route to Hong Kong.

On our return we had a small Reception for Gerd and Fiona for all their Hong Kong friends who had been unable to get to Austria — and with Suzie doing the catering so beautifully, it was another happy evening.

When Gerd and Fiona were married, Gerd was working in Hong Kong and Fiona was then working at the Holiday Inn. Shortly after the wedding Gerd was posted to Kabul in Afghanistan, to run the hotel there.

# TEN
## *Afghanistan—Kabul*

Afghanistan, which is surrounded by mountains, could be called the hinge of Asia.   It accesses the gateway to India through the Khyber Pass, and the back door to Russia.   It has been fought over by invading armies since earliest times.   The British fought three times to maintain their hold on the Khyber Pass — until Xmas Day 1979 when the Russians invaded the country.

They came to support a weak Marxist Government, and stayed to endure the guerrilla warfare of fierce tribesmen who had handled guns since they were children.   Only two things brought the tribes together — religion — they were all Muslim, and it was their country.

Even five years after the Russians invaded, there was still fighting in the capital, Kabul.   Despite the modern weapons of the Russians, there were large areas the Russians could not control, and some people felt that Afghanistan could become Russia's Vietnam.

Modern Afghanistan dates from the middle of the 18th Century. For most of the 19th century the country was subject to big-power pressures from Tsarist Russia in the North and the British in India in the East.   It was because of suspicions that the Rulers at that time favoured Russia — which led to the two Afghan Wars when Britain was defeated on both occasions.   But the British forces returned to enforce a Treaty that gave them control of the Khyber Pass.

Afghanistan managed to remain independent, though under British influence, by playing Britain and Russia off against each other. Relations with Pakistan, however, had been strained since

398

the partition of India and Pakistan's independence. The Afghans wanted the Pathans of the North West Frontier Province to be given the chance to join Afghanistan.

The monarchy ended in 1973 when King Muhammad Zahir had been overthrown in a coup, and after nearly 50 years Afghanistan was declared a Republic, under President Muhammad Daoud.

In 1978 President Muhammad Daoud was murdered in a second coup which led to a Marxist Government under Muhammad Taraki.

It was obvious that the Soviets were well aware of the preparations for this Coup, in fact people did speculate that some of the planes which attacked the Presidential Palace were flown with such great skill, that they probably had Russian pilots! However, at that time, no Soviet combat units were visibly present in the country or participated in the fighting, although Soviet support and encouragement may have been crucial to its success.

From the above, which gives a vague picture of the political climate in Afghanistan when Gerd and Fiona were posted to Kabul, in July, 1978, you will appreciate that we were not at all happy about their posting to this chaotic political boiling pot.

Fiona arrived in Kabul in September, 1978, having resigned from her job at the Holiday Inn in H.K., Gerd having arrivedearlier. She was travelling on an Austrian Passport and the General Manager at that time told her that if she had travelled on her British Passport, she would probably have been shot!

We took a great interest in the political situation and whilst finding it intriguing I also found it frightening as one realised that if a wrong remark was made to the wrong person, one could "disappear"! Afghans it seemed were fighting Afghans — and the Soviets it would appear were fighting both the Government and the revolutionaries.

There was an excellent German School in Kabul and therefore half the population spoke fluent German, and the staff members could not understand why Fiona's German was so poor! This was pointed out by their driver who actually asked Fiona why it was that her German was so bad as of course they thought she was Austrian having entered the country on her Austrian passport!

Many of the Expats had left Kabul along with the wealthy Afghans who also got out whilst they could.

Obviously the medical facilities during this period were not very good and it was very difficult getting medical attention. Therefore when Fiona discovered she was pregnant — there was a problem. She was very fortunate however, as the U.S. Ambassador had his own Doctor and he kindly agreed that Fiona could have her monthly check-ups done by him.

This didn't last long as Ambassador Dobbs, on his way to a meeting, was hijacked and taken to the Kabul Hotel where he was imprisoned and subsequently assassinated. Whether it was the U.S. Marines trying to free him or the work of the Hijackers, it was never quite known.

After this incident, the remainder of the U.S. expatriate wives were asked to leave Kabul along with most other Diplomatic wives. Although life was obviously a bit fraught, Fiona insisted on staying with Gerd — she had obtained an appointment with Pan Am and continued to work for them, and was very busy organising the despatch of freight and animals for the Expats who had already left. Because she had a Pan Am Pass she felt reasonably safe and continued to travel short distances and would still visit Chicken Street, Banyan, and Jodi Maiwand — the most colourful street in Kabul.

One weekend, she and Gerd had gone for a picnic and the green station wagon in which they were travelling, broke down in the middle of the desert and they were very concerned that the wrong type of Afghan would come along and they might be shot! There was no alternative but for the driver to try to hitch a lift to get the spare part that was needed, from the nearest village. This was quite a distance and could take a considerable time. Ghulam the driver finally managed to get a lift in a truck which was packed with sheep! In the meantime Gerd and Fiona, who was 7 months pregnant, had to wait by the roadside trying to look inconspicuous, as they had been told that the Afghans were a very fierce race, and they had no reason at this time to doubt it!

Subsequently this proved to be very wrong as although they are as, a race, proud and could be fierce, Fiona found they would give you their last loaf of bread — as proved to be the case when some Afghans approached the station wagon and handed over hunks of bread and mugs of tea whilst they waited. So much for rumours! Even so I think they were very lucky — if perhaps a little rash undertaking this trip at that time!

This was obviously not the best place to give birth to their first baby so Fiona came to join us in Hong Kong and Nicolas was born at the Matilda Hospital on the Peak, at 2.02 p.m. on the 25th May, 1979, weighing 8 lbs 2 oz. Fortunately Gerd was able to get an Exit Visa and so was able to get to Hong Kong for the birth. He spent about 10 days with us, but Fiona had to remain a little longer in order to get the all clear from the Doctor for Nicolas to travel.

There had been a slight set back as Nicky who looked perfectly normal when born, developed all the symptoms of jaundice and was so yellow after a couple of days he actually looked black. Nowadays this is quite a common occurrence, but neither Fiona nor I had heard of it and we were naturally very concerned. He was put into an incubator with strong daylight lamps shining on him — had patches over his eyes to prevent damage and had a tube down his throat in order to give him antibiotics every three hours, and as he was either too sleepy or too lazy to drink — he was also fed through the tube.

Quite alarming for a young mother. Anyway there was a prompt recovery and after three days he was allowed out of his sunshine home, the tube was removed and he reluctantly started to feed! He did continue to be rather like "Dolly Dormouse" and kept falling asleep at the slightest opportunity.

As the political situation in Afghanistan appeared to be deteriorating, we did wonder (and hoped) that Gerd would not be able to return to Kabul, but he left on the 3rd June 1979. We loved having Fiona and this super baby, who really was very good. We were sad and of course very concerned for their safety when they returned to Kabul.

However, they invited us to go and stay with them on our next leave, so in October, 1979 Ken and I flew to Kabul and stayed in the Hotel. It seemed to be occupied by quite a number of Russians who were seen in the restaurants and had a lot of their meetings in the Hotel, consequently there were always armed guards in the lobby and the grounds, which we didn't find re-assuring!

One of the worst features of getting in and out of Afghanistan was that one had to go via Delhi and this always meant a wait of anything from 4 to 8 hours. Not really enough time to drive into town and book into a reasonable Hotel — so we were inclined to spend it at the Indian Guest House at the airport which really was "the pits". On this occasion we were so late arriving in Delhi that we missed our connection and were told there wasn't another flight into Kabul for TWO days. However, we did manage to manoeuvre a seat on Air India which only had a weekly flight into Kabul — but was leaving in 8 hours!

So — we booked into the Guest House only to find that there was no hot water, in fact there was no water at all from any of the taps. A very smartly dressed Indian lady who was staying in the next room and obviously heard our complaint about lack of water, suggested that we took a bucket into her room and took some hot water for a wash. I thought this extremely kind of her and marched into her room with our bucket. She and I were bending down over the bath holding the bucket as it wouldn't stand on its own — I turned on the wrong tap which had been left on "shower — and lo and behold we both got drenched! Her beautiful Sari and elaborate hair ornaments were just dripping. I felt awful about this, but had to laugh — and whilst it didn't matter that I got wet as I looked a wreck anyway — but this Indian lady was so immaculate — and so very wet! So much for doing good turns — but she took it all very well I'm glad to say.

The Afghan Government had bought a D.C.10 and it arrived in

Kabul on its inaugural flight at the same time that we did. It had about 30 Americans on board, all associated with the aircraft, and they were all staying at the Inter-Continental Hotel, where Gerd as General Manager, was responsible for putting on some of the most fabulous banquets. We of course were included in all the festivities and so our social life was terrific. In spite of the 11.p.m. curfew each night which meant the local residents had to leave the Hotel by 10.30.p.m. at the latest, the residents of the Hotel which included the crew and visitors connected with the D.C.10 were able to continue the festivities until early in the a.m.

The Hotel had a super small band — Ceylonese and they seemed happy to play so long as anyone cared to listen or dance. There was certainly no shortage of food (or wine) — but again I think we were extremely fortunate that special supplies had obviously been brought in for the D.C.10 Inauguration.

Because of the American visitors the local Tour Agents had arranged a City Tour — and Ken and I were invited to join it. This was something we certainly would not have been allowed to do at that time, on our own — or at least we would have been ill advised to do so!

A few weeks earlier a party of 8 Germans with their children were all shot and mutilated whilst having a picnic about 4 miles out of Kabul. Another party of tourists were ambushed, in spite of their having armed guards on board their tourist bus, when the guard opened the bus door to remove the road block, not only were the guards shot but also the people sitting near the door.

The American Air Attaché was attacked on his way back from the golf club — but was saved by a Russian family who were passing and took him under their wing. The Russians on the whole — or should I say on the surface — seemed to be hated — certainly by 60% of the population — but one couldn't answer for the remaining 40%.

We were in a shop when Russians came in and the shop-keeper refused to serve them. By contrast we were also in a shop which was heavily guarded by military with guns, when a Russian gent was whisked in and shown to the back of the shop where he and the proprietor disappeared behind a dirty old carpet that was hanging on the wall concealing an entrance to a small back room. After five minutes, the Russian and his two guards emerged with a Karakul Fur Coat! He went out into the street where more armed guards were waiting and disappeared into an army jeep!

I asked the Proprietor of the shop what this was all about and he told me that the Russians had no spare money — and this man had wanted a fur coat for his wife so had paid for it in Vodka and Caviar! This shop keeper was not only sympathetic towards the Russians — but obviously enjoyed Vodka and Caviar! Even so he was scared of them being seen in his shop for fear of reprisals, so he whisked the Russian into the back of the shop and they did not re-appear until they were given the all clear!

We were asked two or three times whether we were "Ruskies" and I was foolishly very quick to assure them that we were English. Fiona said to me afterwards that she didn't think we should mention that, as next to the Russians, we were second on the unpopularity scale amongst a large proportion of the Afghanis! However, as far as we were concerned, we met nothing but friendliness.

Ken and I were a little vague as to what was going on in Kabul, — as I might add — most people seemed to be, as there was no "official" communication and rumours were rife — some of course had more than a degree of truth and others only half truths. But we knew all was not well! A masterpiece of British understatement!

Whilst we were in Kabul they had arranged for Nicolas to be christened — and I was surprised how many friends they had already made who attended the christening and party afterwards.

In view of what Fiona had said about the popularity of the British, we were more than a little apprehensive when she decided one morning to take us to the Silver Market! — it was really in the worst part of Kabul and was so crowded with so many troops and people that we could hardly move. It was in the centre of town and I can tell you we received a lot of very strange stares from the locals both Afghans and Russians who were predominantly male. The few ladies that were in the Bazaar wore the Kabaya and the Yashmak, frankly I wished I'd had one to hide behind!

Every male was carrying some form of weapon — and to my mind were far too casual with these heavy guns hanging over their shoulders — and I wondered if the safety catches were on or if they kept the guns ready to use — they seemed prepared for anything!

When we made our way into the depths of the Bazaar, Fiona was recognised and we were quickly ushered into a dirty little shop and shown into a back room through yet another show room and invited to sit on the floor which was covered with the most beautiful Afghan carpet. The room was very dirty but filled with antique silver.

The proprietor greeted Fiona warmly and immediately unlocked two tin trunks which contained all sorts of antique jewellery, trinkets, watches and I am sure had we known what we were doing, there must have been some wonderful bargains. As it was I was too scared not to buy anything after all his hard work in unpacking the trunks, so ended up with a silver ornamental pipe for Gerd. We also bought a couple of small silver nick-nacks for gifts, which at least were "different" if not valuable.

Close by there was a Bazaar where I bought some brilliant blue Lapis Lazuli. Ken had Lapis cuff links given to him by Fiona for his birthday and I had an ornamental ring with the same stone. — but quite frankly I was quite relieved when we were on our way back to the Hotel!

We met the British Ambassador at one of the D.C.10 Receptions and to our delight this was a couple we had known over 20 years ago in Karachi, and they remembered us quite well. He assured me that Fiona and Nicky would be looked after by the British Embassy if there was any trouble, they could move into the Embassy if things became difficult and would be included in any evacuation plans.

Mind you he did point out that it was possible that the aeroplane they were to use to evacuate the 64 British, would not be able to land — or if it did that the 64 British might not be able to get to the Airport. In that event they had planned to evacuate through the Khyber Pass with an armed guard. However, the Army was heavily involved in the disturbances and were obviously divided in their thinking — one couldn't help wondering if the armed guard would be a help or a hindrance!

Fiona said she felt they would be safer in the basement of the Hotel — which was well away from the town — and if they could remain out of the picture for a time, things would be decided one way or another and they could emerge. She felt the trouble was internal and as she had her Austrian Passport and the Afghans seemed very friendly towards the Germans she really didn't think there would be a problem! Naturally we were very pleased when they left Kabul.

Mike, the British Ambassador, did ring one day to advise Fiona not to take us out into the town as there was rioting in one area and gunshots had been heard in another one and fighting was taking place in another — and there were Tanks all over town. We didn't need a second warning so spent the day round the pool which was very peaceful and it was hard to believe we were in the centre of such turmoil. All the American, Canadian and German wives had been evacuated to Islamabad or Peshawar and some had returned home — but the majority of British wives had stayed in Kabul.

Pan American had their office in the Hotel which of course was very convenient for Fiona who only worked a few hours each day. As she had to go out to the airport occasionally, she was given a car and a driver and so had access to top security areas such as the Airport runway! Not to mention free air fares!

When driving around Kabul we saw signs of the damage done by mortar attacks and the streets seemed to be packed with convoys of soldiers. I really felt that all foreigners should be leaving Kabul — most certainly my darling daughter and her family!

We found our trip to Afghanistan extremely interesting AND, funnily enough, most enjoyable — in spite of the politics and my "fears". It has a good climate, and we felt it was a pity that the political situation was so confusing!

The Press, BBC and journalists from all over the world appeared to be covering the Afghan story — and were all staying at the Inter-Continental Hotel. There were different rumours every day, but the Press were kept under strict surveillance and so were delighted to talk to anyone who had the freedom to move around. Gerd as General Manager of the only First Class Hotel, was permitted quite a degree of freedom.

One day when Fiona was going to tennis she took her cine camera with her which she hid under her tennis gear and managed to take quite a lot of footage of the damage done in the area and of the number of armoured vehicles on the move. This was of great interest to the Press who subsequently managed to smuggle the film out of Afghanistan.

They had hired a very nice mature Afghan lady to help with the baby. She was very devoted and couldn't have looked after Nicky better if he had been her own child. Every morning after his bath, she exercised him and moved his legs up and down — bent them at the knees and then worked on his arms and would do this two or three times per day. She was determined he would be fit and strong. One can't help wondering what has happened to this delightful lady and the rest of the staff that were so good to us. Many of the Afghan Army deserted to the Soviets, taking their arms with them. For instance as a result of desertions, casualties and the difficulty of obtaining new recruits, the Afghan Army which numbered 100,000 at the time of the Soviet invasion had dropped to 30,000 by 1981.

The internal politics in Afghanistan had been very confused for some time — and there had been so many splits and much subterfuge in the Government's internal politics — that it was difficult for anyone to know who they could trust. It was obvious that the Soviet Union had more than a little influence in the internal politics — though remaining to all intents and purposes neutral.

In September, 1979, Taraki was replaced by Hafizullah Amin,

but the people of the countryside were bitterly opposed to this. People in Government kept disappearing, and the country was obviously very unsettled; the Government found it could only maintain itself by calling on Russia for help. The Russians were happy to respond, realising an ambition they had had for many years, of controlling their own back door.

Amin took over as Minister of Defence and dismissed some of the trouble makers who immediately took refuge with the Soviets — possibly in the Soviet Embassy compound.

Taraki, who had recently returned from Moscow, asked Amin to meet him at the People's Palace for discussions; Amin refused to go until the Soviet Ambassador guaranteed his safety. Even so when he arrived at the Palace a wild west shoot out occurred and except for the intervention of one of Amins's loyal supporters, (who put himself in the firing line in front of Amin thus losing his life), he would have been killed. Amin returned the next day with many of his supporters and took Taraki prisoner. The following day it was announced that Taraki was ill and, need I add, he subsequently died three weeks later of this mysterious illness! People were told when Taraki was shot with his bodyguard "it was all a mistake" — they were after Amin. Although it was common knowledge throughout the world AND in Kabul unofficially that Taraki was dead — it was three weeks AFTER the shooting that Kabul radio finally admitted he had died but they quoted the time of death as the previous day!

It really had been a most fascinating visit — and other than the political situation, we had enjoyed being with the family and sharing their traumas.

At the end of November, 1979 we returned to Hong Kong and had to again change planes at Delhi, and again there was a water shortage at the Guest House. However, we were fortunate and only had a 5 hour wait on this occasion. Ken was going on to the U.K. for a business visit and I was going to spend a few days with Linda in Singapore who had been having a few problems in her domestic life.

Fiona and Gerd were invited to an auction that was being held when various items from the Palace were being sold. It seemed that the Afghans had no idea of their real value, but they bought one or two items — but of course were unable to get many items out of Afghanistan. She did buy a teapot for twenty pounds which she took to Sotherbys, who sold it for £200 — so obviously — a lot of money could have been made.

You can imagine on our return to H.K. we eagerly awaited letters from Gerd and Fiona.

On the 27th December, 1979, after we had left, President Amin received a courtesy call from the Soviet Minister of Communications, and that night a Soviet Assault Unit attacked Darulaman Palace where Amin was living and after a bitter fight Amin and several members of his family were killed, and the Russians installed Babrak Karmal in his place!

Fiona and Gerd remember the 27th December very well as Fiona was apparently just putting Nicky to bed when all hell was let loose. They went on to the balcony to see what was happening and found that the sky was lit up with flares and helicopter gun ships were shooting in the areas they had lit up — anything that apparently came into sight. Gerd told all the guests (chiefly journalists) to assemble in the Lobby. Russian B.52 Bombers were arriving over the Hotel every three minutes.

Everyone of course was anxious to know what was happening and who was shooting what. Fiona still had her Pan American Pass which permitted her to get to the airport as she was still working for Pan Am, trying to organise the despatch of freight and pets for the Expat families who had evacuated. So she decided to make a trip to the airport to see what was happening. I'm so glad I knew nothing of this at the time!

She was shattered to see just how many troops, crates of supplies, ambulances, ammunition there were piled up around the Airport, obviously from Russia. The curfew which had previously started at 11.p.m. now started at 9.p.m. and the Hotel was continuously surrounded by armed guards with tanks front and rear.

Unfortunately one of the journalists decided to get out of the

Hotel to see what was happening but he was shot and killed in the process.

In addition to strafing and bombing villages and cities, the Soviets used chemical warfare extensively, attacking Afghans with irritants, nerve gases, and numerous incapacitants. However, in the middle of 1981 the Afghan army divisions that had been helping guard Kabul, moved to the countryside and Soviet troops took their place. The Afghan rebels who were hiding in the hills became stronger and more effective against the Soviets.

It was only later of course that Fiona and Gerd heard of Amin's death and the murder of his family — but they knew something desperate was happening on that fateful night, but at the time did not know what.

The troops would try to walk into the Hotel with their machine guns and Gerd had to tell them they must leave their weapons at the door! Not an enviable job I am sure!

About this time all the journalists were advised to leave and Gerd decided that Fiona and Nicolas too must get out — but of course they had no Exit permit, the airport was closed, so the only way was hopefully through the Khyber Pass. Ghulam, their driver, drove them through the Pass — but stopped to show them a plaque en route to commemorate where the British had been shot! They didn't really want reminding of that incident at that particular time!

Gerd and Fiona left Kabul on the 12th February, 1980. Fiona and Nicky came to stay with us in Hong Kong and she said it was her intention to stay for 10 days and then return when she hoped things would have quietened down! However, when the situation deteriorated it was obvious this would be foolish. I think Gerd had anticipated the trouble and sent her on this holiday as he then only had himself to worry about.

Gerd had been unable to get his Exit Visa — but he finally managed to get out on the 16th March 1980. He left the Hotel in his sports gear with only a tennis bag, as he didn't feel he should alarm the remaining staff by announcing he was leaving. Clearance from Kabul had to be authorised before any items or luggage were allowed on a plane. Over the last few weeks, between them, they had managed to get a few of their cases out — one of the advantages of working for an Airline, but these of course still had to be cleared by Customs in Delhi. This is where her Pan Am Pass once again helped.

Fiona went up to Delhi to meet Gerd and to help clear the few pieces of luggage they had managed to get out of Kabul. Even so they had to leave a lot of treasures behind which have never been retrieved.

When she finally resigned from her job with Pan American, they kindly gave her a couple of free tickets for all the work she had done and for her efforts in repatriating pets and personal freight on behalf of all the individuals who had been evacuated earlier.

For anyone interested in history I would recommend reading about this period in Afghanistan — it was complicated, confusing and I have to admit quite frightening when you were there or had loved ones living there.

On leaving Kabul, Fiona and Gerd planned to go to Vienna and on to Gmunden to see Gerd's parents, and of course to show them their new grandson. They then had a three week holiday in Spain and returned to H.K. for a week before proceeding to Port Vila, which was to be his next posting.

They were both delighted about this — a big change to go to a quiet holiday resort after being in a War Zone for so long. Ken and I, of course, were equally delighted that we didn't have to keep our noses glued to the Satellite news in the hope of either seeing them, or the Hotel, or hearing something about the situation there.

Obviously we had not been at all happy about the family being in Kabul and therefore were delighted about this new posting to Port Vila in Vanuatu, in March 1980. We felt this was an excellent posting to compensate for the difficult time they had experienced in Kabul.

How wrong we were!

# ELEVEN
## *Our Leaves From Hong Kong*

Whilst history was being made in Afghanistan, we had flown to Sydney for Xmas, for the remainder of that year's leave and we joined forces with Hugh and Molly Brown, old friends that we had known in Calcutta, Bombay and Hong Kong.

When we heard that the Ireland family, with the three children, were going to H.K. whilst we were in Sydney, we suggested that they might like to stay in our flat. However, the children naturally much preferred staying in the centre of Hong Kong in the Hotel, but apparently they did occasionally come up to the flat for a meal in the evening and Mela, another Filipino maid who took over from Suzie, was delighted to have their company and cook a meal for them.

Suzie had finished her first contract with us and had obtained a superb appointment with the Belgian Embassy in Brussels — and so Mela came to join us (not to be confused with the Indian girl Mena!) Mela was a school teacher but had been unable to get employment so had chosen to come to H.K. as a maid and told me she got paid much more than she would have done as a school teacher!

Brian tells the story that when they first dined with us they couldn't understand how the maid always appeared immediately everyone had finished their course and removed the plates before bringing the second or third course. They thought she must be psychic as the kitchen was well removed from the dining room.

When they stayed in the flat however they of course discovered the small bell that was under the carpet which we used to step on when a course was finished. This rang in the kitchen and the maid appeared immediately! We rather took this for granted and were amused when we came back and they told us they had discovered our secret! We were unaware that there was a "secret".

Brian is a born gambler and so they paid one or two visits to the Happy Valley Racecourse on H.K. Island and to the Sha Tin Racecourse in the New Territories..

He told us when we next saw him that he had a very successful day at the Races and was HK$1500 up on the afternoon. However, when they were leaving the racecourse just before the last race he recklessly put this HK$1500 on an outsider in the last race. Can you believe it — the horse won and the odds were 20 — 1 so he came home with HK$30,000 — merely because he liked the name of the horse!

This time we stayed in the Australian Club for a couple of nights to recover from the air flight. Hugh was rather alarmed when he read a notice in the room requesting gentlemen to wear jackets and a tie in the dining room at all times!

Hugh, who had been led to believe that Australia was always casual, had not brought a jacket with him — and so the boys decided that we would go for breakfast the next day in shifts and that Ken would leave his jacket on the door knob of Hugh's room, when we returned from breakfast.

We had been back in our room some time doing the packing and waiting for Hugh and Molly to finish breakfast, when Hugh rang us to ask if we had returned from breakfast yet — and we assured him we'd been back at least half an hour and that the jacket was on the door handle of their room. Hugh said he had kept looking but there was no jacket!

Alarm and despondency — where was the jacket? It transpired it had been taken by the laundry who saw it hanging on the door and assumed it was for cleaning! It took at least an hour to retrieve the jacket and in the meantime the Club kindly sent up their breakfast

— so we wouldn't be too late in leaving!

We were to drive up to Burleigh Heads in Queensland where Brian had very generously let us use his Unit which was on the beach. The drive up the coast was glorious — we spent one night at Tuncurry/Foster and the second night at Port Macquarie and the third night at Coff's Harbour. People do this trip in one day — but — as we had never been on this coast we wanted to stop and see as much as we could of the coast line which is out of this world.

We had a very happy time in Brian's Unit and were amazed that people would appear on the beach around 6.a.m. in order to secure one of the picnic tables that were dotted around on the grass overlooking the beach. Of course Xmas in Aussie is the height of their season and the surfers started to arrive around 4.30.a.m. There is a channel on the radio which gives the names of the beaches where the surf is at its best, and within ten minutes of this broadcast, the cars simply roar up — the boards are unhooked from the roof of the cars, the surf board receives particular attention having its base waxed — and off they go — always running — which I would have thought was most exhausting when they have to battle the waves for the next hour or two.

By lunch time however, one could hardly see a spare spot of grass as families arrived complete with tents, umbrellas and their own B.B.Q.'s. Obviously Xmas dinner was quite different to that in the U.K. In fact we all went out for a meal and were surprised that the normal menu was produced, which did provide Turkey — but no Mince Pies!

Alas it all passed too quickly and we had to drive back to Sydney and return the car and then had two more days before taking the flight back to Hong Kong.

In January 1980 Ken had to go to Taiwan on a business trip and as I had become friendly with the wife of his associate during our last visit in 1975, they had asked that I came along as well. Another unexpected trip which I enjoyed — even though I had seen most of the points of interest on our last visit — it was good to see the changes that had occurred.

From June to August, 1980, I had not been at all well and had been in the Matilda Hospital in H.K. with a collapsed lung, bronchitis, pneumonia and inflamed Liver.

In September, 1980 we took the remainder of our leave and this time flew to Frankfurt en route to the U.K. where I was to have some medical check-ups. The only comment in my diary at that time was "stayed Intercontinental Hotel, Frankfurt b....y expensive"!

So while we were home I arranged to see Dr. Narriman, who had been our family doctor the whole time we had been in Karachi; he was now in Harley Street. He referred me to the Royal Free Hospital in Hampstead who did various tests and I returned to Dr. Narriman for the verdict.

He told me I had Cirrhosis, which he put down to the Blood Transfusion I had had after my Ruptured Ectopic Pregnancy in Calcutta! His prognosis was not "crash hot" and when asked about it — he said it could be six months or perhaps two years, which didn't fill me full of joy — but I was determined to beat the odds — and so far, although my Liver Function Tests are still alarming — I have proved him wrong!

I still go regularly to The Royal Free where over the years I have had Liver Biopsies, Steroid Treatment and a Liver Scan every 6 months. I have a lot to thank them for — also Dr. Adelle Davis whose book "Let's Get Well" with her recommendations for vitamin and mineral therapy has been my bible! Certainly something is working and I am indeed a very lucky lady.

We spent the first couple of days with Pat and Phil Brewer down in Heathfield, before moving to the Oriental Club. Ken of course had his usual Head Office visits in London and Liverpool but between Hospital visits we were able to visit various relatives and friends.

We flew to New York on the 19th September, 1980 — to visit the Green's who as explained earlier, we knew in Hong Kong. They had now relocated from Tokyo to New York and were anxious to show us New England and the wonderful Autumn colours, which I admit were very impressive. Audrey's Aunt Lucille from Hawaii was also staying with them at the time — so we had a good re-union. Alas "Kona I" the poodle they had taken to Hong Kong had not survived and they now had "Kona II" — another white poodle. I was shattered to find that Kona II had his own mackintosh and little boots for the cold weather! Who said the Brits were stupid over animals?

We left for San Francisco to stay with Frank and Mary Troxel, other friends from H.K. who lived in Lafayette in California, in a large ranch type home which they are still in to-day. It was beautiful, as was the surrounding area.

After a couple of days we went to Seattle for our second visit to Sally and Robin Hodgson, who again drove us all around to see what we had missed on our first visit. From there we had to change planes in Honolulu so spent the night and left the following day for H.K. via Tokyo. We had intended to break our journey in Tokyo, but I wasn't feeling on top of the world, so we flew directly home to H.K.

I have explained that whilst in H.K. I would take our visitors out to the factories where they could buy Designer clothes, bags etc., at a ridiculously low price. One of our U.K. visitors nearly convinced me that I should not do this in future.

She told me she wanted to buy "a couple" of Fake handbags which we assumed were for her own use. We foolishly took her to the market stall where these were sold and introduced her to the owner. Anyway — after introducing her to this supplier, we had nothing more to do with her future purchases.

Apparently, she had gone back to the stall at night and bought a large number of these bags which the stall holder kindly delivered to her Hotel — packed ready for despatch. How she got them in to the U.K. past Customs, I don't know but she then sold them from her flat — rather like the very popular "Tupperware" parties. The people she sold them to were of course all friends, so I suppose she felt she was safe.  Or perhaps she didn't even think about the consequences of selling "fake" items.

It transpired that one of her friends subsequently went out to lunch sporting her new designer handbag and at the lunch party there was someone associated with the genuine handbags.  He immediately spotted the fake and asked her where she had bought it — and she said she'd bought it from a friend.

The outcome of this was that the police traced the bag back to the flat from where it had been sold, and in turn insisted on getting the name of the H.K. supplier.

I learnt about this much later when I went along to buy a handbag for myself before going on leave and the factory manager told me that "my friend" had got him into a lot of trouble.  The Police had come to his market stall and asked him where all the Fake handbags were — obviously there was no point in denying this — so he took them to the factory and all the handbags were confiscated and he received a large fine.  I felt very concerned as it would appear that it was this so called "friend" who had obviously been intent on buying a large stock of handbags for re-sale and not just for her own use.

I commiserated with the man at the Market Stall and immediately assumed he would not have any more fake bags — but he asked me what I wanted and I expressed my surprise that he still had some stock!  He told me then that he had three factories and of course only showed the Police ONE factory, so although he had lost a lot of money and a large amount of stock — he was not daunted and the illegal trade continued!

He was not alone of course — H.K. at one time was full of Fakes — but this practice had been squashed to a large degree by the Government.

In November 1980, my old school friend Ruth Swift arrived for about 5 weeks.  She and I had rather lost touch over the years, our paths going in very different directions, but when I heard that her husband, Seymour had suddenly died, I wrote and suggested that it might do her good to have a change of scene and invited her to come out to stay with us in Hong Kong.

We were delighted when she accepted, because we felt very confident that she would enjoy H.K. and hopefully it would help her adjust to what had to be a new life style.  It was amazing that when we both met after what must have been nearly 20 years — it seemed as though we had never been apart for more than a couple of months — but of course we had a lot of catching up to do, and our tongues worked overtime!

There was the usual round of Cocktail parties, dinners, outings on the Company junk, weekends at Lantau.  Ken was a member of The Hong Kong Jockey Club, so we took Ruth to the new Sha Tin Race Course, which must be one of the richest Clubs in the  world — donating large amounts each year to various charities.  We were told that there was more money put on the last race in Hong Kong than was placed for the whole season in the U.K.

The large Diamond Screen at both Happy Valley and Sha Tin Racecourses enables one to watch the race at close quarters for the whole of the race even when the horses are more or less out of sight.

There is night racing, and of course lunches and dinners are served in the various venues where one can still watch the race on the T.V. and someone will come round and take your bets (and collect your winnings) if you don't want to leave the table.

Ruth had bred horses at one stage in her life so of course was very interested in the condition of the horses, how they were kept and trained.   Although I wouldn't say I was a gambler by nature, whenever I visited the race courses in Hong Kong, my adrenaline took over and I found myself studying form — past performance, weight of jockey, how many wins he had had in the last four times he had run, and where he stood on the Jockey Table, before risking my small bet of probably HK$5!

Altogether I was most unsociable — as this took up a lot of time, and the time passed so quickly.   I was so busy either placing bets, dashing down to look at the horses in the paddock before they entered the course, and occasionally queuing up to collect my winnings!

One amusing story about my betting was that I had carefully studied the next race and decided after a lot of deliberation I would put HK$10 on Horse 9. Whilst waiting to place my bet I noticed that several Chinese were putting large amounts of money on Horse 5 — and when the gentleman in front of me placed $5,000 on Horse 5 — I quickly changed my mind and felt that they must be in the know! Need I add that my Horse No.9 came in at 10-1 and Horse No.5. is still running!

We loved having Ruth, she was so enthusiastic and gave the impression that she enjoyed just everything, when I am sure there must have been occasions when she was bored stiff — but she never showed it — an ideal guest, and we had no hesitation in suggesting that she join us in Australia at a later date. She was anxious to get back to spend Xmas at home.

Some Australian friends who had been visiting us in H.K. had said they would like to buy a Mink coat, so we had great fun going round the factory outlets trying on all the various Minks. Having bought one they then had the problem of how they could take it back into Australia without incurring heavy duty which would probably be more than they had paid for the coat.

I knew that we would be going to Sydney around the 20th December, 1980 en route to Port Vila and would be spending a few days in Sydney, so what could be better than for me to wear her coat down to Sydney and just "forget" to take it with me when I left! Had I been challenged on entering Australia then it was agreed that I would have to return to H.K. with the coat. Rightly or wrongly — I decided to make the offer. I felt it was fitting retribution for all the harassing times I had had with Customs in the past — all for no good reason.

Fortunately, all went well — and we spent a few days with these friends. We had a pleasant lunch with Terry and Otti D'Souza, Pakistani friends who had emigrated to Australia a few years before.

Otti told us the lovely story that when she first started to drive in Sydney — she suddenly found her car had stalled and would not move and as she was on a roundabout she was very concerned. The gentleman in the car behind her, on realising her plight, came to her assistance asking what was wrong? Otti had no idea — she told him the car had just stopped! He quickly looked at her dash board and then said "but you have no petrol — when did you last fill it?" Otti had to admit that she didn't even KNOW that you had to fill cars with petrol as in Karachi the driver always brought the car round to the front door and obviously he always ensured that the tank was full, and that it didn't need oil, or air in the tyres!

I think this poor gentleman could not believe what he was hearing — even so he kindly went off and brought a can of petrol for her and filled the tank!

We also had dinner with our friends the Irelands, but found poor Barbara very sick indeed, in fact this was the last time we would see her.

I was quite distraught about this, as she had been battling with cancer for some time, about the same time that I had been told that I had cirrhosis of the Liver. We had discussed vitamin supplements etc. together, which in my case seemed to be working — but Barbara obviously wasn't so fortunate and I was quite shocked when I saw her.

We'd really become very attached to this delightful couple and their three children. Unfortunately, Barbara did not improve and was a very sick lady, It was not long after our visit that she asked to be taken up to Queensland to their flat at Burleigh Heads and it was here that she died.

She was sadly missed by all her friends and, of course, her family. They had two lovely daughters and a son and I have to say that Brian, who had been a very attentive husband, did a wonderful job being both a Dad and a Mum to them all.

We were very concerned about Brian being left with three children, not to mention the terrible void in his life, but he coped admirably and all we could do was to keep in touch by letter.

# TWELVE
## *Vanuatu and Our Visit to Port Vila— Xmas 1980*

As indicated, Gerd and Fiona were very pleased about their next posting to Port Vila, the Capital and main Port of Vanuatu. Ken and I, were equally delighted as obviously we had not been at all happy about the family being in Afghanistan and therefore were relieved to hear they were going to this new posting, feeling this would compensate for the difficult time they had experienced in Kabul.

The relief I might add was short lived!

Gerd arrived to take up his appointment as General Manager of the Inter-Continental Hotel in Port Vila in April, 1980, just before the militant Jimmy Stevens decided to take the law into his own hands and instigated an uprising, thereby inflicting general chaos and disorder on the islands.

In 1965 Jimmy Stevens had founded the Nagriamel Movement in Santo and in 1975 he proclaimed the Nagriamel Federation and told the British to leave Santo, but allowed the French to stay as they supported his movement — hence the predominance of French.

Fiona arrived in Vila shortly after Gerd, and decided to open up a shop as she found so many things were unobtainable there, and thought there was scope for a business. She had applied for a licence and wrote to me to ask if I would buy certain items for her in H.K. and despatch them to Vila. She thought the Australian and foreign tourists who visited the New Hebrides would snap up these items. So on one of my factory visits I bought a supply of beach wear suitable for the New Hebrides and couldn't resist 40 fake handbags! All the well known names that would sell for a fortune if they were genuine, and certainly would attract the tourists, if not the locals.

In the U.K. of course this was quite illegal (as it was in H.K.) but the suppliers usually kept normal handbags on show on their Stalls and one had to particularly ask for the Designer Label ones. If they knew you, or thought you were "safe" then — they would take you into another area where they kept all the counterfeit bags, watches, sweat shirts etc.

Some of these Stall Holders became quite bold and when you were walking past their stall they would whisper "Designer Handbags for sale" but on the whole, they would wait for you to approach them. I bought these handbags and kept them waiting for Fiona to tell me when to despatch them.

However, not wishing to be caught in the same position as they were in Kabul, when they had to leave so many of their personal possessions behind, she saw the writing on the wall, and decided to postpone the opening of her shop until they could see how "Independence" would affect them.

So guess who ended up with 40 Designer Handbags — which of course I daren't send to my friends in the U.K. — not to mention the Beach outfits!

The same press and photographers that had been staying in the Hotel at Kabul arrived in Port Vila and they moved into the Intercontinental hoping for another scoop, and obviously surprised to find that again they knew the General Manager of the Hotel and his wife! After their experiences together in Kabul — many had become firm friends — but obviously their presence in Port Vila indicated that they were expecting trouble.

On the 30th July, 1980, Independence was officially declared and the New Hebrides was renamed the Independent Republic of Vanuatu, ending nearly a century of joint British and French rule. Two of the eighty Islands made a bid for separate independence when the new republic was founded.

Troops from Papua New Guinea were flown in to suppress the rebellion, when the British and French had failed. They arrested Stevens and hundreds of his followers and in November he was sentenced to 14½ years jail.

Obviously once again, Gerd and Fiona were living with a degree of uncertainty as to the future and arrests were made daily.

We felt at this time, that they had gone from one disaster to another — but fortunately — things did not escalate to the same extent that they had in Kabul!

We still had some leave due and Fiona and Gerd invited us to go and spend Xmas with them.

So on the 23rd December 1980, we left Sydney where we had been for a few days and flew to Noumea en route to Port Vila. We were met by Fiona and Gerd and had a fantastic holiday with them.

Port Vila in the South Pacific, known affectionately as Vila, (formerly the New Hebrides) stands on the edge of a palm studded Lagoon, and spreads across a gentle sloping hillside and around a simply beautiful natural harbour.

Further along the same Lagoon was also an equally impressive Hotel Le Lagon Pacific Resort, part of a Japanese owned Pan Pacific Chain of Hotels. The restaurants were housed under a large thatched roof and Fiona and Gerd took us there to the Tam Tam Lounge one evening where there was music and dancing. A very romantic setting — as was the Inter-Continental of course.

The sprawling town had a number of attractions, most of which could be explored on foot.

The Cultural Centre, next to the Hotel Rossi, the oldest hotel in Vanuatu, houses an interesting Museum. Next door is "Handikraf blong Vanuatu" where one can pick up local handicrafts and artefacts.

Twice a week at the Central Market scores of local women dressed in their Mother Hubbard colourful dresses displayed their wares, from food to souvenirs; we loved this market and the atmosphere associated with it.

The Inter-Continental Hotel stood on this palm studded bluff running down to a delightful Sandy Beach on the edge of the Erakor Lagoon.

One weekend we were taken to the Hideaway Island Resort for a Melanesian Buffet, Hideaway was very primitive, with sand floors, thatched roofs but obviously very popular with the young.  I was relieved we were staying at the Intercontinental with Gerd and Fiona — as, whilst I appreciated the setting, I felt we were too old to cope with the cold showers and confined quarters and the flying insects, but an ideal spot for young people, on a budget.

Gerd drove us round the Island one weekend — which was quite a challenge as part of the roads were tar sealed in places, some were coral-paved and others corrugated with pot holes all over.  Even so it was an interesting drive — (if perhaps a little bumpy), and we stopped at one of the many beaches for a swim.

Fiona and Gerd had joined the "Takara Club", which was a delightful little sailing Club on the most beautiful beach.  Fiona had become quite enthusiastic about sailing after her time in Karachi so we spent a few happy days there watching the yacht racing.

Another day we went to the Mandura Club with its very beautiful surroundings and the following day took a boat to Erakor Island. It was here I saw my very first Star fish in its natural surroundings — not one — but several, and had never realised what a variety of brilliant colours they had, bright scarlet, pink, bluish grey etc.  So I collected several of these colourful creatures as I thought they would look very attractive in our fish tank or on the patio and I was determined to bring one or two back to H.K.  I hadn't realised that once taken out of the water they lost all their colour!  So by the time we got back to the Hotel all their lovely colours had disappeared! Just as well I suppose otherwise I would have brought them back on the plane and the smell would have doubtless caused consternation.

It was very obvious that the majority of the locals spoke French — but I loved the pidgin English that so many spoke — for example:—

Gudmoning (Good morning)
Bagarap      (Broken down)
Wanem taem?      (What is the time)
Haos blong me      (My house)
Pikinini blong      God (Jesus Christ)
Me no save      (I don't know)
Las Wik      (Last week)
Nekis Wik  (Next week)
Graon i sek (Earthquake — Ground he shakes)

Not that I understood it all — but it was a challenge — rather like doing a cross word puzzle!

I learnt that the Bizarre sport of bungee jumping — now touted as a new fad throughout the world, originated hundreds of years ago in Vanuatu.  It was then called "land diving"!

This "Land diving" is reputed to have started after the abused wife of a man named Tamalie, ran away from him and climbed to the top of a huge Banyan tree.   As Tamalie climbed after her, his wife tied vines from the Banyan tree around her legs and when Tamalie reached for her she jumped!   Tamalie also jumped, the vines saving the woman but Tamalie died.   Angered, the other men decided they had to perfect the same feat so no woman would trick them again!

Only men were allowed to learn to land dive and they used it as an opportunity for a public hearing to air their marital problems. They made these Jumps from crude stick towers — sometimes over 80 feet high.   Once the jumper climbed to the top of the tower, his village had to listen to him discussing the disagreement he had with his wife — while she watched silently.   When he had finished — he took his leap.

Obviously there were frequently serious injuries and sometimes even deaths.

Tourists who witnessed this ceremony went back home and using modern equipment — came up with bungee jumping, which now

425

takes place all over the world — usually at holiday resorts — and quite often from cranes hanging over the sea — so the jumper can choose whether his jump is shortened by the ropes to prevent him going into the water, or lengthened when he is "ducked"! Elastic is now incorporated into the rope, so that it is no longer quite so dangerous.

Yet even in modern times, bungee jumping can end in tragedy. Queen Elizabeth witnessed that grisly truth on Vanuatu in the 1970's. The vine snapped during a diving ceremony and a man fell to his death in front of the horrified Queen.

We spent a memorable New Year's Eve on the beach at the Hotel with a full moon, a local band and a superb Buffet.

Just after midnight they announced there was a Cabaret — which would include a strip tease. You can imagine we were quite shattered when they went on to announce that the strip tease artist was none other than our darling daughter — Fiona!

I think Gerd, who knew nothing of this — was equally shattered! I hasten to add that she did not end up "in the nuddy" — and it was very tastefully done, and we were very impressed!

The Hotel had erected a large cloth screen on a wooden stage, behind which there were lights which cast the shadows of two people on the cloth. We then heard what appeared to be a very sensuous voice, saying — "Please take off my shoes Charles", after which a pair of shoes were thrown over the screen. This was followed a few seconds later by a request to "Please take off my tights Charles" and the tights then appeared over the screen. This patter continued until obviously all the female garments had been removed. The lights then dimmed and a naked figure dashed off the stage with Fiona running after him and shouting "If I catch you wearing my clothes again Charles — you are sacked!"

I must say everyone enjoyed this brief interlude — and whilst it may not sound very amusing — it brought the house down — except there was no house — we were on the beach!

In spite of the unrest on the Island — it didn't seem to interfere with their social life — and we most certainly had a memorable Xmas with them, and a delightful holiday.

After this lovely holiday we returned to Hong Kong on the 11th January, 1981, where we had five more months before Ken took his first retirement. We continued to have our usual flow of visitors — which I admit we enjoyed. Di and Ken Bevans our General Manager, on his retiral trip, and then the new General Manager came out the following week for a Board Meeting.

At the weekend we all went over to Macau where we spent a couple of nights and took a day trip into China which was an experience for us all. In those days China had not really opened up and these short trips over from Macau were the only way the majority of us could get into China, unless you had business over there. We visited Sun Yat Sen's house — had a fabulous Chinese meal — visited a commune and a school. Everyone seemed to be on bikes — we had never seen so many — and driving around in this Taxi one felt it would be impossible to miss knocking several over — they popped out of everywhere.

We received a lot of curious glances as in those days of course not so many foreigners had been into China.

It was an interesting and enjoyable trip and made one realise what progress had been made in H.K.

Ken was to retire in May, 1981 — and we both had very mixed feelings about this. It would certainly be the end of an era — we had loved the expatriate life — and most of all the climate! How we would face a U.K. winter we weren't quite sure!

We had the packers in and did a lot of last minute shopping — as never again would things be so cheap. We then moved into the Furama Hotel for the last few days. It was a frantic time — lunch parties every day and farewell drinks parties and dinners.

Imagine how cross I was when the first night in the Hotel having bathed and dressed for a dinner party — I found that I had given the Packers ALL my shoes and bags!

I rang Crown Pacific, to ask if they had crated everything — and was told that the crates were sealed — having been passed by Customs — and therefore there was no way they could extract the box with my shoes and bags in. By wearing slacks I was able to get away with wearing my flip flops I had been wearing all day! Being H.K. of course I was fortunate in that I rang "Pauls Shoes" who had made shoes for me over the years and had just completed a couple of pairs — and I told them what had happened and asked if they could quickly make me a pair of white and a pair of black shoes. You won't believe it — but I collected them the following night!

We were both sad to leave H.K. — in fact I think I could say I was distraught — we'd been in H.K. over 8 years and it was "home" — and of course been in the East over 33 years and really felt this was closing a very pleasant chapter of our life. Living in the U.K. was going to be very different, and most of all we would miss our friends. I hadn't at that stage thought about the weather — as we'd always lived in a tropical climate — and found the cold overpowering!

Having been out of the U.K. since 1948 we obviously had few friends back in England, our family were settled in the East and we knew we would miss them terribly. It would take a lot of adjustment.

I tended to forget that other people retire and come home — and in point of fact we now have a nucleus of overseas friends living here, which has made my attitude to life in the U.K. very different.

In May 1981, we finally got away — and flew to Singapore where we spent a very happy week with Linda. We still had many friends there that we had known in our other postings — so again it was a round of farewell parties.

We went up to Kuala Lumpur to say good-bye to Diane and Ismail and some of our friends who were still there, not having been pushed out! Then back to Singapore for a few days and then we flew to Colombo.

# THIRTEEN
## *Ceylon or Sri Lanka—Visit May, 1981*

We had always planned to re-visit Sri Lanka after our brief visit of 8 days when the Chinkoa was in Port on our trip home in 1955. So we flew into Colombo and stayed at the Inter-Continental Hotel for one night only as we planned to travel round the island.

They say Sri Lanka is shaped like a teardrop that has fallen from the cheek of India and is marred by civil conflict that could well make India weep! One can see why — a beautiful Island marred by conflict.

On arriving at Colombo airport we intended hiring a car and driving round the Island, but we were persuaded that it really wouldn't be safe for us to drive ourselves and for only a little extra we could have the services of a driver!

We tried to argue — but obviously — we had to have a driver or all sorts of things might "happen" to the car! The amazing thing was that every Hotel we stayed at provided accommodation for the driver at no extra cost. I suppose this is a custom left over from the days when everyone travelled with their own private driver. We were very pleased we had employed him as I am sure we saw far more than we would have done if I had been doing the map reading and Ken had been doing the driving! Also we would have been hassled much more by the locals. Added to which we were still speaking at the end of each day!

Ceylon, as it was then known, was indeed a lovely Island. In fact the Muslims believe that Adam and Eve, after being evicted from Paradise, were allowed to meet once more on earth, that is,

Paradise on Earth or Sri Lanka!

The coffee plantations, that the British developed, failed and were replaced by the Ceylon Tea which now brings in more than half of Sri Lanka's export earnings. Rubber and Coconut Plantations were also established and Indian Tamils were brought in to work the plantations.

The need for Tamil workers is quite simple, the Sinhalese (the majority of Sri Lankans) do not like to work in the fields, whereas the Indians have no objection. The Sinhalese are not necessarily lazy but seem to have a different set of values, which attach a high degree of importance to the benefits of leisure!

The conflict between Tamils and Sinhalese surfaced after Independence from Britain in 1948. The Tamils who are of Hindu religion and the Sinhalese who are Buddhists, have never got along too well with one another. Under British rule the Tamils held the majority of responsible white collared jobs, but when Ceylon became the Republic of Sri Lanka in 1972, the Sinhalese claimed these top jobs. This basically is the root of all the present troubles, not overlooking of course the religious problems which came to a head in 1948.

Leaving this aside — it is a wonderful Island and our driver — a Tamil I might add, was most anxious that we saw all that was possible in the time available.

He pointed out the Cinnamon Garden district of Colombo which is the best residential area, filled with lovely gracious houses, all denoting a way of life, once pictured by Somerset Maugham(?) which is now disappearing swiftly all over the world — but remnants still remain in Colombo.

We visited the Mount Lavinia Hotel which we had found so romantic on our previous visit. It is 7 miles south of Colombo with its own private beach surrounded by gardens and palm trees, but since our last visit it had deteriorated and looked run down and neglected, so we opted to stay in the Galle Face Hotel which had been completely remodelled, and only about a mile from the centre of the town.

On our second day, the driver suggested he took us up to Kandy, about 72 miles from Colombo. The drive was interesting — we saw many working elephants and he pointed out the original ones that appeared in "Elephant Boy". All of them seemed to be well trained and performed on the river at Katugastota. For 50 cents we were encouraged to have our photo taken with one of these beautiful animals.

Kandy is one of the world's most sacred Buddhist sites. The great attraction in Kandy is the Temple of the Tooth, said to have an authentic tooth of Buddha, who originated the religion in the 6th Century BC. The tooth is kept concealed in seven jewel-encrusted caskets, each nestled inside a larger casket. Every August the tooth is carried in a procession through the city at an annual festival. The temple itself is not too prepossessing but it was interesting to see how the prayers were conducted and to learn a smattering about Buddhism

In this area there were numerous other Temples, but time did not permit us to visit more than two before we continued the drive up to Nuwara Eliya (pronounced Nur-ehlia) where it was suggested we spent the night.

Nuwar Eliya is about 3,600 feet above sea level and is a resort town with golfing, fishing etc. The British established this as a Hill Station and a refuge from the summer heat of the lowlands. It is the nearest Hill Station where one can get away from the heat of Colombo. The present buildings are mostly in the late Edwardian style.

Here we stayed at "The Hill Club" — which from the outside really looked like something out of the British Raj. There were few guests and so we were allocated the whole of the West Wing which had the most wonderful views. The saddest thing was that on going down to dinner that evening we found the Dining Room with about 40 tables ALL beautifully laid with the most wonderful napery and silver — flower arrangements and two Bearers waiting at each table. But, other than another table of four the place was deserted, and one was left wondering how on earth it could survive, let alone be profitable.

On the way back our driver insisted that we stopped at Anuradhapura which is the greatest of the lost cities of Sri Lanka. Here we saw the Pokunas, the stone baths used for religious bathing. There were many "Dagobas", the Sinhalese equivalent to "pagoda"
.

As we had a day to spare before catching our flight to London, the driver suggested we visited the Polonnaruwa area which was very impressive and we were glad we took his advice. There seemed to be quite a lot to see — inside the Lankatilaka we saw the huge headless statue of Buddha, we also saw a Lotus Bath and the shrine with three Buddhas also the classic Milk Dagoba so called because of its whitish colour.

We were taken to a gem factory where I am sure the driver got commission, but even so, we bought three most beautiful loose sapphires which I had made into a ring a few years later. Although I was suspicious as to whether the stones were genuine, we found they were valued at much more than we paid for them — so — we have to thank the little driver who introduced us to this small but very interesting gem factory.

One very pleasant coincidence was that when driving past the St. Andrews Church just behind the Galle Face Hotel, we saw that Andrew Baillie was giving the Sermon next Sunday. Andrew Baillie was the very nice Scottish Minister who had married Ken and me in Calcutta at the St. Andrews Church. Not quite sure that it was the same person, we tentatively called at the Vicarage and were met by his sister Martha, who obviously didn't recognise us initially, but we explained why we were calling and were invited in for tea. The Rev. Baillie arrived down the stairs of this very old structure and was even more delighted than we were. He and his sister had been there a number of years and were about to leave having thoroughly enjoyed their time in Ceylon as it was then. I think he was also delighted that at least one of the marriages he had performed was so successful. If you remember, no one was very anxious to marry a divorcee in Calcutta at that time, but the Rev. Baillie agreed and performed a very nice service.

I always laugh as I thought it was unusual for a Minister to drink, other than a token to wish the bride and groom well — but Andrew being a true Scot certainly enjoyed his whisky. He told a story about the days when he was first ordained and NEVER drank — but at one function he had had so many glasses of Orange Juice that he felt most peculiar and had to leave. One of his congregation told him if he drank Whisky he would not suffer as he did drinking Orange juice! So he started having the odd whisky and found it did NOT have the same disastrous effect that the Orange Juice had!

Unfortunately our time in Sri Lanka had come to an end and we had to leave and arrived back in London in June, 1981.

# FOURTEEN
## *U.K. — 1981*

Our container from H.K. arrived on 10th July 1981, and it quickly became apparent that there was no way we could unpack the cartons — so they were literally stacked to the ceiling in our second bedroom with an overflow into the Lounge.

So we started to look for larger accommodation realising that as we were to live in the U.K. permanently — (or so we thought) — we would need extra space — not only for ourselves, but if the girls — who were now both married with children, wanted to come back home it was essential we had somewhere for them to stay. I don't know if our days in the East had upset our sense of values — but we really couldn't find anything — in our price bracket — that we would enjoy living in long term. I don't exaggerate when I say we must have viewed between 70 to 80 properties in Surrey, Devon, Sussex, Kent, Norfolk and Oxfordshire. I have to admit that because of my deteriorating sight with the consequent doubts about driving I wanted something that was near a bus route.

The thought of vegetating in the country looking at cows and fields — did NOT inspire me, as whilst the open spaces are fine in the summer — I felt they were pretty grim in the winter. I came to the conclusion I was a "towny" and really wanted something reasonably near a shopping centre, library, Theatre and transport!

We both enjoyed where we lived — there was always something happening on the Thames — and we were next door to a very active Canoe Club, opposite a sailing Club and 4 mins walk from Kingston Rowing Club — not to mention the Lensbury Club on the opposite

side of the river. The flats also had their own swimming pool —
and whilst it was rarely warm enough to enjoy them — we felt we
must occasionally have some warm weather!

Besides enjoying the river — we overlooked playing fields which
we were told could not be built on — so really felt we had our
"country" all around us. Walks on the tow path to Richmond or
Hampton were possible, if we felt energetic — and of course
Richmond Park was about 15 mins walk behind us. We were very
accessible for Heathrow so had many friends arriving in the U.K. to
meet and they in turn were delighted to have a bed so near London.

The tube and the Southern Railway were both quite close — and
in those days it took 30 mins to drive from the flat into Oxford
Street where we could always park at Selfridges for a reasonable
payment. Gone are those days of course — the traffic is hell —
and parking in London is impossible and madly expensive so we
never drive into town but take the tube.

You can perhaps understand why we couldn't find anything that
offered us the facilities we had at the moment — and if life here
became too congested — then we could always move later.

However, we still could not unpack all our freight — and although
we disposed of many items from H.K., the problem was no nearer
being solved, and some of the rooms were packed to the ceiling
with boxes. Our caretaker who had watched with a degree of
amusement all our attempts to get the freight into the flat — told us
that one of the tenants living in a Penthouse, was anxious to move to
a smaller flat. His wife had recently died and he found the present
flat too large, but he did not want to leave the complex.

This really sounded ideal — so we were able to negotiate an
exchange and moved into the new flat at York Court on the 17th
December, 1981 I should add that we moved OUT on the 18th
December, as there was no central heating which apparently had
not worried the previous owner. Mind you he did admit that he
slept with a Baraclava helmet on as his wife insisted on having all
the windows open! As neither of us were prepared to go to these

extremes — we ordered central heating to be installed and some very kind friends, Liz and Dennis Constantine lent us their flat which was empty at the time. We moved back into our flat the following week when the central heating had been installed AND was working.

Eventually the majority of the freight was unpacked — though there were still one or two boxes that were piled into the third bedroom. Decorating, up-dating the kitchen and installing double glazing took up a lot of our spare time.

Whilst missing our family, we enjoyed living in the flat at York Court, there was always something of interest happening on the river. As all the windows had a river view, on race days or when there were evening races, I found myself shouting instructions to the fleet to "go about" or "gybe" even though of course they could not hear my advice!

In the evening we would have the odd Ferry sailing past with a band on board and people dancing — and it seemed that every Friday and Saturday night there was a firework display. These seemed to be instigated by one of the many sailing clubs on the river, when they were having a prize giving or just a social evening and sometimes from Hampton Court or Broom Park.

Because we are so close to the airport, many of our friends coming on leave would call in to see us and perhaps spend the night — so life was not as dull as I'd imagined. The winter was a different matter — people seemed to hibernate — though the activities on the river continued, much to our amazement.

Ken eventually got "itchy feet" and so registered with the B.E.S.O. (British Executive Services Overseas) — an organisation that wanted the expertise of retirees in various capacities, in various parts of the world.

Within a matter of weeks he was asked if he would like to go to the Turks and Caicos Islands to examine the possibilities of their becoming an Off-Shore Insurance Centre.

# FIFTEEN
## *Turks & Caicos Islands and Cayman Islands—June 1982*

Whilst there was no salary with this appointment, we did get our accommodation and meals paid for. There was a small remuneration for out of pocket expenses, so what had we to lose? We had never been to the Caribbean — so this was a good opportunity to see a little of these Islands.

In order to get to the Turks and Caicos Islands we had to break our journey in Miami — which in itself was an experience!

We stayed in a Hotel on the beach — which along with all the other beach Hotels had their own private stretch of sand — and was inaccessible except through the Hotels. Again there were warnings everywhere about crime and the necessity of locking any valuables in the Hotel Safe. At the same time one was warned about the dangers of being approached by strangers. Miami apparently had the highest crime rate in the country and because it is the southern most large city of the continental USA and it's near to the Caribbean, it has attracted a large community of Cuban exiles from the Castro regime. It certainly seemed to me that it was as treacherous for tourists as we had found in similar areas in New York and Washington — and so we spent most of our time on the beach!

We were quite glad we were leaving the next day!

Frankly prior to this trip we had never heard of the Turks and Caicos Islands — I suppose they were relatively unknown. They are 600 miles south east of Miami, first settled by the English more than 200 year's ago. The British Crown Colony of Turks and Caicos had been famous for its wealth of salt with which the Bermudians established a trade that was the basis of the Bermudian economy. When we were there — we saw great mounds of salt everywhere — but there was no sign of it being utilized.

Of the 40 Islands forming the Turks and Caicos only eight are inhabited. There are more than 230 miles of beaches ranging from secluded coves to mile long stretches of sand. Most beaches consist of soft coralline sand. As a result of this "sand" Ken suffered a most painful eye condition and on going to the Dr. it was discovered a particle of coral had got into the eye and scratched the eye ball.

When we arrived on Grand Turk we were met by one of the local Government officials who took us to our "Hotel", the Salt Raker, run by a young couple with whom we became very friendly.

I have to admit this accommodation was rather a shock — it resembled a very large Beach House — and could accommodate about 18 people — but it was never full. It was on the beach — the Dining Room was out in the open under a palm leaf thatched roof — the bar seemed to be busy most evenings with residents — and obviously — there was little to do — but eat and drink, and the Salt Raker had Sing Songs on Friday and Saturday evenings which seemed very popular.

On our first evening there I found to my horror two large cockroaches wandering around the bedroom so asked the Owners for some form of Insect Killer. They looked a little surprised — but grudgingly gave me a tin of spray and so before we went down to dinner I shut the windows and thoroughly sprayed the bedroom and bathroom and turned off the light and went down for our meal. Imagine my shock when we returned to the bedroom that evening and switched on the light, we saw no less than 22 large cockroaches dashing around the walls and ceilings!! I could not sleep until they had all been killed and the room was further sprayed. At this stage I would happily have returned home — but we appeared to have either frightened them as we saw very few in the future — at least not in our bedroom!

I was rather mortified when one morning whilst having breakfast there was a phone call for me.    This was the Chief Financial Advisor's wife who introduced herself and said that she would come round at 10.a.m. and take me out to see a school.    At least that is what I thought she said and I imagined it was her way of entertaining the visiting V.I.P.'s wife.    I wasn't very enthusiastic but felt it would be rude to refuse and after all I could hardly say I had a previous engagement as I knew no one and had only arrived the day before!

I was picked up in an old car — by this local lady who was obviously of Bermudian descent and we drove to a large building which I assumed was the school.    We got out of the car and I thought I was to have a conducted tour of the school to see what progress they had made in their education system — I really could not find out why I was being shown the school.

Consequently, I was shattered when she flung open a door to disclose about 30 ladies — all locals except for two.    My friend said very proudly, "Ladies, let me introduce Mrs. Campbell, she has come to talk to us for the next hour about her experiences"!    I did my best to get out of this — saying I had no experiences that anyone would be interested in.    She then explained to me that all these ladies had never left the Grand Turk — and they would love to hear about England or any of the other countries I had lived in!

How I got through the next hour I don't know — but I did — and as though that wasn't enough I heard this lady then asking for questions for Mrs. Campbell!    Frankly I didn't know all the answers — but decided what I didn't know I would make up or at least brush over the question by talking on another subject.    It was then time for coffee (I could have done with a whisky except that I didn't then drink) and there was no sign of anything but orange juice and coffee.

Finally, the meeting started to break up — and as I had been brought to the school, I had no transport back — so this lady went up to one of the two European ladies and asked if she would drop me off at the Salt Raker Inn.    This particular lady who was very quiet and seemed very unobtrusive agreed to take me back to the

Hotel.  In trying to make conversation I asked her where she lived — only to be told "Government House".  She was none other than the High Commissioner's wife — but had never been introduced to me by my hostess.

I felt more embarrassed than ever about the lift she had been talked into giving me — AND — about the talk I had given.

Anyway — the following morning whilst finishing my breakfast there was a sound of a police escort which seemed to be coming to the Salt Raker.  The next thing I knew — in came a very elaborately dressed individual — in uniform — asking where Mrs. Campbell was?  I really wondered what I had done and why they were going to arrest me — when this well dressed individual in white uniform and many medals clicked his heels at my table and handed me a gold edged invitation to the Queen's Birthday Party!  Obviously this had been prompted by my lift the previous day.

Having been to similar parties in Calcutta, Bombay, Karachi and Malaysia — we naturally assumed that we should dress reasonably well for this celebration.  But this was "different".  It was held in a sports field — with a few portable chairs around the perimeter — and it was HOT.  The only liquid refreshments were glasses of doubtful looking coloured water — and we waited and waited. Eventually an old London taxi appeared and drove round the sportsfield — and we could see the British High Commissioner — splendid in his white uniform and plumed head gear appear, accompanied by his wife, the lady who had kindly driven me home the previous day!

The reason for the use of the London Taxi was that it was the only vehicle that would accommodate the High Commissioner's large plumed hat!

He gave the usual speech — toasted the Queen — (still with the coloured water) — and then left in the Taxi.  We had been asked to the Residence afterwards, with a select few, for a further celebration which was more in line with the occasion.

There were numerous eating places on Grand Turk, all very

casual, often with plain wood tables, but called "The Hong Kong Restaurant" or "Dora's" with its plastic tablecloths.   But they did have more up market eating places — and all the food was unusual and quite tasty.

We did meet another couple from the U.K., also out with B.E.S.O. but they were accommodated in a house as they were expected to be in the Grand Turks for about six months.   There was an American girl staying at the Salt Raker who had come for a six week holiday as she wanted to relax!   (She wouldn't have a problem!)   We were given a car and so were able to drive round the Island — but having done this once — there was really nothing that we felt should be repeated, so a lot of our spare time was spent on the beach.

Cockburn Town is the Colony's capital and seat of Government and the buildings in the Capital reflected the 19th Century Bermudian style of architecture.

The roads certainly were not busy or crowded other than the horses and cattle that wandered around as if they owned the place and the occasional donkey cart would clatter by carrying a load of water or freight and chickens would skatter across them as though they were trying to commit suicide.

Before we left the Grand Turk, it was suggested that to help Ken with his report, it would be a good idea if we also visited the Cayman Island.   So prior to leaving for the U.K. we had a few days in the Caymans which were far more advanced than the Turks and Caicos in many ways.   We stayed in a reasonable Hotel — enjoyed touring round the Island — but we had two calamities.

On our last evening on the Island we went to a seafood restaurant where the waiter was surprised we hadn't eaten "Conch" and so I was persuaded to try this dish as a Starter.   Obviously it is in the same category as Oysters, to which I have always been allergic, and about one hour after getting to bed — I was violently sick and had ghastly diarrhoe and spent the night on the loo with a bucket on my knees.   I really felt I'd never leave the Caymans and certainly would be unable to travel the next day.

However, although feeling "groggy" I felt I could make the trip, but had not taken into account the effect of the air pressure in the aircraft. This caused the most unbearable pains in the stomach — which became so bad that I had to lie down in the aisle of the plane as to sit was unbearable. It was one of the longest journeys I remember, even though we were stopping off in Singapore for the night.

So this, coupled with the Coral Ken had in his eye made our Cayman trip memorable for all the wrong reasons!

# SIXTEEN
## *Singapore*
### *October-December 1982; April-Septemnber 1984*

When Ken got back to the U.K. after his Turks and Caicos visit, he had to submit his Report to BESO and we then started our retirement for the second time.    Not for long!

We had not been back from the Turks and Caicos very long when Ken was asked to do a 2 month Audit in Singapore for SAGI (Singapore Aviation and General Insurance).

We had visited Singapore on numerous occasions, but we found during the time we were there, that actually living there was so very different and to my mind far more enjoyable than merely paying a short visit.

We were met in Singapore by John Kuyper, whom we had met several times before, and he took us to The Goodwood Park Hotel in Scotts Road where we were booked into their Park Lane Apartments.    These were individual units consisting of a living room, a bedroom, a kitchen and two bathrooms — ideal as far as we were concerned.    We had the use of the Goodwood Park Hotel swimming pool and that of the adjoining York Hotel which was under the same family management.

Singapore meaning The Lion City, is one of the world's smallest but most successful countries and it was a joy to live there.

In 1961, the Malayan Prime Minister, Tunku Abdul Rahman proposed closer political and economic co-operation between the Federation of Malaya, Singapore, Sarawak, North Borneo and Brunei.

As a result, in 1963, Singapore became part of Malaysia which consisted of the Federation of Malaya, Sarawak, North Borneo (now Sabah), with Brunei opting out.

This merger proved to be short lived. Singapore was separated from the rest of Malaysia on 9th August, 1965 and became a sovereign, democratic and independent nation.

Singapore itself is just north of the Equator, and comprises of the main Island of Singapore and some 58 Islets. It is linked to the foot of Malaysia by a long causeway which carries a road, a railway and a water pipeline across the Strait of Johore.

Most of the 2.6 million people live on the main Island of Singapore. It is a sleek, efficient international business centre at the cross-roads of Asia and one of the worlds busiest ports. In 1965, Malaysia had been convinced that Singapore could not survive once it became Independent   This appears quite ironical now as Singapore is a politically stable state with a high rate of economic growth!

In to-days world, Singapore is indeed a miracle — and so much of this is due to Lee Kuan Yue who became Premier in 1959 where his People's Action Party held an overwhelming majority in Parliament. It has been said that he is a benevolent Dictator. If this means that he runs a strictly disciplined and regulated society, the cleanest, most efficient and most corrupt-free State in S.E. Asia, with little, if any, unemployment, — then I suppose he is — but does it matter?   It certainly works and I feel the West could learn a lot from this highly successful Premier.

To my mind, Singapore certainly proves that our attitude towards crime in the West — has achieved nothing and perhaps we should throw away the velvet glove and try a little discipline AND introduce punishments that fit the crime.

Why is it that Singapore can achieve such success in preventing crime, eliminating jaywalking, car stealing, chewing gum and litter on the streets, not to mention vandalism?

I think the majority of people approved of his application of the birch when recently used on a teenager who had deliberately vandalised a car.    A senseless crime, which I don't think will be repeated — certainly not in Singapore.    Still our "do gooders" try to convince us that punishment does not pay and a good holiday at the Tax Payer's expense is the answer?

All the regulations that are introduced in Singapore AND carried out, make a lot of sense.    The habit of chewing gum is frowned on as its abolition saves public cleaning bills, everyone is taught not to waste water as Singapore has to buy water from Malaysia and although a fine for not flushing a toilet in a public area brought criticism from the locals when initially introduced — it is now taken as a matter of course and the public amenities are scrupulously clean.

It hasn't all been easy introducing new regulations — as — there is no point whatsoever in making rules if they are ignored and not carried out.    I was in Singapore when the "flushing toilets" rule became law — and they actually had people inside the toilet areas listening for the flush!    The first few months culprits received a warning, but after about six months when it had been publicly advertised in the Press and T.V. — people were fined.

I remember a conversation with a taxi driver when he said that it cost him 10P to go into a public toilet — so why should he have to flush it!    I explained at great length that it was a social necessity — he wasn't convinced at the time, but one never heard complaints after the system was established.

To help overcome the traffic problem, a 175% import duty on vehicles was introduced and in addition, cars carrying less than four people are forbidden to enter the centre of Singapore city during peak hours without a special permit.    Provision is made for people to park their cars outside the city limits and shuttle buses are run to ferry people into the centre.

One controversial move whilst we were living in Singapore was to create "Brighter Babies'.    Mothers under the age of 30 with poor education and one or two children, were offered about US$4500 towards an apartment if they agreed to be sterilised!    At the same time unmarried professionals with University degrees or Civil

Service backgrounds, were offered incentives to settle down and have children! The idea presumably was that well educated people produced brighter children!

I have never lived in such a well disciplined society — where I felt completely safe at all hours of the day. There are few countries one can say that about nowadays and until we in the UK introduce legislation where punishments are related to the crime — and the victim is no longer treated as the culprit — I regret to say this state of affairs will continue.

I must get off my soap box — you'll gather I was more than a little impressed with conditions in Singapore.

Ken enjoyed his job and I most certainly enjoyed my time there. I took a Computer course — as I felt I was really getting behind the times when my young grandsons were computer wise, whilst it all remained a mystery to me!

The two months passed very quickly and so we left for a quick trip to Kuala Lumpur from where we went to Kuala Selangor, the Genting Highlands, Port Dickson, Frasers Hill for old times sake and then returned to Singapore. We spent Xmas 1982 with Linda in Singapore and then flew to Hong Kong on the 27th December. Fiona and family were spending Xmas in Austria with Gerd's parents.

Tony and Val Henderson who were on leave in the U.K. offered us the use of their flat which was at the top of The Peak. Tony had been working with Ken when he was in H.K. We were very appreciative of this generous offer.

Whilst in H.K. Ken was approached about doing a consultancy job in the Philippines. Nothing definite was decided and in early January, Ruth Swift, my old school friend arrived, and spent a few days with us in H.K. before we all flew down to Sydney on the 19th January 1983.

Poor Ruth was a little concerned though when we left Hong Kong as Ken and I were travelling on our last sub-load ticket issued whilst Ken was associated with Cathay Pacific. This meant that we could be offloaded on route AND we never knew until about 15 minutes before take off, whether we would be on the plane!   We were booked on the same flight — but of course we told her we might not be able to get on the flight but that Brian had said he would meet her.   I think Ruth was very dubious about this — coming to a strange country and staying with a strange man!

However, at the last moment we were given boarding cards and when Ruth saw us in the holding lounge she rushed up and looked so happy.

We stayed in Brian's lovely home at Blakehurst for quite a while — and Ruth and I felt that as there was no wife to do the chores we should do all we could to help.   They did have a housekeeper who came in daily but there was a limit to what she could do in the hours available.   The main problem seemed to be the washing and ironing.

How three teenagers could acquire so much washing we never understood but the laundry arrangements were very pleasant — the laundry room was off the swimming pool and so we took it in turns to put on the washing machine and hang up the clothes — and in between we would sun bathe or have a swim.   A lovely life style.

More than once we had emptied the large laundry basket — washed the items, ironed them and put them back on the beds,  and then sat around the pool enjoying the wonderful views and ambience.

The teenagers arrived home from school and on one occasion when Ruth was walking through the laundry room shortly after their return,  I heard her let out a scream — "I can't believe it", she said, "the damned laundry basket is FULL"!

What an admission — if they read this they will doubtless be furious!   They really were lovely teenagers, — but house trained or tidy — they were not!

They had a very happy home life and Brian did all he could to compensate for the loss of their mother.

Whilst staying with Brian we were able to see some of our old friends now living in Sydney and spent a very happy few days meeting up with them.

Brian had a boat called "Mistress" — aptly called he said because it cost him a lot of money but gave him a lot of pleasure! We had a very memorable weekend on this boat when we sailed from Acuna Bay, where Mistress was anchored up the Hawkesbury River — did some fishing, swimming and lots of eating and drinking. Obviously Brian had lots of sailing friends and one night we joined forces with two other boats and had a hilarious evening.

After this lovely weekend we hired a car and drove up to Port MacQuarie where we spent the night and the following day drove as far as Burleigh Heads where we booked into Goodwin Towers for about a week.

We then drove 800 kms to Yepoon and booked into a Motel and the following day joined a cruise to Keppel Island. After a further 400 kms we arrived at Shute Harbour where we spent a couple of days cruising on The Barrier Reef, calling at Hook Island, South Molle and Dreamland Island. We snorkelled and swam and thoroughly enjoyed the warm water and marvelled at the number of fish we saw.

The boat anchored a little way off the Reef — so as not to damage the Coral, but we were told that we could swim to the Reef — as Sharks apparently did not swim near the Coral!

I was enchanted with all I could see through the Mask that I didn't realise how far I had travelled and when I surfaced, could not see anyone else from the boat, or for that matter I could not decide which boat was ours! I felt if I removed my mask and stood up — that someone from the boat would hopefully see me. I am as blind as a bat without glasses, but the magnification when using the Mask enabled me to see the very colourful fish and the coral in the water — but didn't help once I surfaced!

I then found I could not climb on to the Reef — my knees were giving me a little trouble, so decided I would float over the Reef and then I would be able to stand! Need I say that I scratched my "flitties" in this manoeuvre — but fortunately I had no adverse affects. We have since learnt that a scratch with Coral causes immediate poisoning — but — Coral near the surface of the water which gets the benefit of the sun, apparently seems to be safe!

Eventually a young couple from the boat saw me and came to my assistance and we swam back to the boat together.

The following day we drove to Bowen on the Sunshine Coast and decided that we would not travel further north on this trip as Ruth had to get back to Sydney in order to get her flight back to the U.K.

Having had a few more days in Sydney, Ken and I flew to H.K. for a few days before returning to the U.K. Ken had been asked to return to Singapore for a further year with SAGI, and this suited us very well — we both enjoyed Singapore, Linda was there and of course the extra cash was a bonus.

Anglia had just finished installing the double glazing in the Kingston flat, the day before we were to fly to Singapore. We felt they were cutting things rather finely as they had promised to be finished four days earlier, but the bad weather had prevented them from keeping to their schedule. Obviously we could not leave the flat with the windows out — so were very concerned.

We arrived in Singapore in April, 1983 and had again been booked into the Parklane Apartments at the Goodwood Park Hotel, — into the same suite we had vacated in December, 1982 and which had begun to feel like home! We were allocated the same maid "Eng" who was a delight and I am sure we got many more "perks" than we should have. Every day the very attractive toilet basket in the bathroom was filled with Soap, Shampoo, Body Lotion and Bath Oil — and we always seemed to get double rations.

At night we were given a Chocolate Mint on our pillow — but very often would find more than the official allocation!

On the 27th May, we had been invited to spend a weekend with relatives of Dianes at Club Med at Kuantan, so flew up to K.L. on the evening Shuttle service — which was much cheaper than the normal flight, but it was very much a case of first come first served. No seats were booked and rather like a bus you arrived and queued to purchase your ticket. We couldn't get on the first Shuttle but were well in front of the queue for the following one which left in half an hour.

The next day we flew in a small private plane for Kuantan and booked into the Club.   Hamzah, my niece's brother in law was involved in promoting tourism in Malaysia, and had been invited to visit Club Med so that he knew what he was promoting.  Obviously all stops had been pulled out to ensure that he had an enjoyable visit.

Never having been to a Club Med before I was pleasantly surprised.  First of all we were met by a happy crowd of Malaysian ladies singing a welcome song, garlanded, given a delicious cool drink and then shown to our chalets.   Before lunch it was arranged that we would be shown around the Club — and I was very impressed at the number of activities that were available.   Besides the obvious swimming and sailing, there were tennis courts, a 9 hole golf course, Archery classes, Windsurfing, Ski-ing, Sailing.    They also ran courses on Computers, Batik dyeing, lampshade making, dress making classes, language courses, Aerobics, and the full use of a Gymnasium with a trainer to advise you what apparatus would be suitable — so if you didn't want to rest and relax, there was plenty to keep you occupied.   Of course there were similar activities for children — so parents had no need to worry about them.

In the evening, after a sumptuous Malay Buffet, there was a high class of entertainment laid on.

The next morning I chose to have lessons in Windsurfing followed by a short computer course, which lasted about half an hour.

Lunch was also a Buffet type meal, though I forgot to mention that for those who wanted to dine alone, there was a restaurant with a good a la carte menu.

We were very impressed — it was not the Butlin type of accommodation or entertainment we had imagined.

Having left Kuantan we had to fly directly back to Singapore as Ken had to start work the next day, but this had been a very unexpected and pleasant interlude.

We were so lucky being so near both girls and were able to fly up to H.K. to see Fiona and family for a week at the end of June 1983 and in October of that year Ken had to go to H.K. on business — so I went along as well, and had another week with Fiona.

A Typhoon prevented Ken from returning from Kuching where he had gone on business and so couldn't get back to HK on schedule. Our departure for Singapore a couple of days later was also delayed as a Lufthansa Flight had aborted and planes were cancelled, but we were able to leave the following day.

In November of that year, Julie and Tony Jones came to Singapore and Julie came to stay with us whilst Tony went on to Hong Kong.

The Hotel were very understanding and permitted us to have a guest to stay without any charge — even though they provided extra linen for the bed settee in the Lounge. It really was a super Hotel and we so enjoyed the time we spent there.

Diane and Ismail had kindly invited us to go and stay with them for a few days so Julie and I drove up to Kuala Lumpur by coach. It was on this trip that we found conditions so different once we had crossed the Causeway into Malaysia. The bus drivers, when we boarded the coach in Singapore, had been so smart in their blue uniforms and had been helpful when boarding the bus, and told us in very good English where the "convenience stops" would be, asked us which videos we would like to watch on the journey, and were generally very pleasant. But when we disembarked from the coach at the Causeway in order to carry our luggage through Customs before boarding the bus again to continue the journey to Kuala Lumpur, this all changed. We could hardly recognise the coach, the drivers wore dirty looking vests, had no hat or jacket — and for the remainder of the journey appeared not to even understand English let alone speak it! — no one received any help with their luggage, the video was now all in the Bahasa and we found it hard to believe that there had not been a change of crew — and that it was just a change in attitude!

Julie found staying in a Malay household quite an experience

451

and Diane and Ismail went out of their way to entertain us royally. We were taken sightseeing to Malacca, and Kuantan before returning on the train — which was quicker.   Here we had sniffer dogs examining our luggage on the platform when we arrived.   One poor lady must have had a shock when one of the dogs suddenly grabbed one of her shoes from her hand luggage and dashed off with it.   Immediately she was surrounded by Customs officials, just in case the shoe had contained drugs — but it transpired that the dog was under training and decided it was time for some excitement. Even so the shoe was examined minutely and other dogs were used to see if they had the same re-action — but thankfully all was well.

We went down to China Town, visited the wonderful Porcelain factory which had the oldest kiln in the East we were told — it was certainly large and as it was not in use at the time — we were able to walk the length of the kiln which was racked and partially stacked with the pottery waiting to be glazed.

Julie wanted to visit the Bird Singing Contest which was held every morning at 5.a.m., when the local enthusiasts appeared with their covered bird cages, sat and had coffee and waited until all the hooks were filled with these caged birds.   Then the covers were removed and the birds started to sing — we gathered prizes were given for the best repertoire!   Afraid we were not very good hosts as getting up at that hour, with a day's work ahead, did not appeal to either of us, so Julie took herself off on her own.

Xmas 1983 we spent with Linda and family in Singapore and of course in April 1984 Ken's initial contract with SAGI came to an end but they asked him if he would do a further three months after our leave, and so we left for the U.K. spending about 10 days in Hong Kong en route to the U.K.

Our flat in Kingston was still let to the excellent tenants we had and so we spent a week in the Oriental Club and then went North to visit family and friends, returning to Singapore on the 4th June, 1984.

The Hotel knew before we left that we would be returning and so they utilised this time to re-decorate the apartment and it was available when we returned, which pleased us immensely. Knowing we were coming back, we had stored most of our luggage in the Baggage room of the Hotel, so it wasn't long before the apartment looked like home once more.

Whilst I had been in Singapore I had made a point of visiting Cynthia Koeke who was in her 80's but a most interesting and entertaining individual. She was nearly blind and had only one leg — but — she was a mound of interesting experiences.

She has written her own book about her experiences as a P.O.W. after the fall of Singapore, in which she explains how she and her husband were woken by Japanese banging on their door, they commandeered their only car and demanded that they left immediately for the Singapore Swimming Club where all the remaining Expats were gathered. From here they were interned, the men being sent to Changi jail.

The ladies were finally also sent to Changi, but they had to walk from the Swimming Club — a distance of about 8 kms. Cynthia had only one leg, so she was on crutches and obviously finding it difficult. Eventually a Japanese lorry that was accompanying them offered to give her a lift. She refused any help and as this batch of exceedingly brave ladies approached Changi, they started singing "There'll Always Be an England" as they wanted the men prisoners to think they were in good spirits!

There was no communication between the two camps, but Cynthia was told that they were moving the men to another area and that they would be passing the ladies' camp at a certain time. She found some good reason to be near the gate as the men marched past in the hope of seeing her husband, but when the Japanese Guards realised what she was doing they knocked her to the ground!

She reckoned she had an easier time in the camp than a lot of the ladies as she was a good seamstress. Some of the Japanese Officers asked if there was anyone that could mend their uniforms and Cynthia said if they got her a sewing machine she would be able to do this.

She also knew if she had access to a machine that she would be able to make and mend things for the ladies in the camp. A sewing machine was produced and Cynthia repaired uniforms and when she was assured of a little privacy, would also do work for the ladies.

Apparently two of the ladies were pregnant when they were interned, and Cynthia was able to make baby garments for them and to let out their dresses as they became larger. She was a wonderful lady and always had some interesting stories to relate. Her parrot that wandered around her flat was equally verbose and whenever I arrived he let out a groan and said "Good Bye" and would continue at intervals to say "Good Bye" hoping I suppose that I would take the hint!

Margaret Crowther, who had been our neighbour in Bombay, had been recently widowed and so whilst we were on leave in the U.K. we suggested to her that she came out for a holiday to Singapore and were delighted when she agreed. It was great fun having her, because as you all know, when you entertain guests, you also enjoy the entertainment.

Ken and I both took great delight in showing her around all the tourist attractions, and I went up to Malacca with her on the bus, having been there at least twice, I was able to show her as much as possible in the shortest time.

We also spent a night with my niece in Kuala Lumpur and she and her husband took us to Kelang for a typical Chinese dinner — I think we had 10 courses — just a small dinner!

We found that actually living in Singapore was so very different and even more enjoyable than merely paying a short visit. Now we had time to do all the things, that as tourists we had been unable to do.

We were able to enjoy the various Festivals that take place throughout the year — and with the multi-racial society, in which there are Chinese, Malays, Indians, Filipinos and Europeans, plus a few others, all of them keen on celebrating their own cultural and religious holidays, then you can be sure there are endless festivities of one sort or another.

Since Festivals in Asia are based on the lunar calendar — one can't always plan one's visit to coincide with the Festival. But now we were resident in Singapore we were able to see most of these celebrations as they appeared

Chinese New Year is the biggest festival of the year — for the Chinese, and although all the Chinese shops are closed at this time the Indian and often the Christian shops remain open. These Festivals certainly added colour to the city. Living in the Hotel we were invited to join in the festivities — which included the traditional Dragon Dance. At least 10 people could be seen hiding under the Dragon's body with green trousers that were supposed to resemble the Dragon's legs, holding sticks which were attached to various parts of the Dragon. As the drums and cymbals crashed, the Dragon became life like, jumping and dancing and, after about 5 mins. of these contortions, one by one the men would be replaced, those leaving the Dragon's body looking quite hot and weary — but after a few moments rest they were ready to return. The dance would continue for about half an hour in the compound of the Hotel and the finale was usually the Dragon jumping to obtain a cabbage that was suspended on long bamboo poles. This necessitated the men under the Dragon jumping on each other's shoulders in order to obtain the height required to grab the cabbage.

This was not the end. The Dragon would then dance his way through the Hotel and the grounds — with the drums getting louder. Food would be left outside the restaurants which the Dragon would devour. A very spectacular ceremony — and rather noisy!

As foreigners we found it confusing that the actual date for the start of Chinese New Year was never very definite — it depended entirely on when the new Moon was seen. I have to admit in later years it appeared that the moon was conveniently seen on the date that had been forecast! Not necessarily in Singapore, but somewhere in the East!

Dragon Boat races take place on the Singapore River during the Chinese New Year. Each boat is manned by a drummer plus his very large noisy drum. This is to ensure that the oarsmen keep in time and they execute the correct number of strokes per minute in order to win the race. The drumming gets quite frenetic as the race progresses. We were rather amused to find that Dragon Boat Races take place on the River Thames in front of our flat — though nowhere near as noisy as we experienced in Singapore and Hong Kong. Perhaps because, as far as I could see, no Chinese were participating!

Having given their homes a thorough Spring Clean, the Chinese paste their newly spruced homes with red scrolls painted with verses and above all their doors they hang banners and lanterns. As explained earlier, there are family re-unions when the Chinese dress up in their finery — all debts have to be settled before the New Year and Angpows (the little red envelopes with money inside) are exchanged and passed to the younger generation or unmarried children, who look forward to receiving this extra cash

The Buddhist celebration is Vasak Day when saffron robed monks chant verses late into the night at the Temple of 1,000 lights.

Another colourful celebration is the Birthday of the Monkey God. It's held twice a year in several temples around town. This is when Mediums with skewers pierced through their cheeks and tongues, go into trances during the ceremony and write out special charms with their blood. No thought of AIDS!

The Chinese love to eat and on the 15th night of the eighth moon, when according to the Chinese the moon is at its brightest and roundest, they arrange a feast. On this evening they celebrate by eating Moon Cakes — filled with a mixture of bean paste and lotus seeds. On the night of the Festival, children light their lanterns, which are in various shapes, of animals, aeroplanes, birds etc., whilst housewives burn joss sticks and candles and offer cakes to the Gods.

During the Festival of the Nine Emperor Gods the images of the Nine Gods are placed on decorated sedan chairs and paraded through the streets with the accompaniment of cymbals and drums and followed by throngs of devotees carrying yellow flags and banners to the sea.

Twice we saw the festivities at the Mariamman Temple on South Bridge Road during their Thimithi Festival. This takes place in the Hindu Temple and devotees put themselves into a trance and walk over a pit of burning coals to fulfil their vows — and — believe me — the coals are VERY hot. From what we could see the soles of their feet were never burnt — maybe there is something to this going into a trance!

Occasionally one would see the travelling Medicine Man — a Chinese wearing a tatty shirt stands with feet apart. He takes hold of an iron bar with his teeth and his accomplice tells the crowd he is going to bend this 1" thick iron bar! He makes many false starts and grunts and groans — the veins in his neck stand out. He strains and strains — and nothing happens — but wait — his assistant then produces the bottle of elixir which the strong man drinks. Within seconds he finds he can now bend the bar until the two ends meet! I wonder if this is how Popeye originated?

The assistant explains to the audience that it is this special brand of snake oil which gives strength and cures everything! Need I say, this sells like hot cakes!

The famous Padang, where the Cricket Club now stands, was created by Stamford Raffles, who, when he saw the flat land around the harbour envisaged a sports field and foresaw the possibilities of forming a rugby team to compete against the Dutch. This may be a distortion of the actual facts, but one of the first things Raffles did when laying out the town was to leave enough space for a military parade ground where sports could be played.

We were in Singapore in the days when Bugi Street was operating. By day, famous for the food it served, but by night it was the renowned and notorious haunt of Singapore's most bizarre night owls. If we had visitors we would quite often end up after dinner at Bugi Street for a beer. There was little point going there before 10.p.m. and the nearer to midnight, the more atmosphere there appeared to be! On sitting at one of the tables for a beer we would immediately be surrounded by street entertainers.

My favourite was the little boy who asked us to play naughts and crosses with him. He would always let you make the first move — but you NEVER won — don't know how he did this — but he was well trained and of course made quite a lot of money when he found someone who was prepared to bet 50 cents that they would beat him.

Then we would get men coming along with loose jackets, asking if we wanted to buy a watch — and then they would open their jackets and the linings would be covered with all makes of fake watches, Rolex, Gucci, Longines, Seiko etc. Then they would dive into one of their pockets and produce, radio's, rather rude mechanical toys, vibrators, massage machines, and literally about 20 items — and one was at a loss to know where they had been kept.

This was all highly illegal — but in those days the authorities seemed to turn a blind eye — at least on most evenings.

The main attractions were the "ladies" that weren't — and I have to say some of them were so very glamorous. We did witness a rather spectacular fight between a Navy boy and one of these "ladies". We never found out at what stage the sailor had discovered his lovely date for the night, who he had been plying with drinks, was not what she seemed!

However, the excesses of Bugis Street have now been checked by the police, though the place continues, it is a shadow of it's former self. Purged of decadence, with the Police patrolling the streets. Bugis Street, once so out of keeping with the rest of the city, has become a part of ordered Singapore.

We had been in Singapore or visiting Singapore for about eight years before we discovered the most amazing pottery factory, which boasted having the oldest and largest kiln in Asia. The kiln was not in operation the first time we found this craftily hidden factory — and we were able to walk inside the kiln which was being loaded with hundreds of pottery specialities, wonderful umbrella stands, large and small lamp bases, stools, plaques besides all sizes of bowls and ornaments, at ridiculously low prices.

On Sundays we often went out to Pongol Point for a Chinese meal — and in the evenings a visit to Newton Circus was always a must for visitors.    One sat around on stools and could order food from any of the stalls serving a variety of Asian dishes — and the "beer" man came round regularly — but no spirits were for sale.    It was here we saw the largest Crayfish we have ever seen.

An evening to be recommended, which few tourists seem to know anything about, is to go out to Saujana Villa on the north east side of the island.    Saujana Smith is the proprietor, an expat Brit who came to the Far East before the war, was captured by the Japanese and did his turn as a POW and settled in this estate in the country. The drive out to the Villa passes through some splendid rural countryside where Malay Kampong houses still have thatched roofs. At the Villa one can sit in the garden having a drink and watching the sun set over the distant Malaysia hills across the Straits.

After dinner they put on a Cultural Show presented under a thatched roof.   The show represented the three cultures of Singapore, Chinese, Indian and Malay.    You begin to feel you are living in another era.

We spent four years — with a break in the middle — staying at the Goodwood Park Hotel in their Park Lane Apartments.   As we had officially retired from the East and all our household goods had gone back to the U.K. when we left H.K., we felt this was an ideal place to stay as we were provided with everything.   The Hotel was very central — in Scotts Road — only two minutes away from the well known Tang's Department store, which is on the corner of Orchard Road — the up-market shopping area.

The Hotel started many years ago, as a German Club and during the War was a Japanese Hospital.

Whilst we were staying at the Hotel a film company moved in and were filming "Tanamara" — a most romantic story which you should read if you haven't already done so.    I fondly thought I was

IN the film as I was most certainly standing near the rickshaw that brought the leading character to the Hotel, but when I saw the film, I had been eliminated!

Ken's consultancy in Singapore finished finally in September, 1984 — and you'll probably guess that we left for Australia yet again! We had become quite addicted to the country and its wonderful climate. We hoped we could spend most of the winter in Australia — returning to the U.K. in the Spring.

So on the 4th October, 1984 we booked a flight to Perth where we had been invited by Keith and Ida Morris to stay with them at Bateman. Keith had by now retired and they had left Sydney to return to their home in Perth. They made us most welcome — and we met all their family, two daughters and two sons. The dog "Dingho" the Pussy Cat and of course all their friends who were all equally welcoming.

Perth is a delightful spot — rather like England — except of course for the climate! It is on the Swan river but the Port is at Freemantle, we had some very enjoyable trips sailing up and down the river and had conducted tours round the city.

The Morris's had a caravan or should I say a Mobile Home at Busselton which is near the beach and we went down there for four days. They erected a lean-to against the caravan where Ken and I slept — my only concern was that the toilet block seemed a long way away at 2.a.m. and I decided I had to wake Ken to accompany me to the Loo!

There was so much to see — Nannup, Bridgetown, Donnybrook, Pemberton, Babingup. Ida and Keith had climbed The Gloucester Tree where there was a look out, on their honeymoon, so of course we had to visit that. Ken and Keith went fishing one morning — and Ken managed to catch a Shovelnosed Shark along with a lot of crabs. In the afternoon we visited Wrights and Vasse Felix Winery, after which they took us to Cape Naturalist, Bunkers Bay, Sugar Loaf and Heelup. We could have spent much longer there as besides there being so much to see, the sea and sand were very inviting.

When we got back to Perth we accompanied Ida and Keith to the shop they had taken over after Keith's retirement — this was basically a Mail Order Shop for outsize ladies.   We were shattered to find they catered for bust sizes up to 58".   This was quite a change for Keith who had been Manager of an Insurance Company in Sydney — but he seemed to enjoy the challenge.   Ken was quite tickled when he was given the job of pricing ladies knickers!   A big change for him too!

One afternoon we were taken to Scarborough — funny to find so many English names in Australia.   Ken and I then hired a car and went on a tour to Coolgardie and on to Kalgoorlie where we went down a Gold Mine (but found no gold!) then booked into a Hotel and went onto Esperance the next day.

We had an interesting encounter at 11 mile beach where we noticed a Scuba Diver in the water on his own — we continued our drive to Butti Cover, the Pink Lake, Twilight Beach and returned about five hours later to find the Scuba Diver's van still parked with no sign of the diver!   Not being experienced with diving — it occurred to me that no one would be in the water for all that time — and it was getting dark.   We were just deciding to call the Life Guard when we spotted the diver returning up the Cliff.   When he arrived at his van I told him how concerned we had been and how we were about to advise the coast guard or the Life Guard.   He explained that he had been diving for Abalone and had found the shells too heavy to climb up the cliff with his Scuba Gear, so had left the shells in a bag at the bottom of the cliff, brought his equipment up and had gone down later for the shells.

He was very touched at our concern — and I think the fact that we were ignorant Poms prompted him to give me a couple of the shells after he had cleaned them.   The inside of the Abalone shell is the same colour as an Opal.

The next day we continued our tour — Mount Clarence, Mount Melville, Middleton Beach on to Albany and spent the night at Emu Beach.   The following day we went to Frenchman's Bay, The Gap, saw the Blow Holes. I could go on for ever as there were so many beaches, and the scenery was out of this world, but we eventually got back to the Caravan and then returned to Bateman.

We discovered that a couple who had lived opposite us in Bombay had settled in Perth and were living quite near us — so we had a very happy day with them.

We were taken for dinner to the Royal Perth Yacht Club — home of The Australian Cup, by Rose Hammill and her husband Tony. We had known Rose of course in Karachi, sadly her husband had died shortly after their return to Perth. She had now re-married a delightful gentleman also retired, and who was a very active member of the Yacht Club.

Ida and Keith had to leave for Sydney on a buying trip for the shop and asked us to stay in their lovely home, to look after the dog and the pussy — we felt this was above and beyond — and had a thoroughly enjoyable time — with swims every morning and evening in their pool.

We flew into Sydney on the 5th November, 1984 and had a few days staying at Hurstfield, had dinner at the Royal Sydney Yacht Club with Frank and Joy Coyne who had also invited Brian. On the way home we got caught in the most horrific storm and were nearly swept off the road on a couple of occasions — we had lived through Typhoons which had not been so violent! We had another couple of days on the boat and went to a Horse Show and on the 12th November took the evening bus to Burleigh Heads.

Again we booked into one of the Units at Goodwin Towers and had another wonderful visit.

Queensland offers so much — besides the fantastic beaches — which are never ending, there is the National Forest, the Bird Sanctuary, Sea World, Dreamworld, Koala Park, Wet and Wild — and then one can drive up to the mountains, to the Hinze Dam, Mount Warning, Jupiters Casino where they have regular Extravaganza Shows, not forgetting the Twin Towns Club the Seagulls Club where, besides the Poker Machines which not only make the Clubs solvent, but actually produce fantastic profits.

There must be more golf clubs per square mile in Australia than anywhere else in the world. Added to which a round of golf costs so little compared to Europe.

Brian had invited us to spend Xmas with he and the family — and so we flew down to Sydney around the 20th December, and had a very happy time where we were made very welcome and very much at home. On New Year's Eve we were invited to participate in the children's (all teenagers now of course) New Year's Eve party — on condition we left the frivolities shortly after midnight. So in case we were putting a damper on the party we retired earlier than I would have liked, as I was having a Ball!

Ruth arrived on the 8th January, and we had a wonderful weekend on "Mistress" where Ruth was hailed the Oyster Queen as, whenever we went out for a meal, she would order Oysters!

We had already arranged to hire a car and set off for Melbourne staying the night at Eden, on to Sale, Lakes Entrance and 90Mile Beach to Phillip Island. The Penguin Parade was as intriguing as ever, though the number of these delightful little creatures seemed to have diminished considerably from our last visit.

Our accommodation in Melbourne had already been booked — as we felt we may have difficulty in finding somewhere to stay at the last moment. In the brochure they were offering two bedrooms, a large lounge, kitchen and bathroom and we thought the rates were very reasonable! However, we realised it was a very popular Motel and people seemed to come and go all night! We later discovered that we were staying at St. Kilda in the red Light area!

Our visit to Melbourne coincided with Jim Clarke's Farewell Tour. He had been Ken's Overseas Manager for years and now a great chum of ours — so we were included in all the Company entertaining which meant, above other things, we ate in places we would not normally have visited! The first Farewell Dinner for Jim and Margaret, was at The Melbourne Club, hosted by Peter and Julie Duerden, the new Manager for Australia which was excellent.

The next day we were given a car and driver, Marsden by name, to enable us to attend the evening festivities without worrying about the very strict "drink and drive" laws in Australia.

Being included in all these farewells meant that we met up with lots of old friends, some from India and Malaysia, some of whom we hadn't seen for 25 years. One or two had changed partners, but it was great seeing them and catching up on all their chat.

We had a memorable dinner at Burnham Beeches where our arrival was heralded by a Piper who burst into action as soon as the car arrived in the drive. We were pretty tired when the Driver picked us up to take us back to the Motel around midnight — but he was very anxious to show us a little more of the area and, interesting as it was, we dearly wanted to return home to sleep! But there was no stopping his enthusiasm to show off the wonderful countryside, though at that time of night we could hardly see what he was pointing out — but I guess — all this extra "touring" did add to his overtime!

The next day we were driven to Healesville Sanctuary and down through the Dandenongs- beautiful countryside.

Before going to Adelaide we called in to see Sue and Harry Garlick at their lovely Beach House at Anglesea, they were spending more and more time at their Beach house and less and less time at their Unit in Melbourne. We had met Harry when he had come to a medical Conference in Kuala Lumpur, where he spent about two months, during which time we saw a great deal of him.

After a very nostalgic few days with them, we started our drive to Adelaide on the coast road taking about 12 days stopping off and viewing the various beauty spots.

The first night we spent at Port Campbell, which didn't live up to the "Clans" expectations.

It was on this trip that we had a rather traumatic experience. We had stopped in a lay-by to view the Twelve Apostles. Whilst Ken studied the map, Ruth and I viewed the scenery which was just below us. We just could not get over the fantastic sight — mile upon mile of beaches — all deserted and in the foreground these rock formations which constitute the Twelve Apostles, all very picturesque. We thought this particular view was so spectacular that we called to Ken to come and have a look. He got out of the car and without thinking locked his door — and of course the keys were inside! We had just booked out of the Motel and driven about 4 miles when this happened — and all attempts to open the door were in vain.

Ken decided he would have to walk back to the Motel to phone and ask the garage to come to our assistance. This would obviously take time and there were no cars on the road at this time — Australia can be very quiet! After Ken had been gone about 15 minutes — along came a car with a couple of surf boards on the roof — and seeing Ruth and me standing by the car looking pretty helpless, the driver kindly stopped and asked if he could help. We told him the problem — and he went to the back of his car and produced a piece of nylon strapping — which he pushed down the side of the window and within seconds had opened the door! Obviously he had done this many times and he sweetly left us the strapping in case this happened again! One could not help wondering why we bothered to lock cars.

Ruth and I immediately drove off trying to catch Ken who had made a great deal of progress — but we got as far as the Motel without seeing him and so went in to the Motel to enquire if Ken had been there. They told us he had left for the Garage down the road — and we caught him before he had had time to reach the garage. He couldn't believe his eyes when he saw the car and wondered how on earth we had gained entry!

The following day we went down the Princess Margaret Caves, the likes of which I have never seen before or since. They were 6½ miles in length — but of course we didn't cover all that distance but it gives you an idea of the size. One was completely lit by Glow Worms — fantastic what light these small worm like creatures produce That night we spent at Mount Gambier.

We had not pre booked our accommodation in Adelaide, but had arrived reasonably early, but not early enough, as we had the greatest difficulty in finding a Motel, and in the end accepted rooms in a rather third rate establishment — it was clean — but on the Pacific Highway and rather noisy.

Adelaide reminded us of Scotland — we again had friends there whom we had entertained in Hong Kong and they invited us to their home for a meal and advised us where to go and what to see the next day.

We were invited by yet another Company friend to his home for a B.B.Q. — though the mosquitoes drove us inside and we were all bitten to death — guess they liked Pommie blood! (the Mosquitoes).

On Sunday the 27th January, 1985 we drove to Mount Lofty which has a really super Game Reserve, and were taken to the Barossa Valley where those that could drink sampled their wines -and bought several bottles! We also visited a Mohair farm where Ruth and I bought a Stole.

Adelaide was indeed, yet another lovely city which we thoroughly enjoyed exploring. It is the State Capital of South Australia and the broad streets in the city centre appeared to be completely surrounded by the most beautiful parks. The Torrens river has been dammed to form a lake in one of the Parks. Mount Lofty, which is over 2,000 feet can be easily seen from the Eastern Suburbs.

We were told to visit the Town Hall, Government House and Parliament House, all looked upon as historical buildings, but none older than 1863 which by European standards is not classed as very old.

We'd decided in order to save time that we would return the car to Budget Rent a Car and continue the rest of the journey by coach, which took an inland route and would be cheaper and quicker.

We had five days in Adelaide and then had booked on the coach to Canberra. These coach trips are very reasonable and most enjoyable. Two drivers take it in turn to drive — and there is a small compartment curtained off for the alternate driver to get some sleep. There were videos on board to entertain the passengers en route, and of course they had toilet facilities. The coaches made "convenience stops" en route where we could get something to eat, and sometimes to pick up more passengers.

We had three days in Canberra, which is 155 miles south west of Sydney. The City was planned by an American and the Australian Parliament had moved there from Melbourne in 1927 — and later, the Federal Government Departments from Sydney and Melbourne had also transferred there — so — it was not the usual well established capital as Melbourne, or any other capital was. Rather like Islamabad I suppose — a created capital. We went round the "Beehive" — the new Parliament House — a very impressive modern building. On this visit we found Canberra much more interesting than we had done 10 years earlier.

We also had quite a few friends in Canberra — that we had met in Kuala Lumpur when we were there. Jeanne and Norman Mason who had been with the Australian Embassy. It seemed hard to believe that there were three other couples from Kuala Lumpur living in Canberra, with whom I used to play bridge. They all entertained us, either at home or taking us to various places of interest which made it a wonderful visit and we crammed so much into it.

We were very impressed with ALL the homes which were so much better than we had in the U.K. but I suppose with the climate they could afford to have larger rooms — with large patios, swimming pools and the like. In the U.K. it seemed our one thought was to get something small that we could easily heat — and as for swimming pools — who would want one unless it was heated — and that would cost a bomb.

The next day we hired a car and visited the Art Gallery, the High Court, Black Mountain, toured the National Museum, the American Monument, and visited Blundells Cottage. We wondered why we hadn't visited these tourist spots on our earlier visit.

It was time for us to get back to Sydney in time to catch our flight to Auckland, so had booked on the De Lux coach again. When the coach drew into the station, they were the same drivers that had brought us from Adelaide.    They recognised us whilst we were having a coffee at the Coach Station and came over and quietly suggested that we wait until the following day to return to Sydney, as they had a lot of "junkies" on board — and they thought we'd be upset!    We couldn't wait for the next day's coach as we had a plane to catch, so — joined the coach and hoped all would be well.

There were five of these youngsters on board, all with a glazed look and I saw two of them injecting themselves which really alarmed me.    I was even more alarmed when one of them came and sat next to me!    He said I reminded him of his Mother — and I just prayed he loved her and hadn't got a "hate Mum" campaign on at that time!

However, on the whole they gave us no trouble — they did wander up and down the coach repeatedly and kept falling over and changing the cassette on the coach, then turning up the volume, which the driver carefully turned down as soon as they went back to their seats. They were too far gone to even notice — but how sad that youngsters can become so addicted and consequently so stupid.

We were more than glad when we got back to Sydney with no undue incidents.    On arrival we spent another super weekend with Brian and and managed to catch up on our washing in readiness for the flight to New Zealand on the 5th February, where we were met by Lillian and Bill Hamilton at Auckland — dare I say — "also Karachi Yacht Club members".

We drove up to the Bay of Islands along the popular Hibiscus coast through Walkworth with its Satellite Tracking Station and once off the main highway, visited the historic Matakohe Kauri Museum. Lillian had booked for us all to stay at Paihia for five days which was heavenly.    During this time we went to view the Karri Tree, the Museum at Waimemku, Waitangi and Kiri Kiri where the Maori Treaty was signed.    We took the Ferry to Russel and back in the same day.

Then the most exciting trip was on the coach to Cape Reinga, the northernmost tip of North Island.    The coach returned on the beach — all 90 kms of it!    Quite exciting as we had huge sand dunes, as high as a three storey house, on the left of us and of course the sea on the right and at times we were actually driving IN the sea — with no alternative. We saw one lone Penguin sitting in the middle of the beach — and the sight of a solitary penguin standing in the middle of nowhere caused the coach driver to stop and approach the wee fellow who didn't move, even though the coach passed within 10 yards of him and you got the impression he was waiting for the bus!

We left Lillian and Bill at Paihai to continue their holiday, and we drove back to Auckland and then on to Hamilton where we met up with Ian and Jean Strachan who we also knew in Karachi.

The following day saw us at Rotorua — the Thermal area. We booked into a super Motel where we had our own Thermal Pool on the verandah and there was nothing nicer than plunging into the pool at the end of a busy day — it was invigorating. We toured the official Thermal Pools with geysers, which kept erupting and were obviously piping hot. We saw a couple of Maori Hakka Dances which are very spectacular; the only other time I had seen this was at the beginning of the All Blacks Rugger matches.

Our route was then on to Lake Taupo where we spent a couple of nights which we loved — the Motel was actually on the Lake and the amazing thing was that when we wandered outside with our cup of tea at tea time, we met the people who had moved into the Chalet next door to us. Would you believe it — they were people that knew Ken from his days in Calcutta, so there was a lot of chatting and catching up on news.

Taupo is a tourist centre, half way between Aukland and Wellington and is used in the summer by tourists to explore the Volcanic Plateau — and in winter — it is a wonderful centre for Trout fishing.

That evening we had dinner at Taurango with Leslie and John Michael Davis, whom we knew in Malaysia — they are New Zealanders so naturally returned here when their tour of duty in Kuala Lumpur was over. He is now running The Kiwi Fruit Wine Co.

Then on to Napier, Hastings and down to Wellington which was a disaster from the point of view that it was the only place we had difficulty in getting accommodation. We'd actually started looking for a Motel just after lunch, but where ever we went we were greeted with "No Vacancy" signs and by 5.p.m. we had stopped being fussy about wanting something overlooking the water with two rooms. In desperation around 6.p.m. we managed to get a cancellation — but all had to share one room!

We did have time that evening to meet Brian Sivell — the last time we had seen him was at a Xmas party in our flat in Karachi when he entertained us with his version of "Lemon Clapping" — and I can tell you if you haven't played this game with Brian — you have missed a lot! We also met up with Audrey and Mike Thomson, also ex Karachi who had been transferred to Wellington.

They invited us to their lovely home overlooking the Bay and have since decided to retire in New Zealand, though they are both Scots, but obviously the allure of New Zealand supercedes that of Scotland.

We were told by the Motel in Wellington when booking in that we could only have the room for one night and as we could find nothing else decided to take the Ferry over to Picton on South Island, where we hoped accommodation would be easier.

Incidently, three quarters of the New Zealand population of 3.3 million live on North Island, so you will gather that south Island is very sparsely populated. The mountainous south Island is fringed by extensive plains. Running the whole length of the Island are the snow capped peaks of the Southern Alps. Twenty of these peaks exceed 10,000 feet, and at the higher levels there are ice fields and glaciers. It is quite breath taking.

The American Motel at Picton were very happy to give us a couple of rooms — and the next day we hired a car and drove to Nelson to the home of Phyl and Tony Bennett — also from Karachi. They had arranged a BBQ for us with some of their sailing friends in one of their favourite picnic spots. But the weather was terrible so this had to be cancelled and we all gathered at their home and had a good party — which Phyl and Tony are renowned for.

Unfortunately they only had one spare bedroom and so Ruth was booked into a Guest House nearby. I was very concerned about this as I felt we should have all stayed together in a Motel but the Bennetts had prepared our room and made the booking for Ruth so really couldn't do much about it.

We had planned to spend a couple of days with them, but the weather was terrible so we decided to use the time to drive to our next port of call. We were glad we decided to do this as it gave us more time to investigate other areas.

We went to Westport, and Greymouth where we spent the night at the Ora Nui Motel which was super, as were all the Motels in New Zealand. The next day we continued to Hokitika famous for its greenstone. We drove through the spectacular gorges of the Waimakariri River on to Arthur's Pass, and booked into the Glazier View Motel in Franz Joseph.

The owners persuaded us that we couldn't possibly leave the area without taking a Helicopter flight on to the Franz Josef Glacier. Whilst we thought it was rather expensive, we certainly had our money's worth and share of excitement as the Pilot flew virtually INTO the side of the cliff of ice and took evasive action at the very last moment, missing the cliffs literally by inches, and then zooming up and down all the various gullies.

Finally we landed on the Glacier and walked stealthily on this mighty mass of ice and saw the effects of its unbridled power, whilst slipping and sliding on sheets of thick ice. The ice formations on the top of the Glacier, when the sun was shining, were really spectacular. We could see Mount Tasman and Mount Cook, the latter is the highest mountain in New Zealand over 12,000 feet. It was thrilling and mind boggling and we declared we would do this again, but of course time did not permit.

After this excitement, we drove to Queenstown where we had wonderful accommodation at the Aroha Motel flats — with two bedrooms a large living room, kitchen, two bathrooms and near some good eating areas.    Frankly — if anyone was restricted in time when visiting New Zealand, I would recommend their making Queenstown their centre, there is so much to see and do in that area.

On the 19th February, 1985 we left the Motel at 7.a.m. to take a coach tour to Milford Sound the Glacier-sculpted inlet of the Tasman Sea about 160 miles north west of Dunedin.    The spectacular cone of Mitre Peak rising 5551 feet from the sea dominates the entrance to the Sound.    There is a very high rainfall in this area, which feeds hundreds of streams and waterfalls — hence the high Bowen Falls which are over 500 feet high and are spectacular.

Several of the people on the coach were going to walk the full length of the Milford Track — which is 34 miles long and is described as the most beautiful walk in the world.    We were so lucky with the weather as so often the Milford Sound is covered in mist and you can't see a thing, but we had gorgeous weather and had two hours on the Sound in a launch which meant we saw it from both angles — both spectacular — overlooked by "The Remarkables".

Our tour guide tried to persuade us to go to Kevin Heights to see a Deer Park there — but as we live two minutes away from Richmond Park in Surrey, which abounds with all varieties of Deer — we weren't very enthusiastic about this proposition and much preferred absorbing the sheer beauty of the Sound, and enjoying the launch trip.

On our return from the launch, we sat and had coffee and watched the people who had actually walked the Track return, and receive their certificates to prove it.    These were the people who had started the walk three days earlier!    Not all the participants were young by any means — one old duck was nearly 70!    I suppose people get their kicks in different directions — but that wouldn't be my scene. The cost was prohibitive as of course you have accommodation at the Camps en route and they charge you over NZ$480 for the privilege!

For my part — I was quite happy to take in the wonderful scenery and had no desire to participate in the walk.    Perhaps if we had had more time AND were a little younger, it would have appealed.

One evening we had dinner at Gondola and went up in a cable car, which was cold, but exciting.

The most exciting event of the whole trip though — which in retrospect, I think we were MAD to have done — was a trip on a Jet boat on the Shot-over River! Twenty five minutes of sheer excitement or perhaps "terror" would be more apt, whilst this boat skidded and weaved its way at fantastic speeds through narrow gorges with over-hanging cliffs, which the driver missed by TENTHS of an inch — not even inches! As if that was not enough excitement for one day, we then saw another jet boat approaching, head on, at high speed, but just before we crashed — which appeared inevitable, the drivers seemed to reverse throttle until both boats were facing the other direction on one long skid. The drivers added to our terror by pretending that they too were worried and let out a few expletives! The passengers in both boats audibly sighed with relief and amazement when we didn't actually collide!

Our driver really did everything but turn the boat over — but told us that he had actually done that the week before! The crew admitted that they had had one or two fatalities AFTER we returned! It is something I wouldn't have missed, but wouldn't agree to do again!

After this, with literally trembling knees, we walked to Arthur's Point and watched the White Rafters return. We were told by one of them that White Rafting was even more hair raising than the Shot-over Jet!

We were sad to leave Queenstown — as it had been the centre for a number of beautiful and exciting trips.

The next day we drove to Invercargill — which is on an inlet of the Foveaux Strait in the extreme south of South Island. All I can say, after all the beauty we had seen, is that Invercargill was very disappointing.

We decided to go to Timaru via Dunedin, hoping to see Keith and Nanette Wilson again before leaving New Zealand. I think I mentioned that Keith and Nanette were the first people I had known to have three babies under the age of 12 months. The twins were born in Calcutta and they already had a wee girl of under a year. I was shattered at what was involved in coping with three babies! It was rather like a conveyor belt — as soon as one was fed and changed — the next one needed attention and after that the third, by which time the first baby was again yelling for attention! They coped admirably, but it was wonderful to have seen these three babies now grown up into beautiful young ladies.

Keith is a very gifted artist and there is no end to the scenery that New Zealand offers in that direction, though he and Nanette seemed to go overseas fairly regularly where he had more "inspiration". This same "inspiration" prompted Keith to write a very illuminating book covering Nanette and his travels which is beautifully illustrated with some of his excellent paintings and sketches.

Nanette had her own hobby — she bred and reared Deer which, let's face it, was unusual, but interesting and obviously lucrative.

Unfortunately this time we found the Wilsons had gone on one of their overseas trips but we were welcomed by Nanette's sister who took us round the farm and gave us afternoon tea. We gathered Nanette was still breeding Reindeer — and Keith was still painting, but they continued to go overseas about once a year so that Keith could complete a portfolio on another part of the world.

We then headed off to Christchurch which is a lovely city but we could not dally for long as we had to keep up with our itinerary, in order to meet Tony Bennett, so that he could take us to his brother's property at Medina.

Tony was waiting for us when we arrived at the rendezvous and he took us to Sally and David Handyside's farm (his nephew and wife) at Canterbury. They made us so very welcome and we spent a very pleasant evening with them.

This property was really in the "woop woop" — and to get there we drove off the main road onto a dirt track, for what seemed to be miles (and obviously was). Their children Selena, Peter and Anna were taken to school by plane, piloted by their father — in fact it seemed they used the plane as we use a car.

It was a lovely spot to visit but I would hate to live so far off the beaten track. I reckon that I am a "townie" and whilst I enjoy the countryside — I would not be so keen to live in it and would feel "cut off" from the outside world.

Mind you in this day and age with all the crime, drugs, murder, rape, graffiti, and bashing of grannies, or anyone else that gets in the way of to-day's young offenders — perhaps this is the only sensible way to live!

We then drove back to Picton, stopping to see the seals frolicking and cavorting just off the shore in their hundreds, they really appeared to be putting on a cabaret for us! This delayed us a little whilst we took some photos of these cute little creatures. Tony left us at Picton which is a very picturesque town on the head of beautiful Queen Charlotte Sound.

We handed the car back here and again took this enjoyable Ferry trip back to Wellington where we picked up another hire car. They had this very good arrangement to avoid having to take the car on a car ferry, you left it on North Island and took the ferry to South Island where you picked up another car, and vice versa.

Lillian and Bill were still up North and so we drove up to Palmerston and Wanganui on to Lake Taupo where we booked into a very pleasant Motel on the Lake. We all took our cup of tea and sat at the Lake side and were joined by a group of other visitors who it transpired Ken had known in business. What a small world!

We then drove to Tokaanu, south of Lake Taupo where three active volcanoes, Mount Tongariro, Ngauruhoe and Ruapehu dominate the area. We decided this was such a lovely area that we would spend another night at Lake Taupo This is a very popular trout fishing lake and nearby are the thundering Huka Falls, and we booked into another super Motel on the south side of the Lake. (Previously we had been on the North side) Again we wandered down to the lake and were joined by a couple of visitors staying in the next Unit.    Would you believe it we discovered the husband was a great friend of Gordon Petrie.    Gordon was Ken's old school friend from Aberdeen.    What a small world it is, that on our two visits to Lake Taupo we should meet up with U.K. friends staying in the same Motel!

The next night we spent at Ngabawania, north of Hamilton and visited the Waitomo Caves, and the Glow-worm Grotto.    We went round these in a boat and were really thrilled and intrigued with the glow worms yet again.    They fascinated us just as much as they had done in South Island.

Then back to Auckland, the "City of Sails" and in the evening went down to the harbour where Peter Blake's boat the "Lion of New Zealand" was anchored.    We booked into a Motel for the night and handed back the car at the airport having had another fascinating visit which I thoroughly recommend.

We felt sad that our time in this superb country had come to an end.

We all flew back to Sydney, Ruth going on to the U.K. on the 2nd March and we left on the 7.p.m. bus the same evening for — yes, you can guess — Burleigh Heads!

On arrival we found "The Stubbies" competition in full swing which took place immediately in front of Goodwin Towers where of course we were staying yet again!    This is an international surfing competition — and believe me the standards are very high.

After several heavenly weeks in Burleigh, during which time Ken was approached by a General Insurance Company in Manila enquiring if he would do a job for them in Manila.    This sounded a challenge and what we had seen of Manila we had enjoyed.    We therefore returned to Singapore, via Sydney, and stayed with Molly and Hugh Brown for a few days.

We were able to see quite a lot of Linda but heard from my niece Diane that her husband Ismail was ill and she asked if we could go up to see him.    So we had a very quick trip to Malaysia — where there were still a lot of old friends that we knew — and Diane

476

entertained us as Ismail had been unable to return home from hospital.

I was shocked to find when we visited Ismail, that there was an anteroom or general waiting room, outside his private room, which was PACKED with visitors, all waiting to see Ismail! Most of whom I gathered visited daily. Had he not been feeling ill when he entered hospital I was sure that this invasion would certainly make him feel worse! I suppose this is one of the differences in our different cultures. If we are ill, only our very nearest and dearest would be welcome at our bedside — or for that matter "allowed" by the hospital to visit. I really shuddered at the noise and time these various visits took — which I am sure could not be appreciated by the patient!

We had two weeks in Hong Kong as we had planned to spend this time with Fiona, though sadly she was not there when we arrived, having gone to London on a business visit — but we managed about ten days with her and she actually had to leave for Shanghai the day before we departed for Manila on the 29th April,1985.

## SEVENTEEN
### *Time in the Phillipines*
### *29 April 1985—22 August 1987*

As indicated, whilst in Burleigh Heads, Ken had been asked whether he would be prepared to go to Manila as Consultant to a General Insurance Company for a two year period. After our holiday in Australia, rather than return home, we thought this an attractive suggestion — and deferred retirement once again!

To help us settle in the Philippines we had been sent a very informative booklet about life there and I feel the chapter on "The Do's and Don'ts in the Philippines" is worthy of note.

We were told to give Philippinoes or, as spelt in the book, Filipinos — a way out of a situation so that he can save face and avoid embarrassment. Embarrassing him will cause "hiya" or loss of face.

### Do's

*Do* avoid wearing rubber sandals on special occasions. Shoes are a sign of importance to the event. (Hence Imelda's 3,000 pairs)

*Do* issue invitations, especially for food, at least three times: villagers are taught it is proper to refuse the first time or two. Insistence is a sign that the offer or invitation is genuine.

*Do* remember that a snack (merienda) is always served as a sign of welcome and friendship.

*Do* taste a little when food is served, even if you don't care for it. When served a meal, leave a small amount on the plate. This is a sign you've had plenty and their food is enough.

*Do* give food as a gift to the sick, but not flowers. The latter is associated with death.

*Do* befriend children. This is an easy way of reaching the parents.

*Do* give little gifts (candies etc.,) to the children in the household when going home — this creates a warm feeling of caring.

*Do* respect age, as, in all Asia, age has rank over all else.

*Do* remember that the family is the most important decision-making body. No matter what the issue, whether work related or whatever, the ultimate decision will be reached by a consensus of the family members.

*Do* go to your room or where you can be alone if you wish to be quiet. Silence with company suggests your dislike for something or someone.

*Do* remember to bring a small memento or remembrance (pasalubong) for your employees when returning from a trip.

*Do* use the term, "you be the one" if you want something done, and not "you do it". In their language there are special phrases for commands.

## Don'ts

*Don't* admire an item in someone's home because the owner becomes obligated to give it to you. This seems to be more true the poorer the people.

*Don't* call anyone stupid. To villagers in particular, it's worse than cursing. Never refer to a person as an animal "you are a pig" or "you look like a monkey".

*Don't* correct an employee in public: it should be done privately or through a third person.

*Don't* ever leave without telling your host or hostess you are leaving and give a reason. This is called "getting permission".

*Don't* open a gift in public without permission from the giver.

*Don't* be surprised when children are afraid if you have a moustache. In some provinces parents scare their children into obedience by threats of being eaten by strangers with moustaches.

*Don't* use the common American signal for "O.K." — here it means money.

*Don't* use your first finger upward to call someone.   It is very degrading.

*Don't* be confused when somebody says, "he had a baby" because there is no gender in Tagalog.

*Don't* yell loudly to attract someone's attention — "psst" is the popular way.

The Philippines is the only predominantly Christian country in Asia, but even so, when Pope Paul visited Manila in 1970, an attempt was made to assassinate him.

In order to get an idea of the political background when we arrived in Manila, I give below a brief synopsis which led to the situation we found.

To regress a little, the Philippines was invaded by the Japanese in 1941.   Japanese troops conquered Manila on the 2nd January, 1942 and the brutal Japanese military rule continued until 1944 when General Douglas MacArthur fulfilled his promise to return, and liberated the Philippines from the Japanese.   The greatest sea battle in history was fought off the island of Leyte in 1944.

In 1946, the Philippines received full Independence, and the first President of the Republic was Manual Roxas.   The Republic was often referred to as " a piece of Latin America in the Pacific".   There was no doubt about it that the American influence was very obvious.

It has been a mystery to many people how Ferdinand Marcos and his wife Imelda ever got a foot in the door of Malacanang Palace in the first place.   It was said that Ferdinand, whilst at Law School, had been charged with murder and was released on bail in order to take his Bar examination.   Imelda was brought up in dire poverty and had no qualifications other than good looks and unnatural energy. They were married in May 1954 when she had become the beauty Queen of Manila, after, I understand, she had a scene with the umpire!

It appears that the careers of President Marcos and his First Lady owed more to the United States than anyone else. When the Philippines were in the hands of General MacArthur it was a time of opportunity and a time to accumulate fortunes by unorthodox measures — and Marcos excelled at this.

After the fall of South Vietnam, and the removal of air bases in Thailand, Marcos was indispensable to the Americans and received millions of dollars in cash from "unvouchered Funds". The only significant military installations were Subic Naval Base, on the west coast of Luzon, and the Clark Air Base. They were the twin pillars of American Military power in the Pacific, the bases from which the United States could extend its power into the Indian Ocean and the Persian Gulf.

The rapid expansion of Soviet Air and Naval bases in Vietnam ended that dominance, and the bases in the Philippines were not merely important — but priceless. Marcos made the most of this.

The U.S. tried to stop the military torture of civilians and other human rights abuses. But Marcos was a skilled blackmailer and reminded the U.S. that without their continued support, these leases might not be renewed! That is why, as late as March 1985, the State Department did not want to see the basic alliance disturbed and therefore did not want Marcos out. A State memorandum at that time pointed out that "while Marcos was part of the problem, he was also necessarily part of the solution"!

The U.S. never feared an outright military victory by the Communists — not so long as they lacked a supply of foreign weapons — but they did fear a political victory if the Communist Party should become strong enough to impose an anti-American orientation upon any Government which succeeded Marcos.

No wonder that Imelda and her eldest daughter were able to spend $3.3 million in three weeks on a visit to the U.S.A. and doubtless the reason that the Marcos family were able to flee to the United States when Marcos was overthrown!

When we arrived in the Philippines in 1985 President Ferdinand Marcos had been President since 1965. When he came to power he found the country to be in a chaotic state, corruption and crime had become the order of the day. The situation didn't improve, so in 1972 Marcos declared Martial Law and within a short time changes were apparent, and we were told that guns disappeared from the streets, crime decreased and some improvement in public health was made. However Martial Law was abolished in 1981, but Marcos continued his dictatorial form of Government with so called "Presidential Decrees".

Marcos was confirmed as Head of State in 1981 and Parliamentary elections were held in 1984, but the result was contested and allegations of vote-rigging were loud and many.

The reason for the surprising success of the opposition was not only the dissatisfaction of a large proportion of the population, over the state of the economy, but also the response of many voters to the murder of the Opposition politician Benigno Aquino as he arrived back at the airport on his return from exile in August 1983.

This dissatisfaction caused the snap election of 1986, where the Opposition united for the first time under Aquino's widow Corazon Cory Aquino.

Ken took up his appointment with this General Insurance Company on the 29th April, 1985, and we found all this intrigue most interesting, though at times — alarming.

Our introduction was quite amusing. We were put into the Peninsula Hotel, and when booking in we were asked by the Reception Clerk, if we would like a room on the top floor which had the advantage of a Helicopter Pad — or we could have a room on the 4th floor, where in an emergency we could jump out of the window onto the roof of the second floor restaurant! Of these two alternatives we opted for the 4th floor — as judging by the time it took for a porter to take our luggage when we arrived at the Hotel, — we didn't feel that a helicopter would give us all that advantage in a crisis! At least this gave us an idea of what we could expect!

As Ken had not yet been issued with a Work Permit — (in spite of their having known for three months that we were arriving in the

Philippines) we were not allowed to bring in our freight, but as we were to learn — decisions took a long time in the Philippines! This meant we had to live out of the two suitcases we'd brought with us.

Our Passports had also been taken off us as they told us these were required for the Work Permit application. I hoped to go to Kuala Lumpur in July for a relative's wedding — but was told that it may not be possible to get the Passports back in time. We hadn't yet learnt what they really meant was that there was a price for getting them back!

The people involved in getting Ken's Work Permit also told us that we may have to return to the U.K. before the Permit could be issued! Frankly, this didn't worry us unduly — as all our expenses would be paid for the trip AND we were flying First Class on this Contract. When the "powers that be" discovered that we were not prepared to grease anyone's palm — they suddenly decided that the Permit could after all be issued whilst we were in the Philippines! We soon caught on to the fact that everything had its price.

Most of our friends lived in one of the "Villages" — which did not mean a village as we think of it — but a large enclosed area where people lived in lovely homes. There was a security wall around the village with only one or two entrances which were patrolled by guards at all times. The guards took the number of your car when you entered the village and when you were leaving and asked you who you were visiting. If they had any doubts about your intentions, they would ring up the house and ask if you were expected?

A good system — but surprisingly enough there was still the odd burglary — but all in all it worked quite well. Only once did we have trouble going through the barrier when we were questioned as to our intent — guess we must have looked particularly scruffy that day — or perhaps the guard was hoping we'd "pay an entrance fee!"

Accommodation was a problem, and it took us some time to find something suitable. As there was only the two of us, we really didn't want a house — as they all seemed so large with even larger gardens and we'd already realised that security would be a big problem, so we opted for a flat. However, all the flats we liked were way above our Rent allowance and it seemed that landlords would rather keep their properties vacant than reduce the rent. In the meantime we continued to live at the Manila Peninsula.

Eventually we found a very pleasant penthouse flat in Twin Towers near the Inter-Continental Hotel in Makati. As flats go it was quite large — with three good sized bedrooms, two bathrooms and a patio which stretched all the way round the flat. But of course the rental was far above our allowance.

We indicated to the landlady our problem about the rent but she refused to take less. Therefore I was more than surprised when a few days later she came to the Hotel when I was in the pool swimming. After waiting for me to come out, she said that on consideration, if our Company would pay two years' rent in advance, we could have the flat for the reduced rental!

We weren't quite sure about the two years' rent in advance, that was a lot of money in a troubled Manila where one never knew how long any of us could stay — so there was a compromise and finally the landlady accepted one year's rent in advance!

The flat was on the corner of Ayala Avenue and E.D.S.A. (Epifanio delos Santos Avenue). It was central — modern, nicely furnished, fully carpeted and air conditioned throughout with a swimming pool, Gym and Sauna — so there really was no need to join a Club.

From this penthouse flat we had an unrestricted view of EDSA — the main thoroughfare north, and from the back of the flat views over to Makati.

It was a fairly regular sight to see Imelda Marcos arrive at the Makati shopping centre in a single decker bus, which had been converted into a changing room with toilet and bathroom facilities. She would permit her driver to park this in any "No Parking" area for as long as it suited her. Often she would leave the "bus" in an entirely different outfit to the one she had been wearing when shopping. This obvious ostentation did not go down well with the Filipinos who were struggling to make ends meet.

But — in spite of all the corruption and favouritism shown to a few by the Marcos's — there was still a nucleus of their followers who supported them. Chiefly I might add from their home town of Ilocos Norte, as the people still remembered how Marcos rewarded his province for their support, by providing roads and facilities which were the envy of the neglected areas elsewhere in the Philippines. They also received handsome gratuities for voting for him!

Socially, I had a very busy time: I played a lot of bridge and made many new friends and several of us would get together during the week and plan a visit to Angeles City, where the U.S. forces Clark Air Base was situated. I hasten to add — not to see the airmen but because there was always a ready market with the forces in situ — prices were reasonable and one could obtain items you did not see in Manila.

The Filipinos are renowned for their intricate sewing detail and handicrafts — and at Xmas time a trip to Angeles City was a must.

Here you could purchase the most beautiful hand made items which one rarely saw in a city — or if you did — you couldn't afford them! I was continually being asked to send boxes of these items to a friend who had a shop in H.K. — but found the prices in Manila cheaper than she could get them for in H.K. or elsewhere. She was very sad when we finally left.

Golf could never be easier or cheaper to play than in the Philippines where there were so many golf courses. We never booked a time and rarely did we have to wait to Tee off. We were also permitted to play on the golf courses attached to the Military camps at Vilamore Air Base and Bonafacio for a ridiculously small fee, and as these were very close to where we were living, we were inclined to use these. In fact Jane Roberts and I had just left Vilamore Golf Club when a bomb was dropped — presumably by the Guerrillas. The course was closed to the public after this incident for quite a time!

The Filipinos are a happy race and just as the Japanese had difficulty in pronouncing the letter "r" and confused it with "l", I found the Filipinos had difficulty pronouncing the letter "p". The first time I was out with our very nice elderly driver and asked him to park the car outside the supermarket, I was a little surprised when he said "you can't fart here Ma'am"! It took me some time to realise the problems they had in pronouncing "p" — and was equally amused when Lourdes the maid, asked me if I was going to a "farty" that night!

When I told her the correct pronunciation she looked puzzled and asked me why we said "foto" when the word began with a "p" and was spelt "photo" and so why couldn't she say "farty" when the word also began with a "p"????

One of our friends had been driving south through the cane fields with his wife and young children when they were stopped and asked to get out of the car at gun point. Money and the keys of his car were demanded — and the insurgents drove off leaving our friend in this remote area. It was unwise to approach any of the villages as they too might have been involved. About two hours later another European picked them up.

Only a fortnight after this there was a similar incident when the driver had been stopped and shot! When we heard of these incidents we decided home was best, and we would restrict ourselves to exploring the immediate vicinity!

Shortly after arriving in Manila in July 1985, I went to a Malay wedding in Kuala Lumpur. The mother of the bride was English but had to become a Muslim before her marriage to a Malay — funnily enough the bride who was also part Malay was marrying an English boy, who too, had to become a Muslim before the wedding would be permitted.

The bride had been at school in England since she was 10 and then went onto Medical College in the U.K. She and her fiancé had been studying medicine in London and had both now qualified. As I was the only really close relative on the bride's side, her mother particularly wanted me to attend the wedding. So I was delighted when I got my Passport back and was able to attend.

We had seen quite a lot of the bride and her fiancé during our time in the U.K. and had become very attached to them both. She was a very loving, caring individual and in many ways like her Mother. It was obvious to me from the start that there was a good possibility of her marrying this English boy — though I realised there would be many complications.

Whilst she had been educated in England — she had been brought up as a strict Muslim and therefore could not marry anyone that had not embraced Islam. Her fiancé, realising this — had become a Muslim the previous year by attending a Mosque in Woking where he received tuition and the religion was explained in great detail. He was eventually accepted into the Muslim faith and was given an additional name of Mohammed to add to his own.

When he arrived in Kuala Lumpur for the wedding, the certificate he produced from the Imam at Woking was not acceptable — and even though the previous year when out on holiday, suspecting that there might be a problem with the Certificate he had from Woking, — he had again attended the Mosque in Kuala Lumpur and obtained a further certificate. He therefore had two "pieces of paper" with official seals from the respective Imams. They naturally assumed this would be acceptable.

All plans for the three day wedding were well on the way — in fact the preparations had started months earlier. Many of the relatives and close friends had spent literally hours making artificial flowers which had to be created so that a hard boiled and beautifully decorated egg could be added a couple of days before each ceremony. One of these flowers, with egg attached, would be given to each guest at each of the ceremonies. This meant that over 3,000 flowers had to be made, not forgetting of course all the flowers required for the decoration of the house, garden and Hotel, where the third ceremony was to take place.

The colour of these flowers and the decoration on the eggs,

matched the colour scheme for each ceremony, which of course was very different! Obviously a lot of hard work went into this, and a great deal of colour planning.

Whilst these floral arrangements were beautiful, I couldn't help thinking that had it been left to me, I would have gone out and bought some arrangements! As it was there were at least 20 relatives in the house each day making the flowers, and of course they had to be provided with a meal! A tremendous amount of work was involved.

The 3,000 eggs could only be boiled a couple of days before the ceremonies to assure freshness — and then painted gold, silver, red and white and glued to the stamens of the flowers. (We all got in on this act which took hours squatting on the floor with about 50 close relatives and friends). I am ashamed to say that my production rate was by far the worst, but then the Malay ladies had all been brought up and shown how to do these from an early age. The eggs of course are a sign of fertility.

Whilst living in Malaysia we had been to many such weddings — but always as a guest — just partaking of the meal, leaving our little red packet (given in place of presents) received our egg and then left. I never realised how much work had gone into the Reception. I was quite exhausted the two days before the wedding as we started at 7.a.m. and, besides the "work party", various guests kept appearing to wish the happy couple well and to enquire if they could take part in the decorating, and they all received "makan" (food) of some sort.

Enough of that — the real excitement started when I was met at the Airport by the bride apologising that her parents and the groom were not there to meet me. There had been this crisis that particular day (three days before the wedding) when the Imam (Priest) had refused to accept the groom's certificates and wanted him to sit an exam, which would be wholly conducted in Arabic — AND — horror of horrors, he wanted evidence that he had been circumcised!

I think at that stage the groom must have wished that they had eloped in the U.K. — but the bride being a dutiful daughter would not dream of doing this.   So.. the poor groom had started to learn the prayers and responses that he would have to make in Arabic at the ceremonies.   Not speaking the language he had to have the words translated into Pidgin English so he could get his tongue round the pronunciation!   The bride's father acted as an interpreter but there was no way in the world that he could possibly learn all he had to in the time available.

So..... this is when I really get very cynical about the religion and its requirements.   Through influence — pressure was brought to bear on the Imam at least to indicate which questions the groom would be asked at the exam — so he didn't have to learn everything in Arabic.   They settled on three questions and of course the responses he should make!

As for the circumcision — devious methods were used which made it possible for a Certificate to be issued by a Malay Doctor to say that he had verified that the groom had been circumcised! Naturally he hoped this would be accepted and further proof not demanded as — he had not been circumcised and he didn't feel that prior to going on a honeymoon was quite the right time to have it done!

For the next three days we saw little of the poor groom — he was up early studying with a tutor in the mornings from 8.a.m. to 1.p.m. and then again in the evening from 6.p.m. to 8.p.m. and he would then stay up until the early hours trying to memorise, what, to him, seemed like Mumbo Jumbo.

His exam was Friday morning and I'm glad to say he passed with flying colours — (perhaps droopy flying colours) so the Wedding could proceed.   He still had to get the responses for the actual Nikka (Wedding ceremony) mastered.

In the meantime the rest of us collected the various wedding outfits that had been made for the various ceremonies — all very spectacular and collected the tickets for their honeymoon on a tropical island off the coast of Malaysia.   We were then asked to collect literally over one hundred Persian rugs from the homes of friends and relatives, which would cover all the floors — not only in the house but in the Shamiana (large tent in the garden). All the family members produced as many rugs as they could spare — and then the Throne had to be arranged with all its various decorations and a yellow satin cushion for the Malay Queen Mother who was to attend the final ceremony. She was a close friend of one of the Aunts and of the bride and had participated in the engagement ceremony.

She was the First Malaysian Queen and her presence did make things even more complicated — as protocol had to be observed and I was given instructions on how to greet her when presented and told it was considered rude to turn your back on The Queen when leaving the rostrum! As I have the greatest difficulty getting up and down steps when I can see where I am going — doing this backwards was hair raising!

This was coupled with the formalities of approaching the Throne to bless the happy pair — first with rose petals which had to be showered over their hands which were cupped on an ornate pillow (which had also been made in the house)— then the happy couple had to be sprinkled with rose water — we made the usual "amnesty" (hands together) and retreated, — acknowledging the Queen on the return to my special spot on the floor! Everyone sat on the floor — and we " old ducks" had the greatest difficulty getting up and down and realised just how stiff the old bones had become!

For the first ceremony which was the Nikka ceremony, the Bride had to remain in the Bridal Chamber. (I should add that all the female members of the family had been involved in decorating the bridal bed with flowers and ribbons — it really looked beautiful and far too elaborate to actually sleep in!) The bride was dressed by the female members of the family — and for this occasion wore a very ornate pale blue lace Baju with a lace veil over her head and part of her face.

Whilst she stayed alone in the Bridal Chamber, the bridegroom was sitting cross legged on the floor in one of the living rooms, dressed in a white Malay outfit with a black topi in front of the Amir who was chanting away in Arabic. You can imagine the tension amongst all of us who knew what an ordeal he had been through — wondering if he would "muff" his responses. Praise be — he got through the ceremony with only one slight stumble which was quickly corrected by one of the male family members.

At this stage the bride was brought down the stairs and was seated on a bridal type throne in the other section of the very large "L" shaped Lounge. The groom was then brought into the section of the room where the bride was sitting and they exchanged wedding rings. During this whole ceremony the participants looked very serious and subdued — in fact B....y miserable — but it would be considered precocious of the bride to look happy! After this short ceremony the bride went back to the Bridal Chamber on her own whilst the Groom returned to his half of the room when food was produced by the female members of the family. A most wonderful mixture of Malay goodies — plate upon plate all of which had been made in the home.

This short ceremony was only for family members and very close friends, and I suppose no more than 80 people attended. After all the guests had left the bride was allowed down to join the rest of us. I was told that in a traditional wedding this would not have been permitted and I remember the bride's mother telling me that at her wedding she was locked in a room for five days and only allowed out to participate in the various ceremonies!

The bridegroom was then despatched to the bride's brother's house, where he had been staying — not having any family in Malaysia.

He subsequently confessed to me that he had no idea that he would have to do so much in order to become a Muslim, and he had not told his parents of his change of faith, which he knew his Mother would object to as she was a Pillar of strength in her own church — not to mention being a Sunday School teacher!

The following evening there was a further ceremony which took place in the house and which seemed to be for friends who would not be attending the Banquet at the Hotel. The Bride was dressed in a white wedding dress as one would do in Europe but had a diamond Tiara on her head with the veil attached. She was literally "dripping" with diamonds, all but one having been lent by the various family members. I was later told that between the bride and the groom they were wearing over a Million Pounds worth of jewellery

I found the whole occasion fascinating and was actually invited to be present when the various Aunts arrived in the bedroom to dress the bride, each bringing their own little boxes of jewellery — and she was permitted to chose what she would wear for each ceremony. The same ritual of choosing the jewellery took place for each ceremony.

The bridegroom for this occasion wore a suit and looked like a normal bridegroom and these were the photographs that were subsequently sent to his parents. The other ceremonies when he was wearing the Malay ceremonial dress — were not sent home even though he looked rather splendid!

This was a very nice ceremony — no hassles with Arabic prayers and the speeches were given in English, (the only part of the ceremony that I actually understood). There were a few prayers in Arabic and then a Reception dinner for about 300. Tables had been arranged in the garden under a Marquee and all the food had been prepared in the house!

Even though this was considered the "actual official marriage" the bride and groom were not allowed to spend the night together — which I thought was very hard. But the groom returned to the house he had been staying in for the whole visit, quite bemused at the number of guests there had been in spite of being told it was a "small" gathering!

In the late afternoon of the following day, I was asked if I would go over to the other house where the bridegroom was staying. I think the idea was that as his parents were not there and I was the only English lady in the party, they felt it would be appropriate for me to arrive with the Bridegroom's entourage. As this meant I had to leave the Bride's house in evening dress ready for the evening festivities which were scheduled for 8.p.m. — I was not too enthusiastic — as it was extremely hot and I had hoped to remain in the air conditioning until the ceremony started, but felt perhaps the bridegroom would appreciate a little moral support. As it was I nearly ruined the ceremony for him!

The house I was taken to, which was about 15 kms from the Bride's home, belonged to one of the Bride's Aunts who was kindly holding a Reception there on behalf of the Bridegroom's family. A meal was laid out, Buffet style and I suppose about 100 guests were in this very large house.

There was no sign of the bridegroom, and I knew very few of the guests — but I gathered that he was upstairs being "prepared" by the Aunt (acting as his Mother). After being washed in oils (don't quite know who did that!) he was dressed in the full Malaysian Formal Dress in blue and silver brocade, including a turban like adornment on his head which was decorated with a 4.1/2 carat diamond! — so obviously all this took time!

Eventually he appeared and seemed quite delighted to see me, and after the usual formalities he came and sat next to me. We had a good old natter and a surreptitious chuckle together — he wondered what his contemporaries at the Hospital back in England would think if they could see him now — and we had quite a long time to sit and talk.

Frankly, I learnt far more about Islam and Mohammedism from him, after all his lessons, than I had done from my neice over many years, in spite of our being very close. But then I think she and her parents obviously viewed it far more seriously than the groom did!

At last I learnt why so many Muslims I met were continually washing their hair! A good Muslim would bathe before Prayers and as they should Pray five times per day — a lot of time is spent in the bathroom. I also learnt that they should wash their hair before and after sexual contact — hence a lot of time was spent with wet hair!

The time came for us all to leave for the Bride's house — and it

493

was here I very nearly committed a frightful faux pas. He seemed very nervous and pent up and therefore in wishing him well, I raised my arm to give him a re-assuring pat on the back and to tell him it would all be worth it in the end. Fortunately he anticipated this expression of good will on my part and quickly moved and THEN told me that had I touched him — he would have been considered "unclean" and the whole rigmarole of being washed and dressed would have had to be started again!

As you can imagine there was quite a convoy of cars to get all these guests to the Bride's home. It was agreed that we would all congregate at the La Salle School which was within walking distance of the house — there was plenty of parking in the grounds of the school and we would wait there until we saw the Queen's car pass as it was essential we didn't arrive before the Queen. The road between Petalin Jaya and Kelang is always crowded and the addition of this convoy merely added to the confusion — but we got there in good time — and waited. Eventually a messenger came to confirm that the Queen had arrived — so our procession could start.

A band was waiting to lead our party to the house — the noise was unbelievable — and there were numerous children all carrying gaily coloured tree-like banners. The Best Man had a huge fan (don't really know how he could hold it) to fan the Groom with, not only now whilst walking to the house, but all through the ceremony. The Bride had a similar fan held by her sister, the Chief Bridesmaid.

As I was representing the groom's mother I was pressed to the front of this rather long procession which of course meant that when we got to the house I was the first to greet the Queen. I hadn't anticipated this until much later in the ceremony, and suddenly realised that whilst I was concentrating on the order of the formalities when greeting the Bride, I had completely forgotten the Malay word which I had been told to address the Queen. So — I thought the only thing to do was to greet her as though she were our Royal family — addressed her as "Your Majesty" — did a little curtsy and went on my way to make the official greetings to the rest of the welcoming party.

I then took up my position on the floor with the rest of the VIP guests; there were over 600 guests seated outside at tables waiting for the Banquet to start AFTER the bridal pair had been blessed by the close family and guests inside the house.

The ritual for this blessing was again to approach the Throne on which the pair were sitting, scatter rose petals in their cupped hands, then sprinkle them with a little Rose Water, take a pinch of caraway type seeds to eat, and I gave the bride a peck on the cheek before turning and walking down the steps to my spot on the floor, taking care that at no time did I turn my back on the Queen!

After this ceremony we were led to the Banquet Table, the Bride and Groom sitting with one chair between them, which was for the Queen. I sat on the right of the Groom but neither the bride or groom sat for long at the Banquet but mingled amongst the tables along with many other family members, seeing that all went well.

After the "Makan Malam" (evening dinner) — more coloured eggs were distributed and then the Bride and Groom accompanied by the bride's parents stood at the gate to take farewell — of the Queen and then within the next hour the remainder of the guests slowly left.

This left only close family members who then went inside the house and very soon started "Ronging" (the Malay dance). It was a long time since I had "Ronged" but the atmosphere — was now much more relaxed.

The next day everyone was up early — The Henna lady who came for the first ceremony arrived again to paint the bride's hands and feet with henna — and the ladies present were in turn asked to have their nails painted with Henna. I declined for as long as possible — as I knew it would take a couple of weeks for this to fade — and it did rather look like a Nicotine stain, but in the end I had to succumb. I immediately visited the ladies room and tried to remove the excess henna — merely leaving a couple of nails looking ginger. These I covered up with elastoplast after the ceremony, until the colour looked more normal.

The morning was very busy even though on this occasion the Banquet was being held in a Hotel and the food was supplied. Even so apparently, it is the custom for the bride's family members to do all the vegetable carvings for the tables, the food and the Buffet. For this, the ladies all sat out in the open, cross legged, on carpets — and although it was a covered area and therefore shaded — it was very hot and humid.

From the start, it was quite apparent that there was no way I could contribute to this very skilled art, though I kept being spurred on to at least "try".   But my Roses snapped before being finished and the Doves, which they told me were simple — looked like Boeing 707's!   Obviously Malay children learnt this art at a very early age — and the old adage that "practice makes perfect" would confirm that they had attended many similar ceremonies — and the carvings were fantastic.   Certainly professionals could not have done better than all these ladies — some of whom were very old, but very skilled.

Even so, I couldn't help thinking how much easier it would have been to forget tradition and let the Hotel's ice and vegetable carvers produce whatever was necessary!

I forgot to mention that every day the Make Up Lady came to the house to do the Bride's hair and her make up — and for each ceremony a different hair style was produced.   This last night the bride had her hair held up by 30 GOLD Ornamental Pins — and this took at least 3 hours to do!   It looked fantastic as you can imagine. For this occasion, the bride and the groom were dressed in dark blue brocade, the groom wearing a flamboyant turban or Pugri and looking very regal.

After this the bride changed into yet another lovely outfit and the groom appeared in what looked like pyjamas — but was the casual dress Muslim men seem to wear around the house.   There was more food and then around 1.30.a.m. I was asked if I would join the bride's mother and her Aunts in preparing the Wedding bed.   This meant removing all the floral decorations, taking off the elaborate cushions and covers and finally we all went to bed. I was exhausted — but the drama doesn't end here.

About 3.a.m. I was vaguely conscious of a lot of noise, but was really too tired to do anything about it. The next morning when we all gathered for breakfast I discovered that during the night they had been burgled! The burglars obviously knew that there would be a lot of money and jewellery around after a wedding as there had been no time for it to be returned to Safe Deposit boxes. Fortunately the bridal couple had turned off the air conditioning as it had been on for four days and the room was very cold — also I think they were "washing their hair" when the burglars tried to break open the locks on the outside doors.

As I mentioned earlier the bride and groom had more than 1 million pounds worth of jewellery on, not to mention the jewellery worn by the family AND all the red packets which contained money gifts. So, if the bride and groom had not been awake, the burglars would have had a wonderful haul as everyone had their air conditioning on in the bedrooms, so it was difficult hearing anything above that drone.

The burglars ran away and unfortunately were not caught, but apparently everyone gathered back in the Lounge and had copious cups of tea around 5.a.m. — but I knew nothing of this.

There were other problems associated with the wedding! There were over 16 people staying in the house and there was a water shortage in Malaysia at that time — so you can imagine how difficult that was. The bride's father bought extra water, ordered a water container to be parked at the bottom of the garden and had two lorry loads of water delivered, which at least meant we could all have a shower!

The next morning the bride and groom left for their honeymoon which was to be spent on one of the many Islands off the coast of Malaysia.

I returned to Manila via H.K. and hoped to persuade the Packers

— who were storing our freight, to allow me to remove certain items of equipment which we felt were essential for Manila. Until Ken's Work Permit was issued, the freight could not enter the Philippines. I decided when in the storage shed that, rather than open yet another crate containing the linen, that as linen was so cheap in H.K. that I would buy more sheets and towels in H.K.

In the past I had always bought linen at the Chinese Emporium in Causeway Bay, so I took a taxi down there but was shocked at the cost which had more than doubled from the time we lived in H.K. I decided that when I had finished my shopping I would try out the new section of the MTR (Mass Transit Railway). I thought it would be quicker and considerably cheaper, and I wanted to see how the new section worked!

I carefully checked the new Direction Board and found I could actually get through directly to Central where there was an exit just outside the Furama Hotel where I was staying with Gerd and Fiona in their flat.

I got settled in the train and decided I would make a note of what I had spent on all this linen. I was conscious that the train had stopped at Wanchai and I knew that there were two more stops before I got out at Central.

At the next station, Admiralty, I was suddenly aware that everyone seemed to be vacating the train — so I quickly jumped off. I asked an MTR official which train I should get for Central, and he promptly pointed to the train I had just vacated, so I jumped back in again just as the doors were shutting.

When I had time to gather my senses I suddenly realised that on this long long train in congested H.K. in the rush hour there were no other passengers! The train moved off and stopped and started a couple of times in a tunnel — and then to my horror the air-conditioning was switched off and then the engine! The thought immediately struck me that the Driver had parked the train for the evening and his shift was over!

I panicked — and started running down to the front of the train in order to catch him before he left the train. I realised I had a long way to run as the train was LONG — so I decided to press the emergency buttons hoping this would attract his attention if he hadn't left the cab. There was no response so I ran down the train pressing more buttons hoping that if I had missed the train driver then "someone" would realise there was a problem!

After running down more than three quarters of the train, I eventually heard a clomp clomp clomp of feet and so shouted "help". To my relief I spotted the train driver walking up the remainder of the train and, sounding quite cross, asked me what on earth I was doing as the train was out of service? I told him I was trying to get to Central and had got off the train at Admiralty only to be told by a member of the MTR staff to get back on again. Mind you, all the announcements were in Cantonese and very distorted. He seemed very bewildered and cross and said he didn't know what to do with me! I might add that his English was not crash hot!

He then said he would go to the cabin and ring up for instructions and told me to sit down and wait. I decided I preferred to walk with him just in case he went home leaving me in the train all night and I felt very lonely in that long empty train and it was getting very hot without air conditioning and really no fresh air!

We got to the driver's cabin and he went inside and locked the door leaving me outside. He appeared shortly and told me he was taking me back to Admiralty and back he went into the cabin. Nothing happened! He came out and said he couldn't understand it but the train would not start and asked if I had pressed any of the emergency buttons. I told him I had pressed lots! He then told me he would have to find them and turn them off or the train would not start — so would I show him the buttons I had pressed? Frankly I had pressed so many I really hadn't got a clue — but we walked down the train together and found some of the buttons I had pressed into which he inserted a key and then walked back to the driver's cabin.

I told him I had pressed many more buttons but he said he thought his key would adjust them all.   Well it didn't!

He then re-appeared muttering that this sort of thing had never happened to him before — people usually only pressed ONE emergency stop button so it appeared he would have to turn them ALL off.   He wasn't amused- and neither was I as I was expected at my Grandson's school concert and knew I would be late, and that Fiona would be concerned that I hadn't appeared.   So we walked down the train and found what we hoped were all the buttons I had pressed which he turned off.

Eventually, and that is after at least an hour he returned to the driver's cabin — rang his superiors to tell them what had happened and that he would be bringing the train into Admiralty within a few minutes.

When we arrived at Admiralty, where I was to change trains, we found the platform absolutely PACKED — this had obviously caused havoc on the line and everyone was staring at this strange lady who had the train to herself and was laden with parcels!

When I finally reached the Hotel, Fiona was quite cross as we were late for the school concert — I was told I couldn't bathe or change and must come as I was.   No one was the slightest concerned as to WHY I was late or terribly interested in what I was trying to tell them.

I felt quite hurt that no one was concerned as to what had happened to "Granny" until much later when I confess they all had a good laugh and I did get a little sympathy!

On returning to Manila after this trip, I was well over my luggage allowance and was concerned that I wouldn't be allowed to bring all my purchases back.   I did have to pay about HK$750 excess — but I could have been charged twice that amount!   The annoying thing was that having paid this excess I met a great friend who was on my flight but was travelling with no luggage — only his brief case, and he would have been more than happy to take my excess luggage!   C'est la vie!

When I got back to Manila (in July 1985) with all this equipment,

I found that because of the typhoon we had when everything in the flat was flooded, we had had to have a new transformer fitted in the flat. In doing this they had re-wired and changed many of the electrical outlets but did not tell us they had not changed them ALL, and we now had some sockets that were wired to 210 volts, but others left at 110 volts — (a legacy from the Americans) whilst the others were 220 volts. As a result when I plugged in the new equipment to the socket which had been 110 volts I found everything blew — including the new equipment! A costly and infuriating business.

One of the many things that surprised me when we first arrived in Manila, was being searched when we went IN to the local supermarket. In the U.K. at that time one could be searched when leaving a store, but never when arriving. Having established you were not carrying fire arms you were allowed to enter the Super Market — but — if you were — then the gun had to be held by the store until you left. I was quite shattered at the number of weapons that had been left at the entrance — and wondered how good their security was!

In most foreign countries the ladies were encouraged to join the British Women's Organisation. Each week there was a meeting where one could exchange library books and meet new members and then once or twice a month an outing was organised to some place of interest. There was usually a guest speaker — coffee was served and various items could be bought — the proceeds of which went to charity organisations. Besides the help they gave to local charities, it was a wonderful organisation to help people who might be feeling home sick in their new environment, and to meet other people in the same position.

We had an interesting trip to Las Pinas, a small town famous for its bamboo organ. It had been made from bamboo to save money and was overhauled in Germany between 1973 and 1975.

In Las Pinas we also visited the factory where the Jeepneys were made. Jeepneys are a form of transport peculiar to the Philippines

— resembling a large jeep — with seats down each side. They will stop anywhere and there seemed to be no end to the number of "bodies" that would shove or push their way on board. One paid the driver when you got off — or perhaps I should say "if" you got off as the standard of driving in Manila is hair raising and it must be one of the worst cities in the world to negotiate one's way around. We thought the driving in the Seychelles was bad — but this took the biscuit!

Added to which it is noisy and chaotic but worst of all, the condition of the roads left a lot to be desired! They were full of pot holes — LARGE pot holes. When these became too deep to permit a car or bus to negotiate, they filled them with loose soil or sand, with a thin layer of bitumen! This meant that once it rained the roads were back to the status quo and the whole operation had been a waste of time and money! I remember that on the road to the airport there was a hole at one time that the car could have disappeared into. It really was quite dangerous, particularly at night as there were no warning lights.

Buses and the famous Philippine Jeepney seemed to stop wherever they saw a passenger, irrespective of any traffic behind them. Bus stops are rarely used and taxis are forever trying to get ahead of each other in order to pick up the first available fare.

Horns are used repeatedly, brake lights and blinkers rarely and traffic lane markings never! It seemed that the traffic lights were permanently out of order, and you really felt you took your life in your hands when venturing onto the roads. The cars and buses are often battered — but they seem to survive!

At the weekends Ken and I occasionally went down to Matabunkay which is the most popular beach in the area. The sand is not very white, but the water is clean!

I think the greatest "fun" trip that we did was to Pagsanjan. Here we were paddled up river by two "Banqueros" — in a strong current — in a banca (small boat) or sometimes a canoe. It really is a feat of strength on the part of the boatmen. At the last waterfall you could get out and be paddled on a bamboo raft under the waterfall — which was fun. Then they would turn the boat around and you hurtled down stream at a thrilling speed, shooting the rapids, and fortunately missing the rocks, sometimes by inches, guided by the Banqueros.

The Magdapio Waterfalls are only part of Pagsanjan's attractions as the river trip through the picturesque tropical gorge is really beautiful. We took all our visitors to Pagsanjan if they had sufficient time.

Another popular tourist attraction was a visit to Tagaytay to view the Taal Volcano which is 600 metres above sea level, consequently it is cool and offers visitors superb views of the volcanic island and its crater lake. The volcano is the smallest in the world. About 10 kms from Tagaytay is Mount Sungay where we saw the ruins of the Palace in the Sky, a villa built by Ferdinand Marcos for the State visit of Ronald Reagan! From here there were marvellous views of Laguna Bay and Lake Taal.

Not long before we left we discovered Hidden Valley in Alaminos. This is a fascinating private property and resort where we had lunch which was served on a banana leaf and the tables were built over a lake where one could dangle one's feet in the cool water whilst eating, surrounded by lush tropical vegetation. We were picked up from the car park by a Buffalo cart which slowly meandered to the lunch area — and took us back again via the village.

Because of the unrest we never travelled very far and all these trips could be done in a day. There is so much to see further afield — but the British High Commission did not recommend travelling very far at that time.

I got the impression that everyone was "trigger happy" in the Philippines and had an alarming experience when in a shopping complex. As I was walking through the arcade I heard shouting and the next thing I knew was a bullet whizzed past me and I was suddenly surrounded by about 5 police who were trying to catch a bag snatcher. As he was getting away, they decided to shoot —

and the fact that I was walking in the direct path of the offender —
was too bad!    A shopkeeper shouted at me to come inside his shop
and hide under the counter — and I can tell you I didn't need a
second bidding!    The thief, I might add, was not caught!

On another occasion, friends of ours, Helen and Richard Groves
were leaving Manila and were having a Garage Sale.    They had
advertised in the local press the previous week their larger items
such as refrigerator, air conditioners, Hi Fi, T.V. etc., and this sale
was really for the small items AND let's face it — a lot of rubbish
that in any other country one would have thrown out.

In Manila it seemed that anything would sell!    I offered to help
her with her sale and arrived at the house at 7.a.m. (which I thought
was very early), to start setting up trestle tables on which to display
the smaller items.    The crowd that greeted me when I turned into
her road initially startled me — thinking it was another coup!    I
then realised it was a queue of people waiting to get into the Garage
Sale!

She had a watchman — as all houses had — and this time he was
awake and trying to soothe the crowd who were clamouring to get
in before their neighbour.    We told him to only let 6 people in at a
time as it was impossible to control more — and so it started!    I
might add at these Sales one did not put high prices on anything —
10 Pesos or 20 pesos — but of course if someone was particularly
anxious to buy an item and there was any interest shown by a second
party — they would start increasing their offers.

Helen had decided that all the takings from this sale would go to
charity, after she had paid her maids and watchmen a small gratuity
for their help.

I remember a particular transaction when three people were
bidding against each other for a cracked cup and saucer!    It finally
sold for a ridiculous amount — but we were delighted as the Charity
would benefit even more than we imagined!

Later in the afternoon when things had quietened down a little
— I was sitting at the trestle table holding my friend's baby and just

watching the three people that were hanging around the table, when suddenly a military jeep drew up outside the house and four armed soldiers got out and demanded to get into the compound. The watchman obviously didn't resist — but I was more than a little annoyed at their attitude.

One of these soldiers had apparently been to the house the previous week, wanting to buy an air conditioner which Richard didn't want to sell — after all they needed this to the last moment. This soldier had come back to "negotiate" — and he put down his gun on the table where I was sitting with the baby with the nozzle pointed at me. His small son was also with him and he kept dashing around looking at this and that and then picked up his father's gun — which was still pointing at me and the baby — and I then got up and asked his father to please take the gun off his child as there could easily be an accident. The father did not seem in the slightest concerned, but finally handed the gun to one of the other soldiers.

Can you imagine any army vehicle permitting one of the crew to bring their son with them?

The negotiations over — the jeep departed — and I gathered from Richard he had been told that if he brought his money the following Wednesday he could have the air conditioner. When he returned of course, I gather he haggled some more about the price — as the possession of a gun seemed to indicate to these people that the price MUST go down! It didn't — and we weren't shot!

We flew over to H.K. for Xmas to spend it with Fiona, Gerd and family and remained until the 2nd January. New Year's Eve was spent in the Hotel, where Gerd was Manager — drinks in their flat and then we had dinner at the Rotunda Restaurant which was always a favourite of mine. As it revolves one gets a fantastic view of the H.K. harbour and then of course, as it revolves further, magnificent views of The Peak and over to the South of the Island.

When we returned to Manila, we had a visit from Linda, who brought her new boy friend to be introduced and whom she subsequently married.

At the time I had a very devout Catholic maid — and when I told her to make up the bed in the Guest room as my daughter was arriving — she seemed quite delighted. After meeting them — she seemed confused and asked me if Tony was her husband! I thought it preferable to avoid answering this in view of her strict religious background — so changed the subject quickly by asking her if she had got the fish for dinner!

The next morning Linda and Tony were rather late arising and the maid asked me what my son-in-law liked for breakfast — and did he have tea or coffee? I hadn't a clue of course as I had only just met him and at this stage there was no talk of marriage. I took a chance and said he would like tea, but of course when she subsequently asked him, he asked for coffee! However, we got through the few days without my having to tell any "porkies" as I just avoided any questions about Linda and Tony and let the maid draw her own conclusions!

Imagine my confusion though when Linda rang the following week to say she was coming to Manila with yet another boy friend as BOTH these gentlemen had proposed marriage and she didn't really know which proposal to accept! She would like our opinion — or at least I assumed that was the reason. I decided I could not go through the same nonsense with the maid asking personal questions and I knew she would be horrified if Linda had another man in her bedroom, when she thought the first one was her husband — so I decided I would give her a week's leave.

As things turned out though, the next boy friend arrived on his own as Linda could not get away — so I was spared explanations!

Whilst Linda and Tony were in Manila, the yearly Trade Exhibition was in progress and I managed to get them introduced as "buyers" and they were able to buy a rather lovely Ratan Lounge Suite wholesale, and arranged for it to be shipped to Singapore. Even with the freight it apparently cost less than half it would have done had it been bought in Singapore.

Ken and I were very amused at the Golf Clubs, by the number of

Japanese who flew into Manila for the weekend — purely to play golf! (or so they said). They would arrive on a Saturday morning — hire a Caddy AND would, more often than not, engage a Filipino girl who would walk round the course holding an umbrella over them until they actually played their ball!

Having to follow a Japanese four ball — always slowed down the game — and we discovered one of the reasons was that whilst waiting for their opponents to putt their ball — they would be having a snogging session with the umbrella ladies!

The Japanese would thoroughly enjoy Manila's night life — then have another 18 or 36 holes of golf the next day and fly back in time for work on Monday morning. They told us that these weekends cost them less than paying for a round of golf in Japan!

Conditions in Manila seemed to deteriorate even more, and it is difficult to attempt to explain the sequence of events there at that time.

Perhaps I should go back to give some background — though as I type as I speak — this may be a little disjointed — but it was a memorable time which I feel should be mentioned.

In July 1972 the military announced a great shoot-out with a contingent of Guerillas who were trying to land a shipment of weapons from some unidentified foreign power. After this there was a series of bomb explosions and a plot was revealed to kill many political leaders.

How much of the pre-martial law turmoil was real and how much was orchestrated we'll never know. Defence Minister Enrile was reputed to have been ambushed and his car shot up. In truth Enrile subsequently admitted that the attack on his car was staged and that he had actually shot up the car himself!

Another Marcos aide before his sudden "disappearance" had disclosed that military crews planted many of the Manila bombs — including that at the Manila Water System plant.

It seemed likely that the NPA's (New People's Army) attempt to land arms was real. Enrile subsequently acknowledged that the

# A CALL TO ALL OFFICERS AND MEN OF THE AFP AND THE INP

WE ARE CALLING ALL OFFICERS AND MEN OF THE AFP AND THE INP TO EXAMINE THEIR CONCIENCE AND BE GUIDED BY THEIR CONVICTION.

IF THEY BELIEVE IN WHAT THEY STAND FOR, WE ASK THEM TO JOIN US. WE ASK THEM TO BRING THEIR TROOPS WITH THEM AND JOIN US HERE IN CAMP AGUI-NALDO OR CAMP CRAME AND IF THEY SHOULD DECIDE OTHERWISE, WE ASK YOU TO STAY FOOT AND NOT TO OBEY ILLEGAL AND IMMORAL ORDERS: FROM ALL THE THOUSANDS OF OFFICERS AND MEN COMMITTED TO FIGHT FOR TRUTH, RIGHTEOUSNESS AND JUSTICE AND ARE NOW GATHERED AT THE CAMP AGUINALDO AND CAMP CRAME.

guerillas numbered between 500 and 900 at that time.

In September, 1972, Marcos declared Martial Law — 80,000 people were jailed, thousands tortured, killed or disappeared. A number were subsequently released, but 5,000 were detained as subversives.

The American Chamber of Commerce sent telegams praising Marcos for instituting Martial Law because it would mean stability! But it also meant more freedom for Marcos's friends and foreign firms to exploit the country's resources.

Ninoy Aquino was arrested and was detained in Camp Bonifacio — a military camp at the edge of Manila, where we often played golf. Marcos, however, felt that Ninoy, even in jail, was a profound annoyance and a potential threat, so he offered to free him if he left the country.

Before he could go into exile however, he developed heart problems and after 7 years and 7 months in military confinement he was allowed to leave the country for a Triple Bypass operation in the States. Whilst he offered to return to the Philippines after his surgery, he was told he could stay away as long as he liked, as Marcos felt he would always be a threat to his Presidency.

However, after two years, which Cory Aquino described as the happiest in her life, Ninoy felt it was time he returned to the Philippines. He had been told that the Guerillas were preparing to move and in any case it seemed doubtful that the US would renew his Visa. He was sure that he would be jailed on his return but with Marcos's illness he felt it would not be for long and therefore he wanted to be in the Philippines when this happened.

Armed Forces Chief, Fabian Ver, had reportedly said that once Ninoy was in the plane he would be a dead duck!

As it was, Enrile asked Ninoy to defer his return for two weeks to enable the military to foil the rumoured assassination plot.

Even so — the threats that had been made — did materialise. Those of us who watched Ninoy's return on T.V. saw the shooting — as he was coming down the steps of the plane. The prosecution failed to introduce evidence against the defendants and the court ruled out whatever incriminating testimony slipped through. The judges ignored the eye witness account from a passenger who was on the plane and witnessed the shooting of Ninoy.

Marcos denied any prior knowledge of this murder and the trial of Armed Forces Chief, General Ver, and his co-defendants lasted seven months, but the case was heard by a three-member court which Marcos appointed!

On the 1st October the court that was hearing the murder and conspiracy case against Ver and twenty five others — handed down its verdict. Not guilty!

Ver was suspended after his indictment but Marcos took him back at once and announced a re-organisation of the military!

Rumours were spreading that Marcos's poor health might force him to call an early Presidential Election before the end of his term of office in June, 1987.

The U.S.A. was becoming embarrassed and worried about Marcos's inability to contain the communist insurgency which threatened the U.S. Air and Naval bases in the Philippines. They were looking for political and economic stability which Marcos was not providing.

Marcos had been confirmed as Head of State in 1981 and Parliamentary elections were held in 1984, but the result was contested and allegations of vote-rigging were loud and many.

The dissatisfaction over this vote rigging caused the snap election of 1986, where the Opposition united for the first time under Aquino's widow Cory Aquino.

There were of course many Opposition leaders waiting to take Marcos's place. In November, 1984 the Opposition had formed a group of people who would not be viewed as candidates for the Presidency but who would agree on a selection process. Cory Aquino was one of this group and she was asked at one of the first meetings if she would stand as the Opposition candidate.

She dismissed this as she felt she was not suitable — and did not have the necessary political background. But when the candidates were asked to sign a declaration of unity all but Laurel and Eva Kalaw — a cousin of Ninoy Aquino signed. Laurel said he had a problem over a paragraph calling for the removal of U.S. bases whilst Kalaw thought the process was undemocratic! Laurel of course had been preparing for the Presidency for years. This convenor group agreed that if an election was announced they would chose a candidate.

Numerous candidates suggested that Cory run for President as it was thought only she could end the squabbles on who should lead the divided Opposition. Cory thought this a crazy idea and said they needed a minor miracle.

In time it became quite obvious that Cory was the chosen candidate for the Opposition which she continued to resist on the grounds that she was not suitable and she didn't feel she was the right person.

She was persuaded however to "re-think" and finally she said that if they could get a million signatures on a petition indicating that she was the chosen candidate, she would stand. She was convinced that they would never get a million signatures!

Cory was a very religious person, visiting the Church regularly, where she would often ask for guidance. She finally realised that she could never forgive herself knowing she could have done something and did nothing. Added to which they got the million signatures! So she allowed her name to go forward.

Her decision was not without conflict as Laurel still harboured hopes of being President. He was accused of being overly ambitious and hungry for power, not very different from Marcos. Cory felt that Laurel was blackmailing her and so she went to Cardinal Sin, who having established her reasons for running for the Presidency, said she was a "Joan of Arc". He played a great part in her decision.

After this visit Laurel saw Cardinal Sin who told him that whilst he was wise in the ways of politicians, he was not an attractive candidate and nobody would vote for him. The fact that Cory was a victim of injustice, meant that the sympathy of the people would be with her. He advised Laurel to support Cory and they would win. Cory offered Laurel the Vice Presidency — but he said he would think about it!

When Cory finally agreed to stand, the people were overjoyed and crowds filled the streets shouting Cory, Cory, Cory. They carried yellow banners, ribbons and placards that said "We love Cory" and "We shall never forget or forgive the killers of Ninoy" and a photo of Marcos under which was written "Prime Suspect".

A group marched on Malacanang Palace and burned an effigy of Marcos at the foot of the bridge leading to the Palace. Protestors banged pots, exploded firecrackers and drove cars up and down the streets where piles of tires were burning, sounding their horns and dragging tin cans behind their cars. It was a noisy demonstration which we watched from our flat and we really felt we were in the middle of all the commotion and wondered where it would all end.

In the past Marcos had been in a position to decide the outcome of any election, but this time events were being closely monitored by both internal and external sources.

In December 1985, the Marcos owned T.V. Channel (Channel 4) — and I suspect other channels — only gave news from the Government angle — as did the radio over which Marcos also had full control. So, if we wanted to know the truth we had to listen to the BBC or Channel 6 on the local TV which emanated from the American Clark Air Base and broadcast 24 hours a day! Even then of course some of their reporters stationed in the Philippines had been misled — but on the whole the news had been verified or substantiated. But it became very very confusing.

The US sent Senator Richard Lugar to Manila, at the head of an official American Observer Delegation and delivered Reagan's message that credible elections could produce an increase in US aid.

NAMFREL, the National Citizens Movement for Free Elections, had been set up in 1984, and had limited fraud, sufficiently to allow the Opposition to win a third of Parliamentary seats. NAMFREL therefore would play a crucial role in the election. Marcos accused it of being part of the Opposition and that it was financed by the CIA.

After what appeared to have been weeks of talks, campaigning and Rallies, the election took place on the 7th February, 1986, and in spite of NAMFREL who had over 800,000 volunteers to cover the 90,000 Polling places — thirty Opposition workers were murdered.

The result was not really a surprise to anyone even though the preliminary count indicated correctly that Cory Aquino was in the lead. We then watched the counting of the Returns — all supposedly duly certified by the Board of Canvassers of each province or city which took place in the Batasang Pambansa.

This really was like an episode from one of the Goon Shows — quite unbelievably mis-managed. As the certificates were opened — every single one seemed to be under suspicion — either the seal had cracked — the Certifying Officer's signature was illegible or was suspected of being forged.

Then the final trauma when the NAMFREL vote (National Citizens Movement for Free Elections) which had been formed to organise "poll watchers" to report Ballot results early, in an attempt to prevent fraud in the Vote counting. In their early count they showed a large majority for Cory Aquino, which of course did not agree with the final published count by a few million votes!

However, when the National Assembly (in which Marcos's Governing party held two thirds of the seats) completed the official vote count, they declared Marcos the winner by 1.5 million votes!

It was discovered that $1 and $5 bribes were handed out by Marcos supporters! Soldiers demanded that NAMFREL left their posts.

The result therefore was not really a surprise to anyone even though the preliminary count indicated correctly that Cory Aquino was in the lead.

The reason for the surprised success of the Opposition was not only the dissatisfaction of a large proportion of the population over the vote rigging and the state of the economy, but also the response of many voters to the murder of the Opposition Politician Benigno Aquino (Ninoy) in August, 1983.

The next two days were declared as Public Holidays as I think the Banks were frightened that there would be massive withdrawals. Marcos made a further appearance having gained partial control of one of the T.V. stations — and whilst looking very dejected he said he was still confident he had the situation under control, but declared a State of Emergency with a Curfew from 6.p.m. to 6.a.m. Ramos told the people to ignore this!

The following day — Cory Aquino, having been asked to return to Manila from Cebu, was sworn in as President. She had difficulty leaving her house which was surrounded by Government troops — but she finally made it.

Following the election, both candidates claimed victory and both were sworn in as President in separate ceremonies.

Marcos was sworn in as President in a private ceremony in the Palace. He said he wasn't inviting anyone to witness this — as of course he knew that all Foreign Governments had refused to come! So at this stage, the country had TWO Presidents!

Cory Aquino then rallied the people to join a campaign of non-violent civil disobedience and national protest of the non-violent kind, aimed at pressuring Marcos to resign. Banks, newspapers and Companies favoured by Marcos, were boycotted and "People Power" began to make itself felt.

There was nothing terribly startling — a few Rallies — demonstrations — selling of yellow ribbons which represented the Aquino party — and of course the singing of "Tie a Yellow Ribbon on the old Oak Tree" which became her party song. The resistance was referred to as "People Power" — very correctly so — as it was their non-violent but positive support for Cory that decided the outcome of what could have been a blood bath.

She had said on the T.V. earlier that she really had no desire to be President, she was after all — a housewife, but if this was what the people wanted — she was prepared to stand.

One had to admire the Filipino people who are not by nature fighters — and their contribution to this revolt was peaceful but effective, chiefly in gathering around the Camps hoping to avoid tank or Government troop penetration. They set up kerbside kitchens to supply the so called "Rebels" — they manned the T.V. stations with volunteers and provided 24 hour coverage. My only complaint was that less English was used and more Tagalog (the local language). Had all the news been in Tagalog, I think we would have accepted it better, but it was frustrating in the extreme to hear in English "We now have an important announcement, please listen" and then — a stream of Tagalog with just the odd English word to whet one's curiosity!

On the 22nd evening — Marcos appeared on T.V. around 11.p.m. announcing that there had been an assassination attempt on his life and the First Lady which had been thwarted by the loyal troops who advised them of the threat, 3 hours before it had been scheduled!

This was followed by two or three soldiers appearing on T.V. and reading their "confessions" and admitting taking part in this plot — but only one Major had the guts to say WHY he had agreed to this attempted Coup. He spoke well and left no doubt that he felt Marcos should resign — as the majority of the people were not behind him.

This prompted yet another T.V. appearance when Marcos put on a very good act — he expressed surprise that anyone could say that the people weren't behind him when he had just won the Election — in spite of the fraud — which he attributed to the Opposition!

The same day he held a Press Conference, and managed to avoid answering any pertinent questions by either asking a question himself — or reiterating that he was the chosen leader of the people. The Press Conference lasted an hour and during this time he indicated that he had heard a rumour that Lt. Gen Ramos, the Armed Forces Chief of Staff AND a relative of the Presidents, and the Defence

Minister, Juan Ponce Enrile, were involved in this plot and had therefore tendered their resignations. Marcos said he couldn't believe this and said he had to check it out as it was unbelievable. It appeared that the two resignations were not necessarily connected with the attempted Coup.

Things became serious for Marcos when this happened and the Commanders together with various military units joined the Aquino camp.

Rumours were rife and events were traumatic and completely confusing. One was forced to the conclusion that neither side could tell the complete truth. The Cory Aquino side however, had been known to apologise when statements they, or their supporters had made, turned out to be incorrect. Not so the Marcos side!

It was when the Coup plot had been discovered, that as a safety precaution, Cory Aquino had gone into hiding in a Convent in Cebu.

We subsequently learned that Defence Minister Juan Ponce Enrile and Armed Forces Chief of Staff, General Fidel Ramos had joined the Aquino camp. Together with the military units they had taken refuge within the protective walls of Camp Aguinaldo and Camp Crame situated on E.D.S.A. — the main road to the North and reasonably close to Twin Towers where we had the penthouse flat.

We saw 40 Armoured Personnel Carriers and Troop Carriers which moved out of Camp Bonafacio, and proceeded up EDSA, towards Camp Aguinaldo. We were amused to see that a few of the tanks broke down on EDSA and as a result, there was a general slowing down — and shortly after they all stopped! We noticed a few of the Tank Commanders going into the houses en route and we gathered they were using their phones, but we imagined there would be a complete massacre once the tanks reached the Camp. We feared the worst.

Channel 4 had been taken over from the Marcos supporters and T.V. Channel 7 was abandoned. Appeals were made on the radio by the Opposition (I should say "Rebels" as Cory Aquino was not associated with it at this time as she was in Cebu) to proceed towards

EDSA and form a human block against the tanks. This they did —
and we were very surprised at the response when literally thousands
of people could be seen camping outside the gates of Camp
Aguinaldo, having brought sleeping bags and setting up portable
kitchens. One was left wondering in which country in the world
would this form of resistance prove successful? But it did!

The Catholic Primate, Cardinal Jaime Sin, also called on the
people to go immediately to Camp Aguinaldo — hoping this would
prevent an armed attack. We were very surprised at the response.
The tanks were halted for over 24 hours.

Ramos contacted Marcos and asked him to keep the tanks more
than a mortar shell away from Camp Aguinaldo whilst they
negotiated. This was a waste of time as Marcos would not surrender,
stand down or evacuate — he still called for non-violence but did
agree with General Ver that small arms fire would be allowed.

There were various attempts to take over the T.V. stations and
the Radio stations by Government forces and the Rebels, as Marcos
was lost without his various mouthpieces! You would be listening
to a station when it would suddenly close down and the opposition
would then start broadcasting. We could see the gun fire from
these attempts, from our flat — but of course did not know until
later — who was finally in control, or for how long!

Things became serious for Marcos when he lost his T.V. and
Radio channels.

Throughout the day, reports and pictures appeared on T.V. of
various "shoot outs" — but all in all — very little real damage
appeared to have occurred. Two fighter jets appeared which alarmed
many people as no one knew which side they were on, but at that
stage it was assumed they were the President's. It appeared there
had been many defections from the Government to the rebels and in
fact these jets had defected and were later to attack Malacanang
(the Palace) where 5 people were hurt.

We went to bed that night wondering what we would hear in the
morning — and confess we had two radios continually tuned into

different stations — trying to get the views of both sides — and of course watching T.V. — switching from the Government Channel which had again been retaken after more fighting, to one of the others. Life was indeed quite hectic trying to keep up to date.

I think the 23rd and subsequent twenty four hours  must have been the most confusing that any country has experienced.

After the attempted Coup, which should have taken place early Sunday morning the 23rd February, the President gave two more Press Conferences.  Other than his obvious shock at the defection and subsequent resignation of his two Generals, he appeared in full control of the situation — though he was rather hesitant and meandered slightly, but this enabled him to avoid answering any difficult or "loaded" questions put to him.  He really was a past master at managing to avoid answering questions which could be embarrassing to him!

Mind you, he was not a well man — though the extent of his illness was kept from the public.

Having temporarily gained control of one of the T.V. stations — on Sunday evening he again spoke to the Press for an hour and gave a very positive picture.  He had accepted the fact that Ramos and Enrile had left the Government and were taking refuge. He actually looked better than he had done for ages — he never hesitated in his speech and had seldom been heard to speak more eloquently or convincingly with no trace of weakness — physical or mental.  He actually said he was prepared to lead his troops into any assault — as like an old war horse he was stimulated by the smell of gun fire!

However, throughout his speech he did stipulate that he did not want bloodshed and that while he could end the whole situation immediately by ordering his troops to attack Camp Aguinaldo with mortars and tanks — he would not do this as he wanted a peaceful solution as, after all, the people had voted him President in spite of the Opposition fraudulently acquiring votes!

He did not associate the Coup attempt or the resignation of Ramos and Enrile with the Opposition — which in fact I don't think it was at that stage. The man's conviction and apparently genuine confusion over the events of the last 48 hours was amazing.

This talk however was cut short as the Rebels had again acquired his T.V. station — Channel 4 — one person being killed in the take over. We could actually see the smoke from this confrontation from our flat — in fact there seemed to be black smoke in the sky continually emanating from one or other T.V. stations.

The next morning the 24th, there were more rumours and one was even more confused. You could see people dancing and singing in the streets as they heard that the Marcos family had been seen in Guam! The next moment they were in the depths of depression — as not only was this not true — Marcos managed to make one more T.V. appearance with the First Lady and his grandchildren, and showed the local morning papers to prove that his appearance was not a recording from elsewhere.

Then another radio station was put out of action and a further T.V. station, and there was more firing to be heard, smoke in the sky and we knew there had been yet another attempt at a take over — and we anxiously waited to hear who was then in control.

We felt very involved in this political drama — as we had a bird's eye view of the proceedings from our flat, which had this wonderful view of EDSA, where we could see a lot of the troop movements.

People had been advised that it was not a good time to venture into the streets and — I was continually phoned by various friends living in the Villages, asking what was happening. They were alarming days!

I really felt the tanks and Government troops, that had been outside Camp Aguinaldo for 24 hours, were about to attack. Instead of this, Nuns, Priests, Men, Women and children held vigil and prayed in front of the tanks — some actually laying down in the tanks' path, whilst others offered the soldiers flowers and cups of tea. It brought tears to one's eyes to see Nuns prostrating themselves in this way and we didn't know what the reaction of the tank commanders would be.

People Power became an international phenomenon: We watched as these young girls and Nuns offered flowers and cups of coffee to the tank crews, — some of whom were initially reticent to accept them.  But finally — when they saw one or two of their comrades accepting the drinks and taking the flowers, then slowly, first one soldier and then another would accept a flower or a cup of tea and one felt an enormous sense of relief and we knew that the Nuns lying in front of the tanks would be safe.

It became obvious that very few of Marcos's army did really support him now.

Our phone never stopped ringing as of course people living in the Villages could see nothing of this and it was difficult to know what was true and what was rumour.

The American Embassy — as they had done in India, Pakistan and Kabul, when these countries had political problems, had very early on, advised their nationals to evacuate.   This I found disconcerting and when I came down into the Foyer of the block of flats and saw all the American residents lined up with their luggage, ready to leave for the airport, I couldn't help wondering if they knew something that we didn't — but I have to say — we never evacuated — though in Pakistan  we did have our evacuation case packed — in case we had to beat a hasty retreat!

By enlisting the services of the maid to translate, we gathered that the Marcos family, and General Ver with his family, fled from Malacang Palace about 8.p.m. on Tuesday evening the 25th February.

Initially they were taken by four helicopters to the American Clark Air Base where they spent the  night and left the next morning for Guam.

We heard this news initially from our daughter Linda in Singapore who had heard it announced on the news in Singapore.  A degree of secrecy was maintained in Manila to avoid any undue scenes or violence.

The tanks and armoured cars left the Palace about 9.30.p.m. and it was then assumed by the crowds that Marcos had left.

Unfortunately the Palace was then invaded and a considerable amount of damage was done — and it was hinted that it was a Communist element that had been sent in to add to the confusion. Certainly there were a lot of people from Ilocos Norte, President Marcos's hometown — who had come for his inauguration, but latterly had been invited by the President to come to the Palace with their guns, to protect the Presidential Palace — and the President!

They were of course very loyal to Marcos who had been more than generous to the people of Ilocos Norte — and it was said that he actually paid people to ensure that they voted correctly — for Marcos!

The people refused to believe the stories of Marcos illegally amassing wealth and put it down to propaganda by the Aquino Government, or they blamed Imelda. One of Marcos's party said at the time that "behind every man's success is a woman — AND behind every man's downfall.

There were skirmishes but, considering the depth of feeling, the problem was reasonably controlled and the mob did not penetrate the upper floors of the Palace.

Cory Aquino became National Leader on 25th February, 1986 and on the same day, Marcos and his family plus General Fabian (Marcos's Armed Forces Chief) fled to America. The people in Ilocos Norte were convinced that the Americans had kidnapped the Marcos family and taken them to Hawaii!

There were of course many people who had lost power now that Marcos had gone, who obviously clamoured for his return. It was felt that they were preparing themselves for the slight chance that he might return and they could then say they had backed him all along!

I was fortunate enough to be included on a tour of Malacanang Palace, the day after the Marcos's had fled — and I actually saw all the opulence that Imelda had acquired. The story of her 3,000 pairs of shoes was not exaggerated, though I didn't obviously count them! She claimed later that she was supporting the local shoe industry —

but, from what we could see, the majority of the shoes were Italian!

Her "wardrobe" was better stocked than many Department Stores, with racks of personal clothing hanging in an adjoining room. In addition there was a huge room stacked from top to bottom with boxes which we were told contained gifts she would distribute from time to time to visiting dignitaries AND her close friends! The boxes contained, amongst other items, Rolex Watches, Diamond Brooches and Tie Pins etc. There was also a whole rack of fur coats and jackets, not forgetting her grandson's mini-Mercedes!

With all the poverty in the country, it was quite nauseating to see such wealth. Rumour had it of course that the Marcos's had already remitted thousands of dollars to Swiss Bank Accounts and to the States — perhaps not in their own names, but the money had gone!

Marcos's bedroom was just like a hospital — with all the normal equipment. The Kidney Dialysis machine was next to the bed — and again — one felt it was criminal that he should have such facilities available solely for his own use, when the hospitals were so desperate for drugs let alone expensive equipment. The hospital bed was half raised — and in the remainder of the Palace one got the impression that the family had left in a hurry — food was still on the table where they had obviously been eating. There was a separate (secret) exit to the roof of the Palace from where the family had been taken off by helicopter.

Imelda's bedroom was as you may imagine, luxurious, even if perhaps a little gaudy. Her bathroom contained several of the largest bottles of perfume I had ever seen — and this coupled with all they had managed to take away — made one realise where all the wealth that the country didn't receive had gone!

At the time of the Marcos's departure from the Philippines they started showing on T.V. private videos that they had uncovered at Malacanang Palace. These showed parties on board their private yacht with Imelda singing and dancing with George Harrison — and a particular rowdy party on the occasion of Marcos's birthday, when a large cake was wheeled on to the deck where they had been dancing, and out of this popped a glamorous looking, scantily dressed girl!

Every night we seemed to be entertained by these videos which did nothing to improve the Marcos image — but — he still had his supporters.

There is no doubt about it that Marcos did a lot for the Philippines initially, but — either through Imelda's influence   or his illness, when he was not always aware of what was going on, but the corruption which he had attempted to eliminate in his early years in office — abounded.

I had a great deal of respect for Cory Aquino.  She took on a thankless task, tackling a job she didn't want and knew little about — but as Marcos had said — "the only thing she could offer the country was sincerity".  This was rich coming from a man that had acquired $26 billion in foreign debts while leaving much of the country malnourished!

Her first year in office was not easy.  She survived 7 attempted coups, and found it hard to differentiate between friends and enemies; Enrile her Defence Minister had denounced her Government as a dictatorship, and Salvador Laurel, her Vice President, did not give up his own presidential ambition and it was hard for Cory to know who she could depend on.    Added to which, it seemed that the disasters that the Marcos's Government had created over a number of years, Cory Aquino was supposed to rectify in a matter of months.

As you will gather, everyone living in the Philippines at that time became heavily involved emotionally in this political upheaval.

We did however, manage to enjoy our time there, though because of the unrest we were not able to travel as far afield as we would have liked.  It seemed that every time we planned a trip out of Manila that there was an uprising of sorts.  But there was a lot to do and see in and around Manila, so the fact we were told not to travel further afield because of the unrest at that time, didn't concern us.

I realise now that there was so much that we should have seen in the Philippines — and it is such a pity that a country with so much to offer was so nearly destroyed economically by a President who became avaricious.

Most of our trips took place when we had visitors to stay — and we became quite familiar with the "city in walls" — Intramuras, which is the Manila of the past. This is where Legaspi erected a fortress after his victory over the Muslims.

Following attacks by the Chinese fleet and a fire, the Filipinos were forced to build a wall with a wide moat all around. Within the walls there were numerous feudal lords' houses, 12 churches and several hospitals. Only Spaniards and Muslims were allowed to live within the walls.

Intramuros was almost entirely destroyed by bombs in World War II, but the San Augustin Church remained relatively undamaged and the Manila Cathedral was rebuilt after the war. There are still a few houses well worth seeing like the Casa Manila and the El Amanecer.

The most important defence location of the Intramuros fortress city was Fort Santiago where thousands of Filipino prisoners lost their lives during the Japanese occupation in World War II. Fort Santiago is now a memorial, there is an open air theatre, the Rizal Shrine, commemorating Dr. Jose Rizal who spent his last days in the Fort before his execution by the Spaniards.

In the Fort area there was a display of really old cars which used to belong to important Filipino personalities. In 1988 Fort Santiago was turned inside out by US gold seekers who hoped to uncover the legendary war treasure of the Japanese General Yamashita which was rumoured to be hidden in the Philippines. All in vain I might add.

We had various friends recommend a visit to the Chinese Cemetery which we had ignored, but prior to leaving Manila for good, we decided we should visit this Cemetery.

This must contain some of the most unusual and ostentatious tombs in the world. These are in the form of actual houses, with toilets and mailboxes — some even have air conditioning which remains switched on at all times! There is a complete village — and we spent over an hour just walking around this amazing cemetery. It seemed crazy that the dead should enjoy such opulence when the living existed in such poverty sleeping on the streets and burrowing through rubbish dumps for something they could salvage.

The most depressing sight in the Philippines — and there were many — were Tondo and Smokey Mountain. This is in shocking contrast to the wealth that one can see in the residential areas like Forbes Park and Dasmarinas. Here poverty is at its most extreme where families live in huts on the Municipal Dump and comb the smouldering refuse tip for anything that could be re-used.

Many of our visitors who had had relatives in the War wanted to see the U.S. Military Cemetery and we were very pleased we visited — yet another cemetery! The circular memorial is built on a rise and on the walls are excellent pictures of the Battles of the Pacific. There are 17,000 U.S. soldiers buried here, who died in the Philippines during World War II. The cemetery is kept in very good condition — financed by the U.S. Government.

In 1981 Imelda Marcos had erected the Coconut Palace, for the visit of the Pope. It is made of the best tropical timbers and was used as a Guest House. It is very unusual, and like everything that Imelda had an interest in — money had not been spared and it was well furnished and very interesting.

During our time in Manila we must have visited all the various Museums, the Ayala Museum which specialises in the high points of Philippine history, the Casa Manila Museum which is a faithful reproduction of a typical Spanish residence, and numerous others.

Rizal Park is a real oasis in the centre of the city and popularly known as Luneta Park, besides the wide lawns and flowers thousand of Filipinos are attracted by the music — as you know Filipinos are a very musical race.

There were many interesting markets but the one I visited chiefly was Pistang Pilipino and, as I became known, I did feel I got some very good bargains. Central Market was another favourite haunt, but getting there presented a problem — it was impossible to park one's car anywhere near the market — and with all the unrest at that time I would not venture on a bus!

Fiona at this time had surprised us all by getting heavily involved in the property business. Initially with a Chinese firm where she learnt a lot and had the title of "Financial Advisor" — obviously all the advice, quite sensibly, was to put money into property. She was then asked to join the H.K. off shoot of a U.K. property firm where she was known as "Property Manager". Whilst with this Company she sold some flats to an Egyptian Jew who owned a Company that had featured in the Press quite a lot. The Chairman was a well known Politician, and she was obviously quite surprised when she was asked to join this Company on a salary far in excess of what she was then earning. I guess it was an offer she couldn't afford to refuse. She had to set up their H.K. office and became heavily involved in their China business.

I think at times she wondered what had hit her — as this guy certainly wanted his pound of flesh — (not physically I hasten to add). She was in China at least 6 times per month with periodic visits to London, Paris and New York. She loved the challenge, though at first she employed her own accountant and solicitor to ensure she didn't put a step wrong — as on the salary she was getting she reckoned she could well afford this "insurance".

Things became very fraught for a variety of reasons, and she felt she had to get out of this — and doubtless one day will write her own account of events as they happened at that time.

I regress — but more of this later.

In May of 1986 we were due for leave and returned to the U.K. I had to have periodic check ups at the Hospital as a result of the Cirrhosis that was diagnosed in 1981, and apparently my condition was a cause for concern, as I was hospitalised and therefore unable to return with Ken after our leave.

Fiona had been getting rather concerned about certain incidents related to her previous boss — and so decided she would come over to the U.K. with the boys to see me and to get away from the traumas in H.K. She and the boys were able to stay at the Inter-Continental Hotel because of Gerd's position in the Company and when the hospital said I could become a day patient after about two weeks of residence, Fiona suggested I went to stay with them — which was a terrific bonus — and wonderful to be with someone that cared.

I arrived at the Hotel from the hospital before lunch and the boys were hungry and so, rather than order an expensive meal in the Hotel, which the boys probably would not eat anyway — she decided to go up to Marble Arch and go into Marks and Spencers and buy some sandwiches, bottles of milk, and as I was on a strict diet, I bought yoghurt and a salad.

Before leaving the Hotel she queued to put her passport, money and jewellery into a Safe Deposit Box, but there was a long queue and the boys were getting fractious — so we took the bus to Marble Arch.

We arrived at the Pay Out at different times and I was actually just about paying my bill when I heard Fiona shout — "someone has stolen my wallet! All her travel money, some U.S. dollars she had been given just before boarding the plane to do some shopping for someone, all her credit cards — and — as she had been travelling she also had quite a large amount of other currencies — all of which had gone. Marks and Spencers were very helpful and efficient — took us to the office and allowed Fiona to ring the Police, and all the credit card offices — and even offered to lend her some money for immediate use. Fortunately I was with her so this was not necessary. However, the police insisted that we went down to the station to fill in a statement — and this took care of the rest of the day — and left us all shattered. Fortunately her jewellery was still in the bag — but of course had there not been a queue at the Hotel to put in her valuables, she would not have had so much money on her. This didn't augur very well for her visit.

I don't think either of us slept very well and the next morning I had to get up to the hospital.

Fiona became concerned when she heard her previous boss was now in the U.K. and might want her to become involved in some business she was not happy about. Her Solicitor suggested that in the circumstances she would be well advised to move out of the Inter-Continental where she would be expected to be staying, and move elsewhere — if possible using a different name. She was friendly, and had recently entertained in Port Vila, the Manager of a rival Hotel. She therefore thought she would approach this gentleman and ask if she could move into his Hotel.

I went off to the Hospital in the a.m. and of course had no idea what had been arranged regarding accommodation — so it was agreed that Fiona would ring my friend Olive and tell her where she was staying. I in turn would ring Olive when I had finished at the Hospital to find out where Fiona was staying.

Olive told me she was at a certain Hotel, but had registered in the name of Mrs. Rubenstein! I went to the Hotel and asked at Reception for Mrs. Rubenstock and was told they had no one of that name registered. I explained that she had just booked in and had two wee boys with her. She still insisted that they had no booking in that name. I decided that perhaps I had got the wrong name so rang Olive again and she confirmed that it was Rubenstein and not Rubenstock. Triumphant I returned to Reception and asked for Mrs. Rubenstein and explained I had the wrong name. The Receptionist — still looking rather suspicious — started to ring Fiona's room and asked me who she should say was calling. You can imagine what she thought when I said "her Mother" and she looked really suspicious that I didn't know my daughter's name!

Fiona returned to Hong Kong — happy that I was feeling better and I went to stay with Olive and her tolerant husband Syd. I had to continue going to the hospital every day for blood tests but thought I would be allowed back to Manila the following week! Well — the "following week" never came and I was in the U.K. for three months!

I was excited when I finally was allowed to leave — getting a flight was not easy and I still wasn't feeling on top of the world. However, I had to ask for a Fat Free diet on the plane which they assured me was very easy and they often prepared "special diets" for passengers. When the first meal arrived — everyone seemed to get their trays — but there was no sign of anything for me. Finally the Purser came along with a bottle of Champagne and his apologies that my meal had been given inadvertently to a Muslim lady who had already eaten it! All he could offer me — that was acceptable from the diet point of view, was an apple which he brought from First Class.

He assured me that this wouldn't happen again and he hoped the bottle of Champers would help me get over the loss of lunch. I explained I was not allowed liquor — but — he assured me that my husband would enjoy it!

To cut a long and unbelievable story short, I ended up with five bottles of Champagne — but no food — as every meal was somehow diverted to a vegetarian — who the airline must have thought was more deserving! I felt too ill to make a scene — but I wrote a very rude letter when I got home and was sent a refund of £50 as compensation. (I had hoped for a free ticket!)

This was not the end of a ghastly journey, because when I arrived in Manila and was going through Customs — thrilled at the thought of seeing Ken after all this time — Immigration asked me to step into a side room where I was left. I ventured out to enquire why on earth I was not allowed to pass through Immigration, and was told that my Visa had expired and they were making arrangements to send me back to the U.K.! This was all too much — and they wouldn't even let me out to tell Ken what had happened.

Fortunately, the plane returning was already over booked — a normal occurrence in the Philippines — and after about 2 hours they said they would let me leave the airport, but would keep my passport and I had to return the next morning.

By the time I got outside I was in tears — and any of you that know Manila airport — will realise — that next to Delhi it must be

529

one of the worst in the world.   There is no Reception area and so I could not see Ken — and by this time I was sure he would have thought I had missed the plane and gone home.   To get a trolley for one's luggage you have to have Pesos — and of course I had none — so was trying to cope with my luggage with tears running down my cheeks, when some delightful lady came to my aid and got me a trolley, so that helped a little.

Eventually I spotted Ken — or to be more correct — Ken spotted me — and of course he was furious when I told him about the journey. The next day he got the Company Solicitor to sort out the Visa problem — as I had a "Dependant's Visa" — and Ken of course had a Work Permit so he didn't have problems!

I think this episode was instrumental in Ken making a decision that he had had enough.

We now had continual black outs — as a result candles were unobtainable — and we relied on torches and hoped we could get batteries.   With no electricity of course we had no air conditioning (and no T.V. or radio) and couldn't read — and this made entertaining extremely difficult as you never knew if you would have the facilities to provide a meal.   It was also impossible to keep cool.

Whilst Ken felt honour bound to finish his contract — he obviously had not bargained for my liver problems — and decided when the time was right — he would give in his notice.

We spent Xmas 1986 in H.K. with the family — very flattered that they continued to want to share Xmas with us and we had a very happy family time, and of course still had many friends in H.K. that we met up with.

After Xmas Ken resigned his Consultancy and we left the Philippines on the 22nd January, 1987, arriving in Brisbane for yet another spell in Australia.   To return to England for the winter didn't seem a very good idea!

I think my only disappointment was that we had working for us a young Filipino girl — called Lourdes.   She was married with four children and her husband was unemployed.   Whilst she was with us

— I naturally became very fond of her and bought things for the children and gave her food which I let her think was left over. She always seemed most grateful.

When I told her we were leaving she was naturally sad — but when I gave her her final salary plus an extra two weeks salary and a month's pay for each year she had been with us, plus an extra month's pay, she looked quite rejected. I frankly thought we had been more than generous as it was not the custom in the Philippines to pay staff a gratuity when leaving. I asked her what on earth was the matter and she told me "she expected more"!

This not only disappointed me, but made me cross! The driver we had, who only received the extra month's pay for each year he had been with us, was simply elated and said we had been too generous! I was even more disappointed when I found that things were disappearing from my cupboards in the last few days — and in the end — asked her to leave early, as we had found her a new employer. But I did warn her future employers about the incident.

So our time in Manila came to an end, and as always I was sad to leave. I realised by the number of farewell parties that had been organised for us that we had made a lot of friends in quite a short time. I think having gone through a Revolution together with all its added problems, had brought us all close together. We left the Philippines on the 22nd January, 1987.

## EIGHTEEN
### *Retirement Yet Again—Visit to Australia*

When we left Manila we both thought that this really was "retirement" and so planned to return to Australia for the remainder of the winter.

We arrived in Brisbane and were met by Iris Jarrold, Brian Ireland's sister, who had not been at all well, she had had a mastectomy the previous year, but had developed blinding headaches and had occasional bouts of feeling dizzy. Even so she was as hospitable as her Brother and had arranged for a friend to drive her to the airport to meet us and take us to Burleigh Heads where again we had booked a Unit in Goodwin Towers.

Unfortunately these dizzy spells were diagnosed as a tumour in the brain and poor Iris really started to deteriorate and finally died. A happy release for her — but she was sadly missed by all her family and friends.

We invited Margaret Crowther, who had also been recently widowed, to come and stay with us. Ken and I were hoping that this visit would help her to adjust to her new status, as it had done with our friend Ruth. She arrived at Brisbane on the 2nd February. and as this was her first visit to Australia, she was naturally enchanted with this wonderful country.

Our friendship dated back to our Bombay days when we both lived in the same block of flats called "Kismet". Margaret and I had never met until our husbands were on a business trip in the south of India and both stayed at the same Club. They met at the bar one evening and started talking and realised they both came from Bombay. It was quite a shock I think when they then discovered that not only were they from the same city, but from the same block of flats! On return from their business trip — we all got together and have been firm friends ever since. They had children about the same age as Fiona — so we had a lot in common. The children went to the same school, they swam at Breach Candy, so Margaret and I spent a lot of time together. It was super that she could come and join us in Queensland.

She couldn't believe what wonderful weather we had, and we spent a lot of time swimming and sitting on the beach just opposite the flat and we in turn of course thoroughly enjoyed showing her what Queensland had to offer.

Very near to us is the Currumbin Bird Park — which has lots of lovely birds, and every day at 4.30.p.m. the Parakeets fly into a feeding area in their hundreds, squeaking and squealing and landing on one's head, arm or anything that protrudes! The Park distribute trays of bread and honey water to most of the people watching, and then the Parakeets just go mad and you find you have so many standing on this tray it becomes too heavy to hold! This feeding time is one of the main attractions of the Park and the funny thing is that in about an hour they will all fly off — and guess where they head to — nowhere else but the trees in front of our flats at Goodwin Towers. Here they continue to chirp and squeak until dusk falls — and then they disappear. The fantastic thing is that they continue to come to the Park at the same time even though the clocks have changed by an hour for summer or winter time..

I think the thing that appeals most, though, is the area of the Park where the Kangaroos and Wallabies roam free and will allow you to feed them. Except when they have young in their pouches and then they become quite aggressive and will box anyone that comes near.

The Koala's also have their own area — and appear from the leaves of the gum trees slowly — there is nothing very fast about a Koala!

Margaret had a friend who had emigrated to Sydney a few years ago — who also used to be in Bombay living in the same block of flats that we did, and so she decided she would pay her a visit whilst with us.

On her return we drove up to Maroochydore, and went to Shelley's Beach at Caloundra for lunch and the following day drove up to Noosa Heads where we booked into a Motel.

This had already become a favourite haunt of tourists, and we had difficulty in finding accommodation, ending up with a Unit just off the beach.

The next day we set off for Gladstone going through Bundaberg and had lunch at Gin Gin.   On the 16th we drove from Gladstone to Rockhampton on to MacKay and stayed at Blacks Beach on the Northern Beaches.   We went for a swim most evenings, but the thing I wasn't enthusiastic about was that the swimming area was usually netted to avoid Jelly Fish, Stingers, Portuguese Men of War etc., which seemed to abound in the seas all over on the north Sunshine Coast.   Having to swim in the netted area restricted one and of course — it was usually crowded in that particular area whilst the remainder of the beach was deserted.

I have to say that our accommodation here was good and very cheap, perhaps March is not a very popular time as the schools are not on holiday.

We finally got to Airlie Beach and were able to rent the same apartment that we had when we visited in 1981.   The following day we had booked a cruise starting from Shute Harbour which called at Daydream Island and Hook Island where we had lunch and visited the Observatory.   Obviously this was under the water and enabled you to see the most amazing fish — including a Shark!   I was very glad that there was this thick sheet of glass between us as it looked evil and hungry!   To attract this number of fish — food is thrown into the water at regular intervals so that one is always assured of seeing a large variety of them.   There was only time to call at South Molle before returning to Shute Harbour.

We had planned to spend longer here and do a different cruise the next day, but Ken announced that whilst we were so far North he would like to drive up to Cairns!

The next day therefore we covered 544 kms leaving Airlie Beach early in the morning and driving through Bowen, Ayr, Townsville, Ingham Tully and spent the night at the Del Rio Motel on Mission Beach. A super spot — but the next day I suffered badly from the effects of the Sandflies that had obviously bitten me when we were having dinner in a restaurant on the beach. Ken and Margaret didn't suffer too badly, but I reckon you couldn't put a pin between the bites on my back — but then I had worn a backless sun dress — so guess I asked for it!

Again we had to leave early for Innisfail and Gordonvale, to Cairns — and I can't say we felt we saw a great deal of Cairns, as Ken immediately thought it would be a good idea to proceed further north to Port Douglas! By this time we felt like American Tourists — who cover so much ground, see virtually nothing, but at least can say "we've been there and done that" !

I am sure Cairns is delightful — certainly what little we saw we liked — but — would have liked to spend a couple of nights there.

Port Douglas was superb — and the drive along the coast from Cairns to Port Douglas, quite breathtaking. The "Resort" at Port Douglas was then under construction and we vowed we would do this trip again, now we knew the best places to stop! We had another night in a super Motel — these places really are first class — and any of them I could have happily spent two weeks in — but the object of this exercise was to see as much as possible — and in the future we would know the best places to plan an extended stay. Margaret's time was also limited so we couldn't dilly dally too long.

We left the coast the next day and travelled inland and up the mountains to Mossman, Mount Molloy, Marceba, to Atherton where we met up with a friend of Brian and Iris.

We spent the night at the Wrights Motor Lodge — which I will always remember. The accommodation was good and they also provided an evening meal. It was much cooler up in the Mountain area so they had a huge log fire burning in the grate in the Lounge. After dinner we were invited to go into the Lounge and have a coffee and a Brandy.

Whilst sitting there I heard a tap tap and then a knock knock at the French window — and was shattered to see a lovely Kangaroo standing on its hind legs, obviously wanting to come in.

Naturally, I assumed it belonged to the owners or at least it was an accepted visitor, so I opened the French Window and in hopped the Kangaroo and to our amazement it stood by the fire for a few moments and then hopped over to the Bar as though waiting to be served! I noticed it had a collar on and therefore thought it was the owner's pet!

When the Proprietor brought in the coffee — he was horrified and screamed at the poor Kangaroo saying "WHO let you in?" I confessed that I had done so as I thought he belonged in the family as he was so friendly. I was assured that he was nothing to do with them, but belonged to a couple who lived about 2 miles away. Apparently he was always appearing at the Motel, because people would feed him — but according to the Manager he made a frightful mess (obviously not potty trained) and often stole food — so out he had to go!

I was just sad we hadn't taken a photo of this — as it had to be seen to be believed.

The next day was a marathon one, calling at Yungabuna, where we saw The Fig Tree Curtain — a thick curtain of Fig Trees, Mallanda Falls, the Bromfield Swamp — mile upon mile of dead trees which appeared to have succumbed to the salt, we saw something known as The Crater and Dinna Falls, Milla Milla and Jackson's Look Out, Innisfail, Etty Beach and then spent the next two days at Kurrimine Beach where they had a swimming pool so I didn't have to brave the Jelly Fish etc., or swim in the net. BUT — again there were Sandflies — which we never saw — but only felt the next day! By this time however we had bought some marvellous antidote — so — we weren't unduly troubled.

We drove from Kurrimine Beach to Proserpine and stayed at Airlie Beach again and booked to go on Traiton II the next day to the Barrier Reef.

We passed Hook and Hayman Islands, Daydream Island and sailed through the Whitsundays. I couldn't wait to do some snorkelling — the water was warm and we had anchored only a short distance from part of The Reef. We were again assured that Sharks did not venture very close to The Reef — so it was reasonably safe — but I noticed they had a continual "look out" and there were many Yachts anchored in the area and people were swimming and snorkelling from them all — so decided it was safe enough.

The Barrier Reef really is out of this world — and you have to get under the water to really appreciate the depth of colour and variety of fish. Just to have two weeks in this area exploring all the Islands and different parts of the Reef would be a fabulous holiday and I do recommend it to everyone before they get too old!

When we left Airlie Beach we drove to MacKay, Sabrina Beach and on to Yeppoon where we saw Turkey Birds in the grounds of the Motel. The next day saw us on the road again driving to Emu Park, Rockhampton where I bought a pair of Sapphire Earings which I thought would make a nice present, then on to Gladstone, Gin Gin, and Bundaberg to Hervey Bay — where again we had excellent accommodation on the beach. Nearly all our Motels were on the Beach — as we never looked elsewhere and only if they were all full would we accept anything else!

From Hervey Bay we drove to Noosa Heads where we found the price of rentals had gone down considerably from the previous visit 10 days ago. After a night there we drove to Coolum Beach, Maroochydore, Mooloolaba, and Caloundra back to Brisbane. Ken certainly enjoys driving!

We arrived back on the 28th April, to find a pile of mail, and couldn't believe that we no loner had to get up early every morning ready for the day's drive!

There was still a lot to show Margaret locally, we had a day on the River at Brisbane, drove up Mount Tamborine — went to Mount Warning, had lunch at the Furniture Factory which sounds rather odd, but its a very nice restaurant attached to the factory where they make furniture. There is a Show Room for the furniture and for other objets d'art — made by local craftsmen. On the days we didn't wander far we had a daily swim — often at Tallebudgerra Creek — as there are no waves in the Creek and one steps from the beach into quite deep water. It is tidal with often strong currents, but this means you get an enormous amount of exercise swimming against the current — and getting nowhere — and there were no sharks! This meant a ten minute walk through the National Forest just behind us — which is a delightful walk.

Margaret returned home on the 16th April, 1987 — very sad to leave Aussie which she had so obviously enjoyed. The weather tried to make things easier for her by raining for the first time!

During this trip to Australia, which was longer than most, we had to change Units about five times and this became rather annoying.

When we commented about this to the Agent who did the bookings for us, he told us that the Unit we were going into in two weeks time, was actually coming on the market for Sale and he wondered if we would be interested?

Whilst Margaret had been with us she and I had actually looked at various properties, not so much with any thought of buying, but really looking at what one could expect — for a similar amount in the U.K. On the whole we were quite surprised how superior most of the houses and flats (they are called Units in Oz) were as compared to the U.K. and of course so much cheaper.

When the Agent told us that Unit 23 in this particular block of flats was available, I became quite interested. Obviously we had been spending a lot of our leaves in Australia and as we assumed this was final retirement for Ken we were hopeful that we would continue to come down for the English winter. We just loved Burleigh Heads and would always return here — and would be able to spend even longer periods. As rents were going up in leaps and bounds — it seemed that we would be well advised to buy instead of renting.

Ken however, did not share my enthusiasm and said he would never invest money in Australia. However, I persuaded him to at least have a look at the Unit that was for sale.

In Australia Units are usually sold fully furnished, so although we knew the lay out, we did not know what this particular flat contained — so — to cut a long story short — we went up to inspect it, and as we are leaving the flat I heard Ken asking what the price of this particular Unit was. Imagine my surprise when I heard him make an offer for it — and — so we became the owners of this Unit on the 11th May, 1987. We actually moved in on the 5th June, having spent about a month decorating it and buying the odd pieces of furniture which we felt needed replacing. Since which time we have had some super holidays in it — and I am sure it has been a good buy.

We were lucky in many ways, as three weeks after we bought it the Australian Government brought in a ruling that no foreigners would be allowed to buy property in Australia UNLESS they bought off the drawing board. Usually of course at prices far above what we paid for our Unit.

Fiona and the family arrived for a holiday on the 9th July, and on the same day Ken received a phone call from the Singapore Insurance Company — (known as SAGI) the Company he had been working for, to ask if he would be interested in returning to Singapore. In principal he was quite interested and as we both enjoyed Singapore, Linda of course was living there, and so he said he was prepared to do another year. After the Philippines — this was a very attractive proposition.

On the 20th July, Fiona, Gerd and the boys left for Shute Harbour where they were hiring a yacht and cruising around the Whitsunday Islands which was a great success.

We flew into Singapore on the 23rd July, as Ken had an interview regarding his proposed SAGI employment and we left Singapore for Malaysia on the 29th July to spend two weeks with my niece Diane and Ismail in Kuala Lumpur.

Linda and Tony had arranged to get married on the 15th August, 1987, at the Fort Canning Registry Office in Singapore, so we arrived on the 14th August and booked into the Tanglin Club.   Fiona flew down from H.K. and was staying at the Inter-Continental Hotel. After the Registry Office wedding Ken took the Chief participants at the wedding to a lunch and Linda and Tony had arranged a Marriage Blessing at their house in Ewart Park in the evening.  This was a lovely service, with an Altar arranged in the grounds, flares all over the garden, and everyone of the guests was given a lighted candle which burned throughout the very touching service.    This was followed by a dinner in the house.   Linda looked lovely and she and Tony were obviously very happy and in love.

The following day Elissa and Shane, now fully grown of course, were departing for New Zealand where Elissa had been living for about a year.    It was not possible for Shane, who was now 18, to remain in Singapore without doing National Service in the Singapore Armed Forces for the next two years, so he decided to join his sister in Auckland where he hoped to get employment.

We returned the following day to Brisbane and then down to Burleigh Heads to the Unit we now owned, as Ken's contract did not start until October.

On the 10th September, 1987 Diane and Ismail arrived for a short holiday with us, which I think they enjoyed, though they both felt the heat, which surprised us, as frankly we thought Malaysia was much more humid and had higher temperatures but of course there is no air conditioning in the Unit — only the sea breezes.   We never find it over hot, but Diane particularly was feeling the heat.

Ken's new Contract  started on the 19th October, 1987 and we moved into the same Unit we had previously had in the Parklane Apartments at the Goodwood Park Hotel.   We received a very warm welcome from all the Staff and it really was like returning home.   Some of the long term residents that had been staying there at the same time as us the previous year, also gave us a great welcome.

We were able to see quite a lot of Linda and Tony — and in retrospect realise how lucky we are having spent so much time in the East where it has been possible to see the girls fairly regularly. I often thought that we saw them more often than we would have done if they were living in the North of England and we were living in the South. Certainly we saw far more of them than either Ken or I did of our own parents. One of the contributing factors of course is that when you are on an Overseas assignment you get more leave than you would in the U.K. in a similar job.

Again we went up to Hong Kong for Xmas returning on the 3rd January, and on the 17th June we flew to the U.K. for 2 weeks as Ken had a business visit and we were able to add on a couple of days leave.

On the 5th August we had a quick trip to K.L. as Mariam, Diane's second daughter, was getting engaged — and rather like a Malay wedding, this was a very auspicious occasion, where both families have to exchange beautifully wrapped gifts. To give you an idea, Mariam received a gold chain, ring and bracelet, three ornate bajus or pakaian (dresses), cakes, fruit, and other items too numerous to mention. The bridegroom in return received a ring, Topi, (hat) Baju Kemeja (shirt) gold cuff links, and as all these were wrapped separately in boxes wrapped in gold or silver paper with bows and ribbons — the display looked quite beautiful.

We'd just returned from K.L. when Nikky and Alexander — Fiona's two boys, arrived for a week's holiday. It was quite a squash having them in this small apartment at the Hotel but we loved having them. We took great delight in showing them what Singapore had to offer — though I suppose compared to H.K. it would not compare very favourably with small boys. But we had visits to the Bird Park, the Science Centre, Sentosa, a trip on the Singapore river, the wonderful Zoo and then of course we had the use of two large swimming pools at the Hotel — so I think they enjoyed it — we certainly did.

On the 14th October, 1988 Ken had completed a year of his Consultancy and so was entitled to Leave and so we left once again for Brisbane. This was the year of EXPO at Brisbane — so we had a couple of visits to that, and of course had no problems with accommodation as we now owned our own Unit. As a result we found we really had no desire to travel very far afield — there were a lot of jobs to do in the flat, but we managed a daily swim, went walking on the beach and thoroughly enjoyed this quieter life style.

We returned to Singapore on the 8th November, 1988 and Ruth arrived on the 20th. She is a most enthusiastic tourist and so we thoroughly enjoyed showing her around Singapore — slightly different to our tours in Australia, but even so I think she enjoyed her visit.

We did the usual things, Visit to Jurong Bird Park, toured Changi, went in the Museum, visited Changi jail, had lunch at the Changi Yacht Club, took her to the Zoo — which is so well organised that one doesn't feel sorry for the animals — its an open plan Zoo and the animals look well cared for and one feels they think they are free! On the return from the Zoo we visited the Mandai Orchid garden and I am sure Ruth had no idea there were so many varieties of this wonderful bloom. We took all our visitors to Kranji War Memorial — which again is a credit to the Singapore Government as it is so obviously well cared for and most attractive. We visited the Singapore Yacht Club where we had lunch — went round China town — did a trip on the Singapore River had a couple of games of Bridge and then of course we ate out, had numerous real Chinese Dinners and swam in the Hotel pool most days.

The fake watchman came round — perhaps I should say the watchman who sold fake watches! I think Ruth was shattered when he produced about 1,000 watches for her to choose from — not altogether of course — he showed us about 20 at a time — and I think we ended up between us buying about 12 as at the price they made wonderful gifts. I have to say that to this day the watches I bought from him are still working! Just as well I suppose, as I

542

don't think it would be easy to get these fakes serviced.

Xmas 1988 saw us again in H.K. which was always a very happy visit, we loved being with the children and sharing their excitement. Gerd, being Austrian, was used to celebrating Xmas on Xmas Eve — and so over the years this has become the ritual.    Initially I found it a little odd and felt that Xmas Day would be a little "flat" but in point of fact it was not — it just made the Xmas celebration that much longer!

Ken's sister Dot and husband John came out for a visit in March 1989, they too stayed at the Hotel but took a room in the main building.    They also did a nostalgic trip to Kuala Lumpur where they used to live and met up with old friends and their old servants.

More leave was due in April, 1989 and so on the 13th April, back to Burleigh we went.

We had found hiring a car each visit rather expensive, so before we did our long tour in 1985 we bought a second hand Holden which did us proud.    But having to leave it for 6 months in an open Garage, which is all we had, obviously did the car no good, so we were given permission to convert our open garage to a closed one.    This we completed on this leave.

Before returning to Singapore this time we decided to sell the car as Ken felt it had reached the stage when money would have to be spent on it.

We flew  back to Singapore on the 9th May 1989 — and once more it was just like coming home.    I think that one of the reasons I settled so well in every overseas posting, was that wherever we were we tried to make our accommodation as much like home as possible.    Many couples merely lived in what was given them and so often we found that the wives particularly never settled and never did anything to improve their living conditions.

On the 8th September 1989 we went to the U.K. on leave, and besides seeing friends we had the flat decorated and did a few minor touch-ups ourselves and left for Singapore on the 27th September.

In October that year there was an official visit of HM The Queen and HRH Prince Philip.

As Ken was no longer the No.1. of a British Company, we were not invited to the British High Commission to the usual tea party to meet them. Being the Royalist I am, I was quite disappointed, but thought of the four other occasions when I had been privileged to be included in at least one festivity to meet them.

On the day of the Royal Tea Party I went down to Centrepoint to do some food shopping, and when I got out of the bus I saw a queue of people outside Centre point, and the Singapore police were preventing anyone from entering. I had completely forgotten that Prince Philip had on his itinerary a visit to Centre Point to mark the official opening of this rather nice Centre.

I was the only white face amongst the crowd waiting on the road side to see him and had a wonderful vantage point and so saw his arrival. He immediately went into Centre Point where the people were lined up to be introduced to him, accompanied by all the V.I.P's. Whilst waiting I had been talking to a very enthusiastic Indian gentleman, who was as fond of the Royal family as I — in fact he had followed them around since their arrival in Singapore in the hope of getting a glimpse of them.

The Security Police still did not want us to go into the shopping centre even though Prince Philip had gone upstairs and we all wanted to go downstairs to the Supermarket. So I waited amongst the crowd for his departure.

Very shortly he appeared at the top of the steps, looked around and immediately made a bee line to where I was standing and said to me "What are you doing here?" I was so overcome, as the way he said this I really began to wonder if he could possibly have remembered the four previous occasions when he had spoken to me. However I suspect I rather stood out like a sore finger as a "gwailo" in the midst of a large number of locals.

Forgetting all we had been told on previous Royal visits as to how to address Royalty, I merely mumbled that I had come down to see him (I lied!) and to do my food shopping.    He then said he hadn't seen any food — and I retorted that I didn't think they would show him that area as it was presently undergoing construction work. He laughed and asked me where it was, and then said how long had I been in Singapore.    I suppose for Royalty, it was quite a long chat and I have to say not only was I thrilled but all the people standing near me were equally thrilled.

A Chinese lady standing next to me said in her Chinese English after he left "Are you his Auntie?" — When I laughed and assured her I wasn't — she then asked "Why he talk you?" which I really could not answer!    The Indian gentleman I'd been chatting to whilst waiting wondered why he had seemed so friendly and also asked if HRH knew me!    He was absolutely beside himself having been so near to Prince Philip.    All the time he had been following the Royal tour he hadn't been allowed anywhere remotely near the Royal party.

Even the Security Police were impressed and asked me what he had said!    I think the only person that wasn't impressed was the Manager of Centre point who knew me well and apparently went back to his wife in the evening to say that Prince Philip had spoken to no one in the line-out but had had a long conversation with me — and I wasn't even a guest!

He did have the grace the following day to ring me up and say that he was sending me a lovely photograph of Prince Philip and I deep in conversation which I felt was a very nice gesture in the circumstances.

On the 23rd January, 1990 we flew to Brisbane on leave and returned to Singapore on the 11th February.

On the 6th February Linda had asked us to meet her son Shane, our grandson, who was coming up by coach to Burleigh Heads to stay in a flat Linda had bought.    He had become redundant in the job he had been doing in Sydney and was unable to get employment there, so Linda thought it would be a good idea if he came to the Gold Coast.    She told us the day, the time and the coach Company's name. However, we went to the Depot and waited for one hour for this particular coach to come in, when we realised we had obviously been given the wrong time, but as it transpired, he wasn't on this coach when it arrived and we subsequently found we had been given the wrong coach line, the wrong meeting place and the wrong time!

He stayed with us for a couple of days whilst we went round the Auction rooms to get the immediate furniture he needed. Altogether we achieved quite a lot in a short time and when we left Burleigh on the llth February, we felt quite happy about his living arrangements.

Employment on the coast however, was more difficult to obtain than in Sydney as of course there is virtually no industry and only jobs related to the tourist trade had any vacancies with literally fifty people applying for the one job. So — this wasn't really a good move.

On the 25th April, Ken had to go to Hong Kong on business which suited me very nicely as once again I could stay with Fiona. We returned on the 1st May.

On the 9th August 1990 we took the remainder of our leave and flew to London. Ken had a business appointment so this gave us an extra two days. As our flat was let we moved into a flat that Fiona had bought the previous year, which was vacant at the time and being in Onslow Gardens was very central and we enjoyed our time there.

Ken's Consultancy expired on the 31st October, 1990 and although he received various offers to do more Consultancy work, this time he felt it was really time to hang up his pen, and enjoy his retirement.

We visited Fiona in H.K. and then went down to Burleigh Heads in November, 1990. Linda and Tony came to the Gold Coast for Xmas where they rented a Unit at Surfer's Paradise — and Elissa flew up from Auckland so we all had Xmas together. Elissa stayed with us and having qualified in Interior Design was anxious to obtain employment on the Gold Coast. She had many interviews and promises of possible employment in the future — but as there was nothing definite, she decided to return to Auckland where she knew she had more contacts.

Fiona and family flew to Austria to spend Xmas with Gerd's parents.

Ken and I returned to the U.K. for the summer and had an enjoyable time renewing old acquaintances — as by this time, many of our friends from overseas had also retired.

We returned to the Gold Coast to escape the English winter and in early December 1991, flew to Sydney for Wendy Ireland's Wedding — and we then went to spend a few days with Bob and Muriel Geddes — our ex Karachi friends who had entertained us so lavishly in Nairobi. They had found the U.K. winters too severe and so had emigrated to Australia the previous year. Unfortunately I had acquired an infection on my ankle and had to spend most of our visit with my leg raised — but we did manage a few outings in the car.

We also found the U.K. winters rather severe and so tended to spend the winter months in Australia, returning to the U.K. in the Spring.

The big disasters were that on the 3rd January, 1992, Linda was operated on for cancer of the Oesophagus — and had part of her stomach removed and then on the 15th September, 1992 Ken had his stomach removed because of cancer. He then had five weeks of chemotherapy and radiation which meant travelling up to the Westminster Hospital every day by bus, tube and another bus — not the easiest of journeys and it was bitterly cold at that time.

On the 28th February, 1993 when Ken's treatment was finished, we resumed our trips to Australia and I have to say that the climate and life style seemed to agree with Ken (and with me) and he looked fit and obviously felt well. How lucky we were.

Since then we have tried to arrive in the U.K. in time to have Fiona's two boys for their half term in the Spring and Autumn terms, which we thoroughly enjoyed.

Before leaving Singapore we went to renew our Australian

Visitor's Visa, and enquired whether it was possible to get a visa for longer than a 6 month visit.

On a previous occasion, we had to get an extension of our Visa as in packing up I somehow put my back out and the Doctor said I could not travel for a further week by which time my visa had expired. Trying to get an extension of a further week was very difficult and expensive. We felt therefore that now we were on no fixed Travel schedule, that to have the facility of staying an extra few days or a week, would be a terrific advantage.

The Visa officer in Southport had suggested that now Ken had retired we should apply in Singapore for a Four Year Retiree Visa. This meant we could stay up to four years and come and go as often as we liked — not that we wanted to do this but at least it would cover any emergency which might mean we had to stay longer than 6 months.

This SOUNDED an excellent suggestion — how wrong we were!

A few weeks before we were leaving Singapore, we made application to the Australian Embassy in Singapore for a renewal of our present visa and enquired about the Four Year Retiree Visa which had been recommended in Southport, (Queensland). They were quite enthusiastic and gave us the necessary forms to complete and asked us to have X-Rays and full medicals.

We returned the forms with the fee, which was considerable, and the medical reports and X-Rays. Having complied with this request we were THEN told we would have to have further medicals undertaken by a doctor chosen by the Australian Embassy. Why this hadn't been mentioned before I can't imagine. We were not particularly pleased at having to repeat what had already been done. It was pointed out that these medicals, which were far from cheap, were entirely at our own expense and of course we had already paid for the initial medicals.

Yet another letter from the Immigration Office, asked Ken to have a further x-ray — as they were concerned about the T.B. he had 40 years ago!

The Doctor appointed by the Australian Embassy had to complete the medical form and to do so, kept asking me questions about my state of health, previous illnesses etc. I had furnished all these details on the form they had given me and so I was appalled when the doctor — suddenly asked me if I'd had rectal sex in the last five years? What a question to ask an "old duck"! I was not amused! Ken I might add was not asked this question.

We were told they would get in touch with us once the Embassy had received the reports from the Doctor. About ten days later we received a letter asking us to go to the Australian Embassy again. Naturally we thought this was to get the Visa stamped in our passport? Oh no — nothing so simple, we were then told that we had to be finger printed and get clearance from the Security Police in Singapore! We went down to the Police Station and had to queue up to have these done and as you may imagine we felt like criminals as there were all sorts of odd looking people — who were as intrigued with us as we were with them!

At this stage we were told we must deposit A$500,000 if the application was successful! Fortunately they did take into account the price of our flat and car which reduced this considerably.

Having done all this, when our next letter arrived asking us to report to the office, we went along quite convinced that this time we would be picking up the passports complete WITH the Visas. Oh no — they now decided on looking through our applications, that as we had lived in several countries that the finger prints would have to be sent to every country we had lived in for verification from the respective Security Police, to confirm that we had no police record! First of all though we had to go to a Justice of the Peace to have the finger prints certified that they were actually ours.

This of course took an inordinate time, particularly when you are dealing with the Philippines, Hong Kong, India, and Pakistan — but eventually the clearances from all these countries were received. We were then told to show our bank accounts and evidence that we had remitted the required amount to Australia.

After 7 months we were finally given Four Year Retiree Visas which were valid until 6th November 1994. These read that they were valid for Entry into Australia until this date. We naturally assumed this is what it meant!

However, the first time we tried to re-enter Australia on these Visas, we were denied entry! Apparently we should have been told to obtain re-entry Permits before leaving Australia, even though our Visas said we had unrestricted Entry! They did however, allow us to enter but we had to report to Immigration in Southport the next day and obtain on payment of yet another fee, the re-entry visa we apparently should have obtained before we left!

I have to admit that after this, we knew that we had to have Re-Entry Visas, in fact we were given one that coincided with our Visa and one wonders why this wasn't issued at the same time.

We did find this Visa helpful and in the next four years were able to come and go into Australia — without having to re-apply every time for a Visa AND of course there was no problem if we stayed longer than the six months. With the Visitor's Visa we had travelled on previously, we had to leave Australia before the end of six months.

Four years later of course this Visa had to be renewed and so we applied to the Southport Immigration Office in February, 1994 thinking that it would be easier to get it renewed in Australia than in London.

We applied for the necessary application forms, but were told that the Immigration Office at Southport had no instructions about the renewal of this type of visa and suggested we contact Immigration Brisbane. We were told to ring them and not to visit — so we rang and were again told that they had no instructions about the renewal of this type of Visa, and said there was no point in our visiting the Brisbane Office.

This seemed unbelievable to me that a Government Department had not made provision for this service, so I wrote to Canberra saying I could get no satisfaction from either their Southport or Brisbane office and what could they suggest?

The next thing we knew was a phone call from Brisbane referring to the letter I had written to Canberra and asking why I had done this as they were the authority for Visa renewals in our area. They then invited us to call at the Brisbane Office and we were both given Visa Application Forms for which they asked a sum of A$200 each. It was explained that this was merely for the application forms and if the Visa was granted we would have to pay that fee at the time of issue.

We were told that as they had no instructions about the renewal of these Four Year Visas it would be necessary for us to make a fresh application and start from the beginning! They did concede that the finger printing could be waived! But we had to go for medicals and X-Rays, which had to be taken to the Doctor of their choice, but again, it was pointed out that we must pay for this service.

When we finally got an appointment with the Dr. they had recommended and had shown him the X-Rays, he said there was no Radiologist's Report and so would we go back and obtain this.

Upon returning to the Radiologists they then said they needed a further x-ray on Ken as they had seen something they were not sure about on the lungs. This of course worried us, particularly as we had had to agree that anything the doctors or radiologists found was purely for the purpose of this Visa and would not be disclosed to us. If we had any doubts about this then we should see our own physician and have fresh X-Rays taken. As we had paid for these medical services, I felt it was irregular to say the least that we were not to be allowed to see the results.

Finally we saw the doctor who asked Ken what had caused the huge scar he had on his chest. He explained that he had surgery for cancer but produced a certificate from the Surgeon saying that not only had he made a fantastic recovery, but that there was no sign of the cancer spreading — and that he had undertaken Chemotherapy and Radiation.

We were told they would let us know when they had any information regarding our Visas. This was by now the end of

March.    The next thing we knew was a phone call saying that because of Ken's cancer they did not think they could issue these Visas.    I pointed out that we had our own medical insurance, we cost the Australian Government nothing, in fact we were an asset as we had had to bring in the equivalent of A$500,000 and we always brought money into Australia for our visits.    Cancer was not infectious or contagious — so — what was the problem?

Well the correspondence and phone calls went on from March until June when we were about to leave for the U.K., when 10 days before departure they wrote asking Ken to have an Endoscopy and a further report from a Cancer Specialist, which meant having a Scan and he had to see a Specialist regarding the T.B,. he had had 40 years ago!

Of course we had to be referred to a Specialist by a Dr. in Australia, so incurred a further Bill with the G.P. to arrange these appointments.    It turned out there was no specialist able to see Ken until after we were due to leave Australia.    For personal reasons we had to get back to the U.K. so there was no way we could hang around for another 2 or 3 weeks for these tests, and one wondered why they hadn't asked for these earlier..

After more phone calls and harassment we were given permission to have these tests done in the U.K. and they had to be sent UNOPENED to Immigration Medical Section in Sydney. Obviously these had to be done quickly — so more expense — and Endoscopies and Scans don't come cheap — nor do Specialist appointments!

This "renewal" was certainly an expensive venture.

These Reports were sent off at the beginning of July — and we sat and waited.

Before leaving Australia we had enquired when we could expect our Visas to be issued, and were told that as long as we got back to Australia before the expiry of our present Visa on the 6th November, we could ENTER Australia, and if the Visa was refused they would at least give us a Bridging Visa to enable us to settle our affairs.

We heard nothing from Australia, so booked and paid for our passages at the beginning of October to be sure of obtaining a seat on a flight.

Imagine the anguish when we received a letter saying that our applications had been turned down on the grounds of Ken's cancer!

I feel this is so insensitive — as coping with cancer is a big enough hurdle without this additional worry about a Visa particularly as it is difficult to comprehend the reasoning for it's refusal.

We sent off a Fax pointing out that when we left Australia we were led to believe that we would be allowed back prior to the 6th November, when the present Visa expired and therefore had booked and paid for our return ticket.   Could they not therefore issue a Visitor's Visa which is how we travelled before we were persuaded to apply for this Retiree Visa?   Also what did they suggest we did about our flat, car and personal items in the flat if we had to leave?

A reply came saying that as we had booked our passages we could return to Australia, so long as we arrived before the 6th November and went to the office in Brisbane on arrival to apply for a Bridging Visa to enable us to sort out our personal problems.

It was not possible to issue us with a Visitor's Visa as we had been visiting Australia regularly for short periods so would not qualify.

Once they agreed to see us, the staff in Brisbane were very helpful — but it is the thoughtless bureaucracy — that we found so infuriating, and very disturbing.

In January, 1995, we had no valid Visa for Australia, but we had a letter saying that we could remain until the Government had come to a decision about the formalities of renewing these four year Visas. If we still could not be issued with a Visa, we were to be given 28 days to sell the flat and pack up    but in the meantime    we could not leave Australia!

There is a reciprocal agreement between Australia and the U.K. for medical etc., and one would assume regarding Visas, but it appears it is effective only in one direction.   I doubt that there is any Australian that has been subject to the indignities and harassment, not to mention the expense, that we have experienced trying to get this Four Year Retiree Visa renewed!

This is particularly galling as a U.K. friend of ours who also had cancer the previous year, approached the Australian Visa Office in London and applied for a Visitor's Visa at 10.a.m. and was issued with a Multiple Entry Visa valid for one year by 2.p.m. for the sum of £16.    I hate to think what this application has cost us with all the medical bills involved — and I wonder why on earth we were ever advised to apply for this Four Year Retiree Visa.

Although we had been warned that we may have to leave Australia after one month if the Government did come to a decision about the general renewal of this type of Visa, and they decided that our application may be turned down,  we did actually stay six months. By this time we had to return to the U.K. as Ken and I had medicals booked, but, we had no valid visa in our passports and we did have a letter saying we could NOT leave, so as things stood — it appeared we had a problem!    However, after various visits to Brisbane — (90 kilometres away), and phone calls, we finally were told to post our passports to their office and they would give us a Bridging visa, which would enable us to leave Australia, and we could return by the 4th November.

Can you believe it that two days after our passports were returned, I received a letter from Immigration saying they had "noticed" that my visa renewal application had been outstanding for some months, and in the circumstances they would renew my Visa on condition that I did not attend University!    However, Ken's visa application could not be renewed!  He could however return to Australia, though the Government might reach a decision about the renewal of these Four Year Retiree Visas, and he would then be given 28 days in which to leave!

We still persevere — but in the meantime continue to return to Burleigh Heads for the winters for as long as we can!  We've also had some wonderful holidays touring Australia, which is such a beautiful and interesting country.

# NINETEEN
## *Final Retirement*

As indicated before, Ken had "retired" three times, and it was in 1992 he decided that it really was time he "hung up his boots" and we returned to live in Kingston- upon- Thames.

The tenants, who had been in our flat for 9 years, had by then bought their own apartment in the same area, so we had a busy time resettling — unpacking boxes that had been packed since we left H.K. on Ken's first retirement.

Fiona's children had been admitted to boarding schools, Alexander attended Port Regis at Shaftsbury, whilst Nicolas had opted for St. Andrews at Eastbourne. They both loved their schools and when we went down to pick them up for half term — they were just full of all the excitements school offered. Nick enjoyed climbing, canoeing, swimming and to a lesser degree rugger and cricket, whilst Alexander enjoyed ALL sports.

Port Regis even had its own 9 hole golf course and on one occasion when we went to pick Alexander up for an Exeat, having waited ages, we found he was on the third Tee quite oblivious of the time and one of the pupils offered to go and find him!

From the time they were picked up — Alexander would keep asking how many days it was before he could return to school! Both Linda and Fiona used to ask the same questions, but for an entirely different reason — they dreaded returning to school and I just could not believe how happy my two grandsons were at their schools.

Nick had a little difficulty adjusting the first term — and as he was permitted to have a small pet — we thought we would buy him a Hamster for his birthday.   Naturally we had checked this out with his Housemaster first who said he thought it was a good idea.

The "generation gap" is very obvious when I say that we would give him £10 for his birthday — but one must remember that in my day I would have received two shillings and sixpence — and perhaps at age 15, ten shillings!   How times have changed and it is difficult for we old ducks to adjust to present day values!   Fiona had asked us to buy him a pair of blades (the equivalent to roller skates in my day).   Well when we asked him to chose these he said he no longer wanted "Blades" but would like to go to Harrods and look around their toy department.   We did this and we also went to Hamleys, but there seemed nothing that Nick wanted that was under £75!   So... this is how the Hamster came into the picture.

As we were passing the local pet shop he went in to look at the animals.   He thought he would like a Hamster and spotted a rather cuddly looking one which was only £8 — so he decided to buy this. Of course the Hamster had to have a cage!   We eventually found a cage which was only £15 and we were happy to get this but the pet shop said that it was too small for the Hamster — so we progressed to something a little larger, and a little more expensive of course! Then we were told the Hamster had to have an exercise wheel to keep it fit, also a small house so it had somewhere to go to if it was cold, a water bottle to prevent infection in the drinking water, a feeding bowl — and of course lots of hay so he could burrow and hide, and lots of oats!

Then it was recommended we bought some vitamins and a tray to prevent the food spilling on the floor!   This was without doubt a most expensive Hamster!   But it was cute and cuddly.

Anyway it was all worth it as "Henrietta", as the hamster was named, was a great success.   When he returned to school after the half term holiday, Henrietta Hamster went with him — and I was told at our next school visit by his Housemaster, that this was the best present he could have had as it gave him an interest after school, and the first term can be a little lonely until a circle of friends is established.

At the end of term Nick was going out to Hong Kong to join Fiona and Gerd — but could not of course take Henrietta, so we said we would look after her till he returned — so we drove down to school and picked her up!

I quite enjoyed having the little creature — but one day when we returned home after a four hour outing, I was horrified to find the cage door open and there was no Henrietta! I was convinced I had closed the cage door after cleaning the cage — and wondered if this clever Hamster had learnt how to open the cage or was this the beginning of senility ?

We searched the flat — and I couldn't find any holes or crannies that she could have disappeared down. However, there was one crack where the large pipe from the toilet in the guest bathroom entered the wall and I felt this could be the only place Henrietta could have gone. Unfortunately when I examined this large crack, there appeared to be a drop, presumably to the ground floor. As we are on the 7th floor I imagined that Henrietta must have met an untimely death — BUT perhaps she had managed to cling on to the wall and so I got a piece of ribbon — put weights at the end and slowly lowered this down the hole.

I then put food on the floor near the hole and hoped that perhaps Henrietta would be able to claw her way up the ribbon.

I then had the job of ringing Fiona in Hong Kong to tell her I had lost Henrietta as I felt that it would be easier for her to console Nick in H.K. than it would be when he returned to school! She didn't seem unduly perturbed and told me that when Nick had a Hamster whilst they were living in the Furama Hotel, the same thing happened, and as you can imagine — besides the worry of losing the Hamster they were also worried that one of the Hotel guests might find the Hamster and mistake it for a rat! This would not do the reputation of the Hotel much good.

However, after 3 days the Hamster suddenly appeared — so she told me not to give up hope!

Having heard this, I immediately put the ribbon back down the hole — put more food out and just left it — hoping that she would appear. Anyway, after about 3 days I had given up hope but decided I had nothing to lose by leaving the ribbon down the hole.

Four days later Ken and I were in the Lounge watching T.V. and suddenly I was conscious of something moving — and when I looked down — there was Henrietta looking very dejected — very thin — and with a distinct brown mark across her back, ambling across the carpet!

We were thrilled to see her but concerned at her emaciated state! We put her in her cage and she immediately drank nearly a whole bottle of her water, I had never seen her drink so much so quickly!

After a few days she was back to normal — and as you can imagine I was very relieved that I didn't have to confess to my darling Grandson that I had lost Henrietta!

When Nick returned from H.K. we drove down to Eastbourne and handed Henrietta over — and he seemed delighted to see her — and I was quite sad at saying goodbye to this rather cute little animal who had proved she was a survivor!

However, the following half term when we drove down to school to collect Nick and the Hamster, the Housemaster said he could not have Henrietta back as she kept the dorm awake all night going round and round in her squeaky wheel. So — as we were going down to Australia, we could not keep her for long, therefore we tried to find a nice home for her and were very sad to say goodbye. Nick on the other hand now had so many other interests I think he was relieved that he didn't have to also attend to Henrietta!

We decided to leave the U.K. as soon as we could get a flight after half term — thus avoiding the English winter. We called at Singapore and Hong Kong en route to spend a few days visiting Linda and Fiona and then came back to Burleigh Heads for the English winter.

We had an exciting visit to Tasmania with Brian and his new wife, Pat, where we learnt so much about the early history of Australia.

Originally Tasmania was called Van Diemen's Land and having been discovered by the Dutch and named after the Governor General. The British subsequently took over the Island and used it as a penal settlement.

I found in many ways it was so like the U.K. but with better weather! I felt throughout Tassie that the first settlers had tried to recreate what they had left behind in Britain both in environment and their life style. English type Pubs abound — and the nurseries contain many English flowers. They have actually recreated the chimes of Big Ben in Hobart, the capital, on their Post Office building.

Tasmania really is a beautiful country — mile upon mile of Rain Forests — lots of rivers, waterfalls and very interesting rock formations and of course — wherever you go there seemed to be an old jail where it all started!

Having flown in to Launceston and picked up a car, we drove through a magnificent Rain Forest to Scotsdale, Derby, St. Helens and spent the night at Scamander.

We were fortunate having only one really wet day — though on a couple of occasions we were fooled by the early morning sunshine and put on light clothing — only to find by lunch time a sudden drop in temperature which prompted us to unpack in a car park and get something warmer! I did a strip tease in the back of the car discarding my cotton slax and squeezing into slightly warmer ones! Brian to the embarrassment of his wife did his strip tease outside the car getting out of his shorts into long pants much to the amusement of several spectators!

Tasmania is quite an expensive tourist area in my view. In the top Hotels in the larger towns, they would charge about A$150 per night excluding breakfast. By ferreting about of course we managed to get rooms at around A$ 65-75 which I thought was still expensive when you can get Motels on the Gold Coast, often on the sea front, for around $25 — A$35.

We drove down the coast taking the turn off to Richmond — which we found very interesting and explored yet another jail etc., and then on to Hobart. The next day we set off for Port Arthur calling at Eaglehawk Neck where we saw the most unique rock formation called the Tesselated Pavement which showed the amazing effect the sea can have on rocks over centuries. It really looked like a man made chess board.

Then we stopped at the Blow Hole, the Tasman Arch and Devils Kitchen — before arriving at Port Arthur.

Had we not booked two nights at the Motel in Hobart we would have liked to have spent longer at Port Arthur, where there was so much to see. It had been the Penal settlement where all the really "naughty" convicts were sent. Mind you — "naughty" in those days was stealing a loaf of bread or something equally trivial.

When the convicts first arrived they were sent to McQuarrie Island where because of the appalling conditions, so many of the so called "convicts" died. Nine prisoners were kept in what should have been the space for three. Added to which it was the bleakest part of Tasmania, and out of every 100 prisoners only 35 would die of natural causes. The rest would die of hypothermia, or as a result of frequent flogging, where they had been known to receive 100 lashes per day. Death must often have come as a happy release.

The female prisoners were kept on a separate Island where conditions were little better.

Eventually all the prisoners from McQuarrie were moved to Port Arthur though they were still taken over to Death Island to dig graves; sometimes they actually dug their own which was kept until needed!

On Philip Island we were shown around the prison where I suppose conditions were slightly better but if the convict committed a further offence then they were put into Solitary Confinement which meant being in complete darkness where each cell had three doors so that when one was opened -the other doors prevented even a strip of light getting into the cell, even momentarily.

When the convicts finally were released from this barbaric prison, they were temporarily blind and suffered from dizziness besides malnutrition, and frequently were insane as a result of their treatment.

Even visits to Church meant they were taken in chains with a potato bag over their heads so they could not see or be seen by other prisoners. In church they were put in to a small cell like pew which was completely boxed in and only when they were installed in the "pew" were they allowed to remove the bag from their head and could then only see straight in front of them! The potato bag was put back before they were allowed to leave.

Whilst the forms of punishment were excessive and cruel for what appeared trivial crimes — I think we have now gone to the other extreme. While the degree of criminal violence soars the punishment frequently does not seem to fit the crime.

We took a boat trip around the Island of the Dead named aptly as it was the old cemetery. Apparently in the mid-19th century, poverty was generally felt to be self-inflicted rather than a result of external economic forces. Charity and welfare were thus sparingly applied!

No more convicts were transported from Britain after 1853 which meant that fewer young prisoners were added to "the system". As the average age of convicts increased, so did sickness and feebleness. Many of the convicts by repeated or serious offences, had remained in custody for decades and finished up poor, unskilled and unemployable. They were thus called paupers and had their own pauper's mess which we were taken around. The mind boggles at the thought of the conditions these prisoners endured.

Whilst depressing it was all very interesting and with hindsight, we really should have spent longer in that area — but it's easy to be wise after the event.

On returning to Hobart we did the Salamander Market which takes place every Saturday and we had been told it was a "must". It was interesting — but then I've always enjoyed Markets

In the evening at sunset, we went for a walk around the harbour area — watching the fishermen disgorge their catch of the day, and we saw the occasional Starfish in the clear waters with their magnificent colours. Here we met a very charming Chief Petty Officer from an R.A.N. Frigate who invited us on board for a look around. How I manoeuvred up and down all the ladders I don't know. My knees had already started to give me problems — and at one time felt I would have to sail with them as getting ON board was easy compared to getting off!

Another evening we drove up Mount Wellington where the temperature got colder and colder as we ascended. We were very amused to see the enthusiasm of a young man with his lady friend, who had brought dinner up to the top of the mountain and had laid a beautiful table, adorned with red candles and stiffly starched napery, and they sat sipping their pre-dinner drink. Whilst it looked delightful — as the sun set it was getting decidedly chilly and the candles soon flickered out and by the time we returned from the viewing area, they were already packing up their tables and chairs — which I thought was sad. The young man had obviously gone to a lot of trouble to arrange this romantic dinner.

The following day we drove to Queenstown — which had been a Copper Mining area which we found VERY depressing and sad — all the Copper Mines had closed bar one which we were told would be closing shortly. This of course had caused massive unemployment consequently it looked rather like a ghost town.

Shortly after we left we heard that the only Bank was closing which would mean residents had to travel 200 kms to get cash — but as the Bank was running at a loss, they felt it was not practical to keep the Branch open.

It was our plan to spend the night at Strahan and do the Gordon River Cruise — but when we arrived we found the place was fully booked — even the two prime Hotels who were charging A$175 per night! For that reason alone I was quite glad we couldn't get in! So we went onto Zeehan — and decided it wasn't worth retracing our steps to try to get on the cruise the next day. There were so many people staying at Strahan — we didn't think we would stand much chance of getting on the boat.

So.... the next day we drove to the North coast and stayed at Wynyard — then went up in the chair lift to The Nut in Stanley which was decidedly chilly. It is 152 metres high and rises from the sea with three near perpendicular sides. From the top there were spectacular views of both the local coastline and off- shore islands.

We went through Rocky Cape National Park on to Penguin which nestles between the Bass Strait and the Dial Ranges. It was named in 1861 after the tiny fairy penguins. We had been assured we would see the Penguins returning to their nests at night, but on making enquiries locally — we were told that the Penguins only appear at mating time — but we might see them at 9 p.m. at Ulverston a few miles further on — but there were no penguins there either!

The whole country has the most spectacular waterfalls — but we weren't of course able to visit them all.

Whilst we found the Tasmanians delightful and very polite, but all in all I think some of them were even more laid back than the Queenslander!

Serving breakfast in most of the Motels had to be seen to be believed — they never used trays but made numerous trips with one article in their hand — presented it with a big smile and told us the next items would be coming shortly. We got the teapot — but no cups — the Muesli arrived — but no milk — there was no toast only croissants which they told us were "being heated" but they eventually arrived cold! Even paying the bill was difficult and one felt that even in a large first class hotel you couldn't have had more interruptions on the phone. Mind you, I think they could have done with more staff as often there was one man doing everything — which of course was impossible.

We spent the night at Deloraine and went to the Tasmanian Wild Life Park where I cuddled a delightful Koala, a baby Wombat AND a baby Tasmanian Devil! These little animals look quite evil, and are very fierce, but the babies were cute!

Then we drove to Mole Creek and King Solomons Cave — which was one of the best we had seen. The Stalactites and Stalagmites were beautiful and one rock really looked like a Sculpture of a King — hence the name King Solomon's Mine.

It was decided we would spend the night at Launceston — in order to visit the Penny Royal World. Here we took a barge ride underground through the Gunpowder Mill and viewed the water driven machinery, as it was early in the 19th century. Then we travelled on a fully restored Launceston tram to the Windmill and Cornmill, these two mills are really working museums. After this we decided to take a river cruise on a paddle steamer on the Tamar River. Time was running short but we wanted to take the chair lift over the Cataract Gorge which was delightful, but we could not disembark at the top of the Gorge as unfortunately we had to get to the Airport in time to catch our flight back to beautiful Burleigh. We really had packed so much into this visit and as a result we nearly missed the plane!

In 1995 we had another memorable trip with Brian and Pat. We had been invited to Melbourne to attend Geoff Ireland's wedding. As you know by now, we had known the Ireland family for many years and watched the "children" mature into very switched on adults, and it was planned we were to travel down to Melbourne with Brian and his really delightful wife, Pat.

We had decided that we would use our Frequent Flyer Points for the return trip to Melbourne, and then Pat discovered that for the same number of Frequent Flyer Points we could also fly to Alice Springs and take a coach trip to Ayers Rock — and then fly back to Coolangatta via Sydney.

Ken had always wanted to visit Alice and Ayers Rock. I have to admit I did not share his enthusiasm — but this did seem too good an opportunity to miss — even though it was NOT on my list of priorities! We knew that travelling with Pat and Brian would in itself be an enjoyable experience. They are such fun.

We flew from Melbourne to Alice Springs and booked into the Oasis Frontier Hotel. Ruth Lamb, an old friend of Pat's, who was now living in Alice, picked us up after lunch, and took us a tour of the area. We visited the old Telegraph Station — and then to Simpsons Gap, Stanley Chasm and John Flynn's Grave. We returned to the Hotel for dinner.

The next morning the coach picked us up early and we drove to Ayers Rock — 280 miles away where we booked into the Outback Pioneer Hotel. We arrived around 1.p.m. had lunch and then the coach picked us up at 3.p.m. to drive us to The Olgas where we took the Valley of the Winds Tour.

The Olgas — 35 miles from Ayers Rock, is an extraordinary rock formation which consists of 36 stone domes. The Aborigines call these Kata Tjuta, meaning "many heads" and like Ayers Rock much of the rock is below ground. These rocks cannot be climbed but we could walk among the rocks to the Olga Gorge, where a lush oasis with trees and a water-hole has sprung up between two large boulders. The Olgas take up 20 square miles — a larger area than Ayers Rock, although the latter overshadows it.

Whilst we were walking through the Olgas — I asked the Tour guide to go on without me — as the actual walk was through a very rocky river bed which had dried out — and I felt it was too much for me as I don't see very well — and the rocky river bed spelled disaster So the Group left me sitting on a rock in the Bush and said like McArthur, that they would return!

After about ten minutes I decided that sitting alone in the middle of the Bush was not for me and that I would start walking back to base. I gave myself one or two frights getting lost and can now well understand how you read of people getting lost in the Bush. The scenery all looks the same — and I decided there and then that I really am a "towny" and would have been much happier waiting for the No. 65 bus or the Underground — than wandering in this spectacular countryside.

I realised I had taken the wrong turning when I found myself having to climb over a large tree trunk which crossed the trail and I knew it had not been there on the way out — so obviously I was on the wrong path! I retraced my steps and got back to the "junction" and hoped I had found the correct one. Was I relieved when I spotted the coach in the distance!

The coaches carried large containers of water and whenever we got out to walk, we were given a litre of cold water in a flask to take with us. We were told we should drink at least a litre of water every HOUR — and very sound advice this was. On one occasion I only drank when I was thirsty and so when we started walking I soon became exhausted and had to return to the coach.

The Courier had left a couple of luggage cupboards open, one containing fold away chairs and the other the two large drums of drinking water, so I was able to sit and have a drink on my return as I had finished all the water in my flask during the walk.

Whilst sitting outside the coach waiting for the return of the Group, another lady came and joined me. I spoke four words to her saying "you also gave up?" and was mortified when she then said "which part of Yorkshire are you from?". Whilst I was brought up in Yorkshire I did kid myself that I had lost my accent

I found the flies were unbelievable — and if you opened your mouth to speak — a fly always flew in and as you were choking trying to spit it out — another would join it. We bought fish net covers at the weekly market in Alice and with these on our hats covering our faces — we weren't troubled until we lifted the net to drink water. In the end I decided to drink THROUGH the net!

It seemed that Insect Repellent did everything but Repel! The b....y flies love it. The coach driver asked us NOT to kill any flies on the coach because we'd find 500 flies came to each fly's funeral!

The main tours concentrated on the longer trips to The Olgas, Ayers Rock, The Valley of the Wind, the Virginia Camel Farm where most people on the coach went for a camel ride. Having had our fill of camels in Karachi we did not participate in this rather expensive ride!

The coach took us across the dry bed of the Finke River, which is reputedly the oldest watercourse in the world, en route to Mount Ebenezer where we had a coffee break in a cafe managed by Aboriginals.

Our Courier told us that some of the cattle ranches that we drove through were larger than a couple of Counties in the U.K.

We were woken every morning around 4.a.m. for a 5.a.m. start — Can't say I enjoyed that! Mind you one had to do the sight-seeing in the cool of the early morning as around mid-day the temperatures were unbearable being 40-45+.

The coaches were superb — air conditioned of course — with very pleasant toilet facilities — delightful drivers who also acted as Couriers accompanying us on all the treks and keeping us continually informed about the local tourist attractions, at the same time giving us a run down on the local flora and fauna, — they really were a mound of information and amusing!

As if this wasn't enough, they then organised our Champagne B.B.Q.'s, did the cooking and clearing away — and then came with us on the evening walks.

After our Olgas trip we again had to be up at 4.a.m. in order to get to The Rock before sunrise as the best time to view The Rock is either early morning or late afternoon. These are the times when Uluru is at its most magnificent. Changes in light, atmosphere and the position of the sun cause the rock's colour to metamorphose through a kaleidoscope of shades from — soft orange to flame red or even deep purple. The early morning tour to view the sun rise over Ayers Rock permitted people to actually climb the Rock. Only about half of the really fit tourists attempted it as the first part is the most difficult and people were literally scrambling on all fours until they could reach the part where there is a rope where you can pull yourself up for the next 100 yards and THEN you are on your own!

Ayers Rock is the geographical heart of Australia — it is also its spiritual soul and held sacred by generations of Anangu Aborigines. It was formed 600 million years ago and is located in one of the most remote areas of the globe. The Aborigines call it "Uluru".

In spite of it being 1143 feet high and one and a half miles long and one mile wide, this is only a small proportion of the rock as they say 80% of it is buried beneath the soil.

The local inhabitants discourage the tourists to climb The Rock. Despite the existence of safety chains, the smooth face of the rock is no easy challenge.   Several people have died in the attempt, either as a result of losing their footing, through heat exhaustion or being blown off the rock — as the winds are quite strong.    There is a total ban on climbing between 10.a.m. and 6.p.m. during the summer months.

On the side of the Rock there are about 6 plaques reminding one of the people who had died on the Rock.    One plaque was to the memory of a 16 year old girl blown off the Rock in a gale.   The aboriginal people want these plaques removed as they say they deface THEIR Rock.

One of the tour operators told us that she had taken about 46 people on a 30 day tour into the outback including The Rock, The Olgas etc., and 8 of her passengers died on one trip!    So she warned us not to attempt the climb at Ayers Rock AND the coach driver gave us a lecture on how dangerous it was AND reminded us that the Aboriginal People don't like visitors climbing, what they consider, is their Rock.   We didn't need any convincing — though Ken did quite a few of the shorter walks which I chickened out on.

We watched a mock rescue as we were told by the Wardens that often people who "think" they are fit, collapse with either heart attacks, heat stroke, or slip and break a bone and so it is essential that they are well versed in rescue.

The sunrise was a fantastic sight and the colours changed every few minutes as the sun rose higher in the sky.   We were again accompanied by a ranger guide who took the more energetic members of the party on the six-mile walk around the base of the rock.    Several of the "oldies" opted to stay at the base camp.

We returned to the Hotel about 7.a.m. had breakfast and then joined the party going on the Rock Base tour, interesting but very energetic, though they had two separate tours — one not so demanding as the second.   We joined the least demanding one!

The coach then took us to the Hotel for lunch and a wee rest and then at 6.15.p.m. we set off again for Uluru on the Sunset Tour. Another magnificent sight and the colours on The Rock seemed quite different to the ones we had seen on the Sunrise tour in the morning.   We had yet another magnificent B.B.Q. the food and drink having been brought from the Hotel — and the Tour Guides cooked, served and tidied up afterwards.   We found them a mound of information and they told us many interesting anecdotes about the area and the Aboriginals and their various beliefs.

After the B.B.Q. there was a Star Gazing Tour.   As I can't see very well in the dark, I decided to stay at the B.B.Q. and sat and watched the Stars.   I have never in my life seen so many,  one could hardly put a pin between them.   I am sure I saw just as many as the people who walked in the dark into the Bush.

Whilst sitting in the B.B.Q. area, I suddenly realised there was a Dingo roaming around the table after everyone had left — but it kept its distance — and I was reminded of the Lindy Chamberlain case when the Dingo reputedly took her baby.

Mind you I felt I should have done this Alice Springs\Ayer's Rock trip, 40 years ago as I really could not attempt all the climbing and even walking through the Valley of the Winds, the Olgas, Kings Canyon or round the base of Ayers Rock — was a bit much for the old duck.

We left the Hotel at 5.a.m. the next morning to drive to Kings Canyon.   We had lunch at Mount Ebeneza Cattle Farm which seemed to stretch for ever.   On arriving at Kings Canyon we booked into the Hotel and then another tour was arranged through the Canyon.   By this time I realised it was going to be another energetic and rough walk — so — four of us decided after walking for about half an hour — that we would take the Helicopter flight over the Canyon which was fabulous.   We saw far more than would have been remotely possible had we completed the full walk.   Mind you

I did get rather a shock when I found the Helicopter didn't have any sides to it and we just sat strapped into a seat and when the pilot banked one had a distinct feeling that you might fall out and there was NOTHING to stop you except your safety belt!

So we had a memorable tour of a very small part of the centre of Australia which we found most interesting and so very different to the other parts of Oz we had seen.

Since then we have had yet another wonderful trip with Pat and Brian, this time to the Whitsunday Passage. We flew to Proserpine, took the coach to Shute Harbour and a launch to Hamilton Island where we stayed on "Mistress" Brian's boat they had sailed up from Sanctuary Cove, Queensland, earlier in the year. We first went on "Mistress" on our first visit to Sydney when it was anchored at Acuna Bay — so she was becoming an old friend!

Hamilton Island is quite something! When we called in there on a launch trip ten years ago — it had not had its face lift and we were very pleasantly surprised at what this Resort now had to offer. When not walking we drove around the Island in little Buggies and because we were anchored on the Island, we were permitted to use all the facilities of the resort.

Pat and I took advantage of a water aerobics class — which took place each morning. The pool was without doubt the largest and most luxurious that I have ever seen, let alone swam in. I think they said the overall swimming distance round the pool was the equivalent to the length of 5 Olympic pools. and it wound it's way between various small Islands — which were joined to the mainland, or each other, by rustic bridges. One of the Islands had a Bar which provided service in the water or on the Island.

Another of these small Islands had a jacuzzi and yet another a coffee bar — so whilst swimming around you could always get out of the water and enjoy the facilities.

We went on a fishing trip, and even I caught a Coral Trout — but the professional fishermen who came with us — wouldn't let me keep it as they said it was too small! It looked far bigger than anything we buy in the market — so I was "miffed". I have a snap of this though just to prove that I DID manage a catch. The wife of one of the fishermen caught something so large it swam off with her equipment and left her with a burnt hand! They thought it could have been a shark!

One day we sailed to Hayman Island where again we were allowed to use their very up-market Resort facilities. Another lovely pool with many exceptional facilities. Whilst superb, I preferred the Hamilton Island Resort.

After a morning in this pool we decided to sail to Blue Pearl Bay in the afternoon where we dropped anchor and spent the night. We did quite a lot of snorkelling where the Coral and the coloured fish were really spectacular. I was rather surprised when some of the beautifully coloured little fish that were swimming around us, decided to have a bite or nip. It appears they are very tame as people are always feeding them — and as I hadn't any food for them, they decided to take a bite out of me which actually brought blood! The fish were only about 6-8 inches in length — so one can understand why the Shark has such a reputation.

Whilst snorkelling Ken had obviously brushed against some Coral He hardly noticed the minute cut — and NO-ONE told us of the danger of a coral scratch which we now know is so poisonous.

As this happened at Blue Pool Bay where we had dropped anchor and were spending the night — it was not possible to get hold of a Doctor, so even when the leg started to swell there was nothing we could do until we got back to Hamilton Island. Then it was an emergency call out — at an "Emergency" price — and the Dr. told us that the risk of infection after a coral "nick" was 100% and Ken should have had treatment within the first 12 hours! Without immediate treatment — people had been known to get serious infections which could cause death!

Certainly within two hours his leg was the size of 3 normal legs and we were very concerned. As a result Ken had to sit with his leg UP for the 3 remaining days of the visit and for five weeks after our return to Burleigh Heads. He was put on antibiotics — and his leg dressed daily and reminded that he must keep it raised. As it became so painful there was nothing else he wanted to do with it — but it was rather restrictive! Three months later the wound still had not healed completely.

Qantas on the flight back to Brisbane were very helpful and placed us in a three seater seat and moved the third person so Ken could keep his leg up during the flight.

In spite of this — we had the most wonderful time on Hamilton Island — and can heartily recommend it — but it is expensive and we were very lucky staying on the boat.

It really was a superb holiday which we both thoroughly enjoyed IN SPITE of the coral!

It was after one of our trips when we returned to Burleigh, and on one of the few wet days we experienced, that I started clearing out some cupboards and came across the initial few pages I had written about eight years ago, about my early life

As explained in the Preamble, I tossed up whether to throw these pages out — as they seemed quite irrelevant but decided to add the contents of the letters that Jeanne Mason returned to me, which filled in quite a few years of our overseas life, and my diaries helped me to fill in some of the missing years.

I had acquired an Epsom Computer before leaving Singapore — so thought it would be simple and good practice to write my "memories" down — and give a copy to both our daughters.

Perhaps the "epistle" may be of interest to some other family members once I have fallen off my perch! I found when my own parents died there were so many questions I wish I had asked them.

Whilst struggling with the computer, a couple of friends visited me and read part of this epistle and they persuaded me to submit these "pages" — or at least some of these pages — to a Publisher. They assured me that THEY had found the "book" interesting and encouraged me to try to get it published. I personally think it will only be of interest to close friends and family, but if you ever read it

— then their suggestion was a good one.

If not — then I have to say, I have enjoyed reminiscing over what has been an interesting and full life, with so many long standing friendships formed, in all the countries where we have lived.   I have been blessed with a wonderful partner and two lovely daughters — so who could ask for more?

THE END